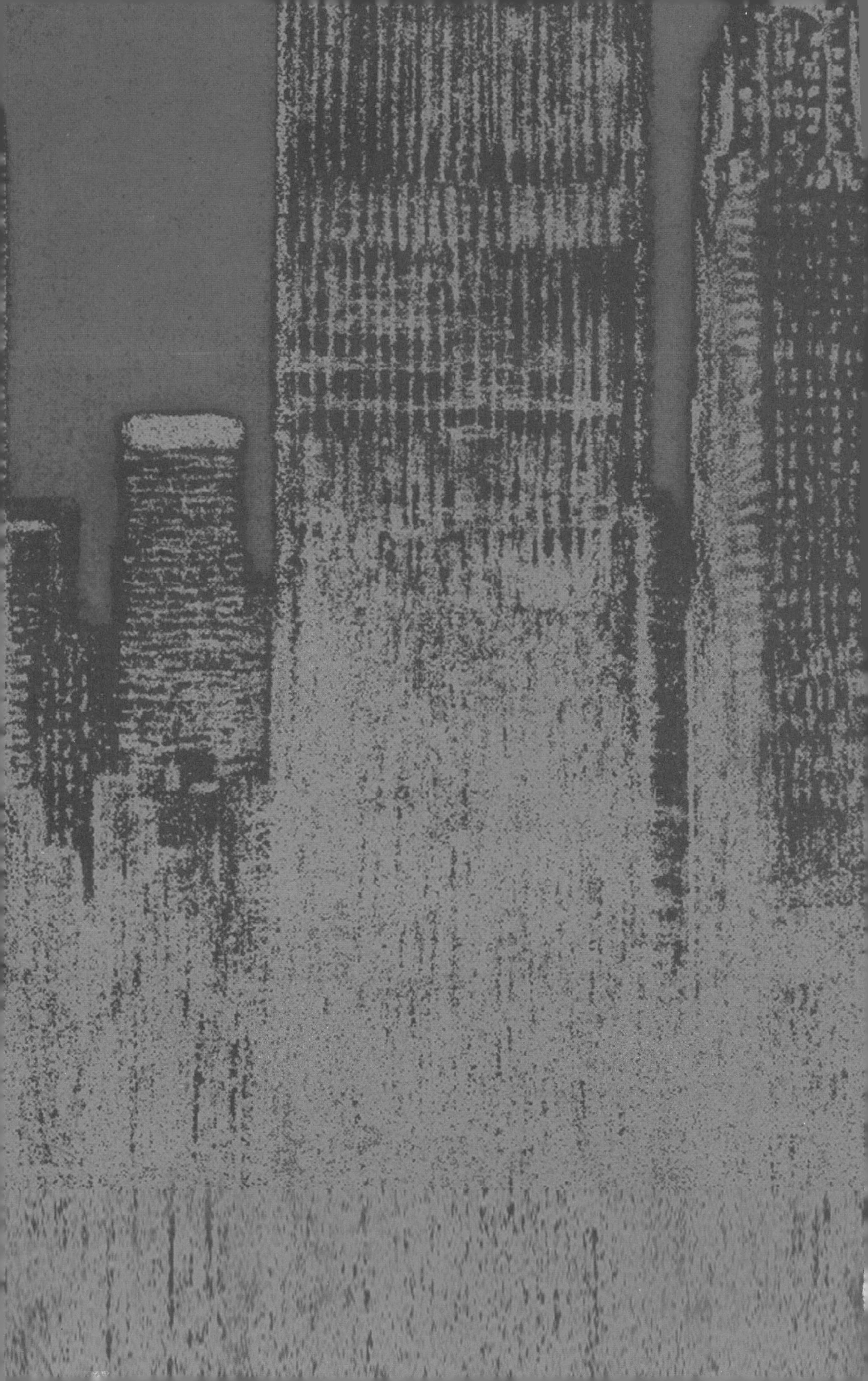

FABLES: THE DELUXE EDITION

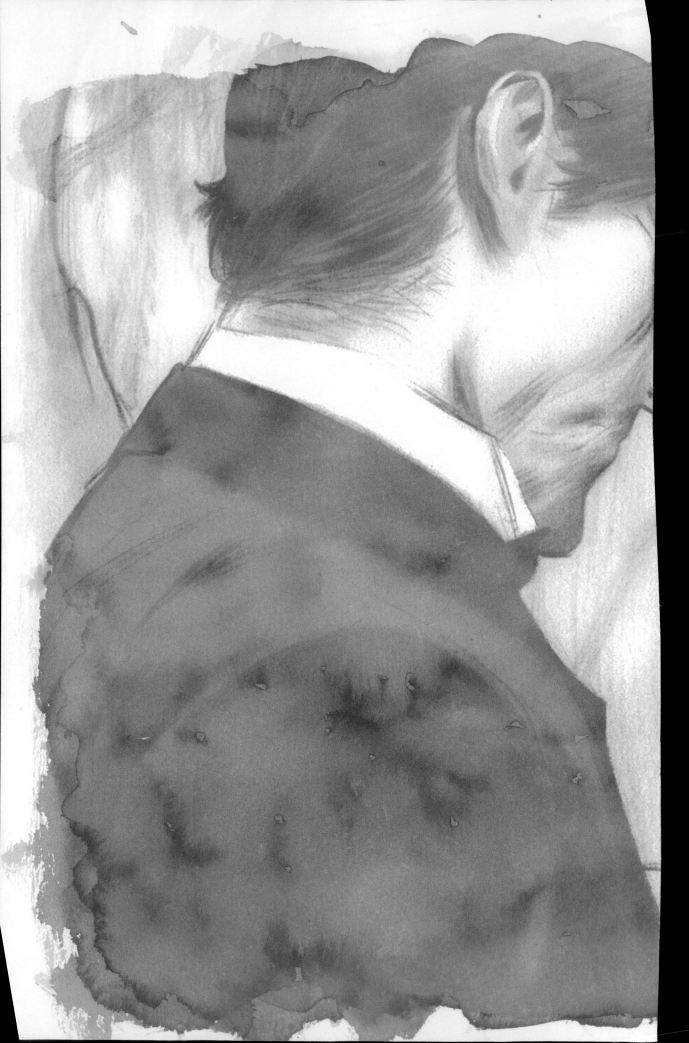

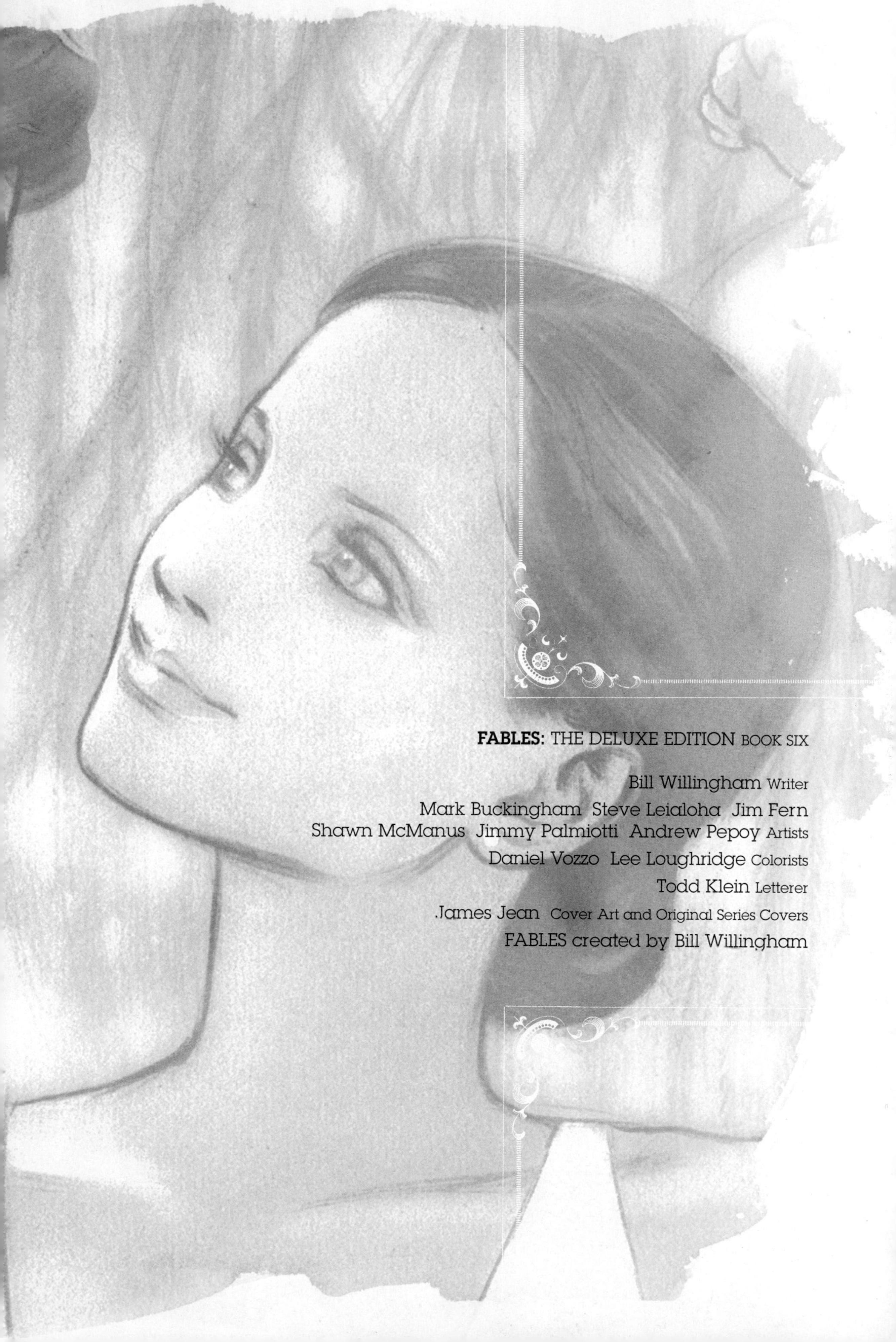

FABLES: THE DELUXE EDITION BOOK SIX

Bill Willingham Writer

Mark Buckingham Steve Leialoha Jim Fern
Shawn McManus Jimmy Palmiotti Andrew Pepoy Artists

Daniel Vozzo Lee Loughridge Colorists

Todd Klein Letterer

James Jean Cover Art and Original Series Covers

FABLES created by Bill Willingham

This collection of pretty lies is dedicated to the mysterious Mrs. Moor, for reasons best kept occluded for now.
— Bill Willingham

This volume is from the year in which events in my life and in FABLES happily coincided, so there is no one else I could possibly dedicate this book to other than my beautiful wife Irma.
— Mark Buckingham

Shelly Bond Editor – Original Series
Angela Rufino Assistant Editor – Original Series
Scott Nybakken Editor
Robbin Brosterman Design Director – Books
Louis Prandi Publication Design

Karen Berger Senior VP – Executive Editor, Vertigo
Bob Harras VP – Editor-in-Chief

Diane Nelson President
Dan DiDio and Jim Lee Co-Publishers
Geoff Johns Chief Creative Officer
John Rood Executive VP – Sales, Marketing and Business Development
Amy Genkins Senior VP – Business and Legal Affairs

Nairi Gardiner Senior VP – Finance
Jeff Boison VP – Publishing Operations
Mark Chiarello VP – Art Direction and Design
John Cunningham VP – Marketing
Terri Cunningham VP – Talent Relations and Services
Alison Gill Senior VP – Manufacturing and Operations
Hank Kanalz Senior VP – Digital
Jay Kogan VP – Business and Legal Affairs, Publishing
Jack Mahan VP – Business Affairs, Talent
Nick Napolitano VP – Manufacturing Administration
Sue Pohja VP – Book Sales
Courtney Simmons Senior VP – Publicity
Bob Wayne Senior VP – Sales

Logo design by Brainchild Studios/NYC

FABLES: THE DELUXE EDITION
BOOK SIX
Published by DC Comics. Cover and compilation Copyright © 2012 Bill Willingham and DC Comics. All Rights Reserved. Introduction Copyright © 2012 Todd Klein. All Rights Reserved. Maps and script Copyright © 2006 Bill Willingham and DC Comics. All Rights Reserved.

DC Comics, 1700 Broadway, New York, NY 10019
A Warner Bros. Entertainment Company. Printed in the USA. First Printing.
ISBN: 978-1-4012-3724-0

SUSTAINABLE FORESTRY INITIATIVE
Certified Chain of Custody
At Least 20% Certified Forest Content
www.sfiprogram.org
SFI-01042
APPLIES TO TEXT STOCK ONLY

Library of Congress Cataloging-in-Publication Data

Willingham, Bill.
  Fables : the deluxe edition, book six / Bill Willingham, Mark Buckingham, Steve Leialoha, Jim Fern, Shawn McManus. -- Deluxe ed.
     p. cm.
  "Originally published in single magazine form as Fables 46-51."
  ISBN 978-1-4012-3724-0
  1. Fairy tales--Adaptations--Comic books, strips, etc. 2. Legends--Adaptations--Comic books, strips, etc. 3. Graphic novels. I. Buckingham, Mark. II. Leialoha, Steve. III. Fern, Jim. IV. McManus, Shawn. V. Title. VI. Title: Fables. Book six.
  PN6727.W52F357 2013
  741.5'973--dc23
                            2012042838

Table of Contents

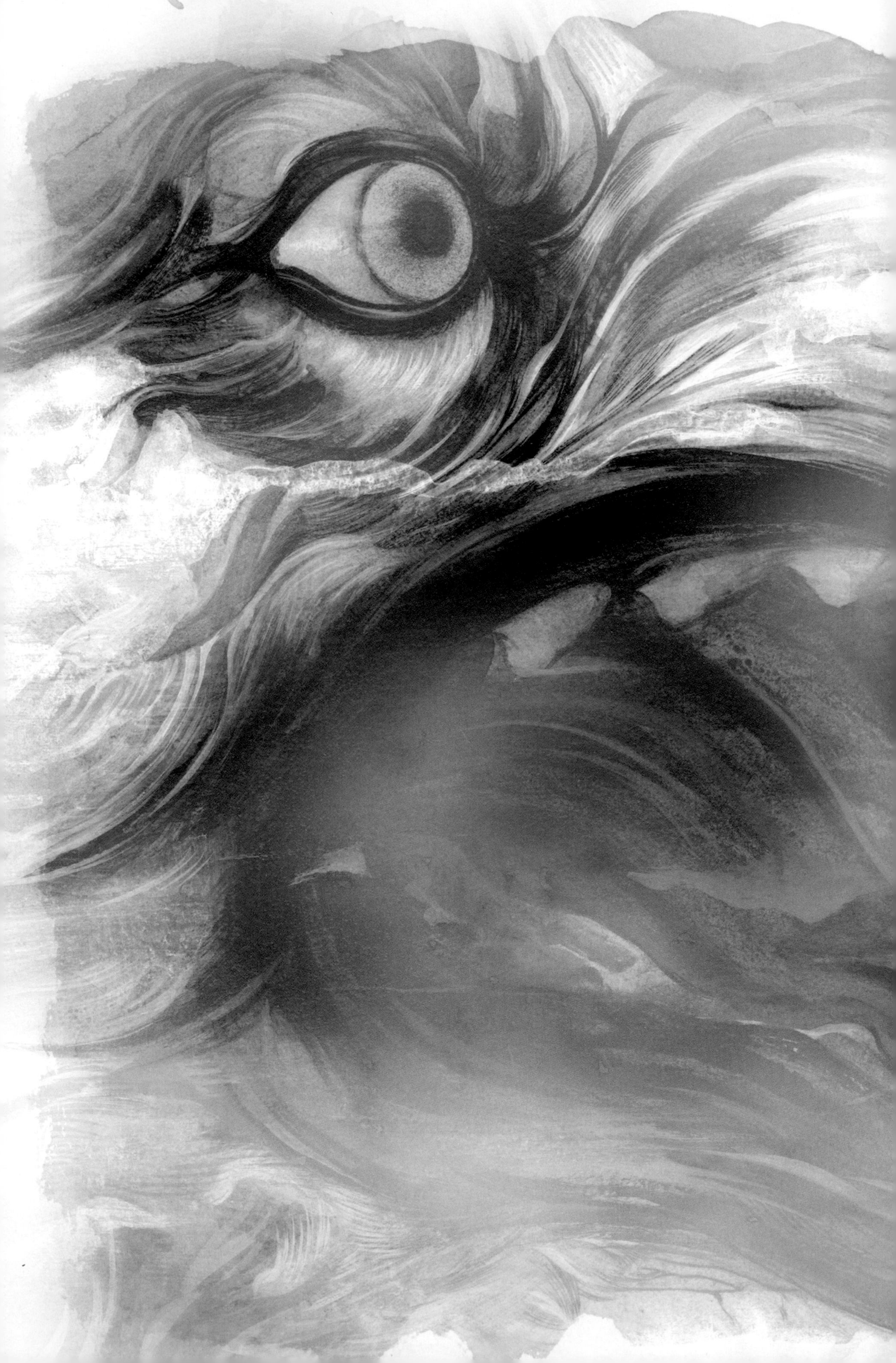

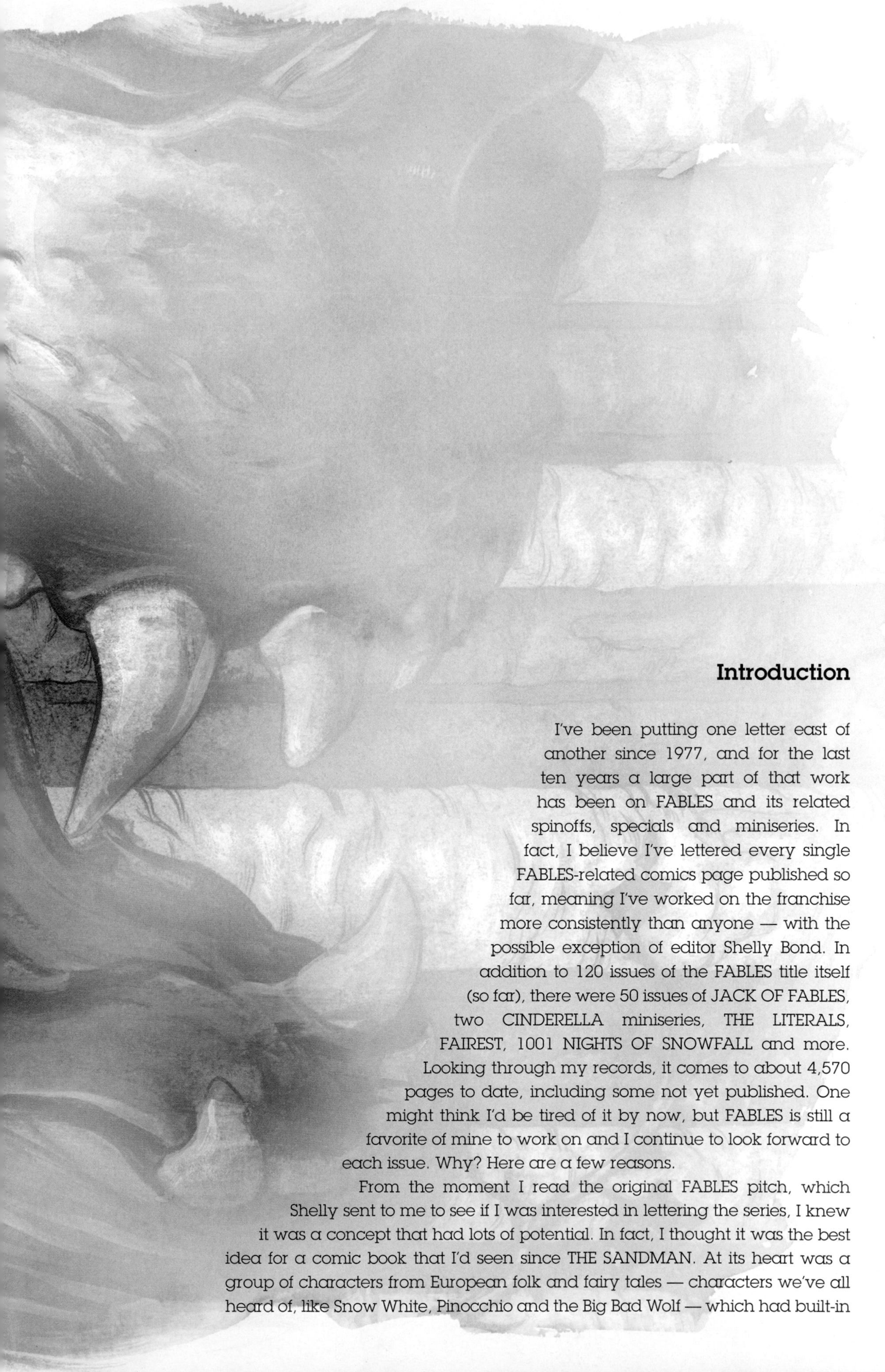

Introduction

I've been putting one letter east of another since 1977, and for the last ten years a large part of that work has been on FABLES and its related spinoffs, specials and miniseries. In fact, I believe I've lettered every single FABLES-related comics page published so far, meaning I've worked on the franchise more consistently than anyone — with the possible exception of editor Shelly Bond. In addition to 120 issues of the FABLES title itself (so far), there were 50 issues of JACK OF FABLES, two CINDERELLA miniseries, THE LITERALS, FAIREST, 1001 NIGHTS OF SNOWFALL and more. Looking through my records, it comes to about 4,570 pages to date, including some not yet published. One might think I'd be tired of it by now, but FABLES is still a favorite of mine to work on and I continue to look forward to each issue. Why? Here are a few reasons.

From the moment I read the original FABLES pitch, which Shelly sent to me to see if I was interested in lettering the series, I knew it was a concept that had lots of potential. In fact, I thought it was the best idea for a comic book that I'd seen since THE SANDMAN. At its heart was a group of characters from European folk and fairy tales — characters we've all heard of, like Snow White, Pinocchio and the Big Bad Wolf — which had built-in resonance and gravitas. Bill Willingham's twist was depicting them as having been expelled from the mythic lands of their original stories and hiding out in America, mostly in New York City and upstate New York. The idea had scope: there are so many characters to choose from, not only from Europe but also from the tales and legends of the rest of the world. And the unknown but clearly epic cataclysm that brought about their exodus to our mundane world? Another engine to drive this story forward.

Beyond the cast's potential, what I liked even more was Bill's approach to the individual characters. Yes, they were recognizably the same folks that we knew from childhood, but they now had new back stories that we *didn't* know before. How did they get here? What troubles and trials have they endured since their original tales ended? How did they come to possess the often quite different attitudes, personality traits, and even physical appearances that we find in the series? Plenty of new stories to explore there! And Bill, who seemed to know and understand all of them thoroughly, had found a unique and perfect voice for each one. He was also carefully weaving, with apparent ease, all of their plotlines together into a single cohesive narrative resplendent in its depth and detail. That FABLES pitch Shelly sent? "Sign me up!" I said.

Of course, every great series needs great artists, and FABLES has had quite a few, though with the second story arc Mark Buckingham hitched his drawing board to the project and claimed it as his own. Bucky's art is a delight in every way, and working over it is always great fun. All of the other artists who have stepped into Fabletown have added their own unique visions, and they have risen to the challenge with excellent work (including the contributions of Jim Fern, Jimmy Palmiotti and Shawn McManus in this volume), but Buckingham remains the artistic center of the series around which all others revolve.

You'll find some great examples of his work in the following pages — particularly in the wedding chapter, which brings together so many of the story and character threads woven by Bill across fifty issues in a brilliant and loving celebration. And I might add that this deluxe edition, with its excellent printing and high-quality paper stock, will allow you to enjoy the art, the coloring (by Daniel Vozzo and Lee Loughridge), and, yes, even the lettering, better than ever before.

When I met up with Bill at this year's San Diego Comic-Con, he was anxious to know if I had agreed to write this introduction, and perhaps a little curious as to what I might put in it. I had agreed but I hadn't had time to start it yet, I told him. "You can do a scathing exposé if you want," he said, with a perhaps slightly nervous smile.

So I considered recounting our first San Diego meeting, years ago, when he told me that he didn't want those fancy styles I used in books like THE SANDMAN, at least not on his work. "I like plain lettering," he said. (I leave it to you, the reader, to see how that has played out!) I thought about revealing how Bill and I learned the hard way how to correctly spell "riposte." I even considered exposing Bill's own super-power: the ability to completely disappear at times when his scripts are most needed. But no, I thought, I'd much rather focus on all of the many positive elements of working on FABLES. So twist my arm as you will, I'll not go down that dark road!

All kidding aside, the FABLES universe is one I feel privileged to revisit each month. It's filled with great writing and delightful art, characters I love (and a few I love to hate), and a creative and editorial team that's a pleasure to work with. I think you'll enjoy what we've prepared for you, so go ahead — turn the page and jump in!

— Todd Klein
July 2012

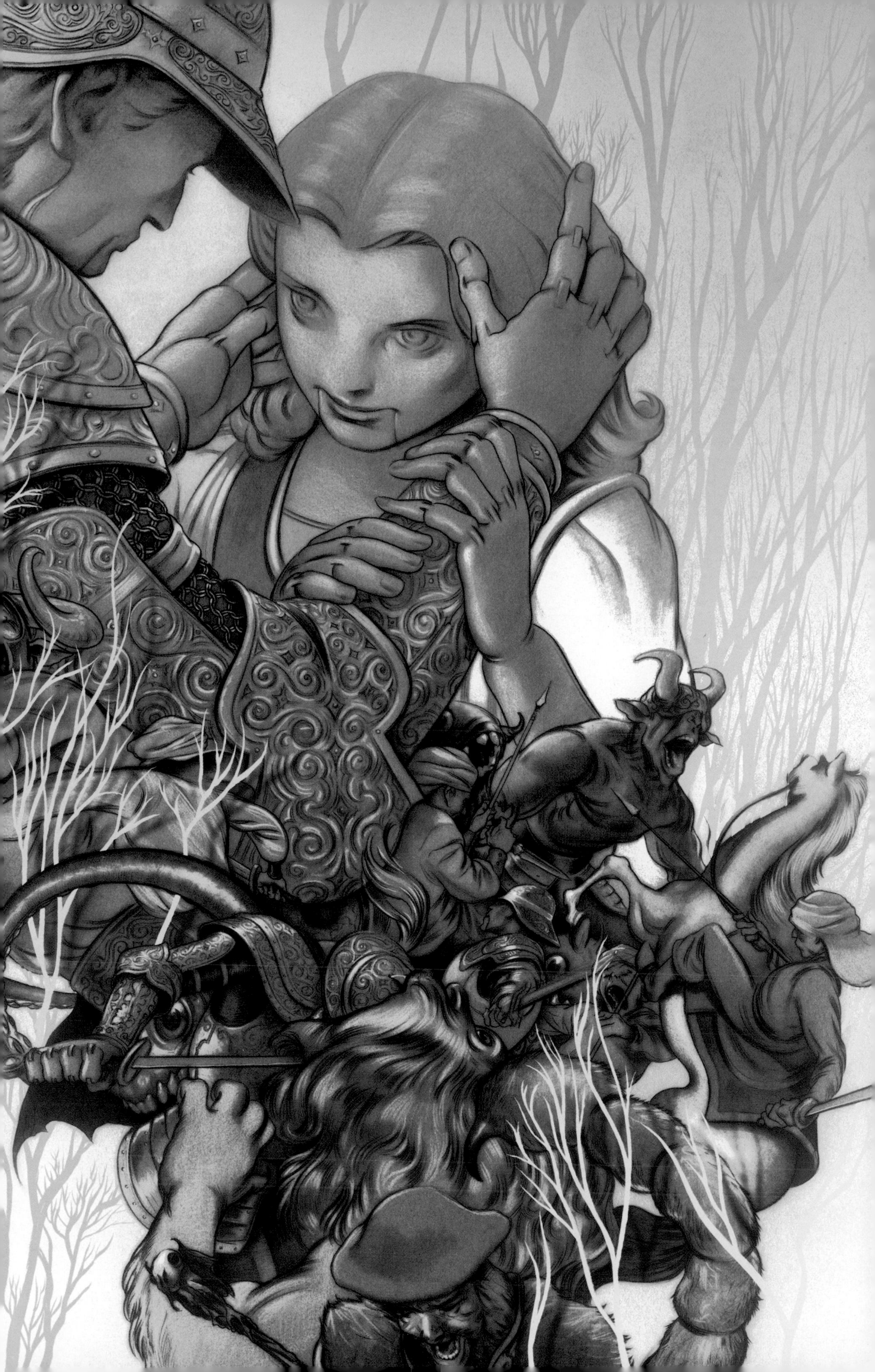

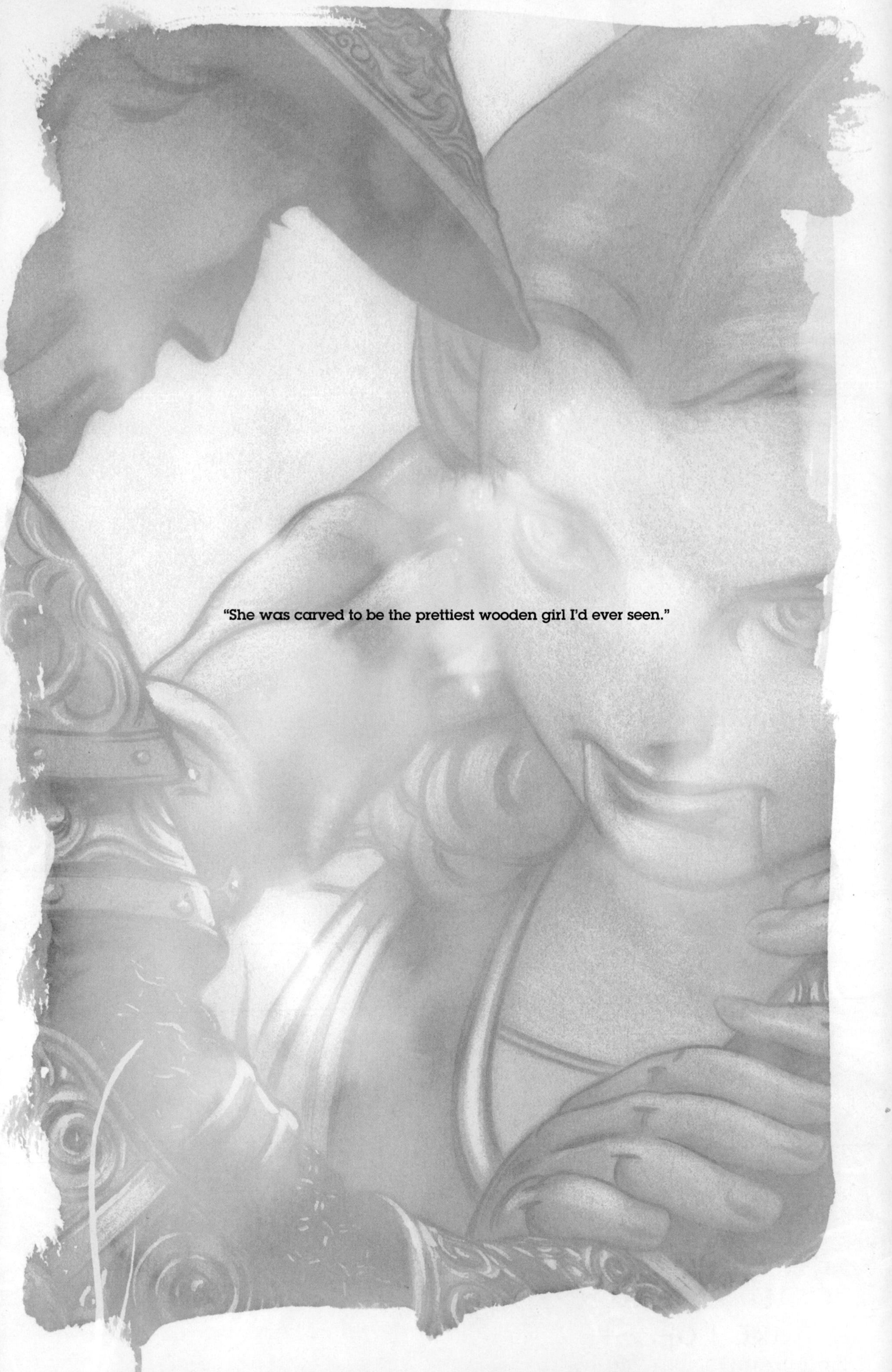

"She was carved to be the prettiest wooden girl I'd ever seen."

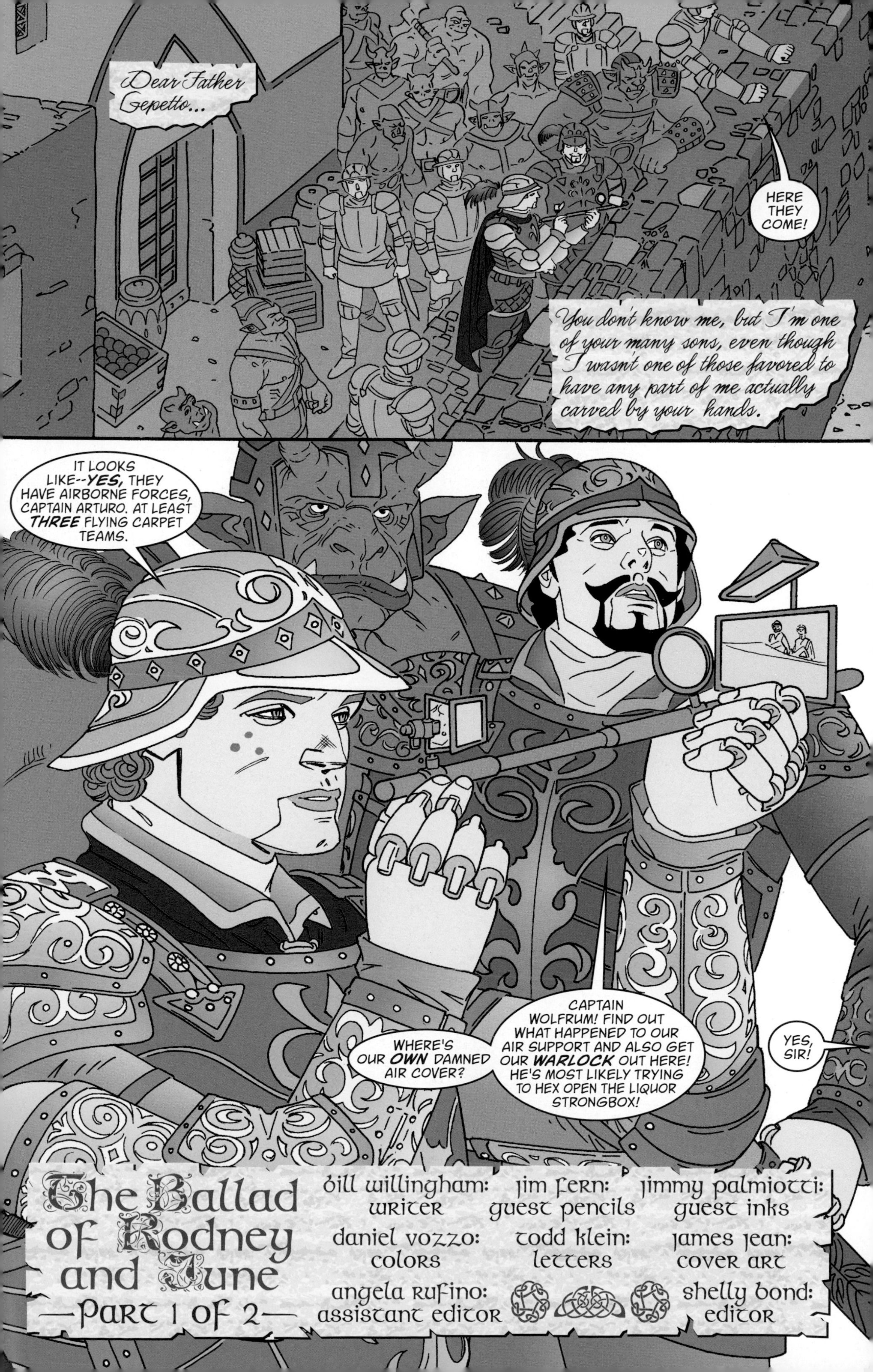

Dear Father Gepetto...
HERE THEY COME!
You don't know me, but I'm one of your many sons, even though I wasn't one of those favored to have any part of me actually carved by your hands.
IT LOOKS LIKE--YES, THEY HAVE AIRBORNE FORCES, CAPTAIN ARTURO. AT LEAST THREE FLYING CARPET TEAMS.
WHERE'S OUR OWN DAMNED AIR COVER?
CAPTAIN WOLFRUM! FIND OUT WHAT HAPPENED TO OUR AIR SUPPORT AND ALSO GET OUR WARLOCK OUT HERE! HE'S MOST LIKELY TRYING TO HEX OPEN THE LIQUOR STRONGBOX!
YES, SIR!
The Ballad of Rodney and June
—Part 1 of 2—
bill willingham: writer
jim fern: guest pencils
jimmy palmiotti: guest inks
daniel vozzo: colors
todd klein: letters
james jean: cover art
angela rufino: assistant editor
shelly bond: editor

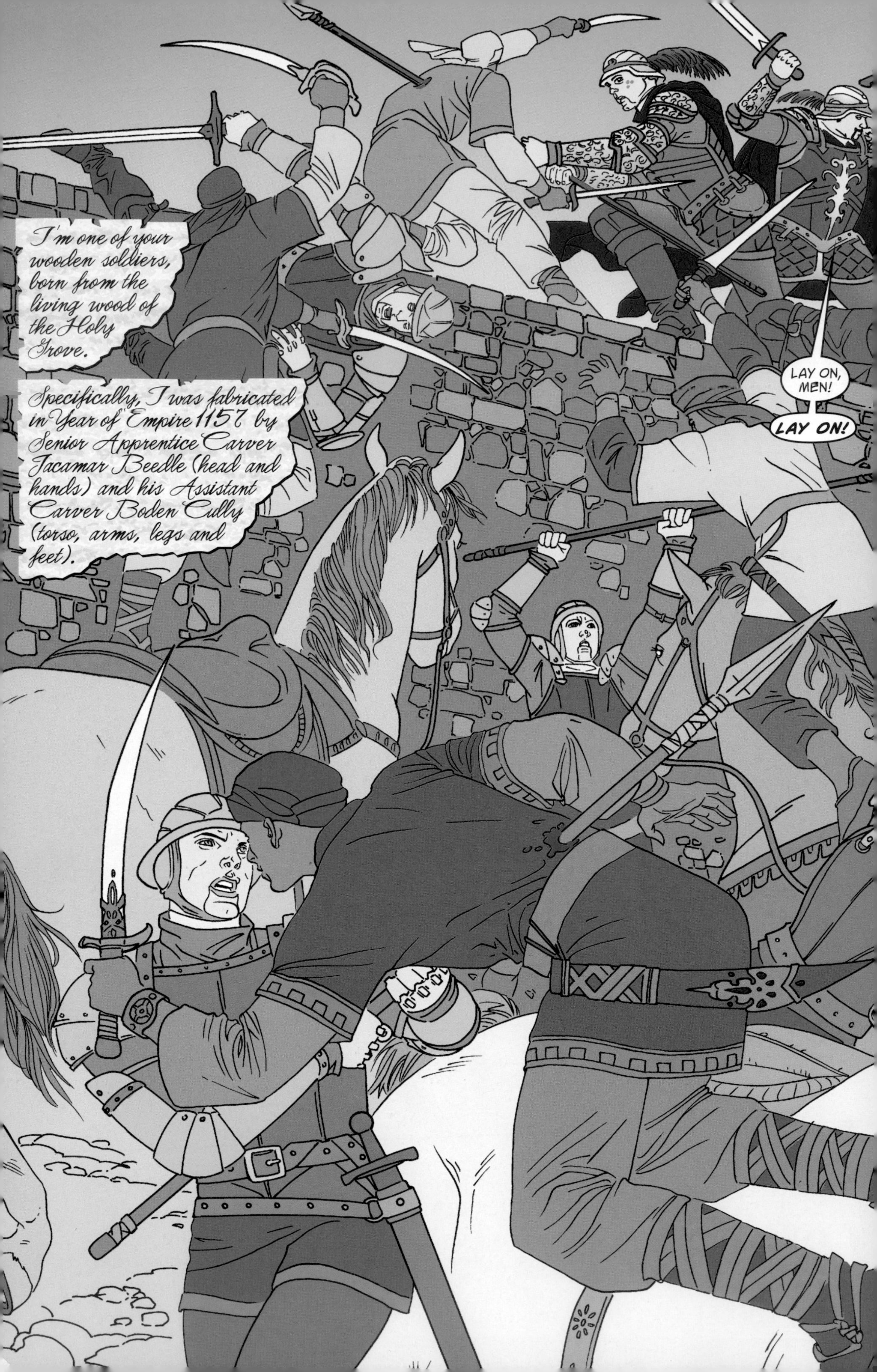

I'm one of your wooden soldiers, born from the living wood of the Holy Grove.
Specifically, I was fabricated in Year of Empire 1157 by Senior Apprentice Carver Jacamar Beedle (head and hands) and his Assistant Carver Boden Cully (torso, arms, legs and feet).
LAY ON, MEN!
LAY ON!

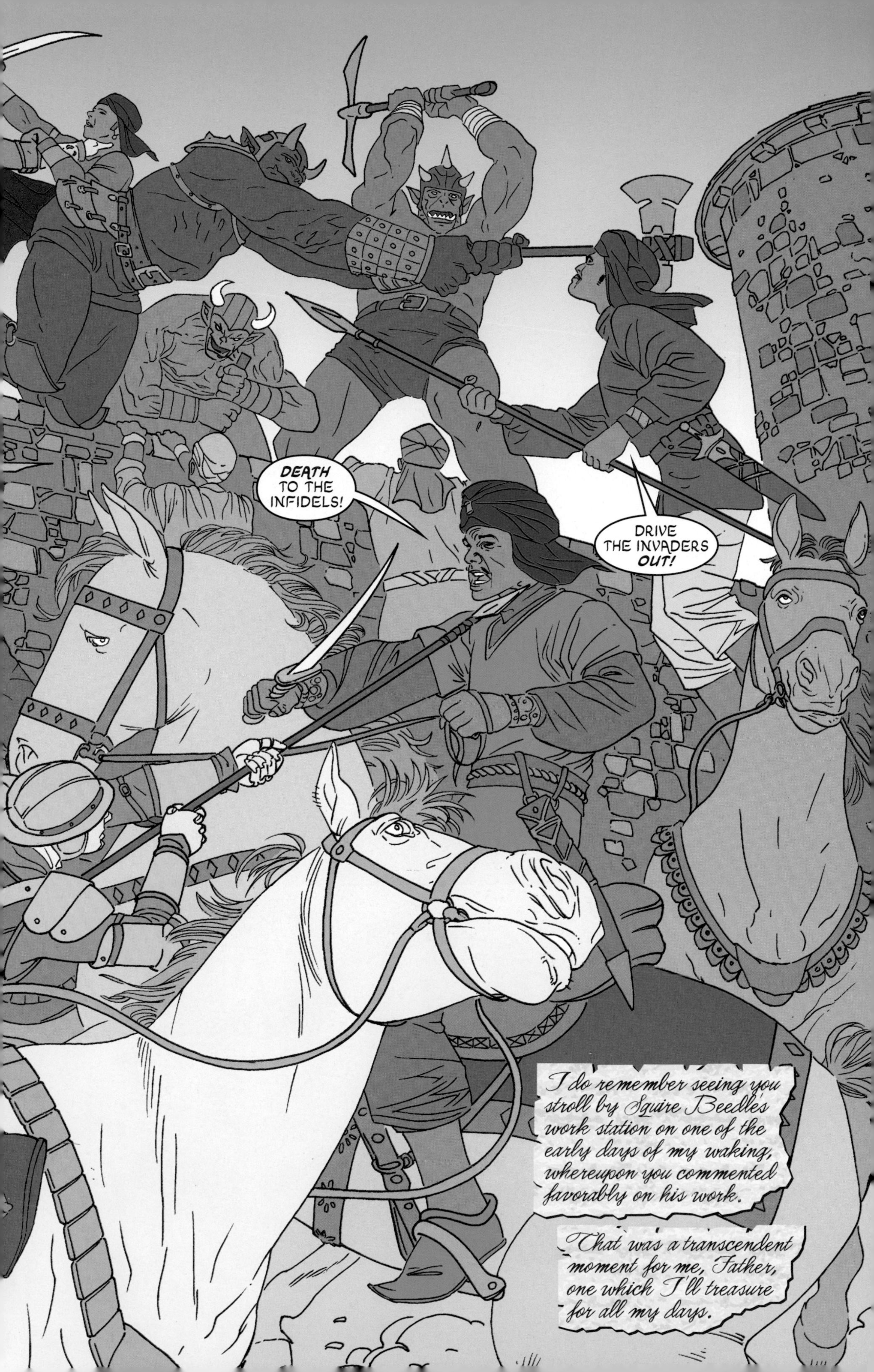
DEATH TO THE INFIDELS!
DRIVE THE INVADERS OUT!
I do remember seeing you stroll by Squire Beedle's work station on one of the early days of my waking, whereupon you commented favorably on his work.
That was a transcendent moment for me, Father, one which I'll treasure for all my days.

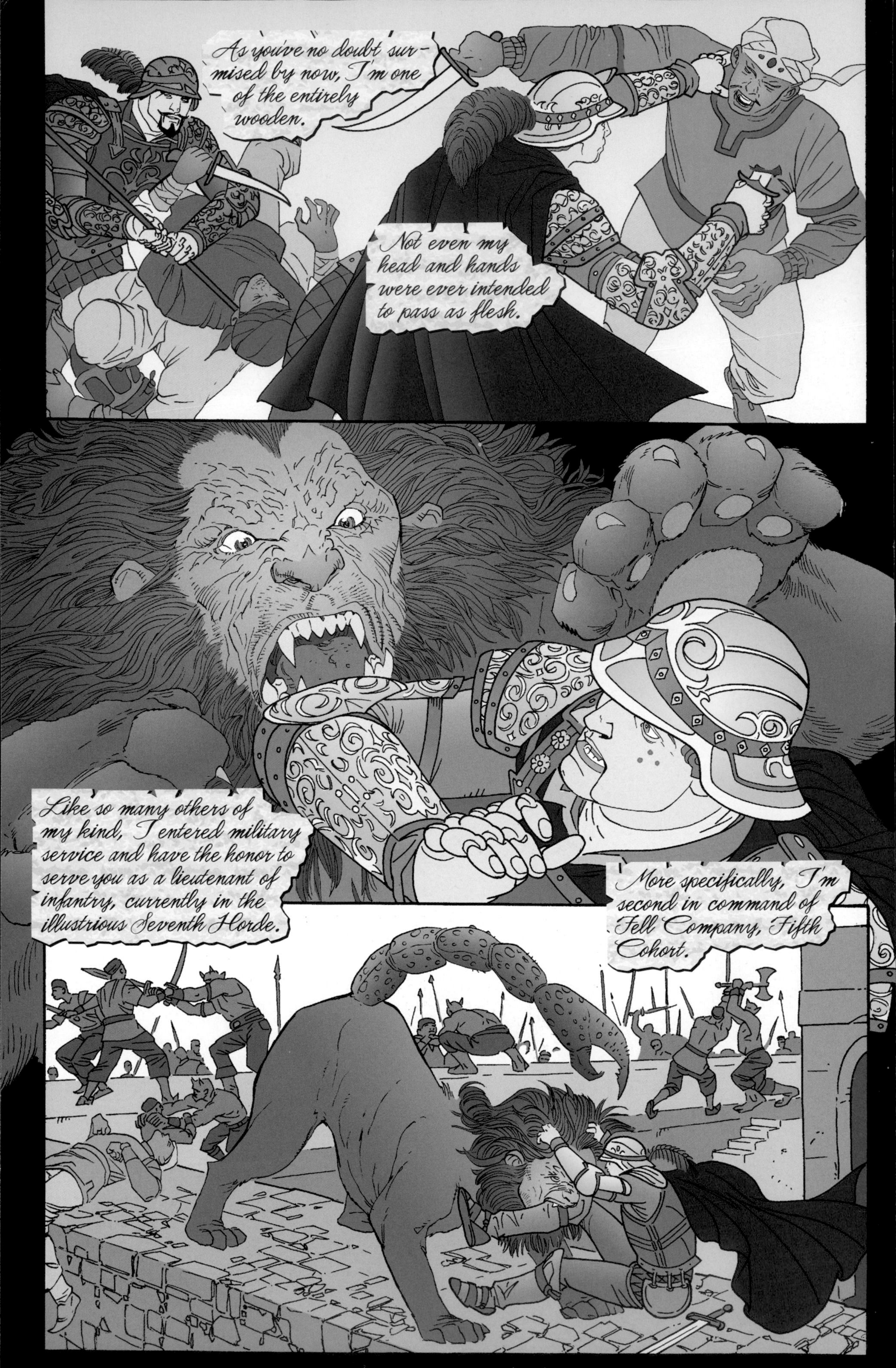
As you've no doubt surmised by now, I'm one of the entirely wooden.
Not even my head and hands were ever intended to pass as flesh.
Like so many others of my kind, I entered military service and have the honor to serve you as a lieutenant of infantry, currently in the illustrious Seventh Horde.
More specifically, I'm second in command of Fell Company, Fifth Cohort.

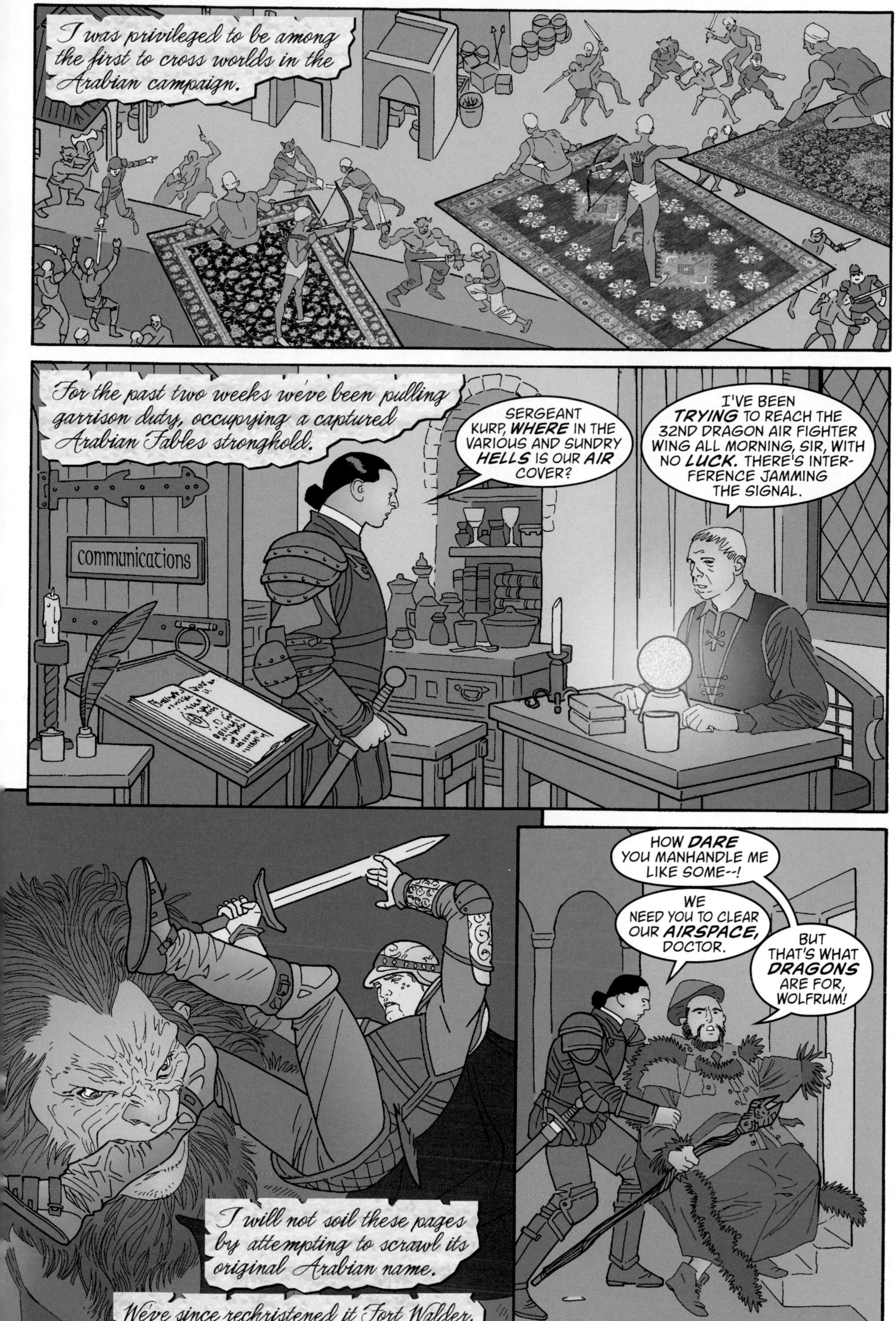
I was privileged to be among the first to cross worlds in the Arabian campaign.
For the past two weeks we've been pulling garrison duty, occupying a captured Arabian Fables stronghold.
communications
SERGEANT KURP, WHERE IN THE VARIOUS AND SUNDRY HELLS IS OUR AIR COVER?
I'VE BEEN TRYING TO REACH THE 32ND DRAGON AIR FIGHTER WING ALL MORNING, SIR, WITH NO LUCK. THERE'S INTERFERENCE JAMMING THE SIGNAL.
I will not soil these pages by attempting to scrawl its original Arabian name.
We've since rechristened it Fort Walder, to honor another of your sons in our company who died in the taking of it.
HOW DARE YOU MANHANDLE ME LIKE SOME--!
WE NEED YOU TO CLEAR OUR AIRSPACE, DOCTOR.
BUT THAT'S WHAT DRAGONS ARE FOR, WOLFRUM!

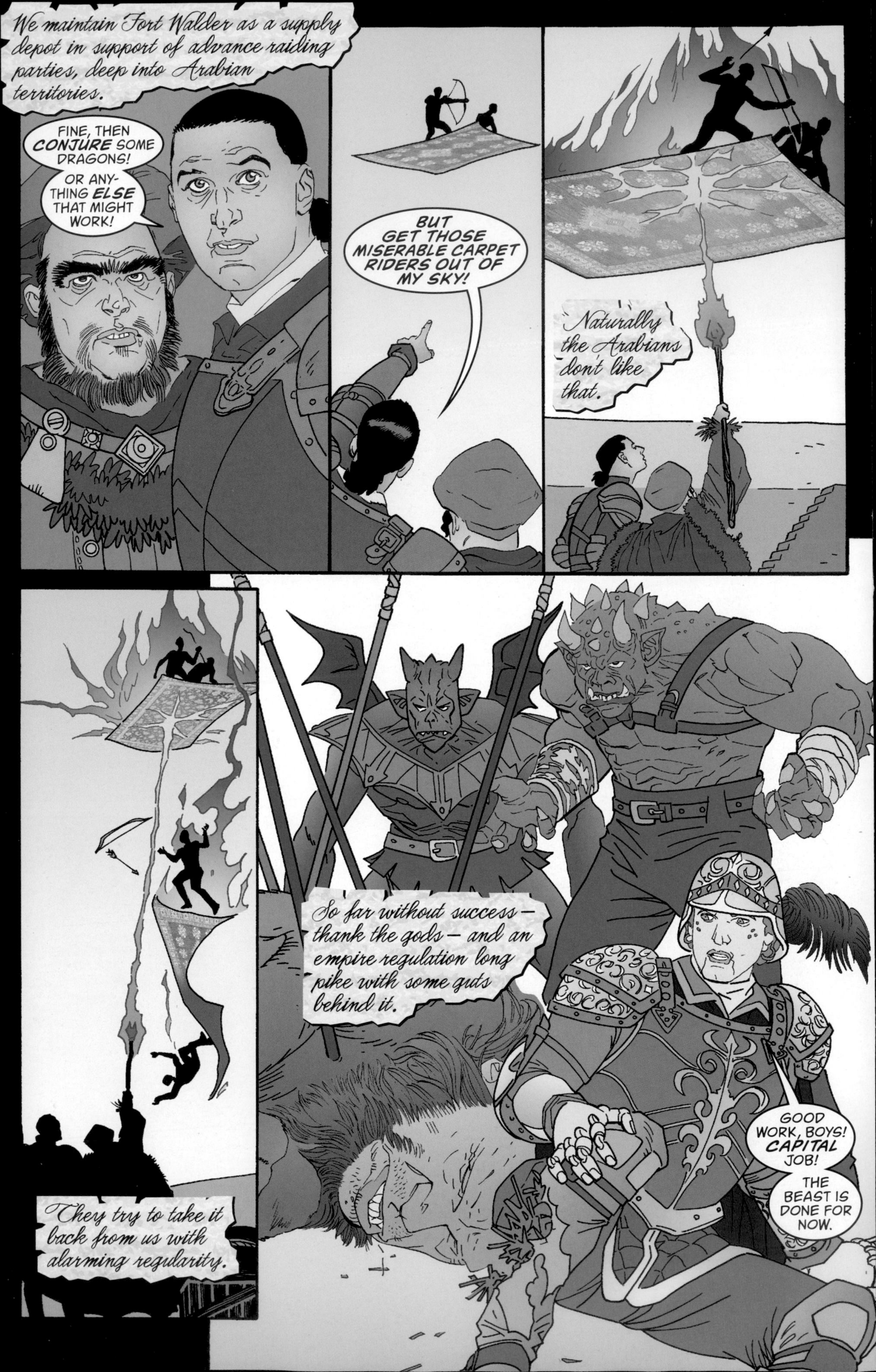
We maintain Fort Walder as a supply depot in support of advance raiding parties, deep into Arabian territories.
FINE, THEN CONJURE SOME DRAGONS!
OR ANY-THING ELSE THAT MIGHT WORK!
BUT GET THOSE MISERABLE CARPET RIDERS OUT OF MY SKY!
Naturally the Arabians don't like that.
They try to take it back from us with alarming regularity.
So far without success— thank the gods— and an empire regulation long pike with some guts behind it.
GOOD WORK, BOYS! CAPITAL JOB!
THE BEAST IS DONE FOR NOW.

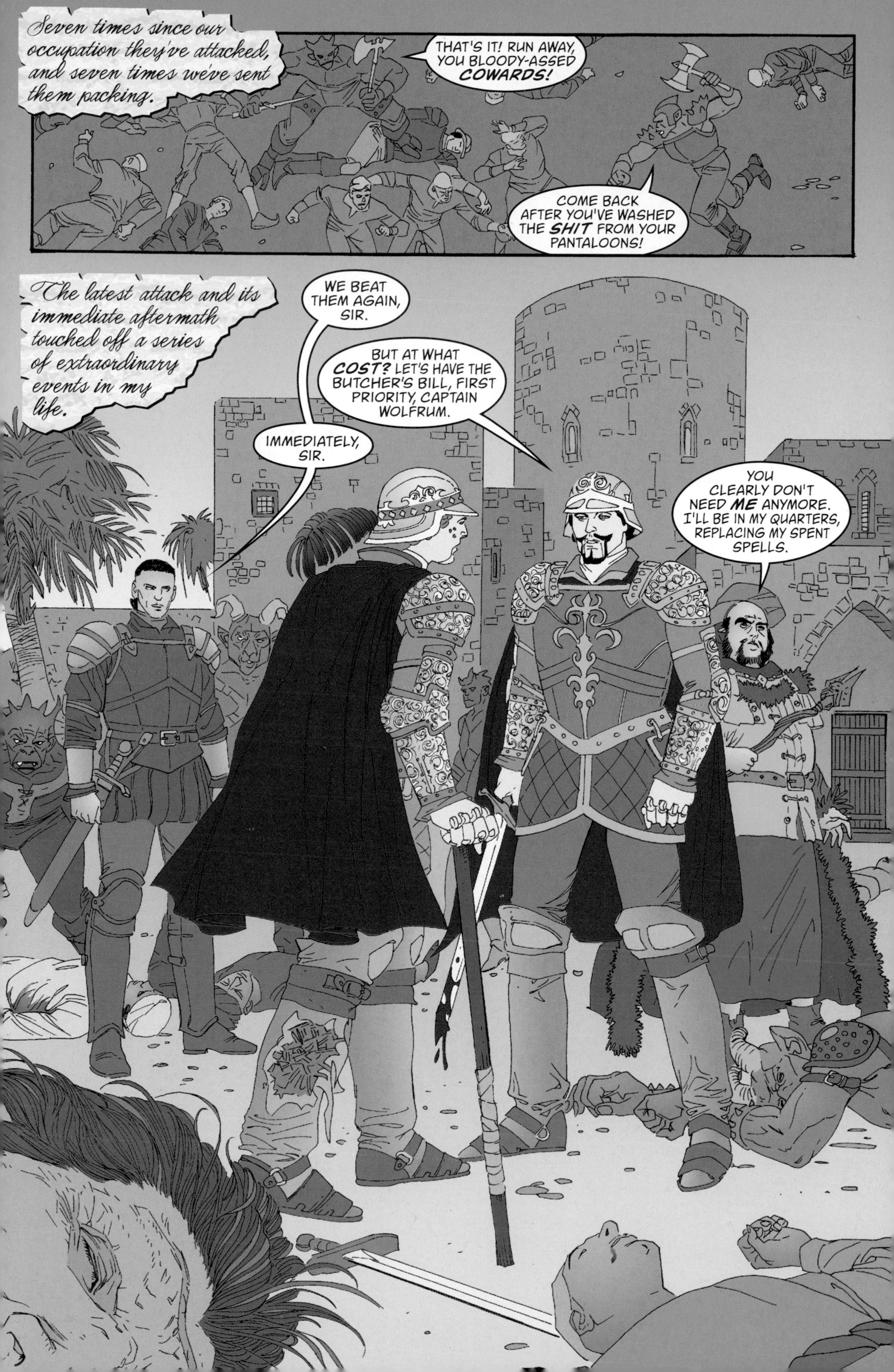
Seven times since our occupation they've attacked, and seven times we've sent them packing.
THAT'S IT! RUN AWAY, YOU BLOODY-ASSED COWARDS!
COME BACK AFTER YOU'VE WASHED THE SHIT FROM YOUR PANTALOONS!
The latest attack and its immediate aftermath touched off a series of extraordinary events in my life.
WE BEAT THEM AGAIN, SIR.
BUT AT WHAT COST? LET'S HAVE THE BUTCHER'S BILL, FIRST PRIORITY, CAPTAIN WOLFRUM.
IMMEDIATELY, SIR.
YOU CLEARLY DON'T NEED ME ANYMORE. I'LL BE IN MY QUARTERS, REPLACING MY SPENT SPELLS.

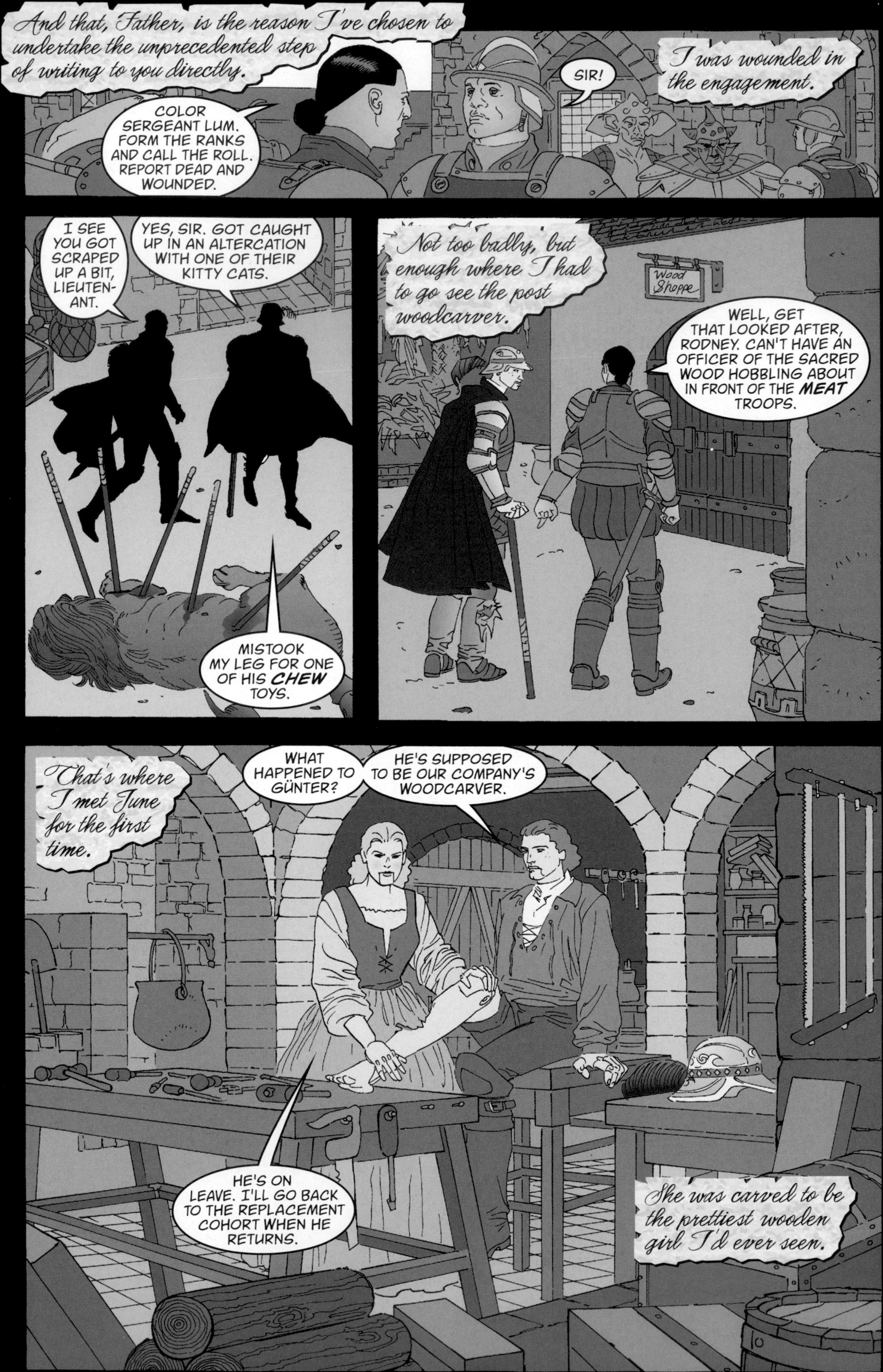
And that, Father, is the reason I've chosen to undertake the unprecedented step of writing to you directly.
COLOR SERGEANT LUM. FORM THE RANKS AND CALL THE ROLL. REPORT DEAD AND WOUNDED.
SIR!
I was wounded in the engagement.
I SEE YOU GOT SCRAPED UP A BIT, LIEUTENANT.
YES, SIR. GOT CAUGHT UP IN AN ALTERCATION WITH ONE OF THEIR KITTY CATS.
MISTOOK MY LEG FOR ONE OF HIS CHEW TOYS.
Not too badly, but enough where I had to go see the post woodcarver.
Wood Shoppe
WELL, GET THAT LOOKED AFTER, RODNEY. CAN'T HAVE AN OFFICER OF THE SACRED WOOD HOBBLING ABOUT IN FRONT OF THE MEAT TROOPS.
That's where I met June for the first time.
WHAT HAPPENED TO GÜNTER?
HE'S SUPPOSED TO BE OUR COMPANY'S WOODCARVER.
HE'S ON LEAVE. I'LL GO BACK TO THE REPLACEMENT COHORT WHEN HE RETURNS.
She was carved to be the prettiest wooden girl I'd ever seen.

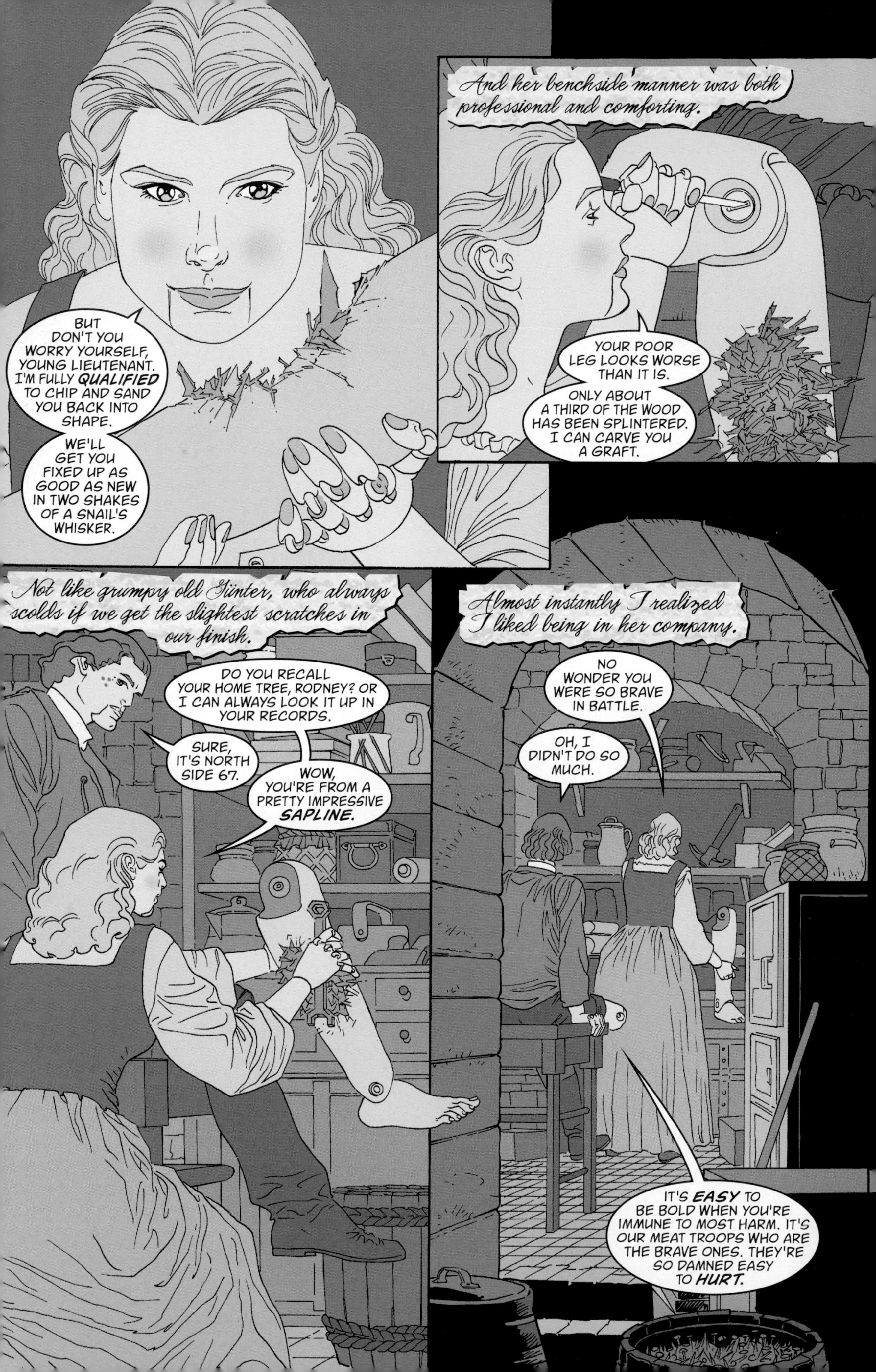

BUT DON'T YOU WORRY YOURSELF, YOUNG LIEUTENANT. I'M FULLY QUALIFIED TO CHIP AND SAND YOU BACK INTO SHAPE.
WE'LL GET YOU FIXED UP AS GOOD AS NEW IN TWO SHAKES OF A SNAIL'S WHISKER.
And her benchside manner was both professional and comforting.
YOUR POOR LEG LOOKS WORSE THAN IT IS.
ONLY ABOUT A THIRD OF THE WOOD HAS BEEN SPLINTERED. I CAN CARVE YOU A GRAFT.
Not like grumpy old Günter, who always scolds if we get the slightest scratches in our finish.
DO YOU RECALL YOUR HOME TREE, RODNEY? OR I CAN ALWAYS LOOK IT UP IN YOUR RECORDS.
SURE, IT'S NORTH SIDE 67.
WOW, YOU'RE FROM A PRETTY IMPRESSIVE SAPLINE.
Almost instantly I realized I liked being in her company.
NO WONDER YOU WERE SO BRAVE IN BATTLE.
OH, I DIDN'T DO SO MUCH.
IT'S EASY TO BE BOLD WHEN YOU'RE IMMUNE TO MOST HARM. IT'S OUR MEAT TROOPS WHO ARE THE BRAVE ONES. THEY'RE SO DAMNED EASY TO HURT.

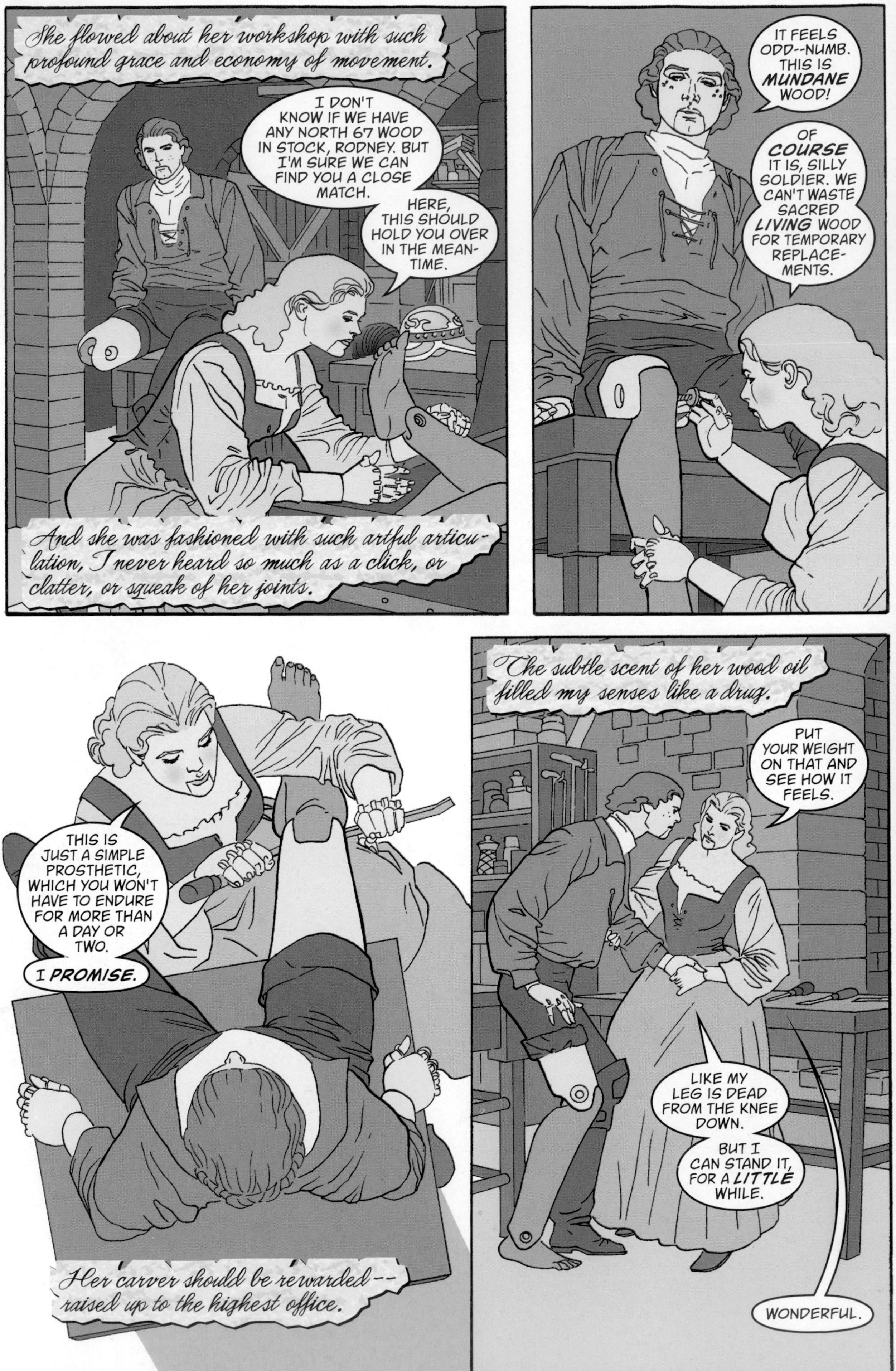
She flowed about her workshop with such profound grace and economy of movement.
I DON'T KNOW IF WE HAVE ANY NORTH 67 WOOD IN STOCK, RODNEY. BUT I'M SURE WE CAN FIND YOU A CLOSE MATCH.
HERE, THIS SHOULD HOLD YOU OVER IN THE MEAN-TIME.
And she was fashioned with such artful articu-lation, I never heard so much as a click, or clatter, or squeak of her joints.
IT FEELS ODD--NUMB. THIS IS MUNDANE WOOD!
OF COURSE IT IS, SILLY SOLDIER. WE CAN'T WASTE SACRED LIVING WOOD FOR TEMPORARY REPLACE-MENTS.
THIS IS JUST A SIMPLE PROSTHETIC, WHICH YOU WON'T HAVE TO ENDURE FOR MORE THAN A DAY OR TWO.
I PROMISE.
Her carver should be rewarded--raised up to the highest office.
The subtle scent of her wood oil filled my senses like a drug.
PUT YOUR WEIGHT ON THAT AND SEE HOW IT FEELS.
LIKE MY LEG IS DEAD FROM THE KNEE DOWN.
BUT I CAN STAND IT, FOR A LITTLE WHILE.
WONDERFUL.

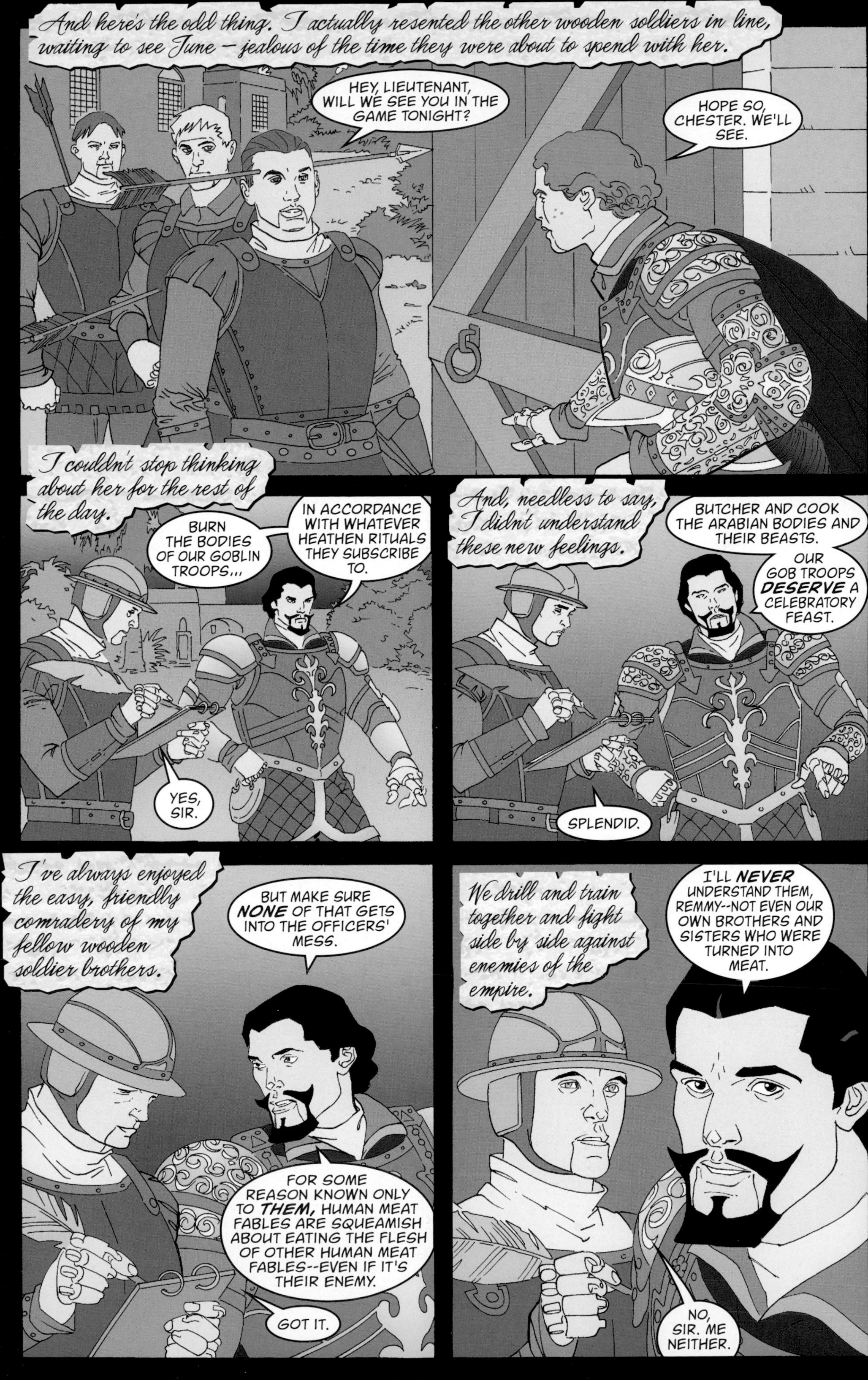
And here's the odd thing. I actually resented the other wooden soldiers in line, waiting to see June — jealous of the time they were about to spend with her.
HEY, LIEUTENANT, WILL WE SEE YOU IN THE GAME TONIGHT?
HOPE SO, CHESTER. WE'LL SEE.
I couldn't stop thinking about her for the rest of the day.
BURN THE BODIES OF OUR GOBLIN TROOPS...
IN ACCORDANCE WITH WHATEVER HEATHEN RITUALS THEY SUBSCRIBE TO.
YES, SIR.
And, needless to say, I didn't understand these new feelings.
BUTCHER AND COOK THE ARABIAN BODIES AND THEIR BEASTS.
OUR GOB TROOPS **DESERVE** A CELEBRATORY FEAST.
SPLENDID.
I've always enjoyed the easy, friendly comradery of my fellow wooden soldier brothers.
BUT MAKE SURE **NONE** OF THAT GETS INTO THE OFFICERS' MESS.
FOR SOME REASON KNOWN ONLY TO **THEM,** HUMAN MEAT FABLES ARE SQUEAMISH ABOUT EATING THE FLESH OF OTHER HUMAN MEAT FABLES--EVEN IF IT'S THEIR ENEMY.
GOT IT.
We drill and train together and fight side by side against enemies of the empire.
I'LL **NEVER** UNDERSTAND THEM, REMMY--NOT EVEN OUR OWN BROTHERS AND SISTERS WHO WERE TURNED INTO MEAT.
NO, SIR. ME NEITHER.

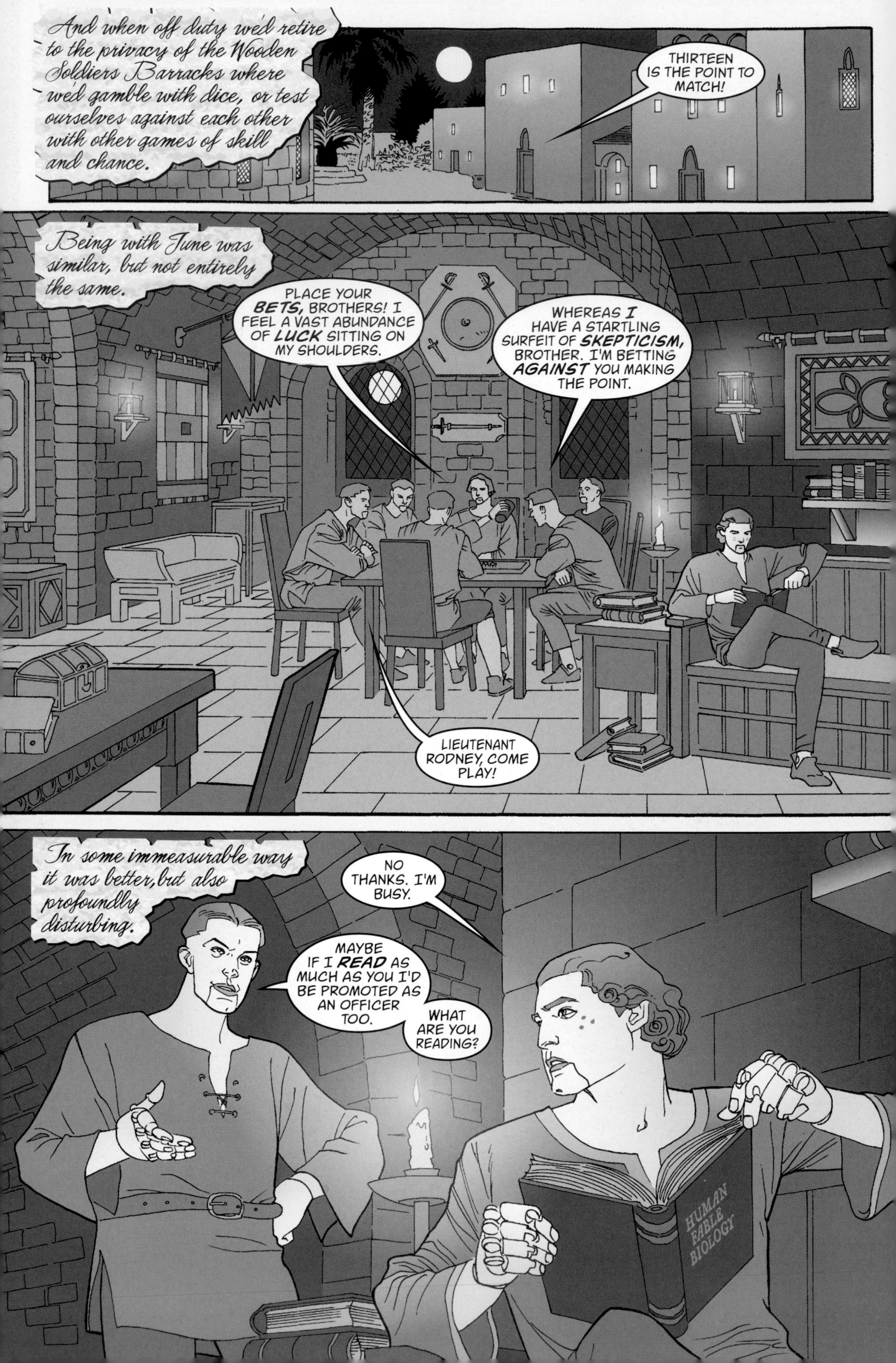
And when off duty we'd retire to the privacy of the Wooden Soldiers Barracks where we'd gamble with dice, or test ourselves against each other with other games of skill and chance.
THIRTEEN IS THE POINT TO MATCH!
Being with June was similar, but not entirely the same.
PLACE YOUR BETS, BROTHERS! I FEEL A VAST ABUNDANCE OF LUCK SITTING ON MY SHOULDERS.
WHEREAS I HAVE A STARTLING SURFEIT OF SKEPTICISM, BROTHER. I'M BETTING AGAINST YOU MAKING THE POINT.
LIEUTENANT RODNEY, COME PLAY!
In some immeasurable way it was better, but also profoundly disturbing.
NO THANKS. I'M BUSY.
MAYBE IF I READ AS MUCH AS YOU I'D BE PROMOTED AS AN OFFICER TOO.
WHAT ARE YOU READING?
HUMAN FABLE BIOLOGY

I tried to make sense of it.

READING UP ON THE MATING HABITS OF **MEAT**, LIEUTENANT?

HEY!

YUCK!

WHY?

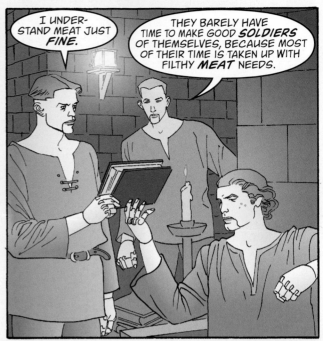

I UNDER-STAND MEAT JUST **FINE.**

THEY BARELY HAVE TIME TO MAKE GOOD **SOLDIERS** OF THEMSELVES, BECAUSE MOST OF THEIR TIME IS TAKEN UP WITH FILTHY **MEAT** NEEDS.

THEY HAVE TO SLEEP A **THIRD** OF EVERY SINGLE DAY.

AND OH, HOW THEY HAVE TO TAKE CONSTANT **BREAKS** TO PISS AND SHIT AND REST AND **COPULATE** WITH THE CAMP FOLLOWERS.

AND THEY HAVE TO **EAT** THREE OR FOUR TIMES A DAY OR THEY WASTE AWAY.

THEY SMELL LIKE A DUNG HEAP IF THEY DON'T **BATHE** EVERY MONTH OR SO.

THEY CAN BARELY RUN A MILE WITHOUT NEEDING TO REST.

AND CAN'T FORCE-MARCH MUCH MORE THAN TWENTY MILES A DAY, AND CAN'T EVEN DO **THAT** FOR MORE THAN A FEW DAYS IN A ROW.

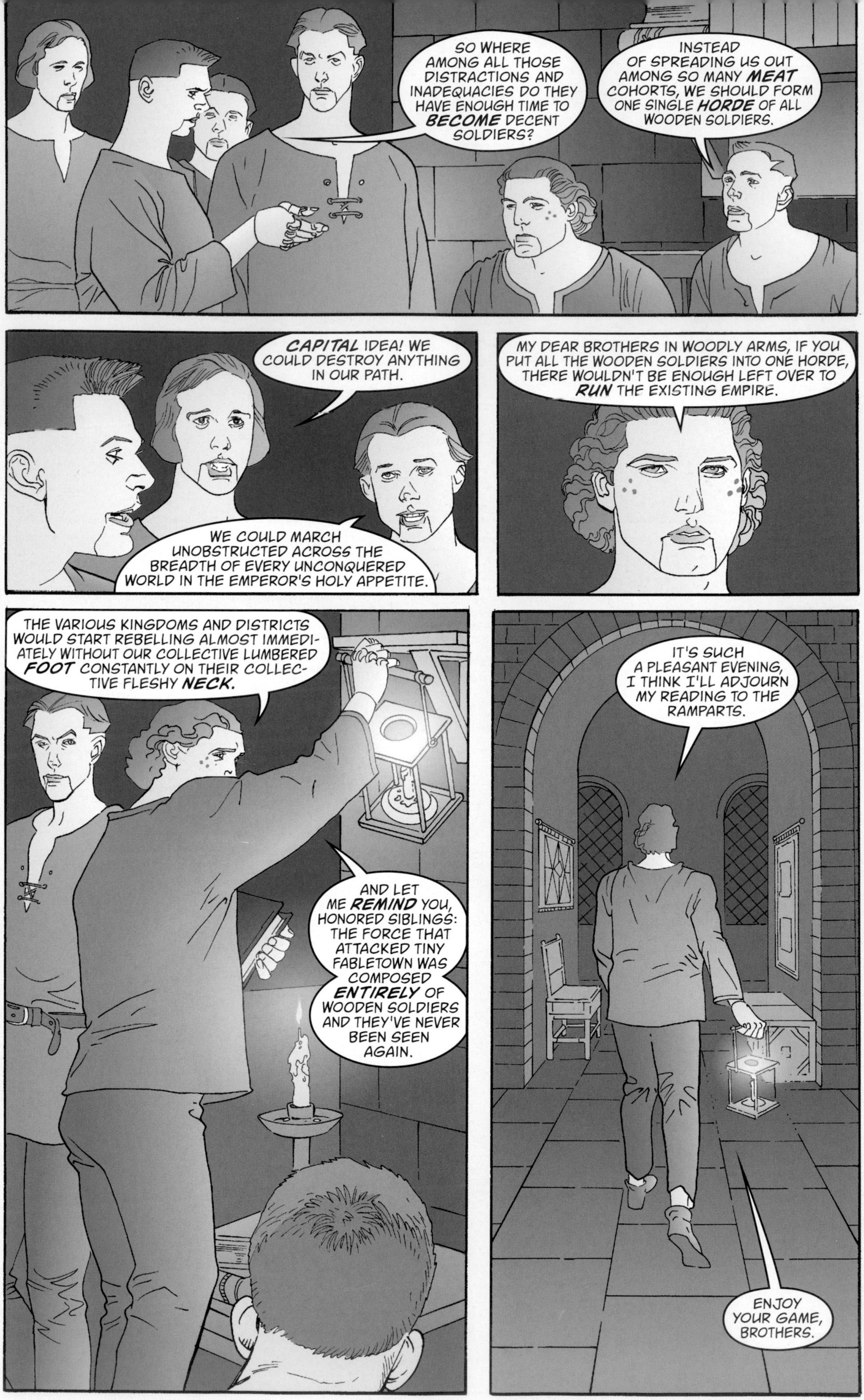
SO WHERE AMONG ALL THOSE DISTRACTIONS AND INADEQUACIES DO THEY HAVE ENOUGH TIME TO **BECOME** DECENT SOLDIERS?
INSTEAD OF SPREADING US OUT AMONG SO MANY **MEAT** COHORTS, WE SHOULD FORM ONE SINGLE **HORDE** OF ALL WOODEN SOLDIERS.
CAPITAL IDEA! WE COULD DESTROY ANYTHING IN OUR PATH.
WE COULD MARCH UNOBSTRUCTED ACROSS THE BREADTH OF EVERY UNCONQUERED WORLD IN THE EMPEROR'S HOLY APPETITE.
MY DEAR BROTHERS IN WOODLY ARMS, IF YOU PUT ALL THE WOODEN SOLDIERS INTO ONE HORDE, THERE WOULDN'T BE ENOUGH LEFT OVER TO **RUN** THE EXISTING EMPIRE.
THE VARIOUS KINGDOMS AND DISTRICTS WOULD START REBELLING ALMOST IMMEDIATELY WITHOUT OUR COLLECTIVE LUMBERED **FOOT** CONSTANTLY ON THEIR COLLECTIVE FLESHY **NECK.**
AND LET ME **REMIND** YOU, HONORED SIBLINGS: THE FORCE THAT ATTACKED TINY FABLETOWN WAS COMPOSED **ENTIRELY** OF WOODEN SOLDIERS AND THEY'VE NEVER BEEN SEEN AGAIN.
IT'S SUCH A PLEASANT EVENING, I THINK I'LL ADJOURN MY READING TO THE RAMPARTS.
ENJOY YOUR GAME, BROTHERS.

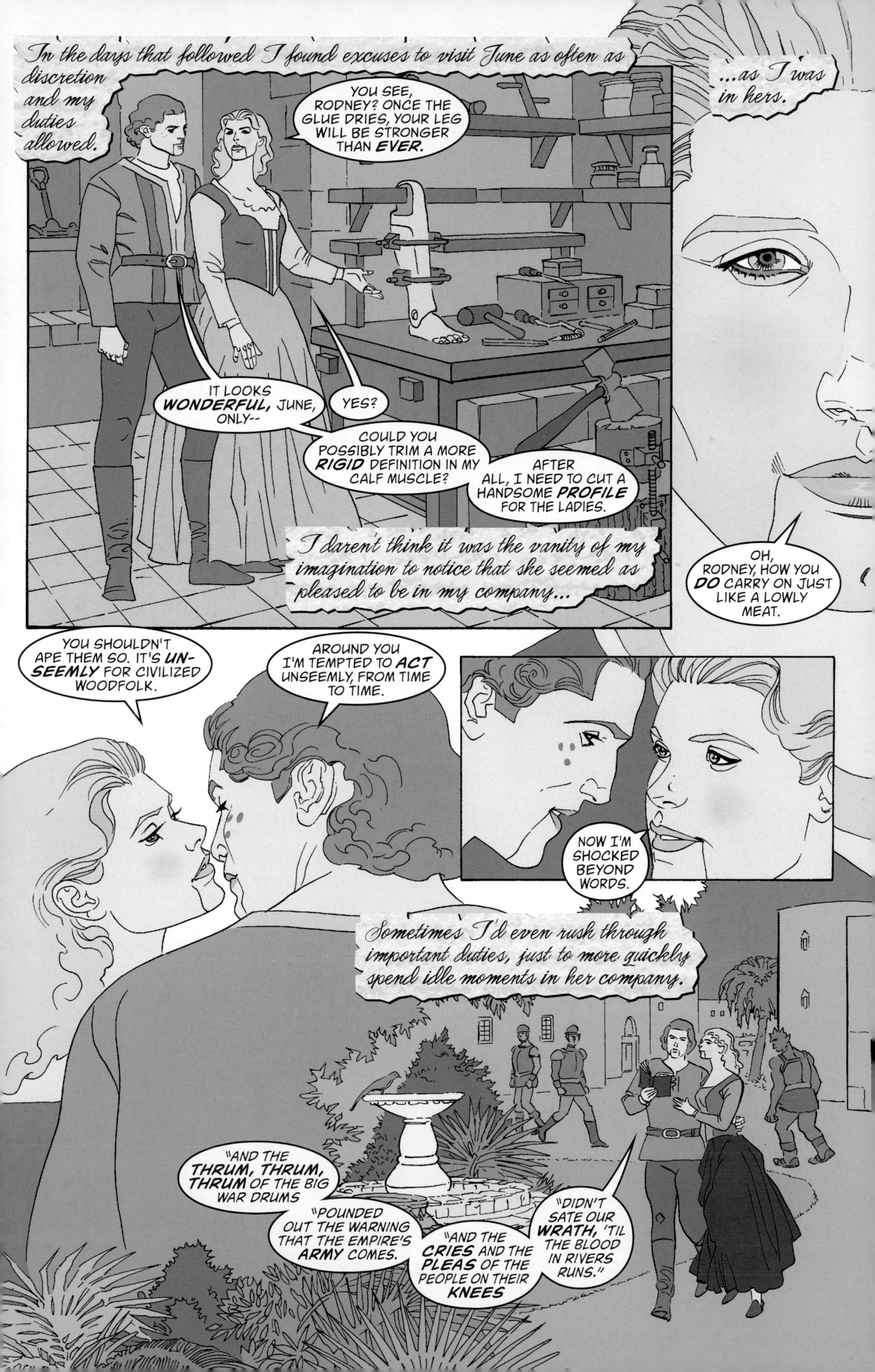
In the days that followed I found excuses to visit June as often as discretion and my duties allowed.
YOU SEE, RODNEY? ONCE THE GLUE DRIES, YOUR LEG WILL BE STRONGER THAN EVER.
IT LOOKS WONDERFUL, JUNE, ONLY--
YES?
COULD YOU POSSIBLY TRIM A MORE RIGID DEFINITION IN MY CALF MUSCLE?
AFTER ALL, I NEED TO CUT A HANDSOME PROFILE FOR THE LADIES.
I darent think it was the vanity of my imagination to notice that she seemed as pleased to be in my company...
...as I was in hers.
OH, RODNEY, HOW YOU DO CARRY ON JUST LIKE A LOWLY MEAT.
YOU SHOULDN'T APE THEM SO. IT'S UNSEEMLY FOR CIVILIZED WOODFOLK.
AROUND YOU I'M TEMPTED TO ACT UNSEEMLY, FROM TIME TO TIME.
NOW I'M SHOCKED BEYOND WORDS.
Sometimes I'd even rush through important duties, just to more quickly spend idle moments in her company.
"AND THE THRUM, THRUM, THRUM OF THE BIG WAR DRUMS
"POUNDED OUT THE WARNING THAT THE EMPIRE'S ARMY COMES.
"AND THE CRIES AND THE PLEAS OF THE PEOPLE ON THEIR KNEES
"DIDN'T SATE OUR WRATH, 'TIL THE BLOOD IN RIVERS RUNS."

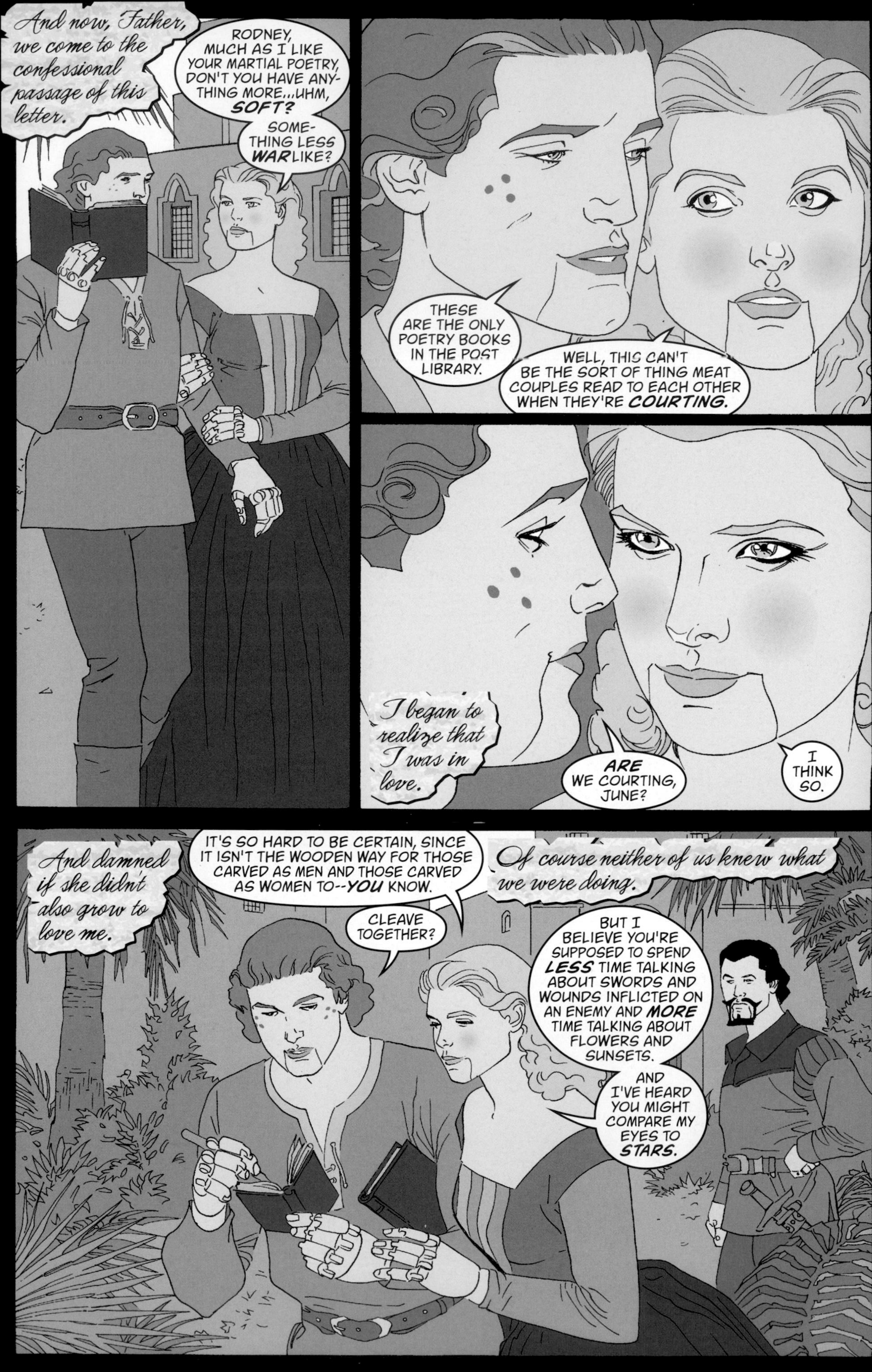
And now, Father, we come to the confessional passage of this letter.
RODNEY, MUCH AS I LIKE YOUR MARTIAL POETRY, DON'T YOU HAVE ANY-THING MORE...UHM, SOFT?
SOME-THING LESS WARLIKE?
THESE ARE THE ONLY POETRY BOOKS IN THE POST LIBRARY.
WELL, THIS CAN'T BE THE SORT OF THING MEAT COUPLES READ TO EACH OTHER WHEN THEY'RE COURTING.
I began to realize that I was in love.
ARE WE COURTING, JUNE?
I THINK SO.
And damned if she didn't also grow to love me.
IT'S SO HARD TO BE CERTAIN, SINCE IT ISN'T THE WOODEN WAY FOR THOSE CARVED AS MEN AND THOSE CARVED AS WOMEN TO--YOU KNOW.
CLEAVE TOGETHER?
Of course neither of us knew what we were doing.
BUT I BELIEVE YOU'RE SUPPOSED TO SPEND LESS TIME TALKING ABOUT SWORDS AND WOUNDS INFLICTED ON AN ENEMY AND MORE TIME TALKING ABOUT FLOWERS AND SUNSETS.
AND I'VE HEARD YOU MIGHT COMPARE MY EYES TO STARS.

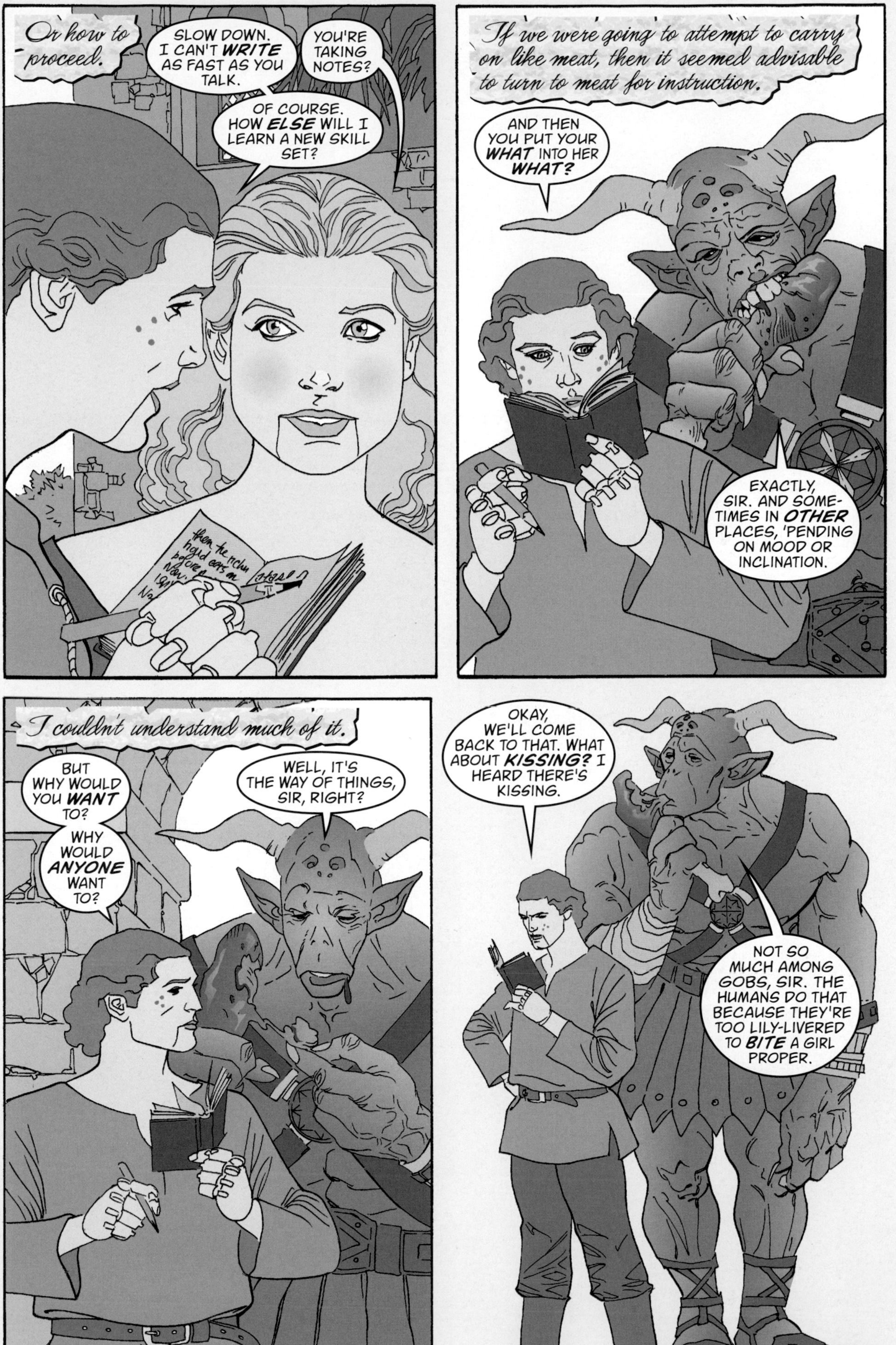
Or how to proceed.
SLOW DOWN. I CAN'T WRITE AS FAST AS YOU TALK.
YOU'RE TAKING NOTES?
OF COURSE. HOW ELSE WILL I LEARN A NEW SKILL SET?
If we were going to attempt to carry on like meat, then it seemed advisable to turn to meat for instruction.
AND THEN YOU PUT YOUR WHAT INTO HER WHAT?
EXACTLY, SIR. AND SOMETIMES IN OTHER PLACES, 'PENDING ON MOOD OR INCLINATION.
I couldn't understand much of it.
BUT WHY WOULD YOU WANT TO?
WHY WOULD ANYONE WANT TO?
WELL, IT'S THE WAY OF THINGS, SIR, RIGHT?
OKAY, WE'LL COME BACK TO THAT. WHAT ABOUT KISSING? I HEARD THERE'S KISSING.
NOT SO MUCH AMONG GOBS, SIR. THE HUMANS DO THAT BECAUSE THEY'RE TOO LILY-LIVERED TO BITE A GIRL PROPER.

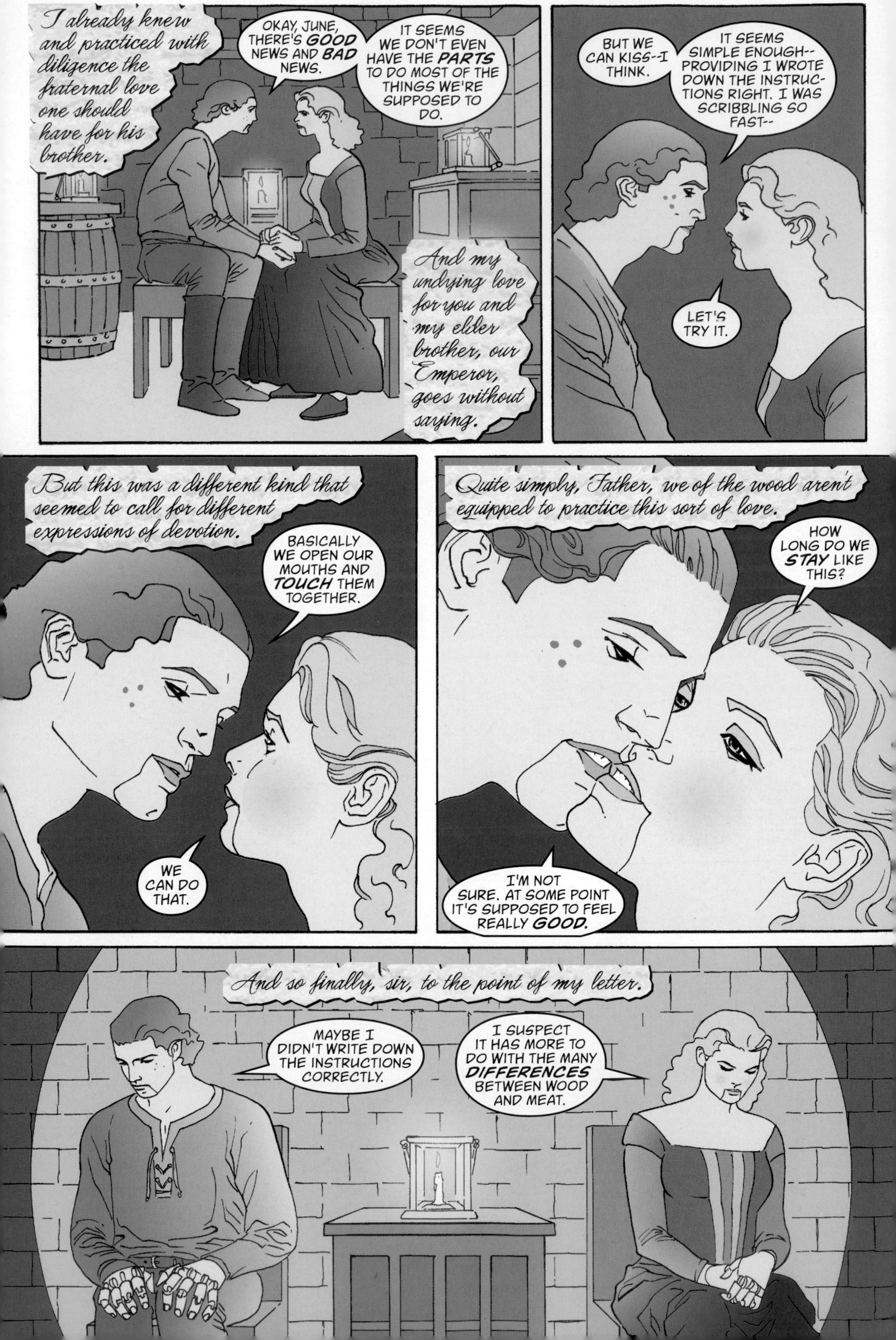
I already knew and practiced with diligence the fraternal love one should have for his brother.
OKAY, JUNE, THERE'S GOOD NEWS AND BAD NEWS.
IT SEEMS WE DON'T EVEN HAVE THE PARTS TO DO MOST OF THE THINGS WE'RE SUPPOSED TO DO.
And my undying love for you and my elder brother, our Emperor, goes without saying.
BUT WE CAN KISS--I THINK.
IT SEEMS SIMPLE ENOUGH--PROVIDING I WROTE DOWN THE INSTRUCTIONS RIGHT. I WAS SCRIBBLING SO FAST--
LET'S TRY IT.
But this was a different kind that seemed to call for different expressions of devotion.
BASICALLY WE OPEN OUR MOUTHS AND TOUCH THEM TOGETHER.
WE CAN DO THAT.
Quite simply, Father, we of the wood aren't equipped to practice this sort of love.
HOW LONG DO WE STAY LIKE THIS?
I'M NOT SURE. AT SOME POINT IT'S SUPPOSED TO FEEL REALLY GOOD.
And so finally, sir, to the point of my letter.
MAYBE I DIDN'T WRITE DOWN THE INSTRUCTIONS CORRECTLY.
I SUSPECT IT HAS MORE TO DO WITH THE MANY DIFFERENCES BETWEEN WOOD AND MEAT.

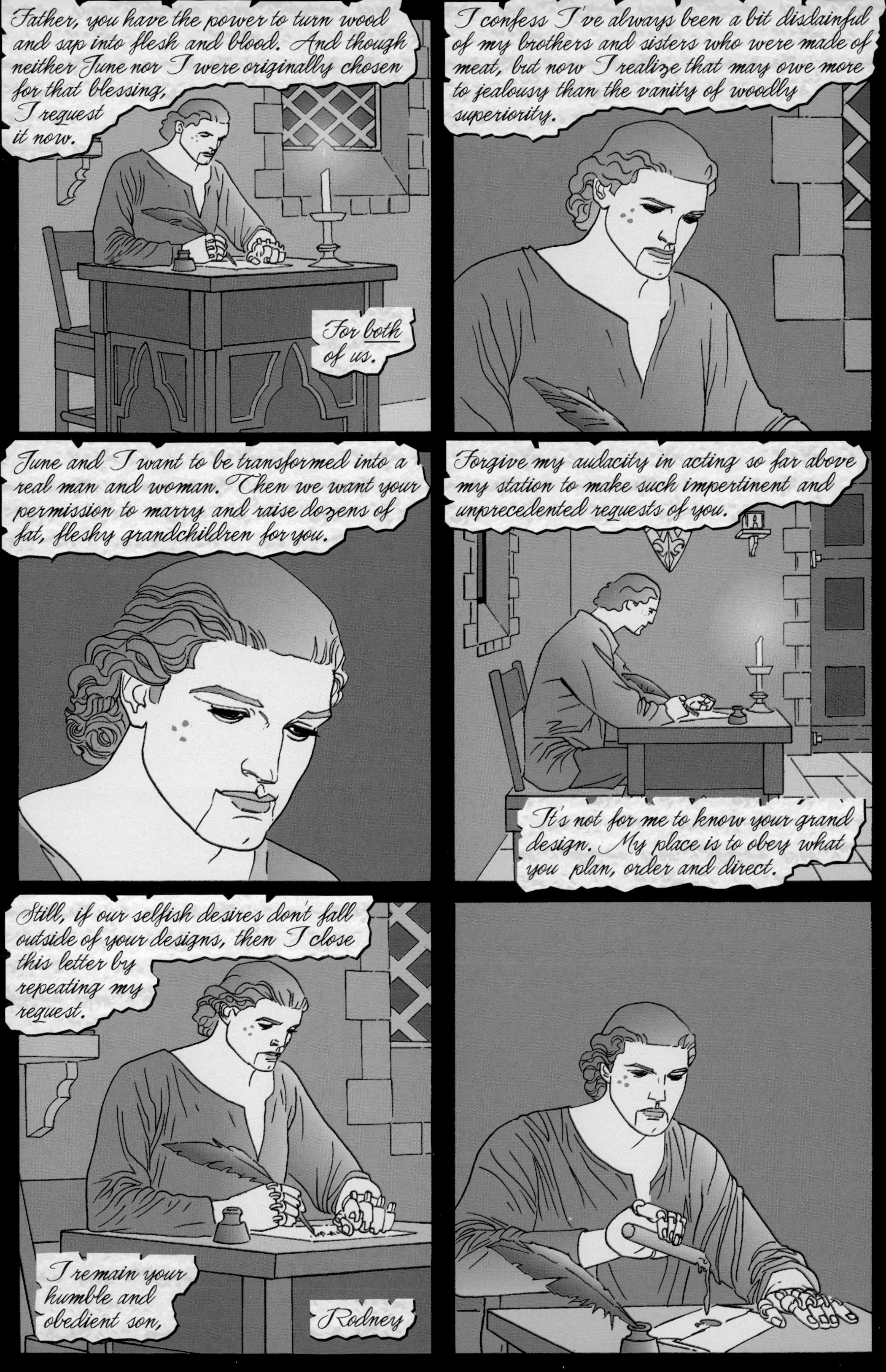
Father, you have the power to turn wood and sap into flesh and blood. And though neither June nor I were originally chosen for that blessing, I request it now.
For both of us.
I confess I've always been a bit disdainful of my brothers and sisters who were made of meat, but now I realize that may owe more to jealousy than the vanity of woodly superiority.
June and I want to be transformed into a real man and woman. Then we want your permission to marry and raise dozens of fat, fleshy grandchildren for you.
Forgive my audacity in acting so far above my station to make such impertinent and unprecedented requests of you.
It's not for me to know your grand design. My place is to obey what you plan, order and direct.
Still, if our selfish desires don't fall outside of your designs, then I close this letter by repeating my request.
I remain your humble and obedient son,
Rodney

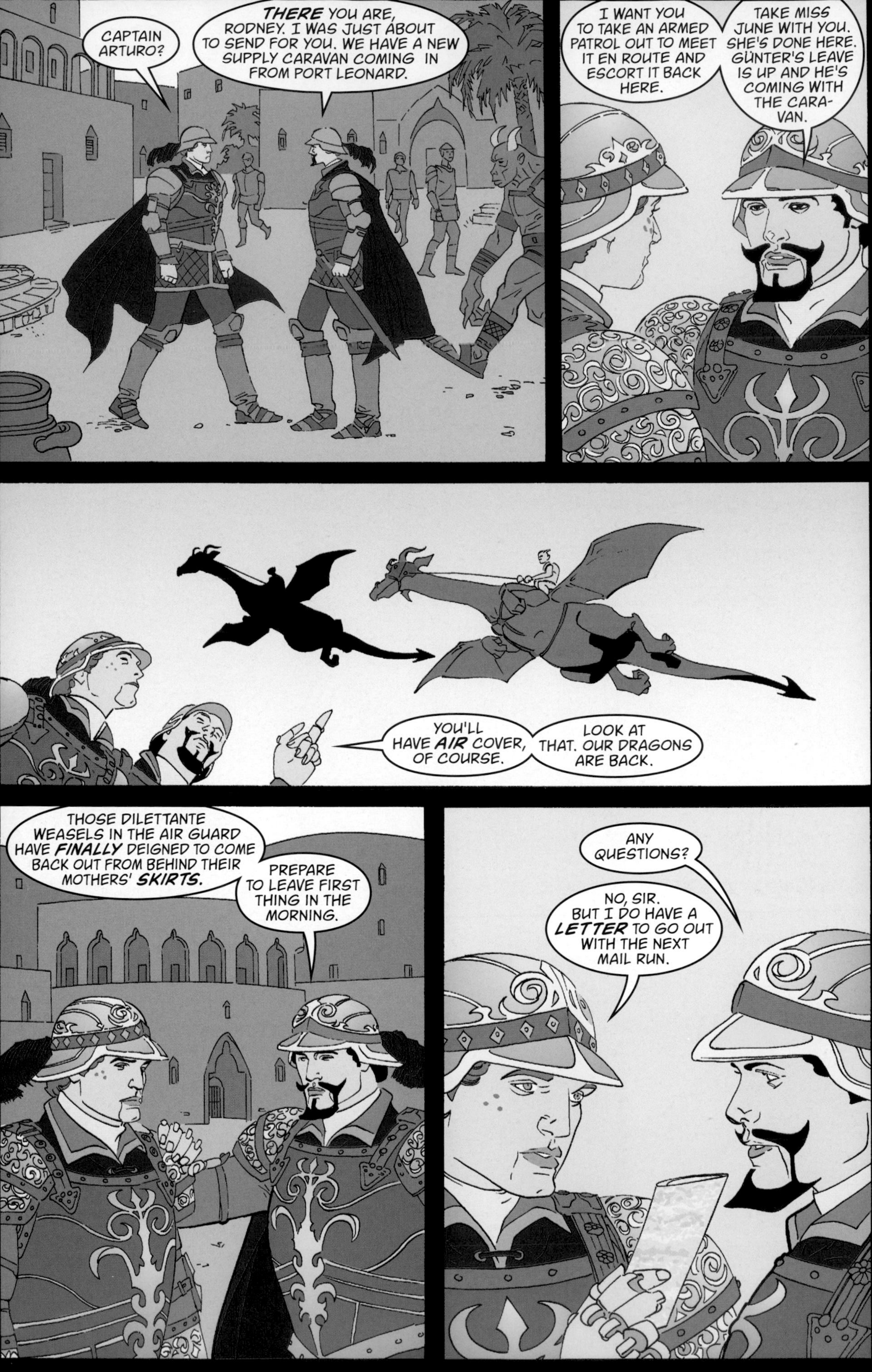
CAPTAIN ARTURO?
THERE YOU ARE, RODNEY. I WAS JUST ABOUT TO SEND FOR YOU. WE HAVE A NEW SUPPLY CARAVAN COMING IN FROM PORT LEONARD.
I WANT YOU TO TAKE AN ARMED PATROL OUT TO MEET IT EN ROUTE AND ESCORT IT BACK HERE.
TAKE MISS JUNE WITH YOU. SHE'S DONE HERE. GÜNTER'S LEAVE IS UP AND HE'S COMING WITH THE CARA-VAN.
LOOK AT THAT. OUR DRAGONS ARE BACK.
YOU'LL HAVE AIR COVER, OF COURSE.
THOSE DILETTANTE WEASELS IN THE AIR GUARD HAVE FINALLY DEIGNED TO COME BACK OUT FROM BEHIND THEIR MOTHERS' SKIRTS.
PREPARE TO LEAVE FIRST THING IN THE MORNING.
ANY QUESTIONS?
NO, SIR. BUT I DO HAVE A LETTER TO GO OUT WITH THE NEXT MAIL RUN.

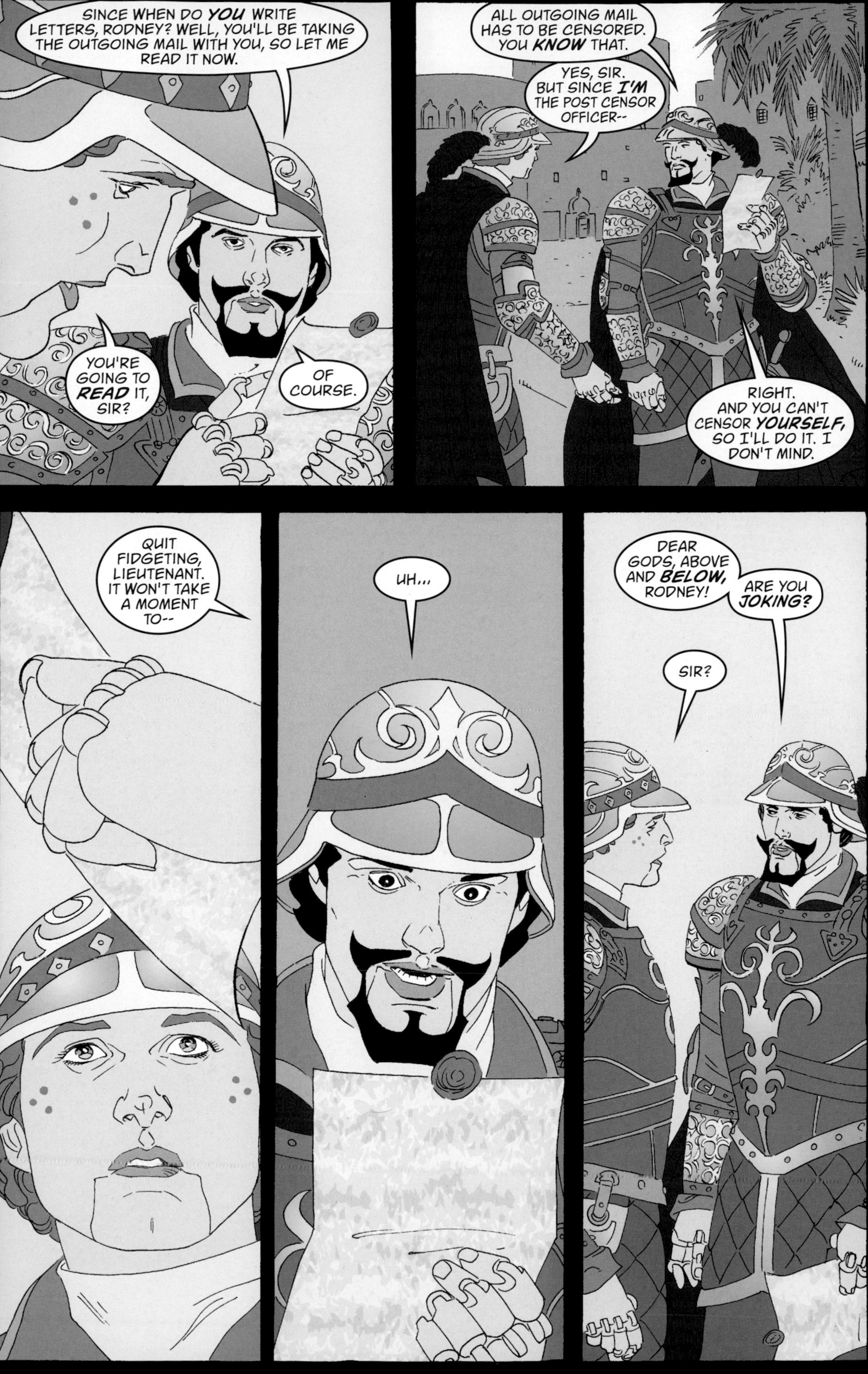
SINCE WHEN DO *YOU* WRITE LETTERS, RODNEY? WELL, YOU'LL BE TAKING THE OUTGOING MAIL WITH YOU, SO LET ME READ IT NOW.
YOU'RE GOING TO *READ* IT, SIR?
OF COURSE.
ALL OUTGOING MAIL HAS TO BE CENSORED. YOU *KNOW* THAT.
YES, SIR. BUT SINCE *I'M* THE POST CENSOR OFFICER--
RIGHT. AND YOU CAN'T CENSOR *YOURSELF,* SO I'LL DO IT. I DON'T MIND.
QUIT FIDGETING, LIEUTENANT. IT WON'T TAKE A MOMENT TO--
UH...
DEAR GODS, ABOVE AND *BELOW,* RODNEY!
ARE YOU *JOKING?*
SIR?

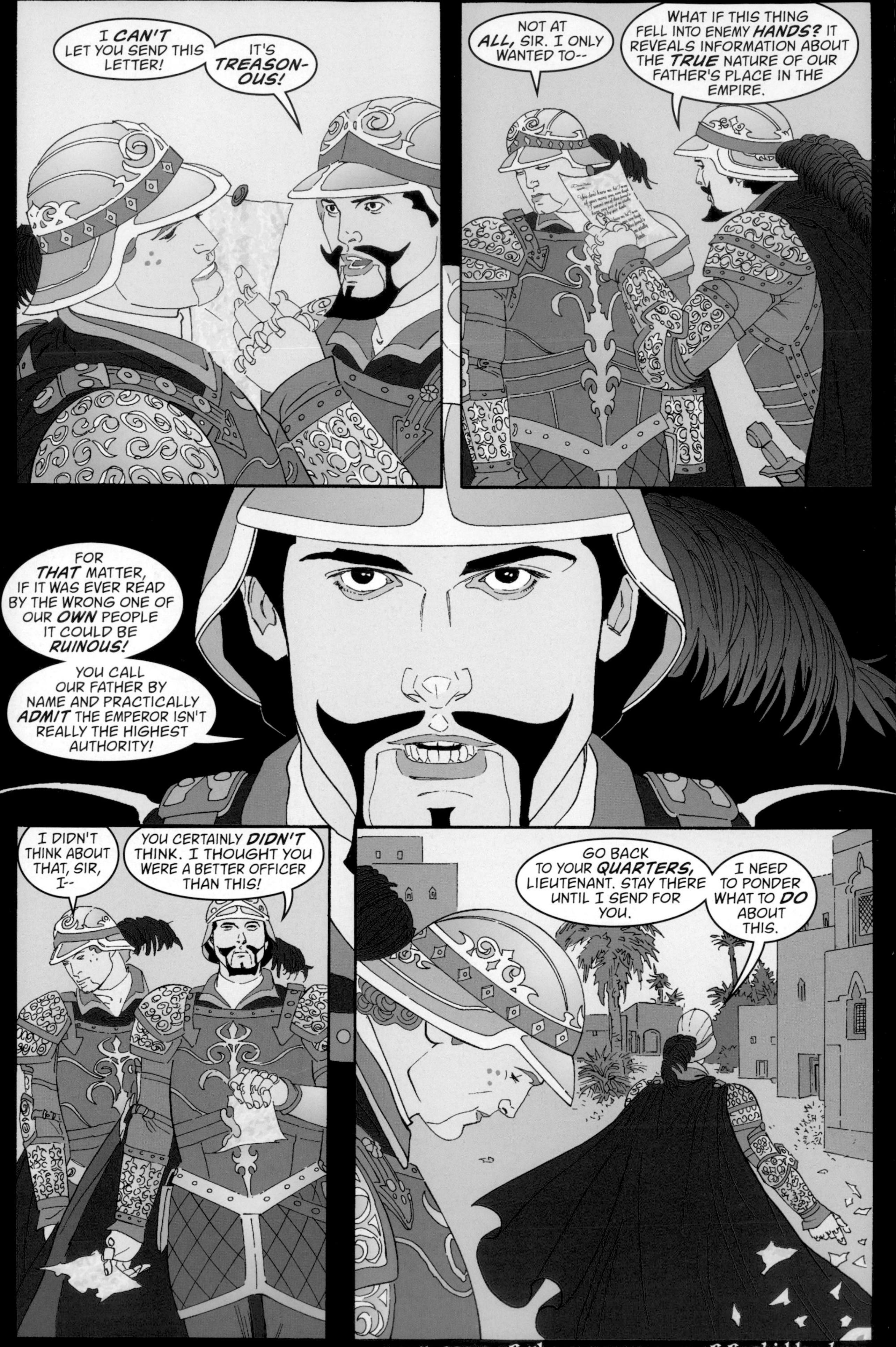
I CAN'T LET YOU SEND THIS LETTER!
IT'S TREASON-OUS!
NOT AT ALL, SIR. I ONLY WANTED TO--
WHAT IF THIS THING FELL INTO ENEMY HANDS? IT REVEALS INFORMATION ABOUT THE TRUE NATURE OF OUR FATHER'S PLACE IN THE EMPIRE.
FOR THAT MATTER, IF IT WAS EVER READ BY THE WRONG ONE OF OUR OWN PEOPLE IT COULD BE RUINOUS!
YOU CALL OUR FATHER BY NAME AND PRACTICALLY ADMIT THE EMPEROR ISN'T REALLY THE HIGHEST AUTHORITY!
I DIDN'T THINK ABOUT THAT, SIR, I--
YOU CERTAINLY DIDN'T THINK. I THOUGHT YOU WERE A BETTER OFFICER THAN THIS!
GO BACK TO YOUR QUARTERS, LIEUTENANT. STAY THERE UNTIL I SEND FOR YOU.
I NEED TO PONDER WHAT TO DO ABOUT THIS.
next: some of the consequences of forbidden love.

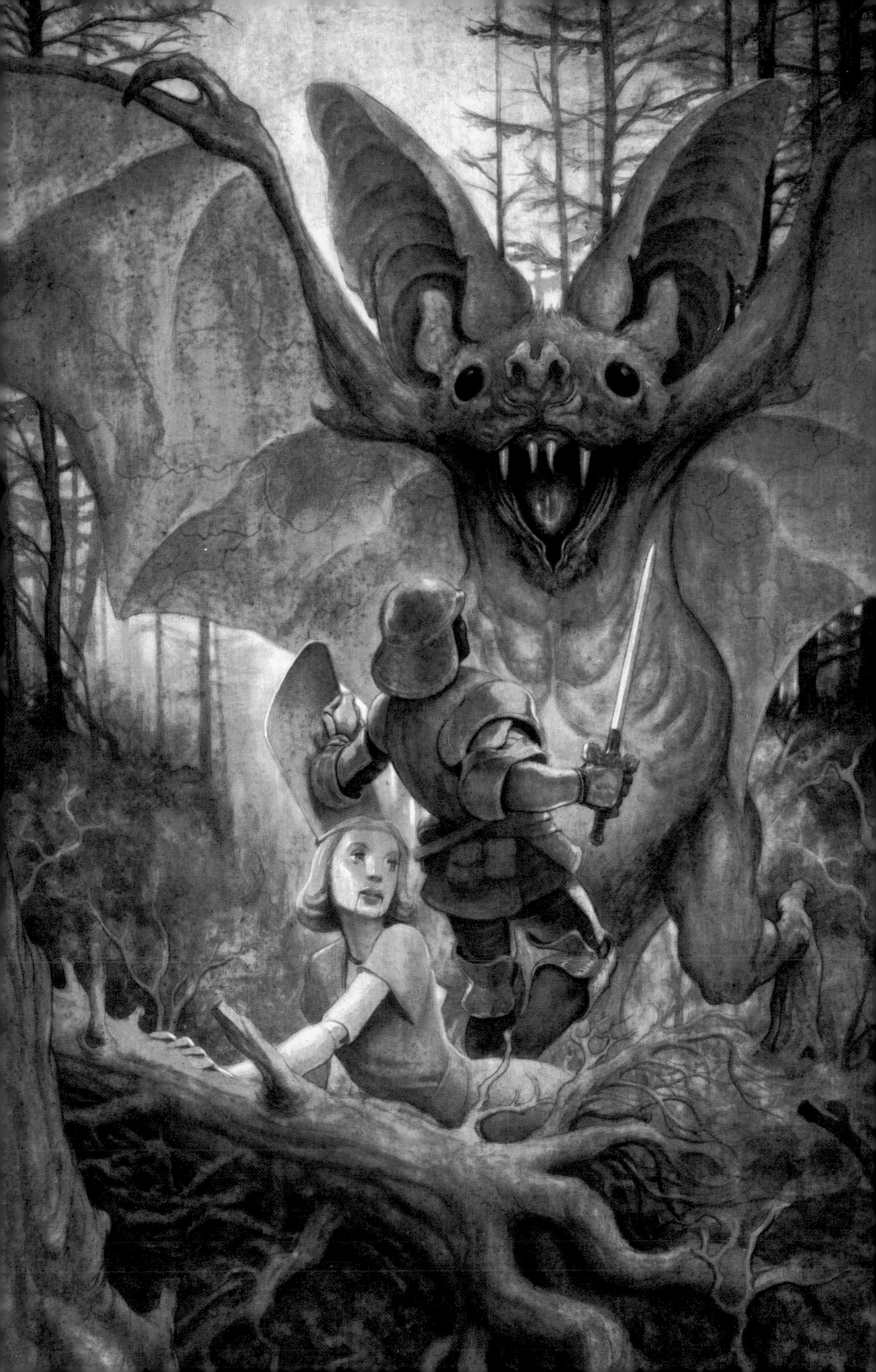

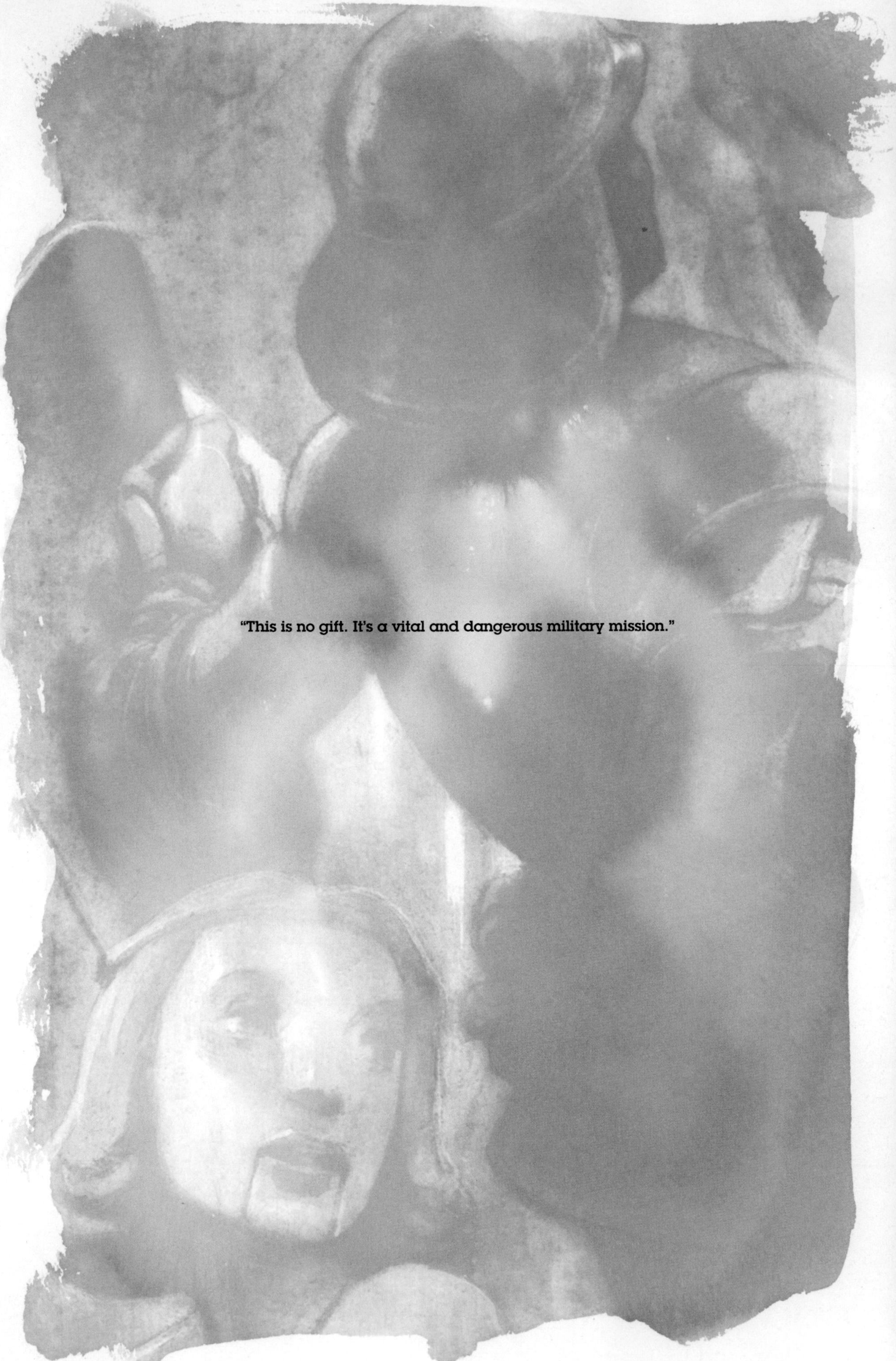

"This is no gift. It's a vital and dangerous military mission."

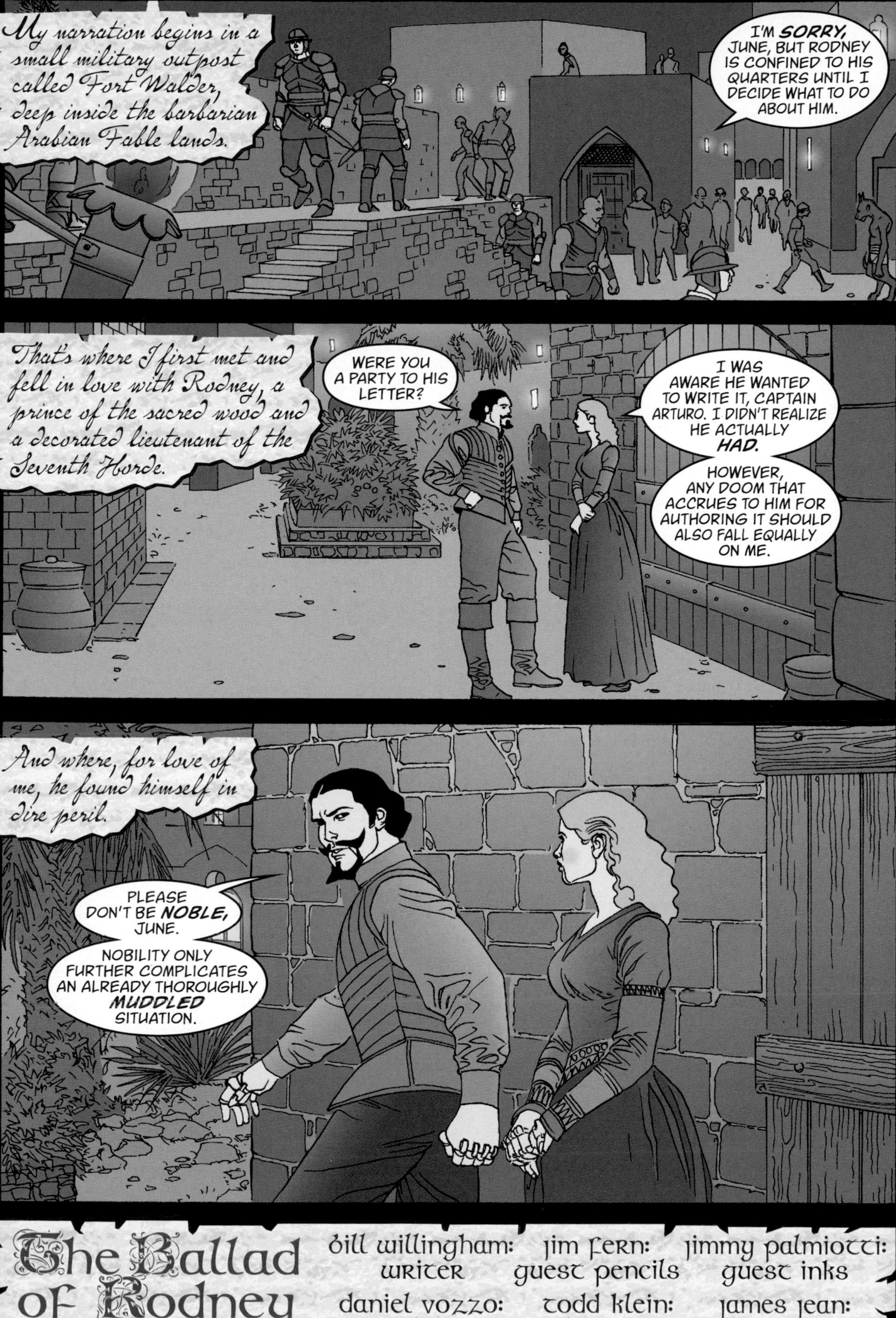
My narration begins in a small military outpost called Fort Walder, deep inside the barbarian Arabian Fable lands.
I'M SORRY, JUNE, BUT RODNEY IS CONFINED TO HIS QUARTERS UNTIL I DECIDE WHAT TO DO ABOUT HIM.
That's where I first met and fell in love with Rodney, a prince of the sacred wood and a decorated lieutenant of the Seventh Horde.
WERE YOU A PARTY TO HIS LETTER?
I WAS AWARE HE WANTED TO WRITE IT, CAPTAIN ARTURO. I DIDN'T REALIZE HE ACTUALLY HAD.
HOWEVER, ANY DOOM THAT ACCRUES TO HIM FOR AUTHORING IT SHOULD ALSO FALL EQUALLY ON ME.
And where, for love of me, he found himself in dire peril.
PLEASE DON'T BE NOBLE, JUNE.
NOBILITY ONLY FURTHER COMPLICATES AN ALREADY THOROUGHLY MUDDLED SITUATION.

The Ballad of Rodney and June

—Part 2 of 2—

bill willingham: writer
jim fern: guest pencils
jimmy palmiotti: guest inks
daniel vozzo: colors
todd klein: letters
james jean: cover art
angela rufino: assistant editor
shelly bond: editor

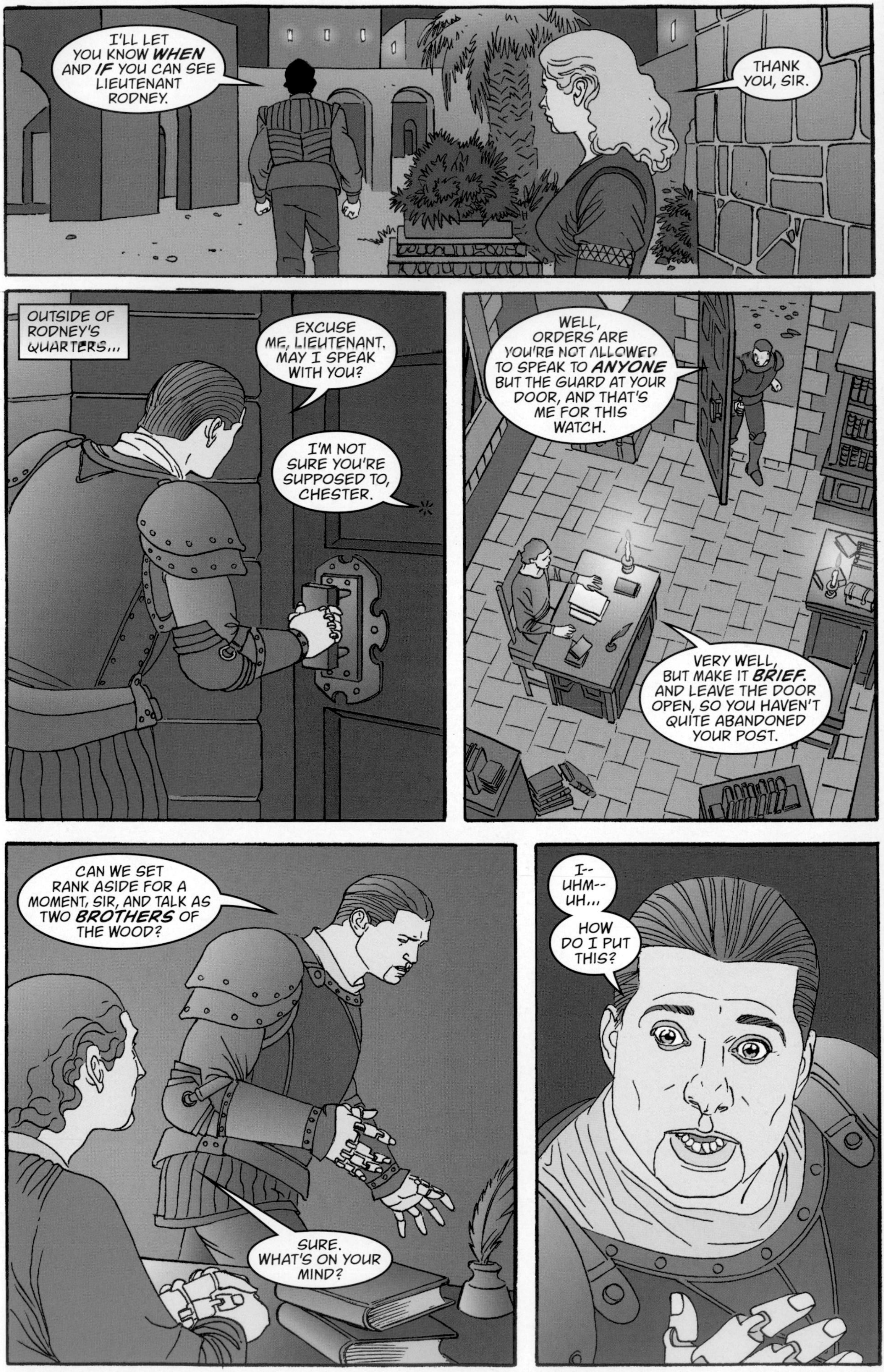
I'LL LET YOU KNOW WHEN AND IF YOU CAN SEE LIEUTENANT RODNEY.
THANK YOU, SIR.
OUTSIDE OF RODNEY'S QUARTERS...
EXCUSE ME, LIEUTENANT. MAY I SPEAK WITH YOU?
I'M NOT SURE YOU'RE SUPPOSED TO, CHESTER.
WELL, ORDERS ARE YOU'RE NOT ALLOWED TO SPEAK TO ANYONE BUT THE GUARD AT YOUR DOOR, AND THAT'S ME FOR THIS WATCH.
VERY WELL, BUT MAKE IT BRIEF. AND LEAVE THE DOOR OPEN, SO YOU HAVEN'T QUITE ABANDONED YOUR POST.
CAN WE SET RANK ASIDE FOR A MOMENT, SIR, AND TALK AS TWO BROTHERS OF THE WOOD?
SURE. WHAT'S ON YOUR MIND?
I-- UHM-- UH...
HOW DO I PUT THIS?

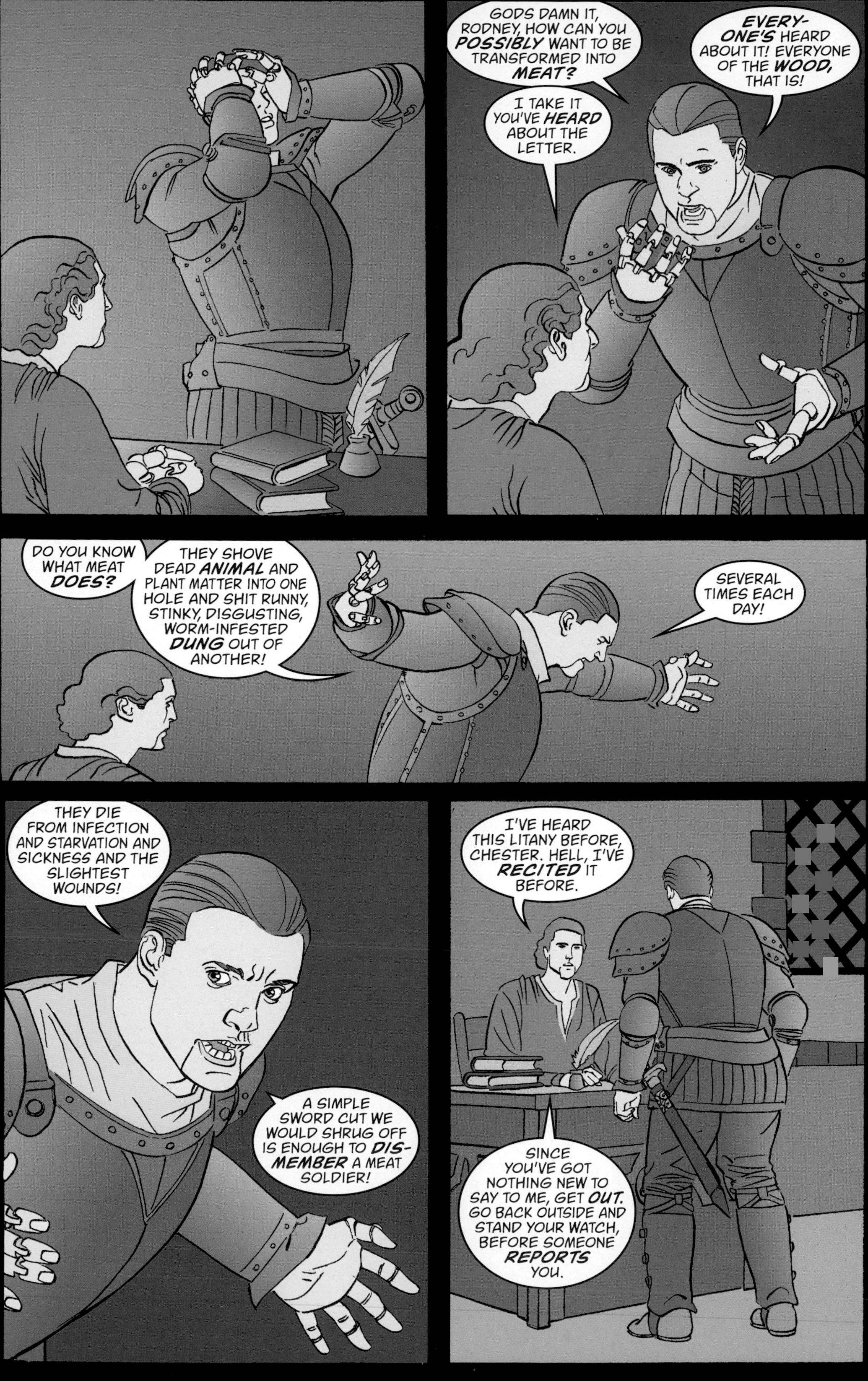
GODS DAMN IT, RODNEY, HOW CAN YOU POSSIBLY WANT TO BE TRANSFORMED INTO MEAT?
I TAKE IT YOU'VE HEARD ABOUT THE LETTER.
EVERY-ONE'S HEARD ABOUT IT! EVERYONE OF THE WOOD, THAT IS!
DO YOU KNOW WHAT MEAT DOES?
THEY SHOVE DEAD ANIMAL AND PLANT MATTER INTO ONE HOLE AND SHIT RUNNY, STINKY, DISGUSTING, WORM-INFESTED DUNG OUT OF ANOTHER!
SEVERAL TIMES EACH DAY!
THEY DIE FROM INFECTION AND STARVATION AND SICKNESS AND THE SLIGHTEST WOUNDS!
A SIMPLE SWORD CUT WE WOULD SHRUG OFF IS ENOUGH TO DIS-MEMBER A MEAT SOLDIER!
I'VE HEARD THIS LITANY BEFORE, CHESTER. HELL, I'VE RECITED IT BEFORE.
SINCE YOU'VE GOT NOTHING NEW TO SAY TO ME, GET OUT. GO BACK OUTSIDE AND STAND YOUR WATCH, BEFORE SOMEONE REPORTS YOU.

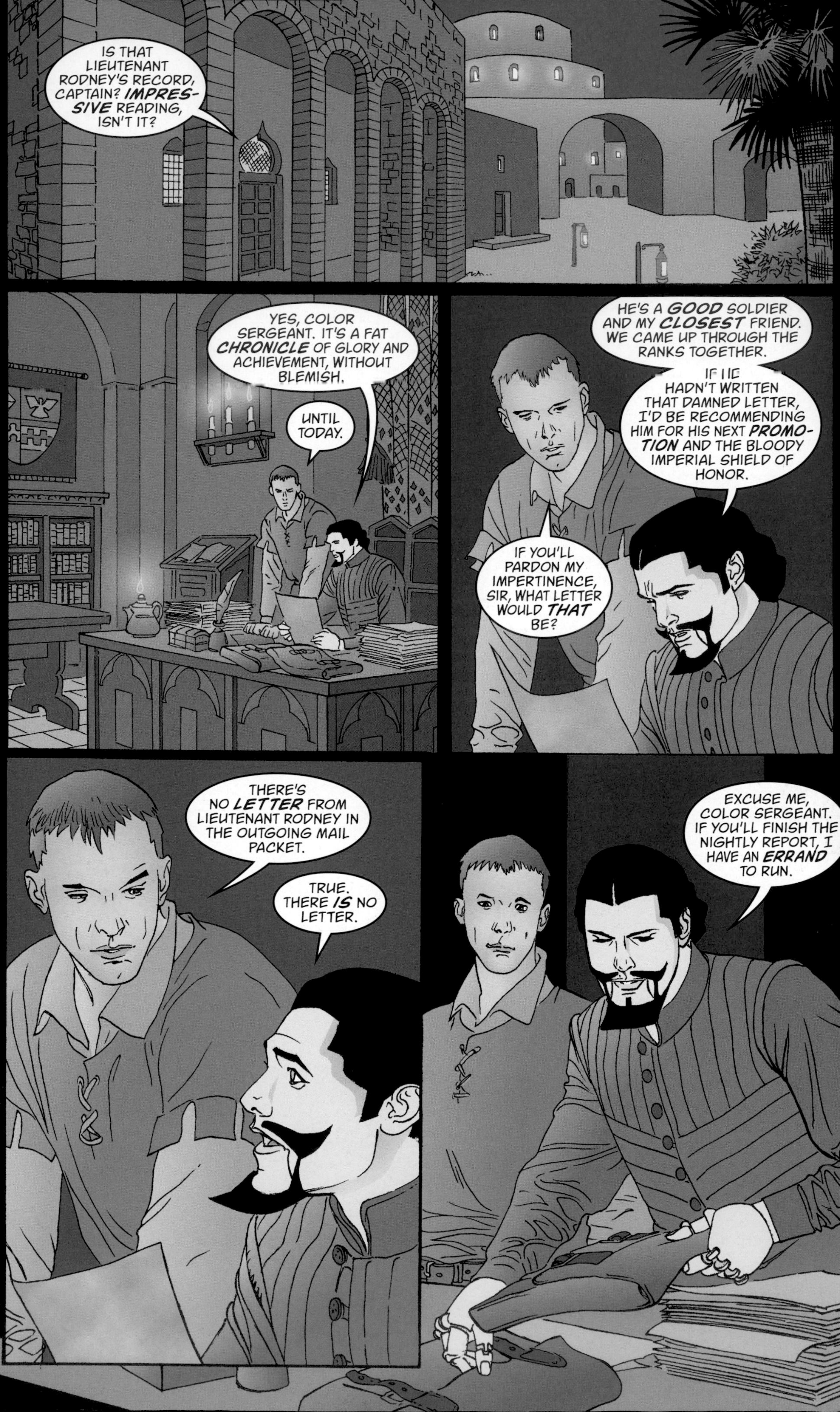
IS THAT LIEUTENANT RODNEY'S RECORD, CAPTAIN? IMPRESSIVE READING, ISN'T IT?
YES, COLOR SERGEANT. IT'S A FAT CHRONICLE OF GLORY AND ACHIEVEMENT, WITHOUT BLEMISH.
UNTIL TODAY.
HE'S A GOOD SOLDIER AND MY CLOSEST FRIEND. WE CAME UP THROUGH THE RANKS TOGETHER.
IF HE HADN'T WRITTEN THAT DAMNED LETTER, I'D BE RECOMMENDING HIM FOR HIS NEXT PROMOTION AND THE BLOODY IMPERIAL SHIELD OF HONOR.
IF YOU'LL PARDON MY IMPERTINENCE, SIR, WHAT LETTER WOULD THAT BE?
THERE'S NO LETTER FROM LIEUTENANT RODNEY IN THE OUTGOING MAIL PACKET.
TRUE. THERE IS NO LETTER.
EXCUSE ME, COLOR SERGEANT. IF YOU'LL FINISH THE NIGHTLY REPORT, I HAVE AN ERRAND TO RUN.

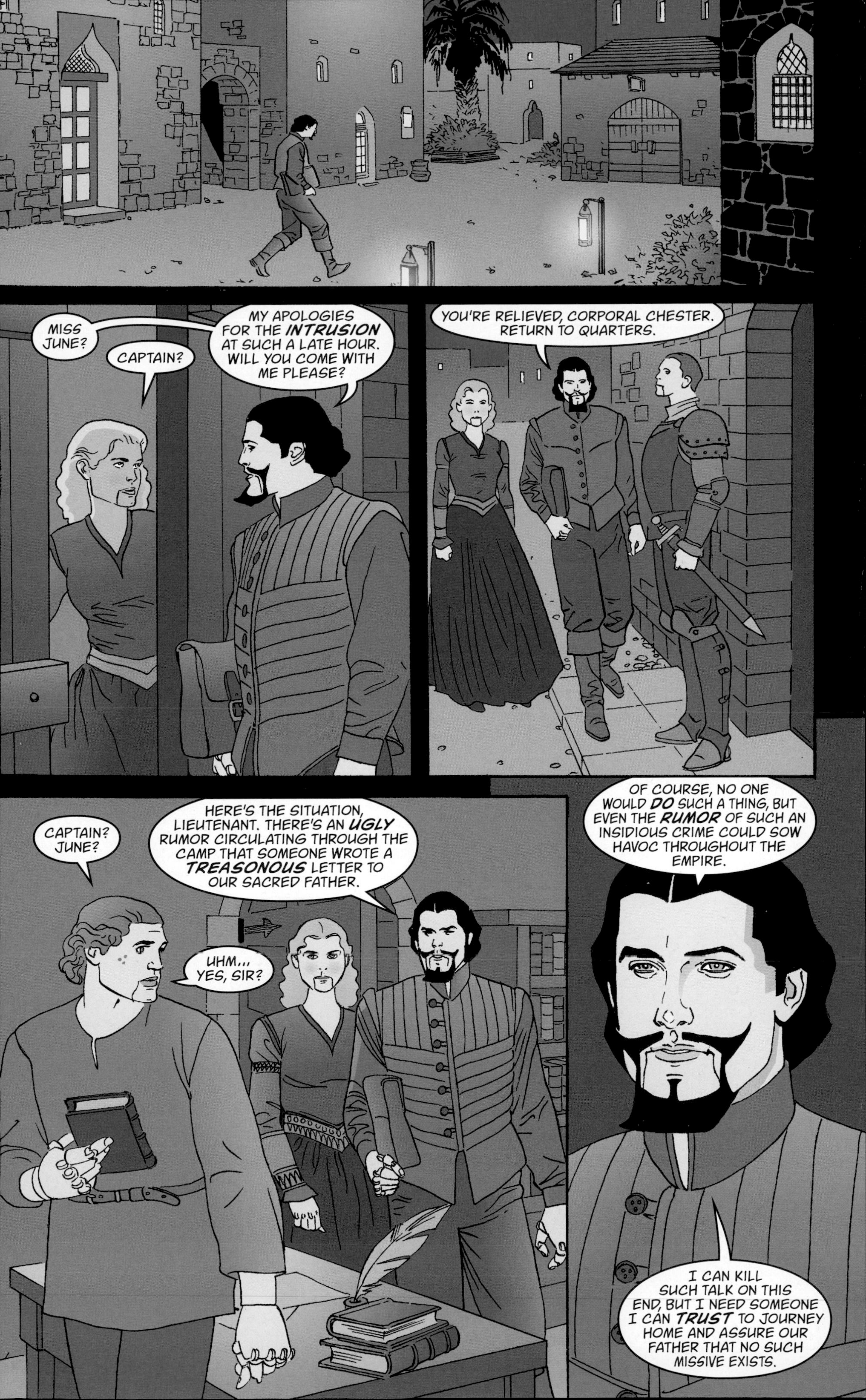
MISS JUNE?
CAPTAIN?
MY APOLOGIES FOR THE INTRUSION AT SUCH A LATE HOUR. WILL YOU COME WITH ME PLEASE?
YOU'RE RELIEVED, CORPORAL CHESTER. RETURN TO QUARTERS.
CAPTAIN? JUNE?
HERE'S THE SITUATION, LIEUTENANT. THERE'S AN UGLY RUMOR CIRCULATING THROUGH THE CAMP THAT SOMEONE WROTE A TREASONOUS LETTER TO OUR SACRED FATHER.
UHM... YES, SIR?
OF COURSE, NO ONE WOULD DO SUCH A THING, BUT EVEN THE RUMOR OF SUCH AN INSIDIOUS CRIME COULD SOW HAVOC THROUGHOUT THE EMPIRE.
I CAN KILL SUCH TALK ON THIS END, BUT I NEED SOMEONE I CAN TRUST TO JOURNEY HOME AND ASSURE OUR FATHER THAT NO SUCH MISSIVE EXISTS.

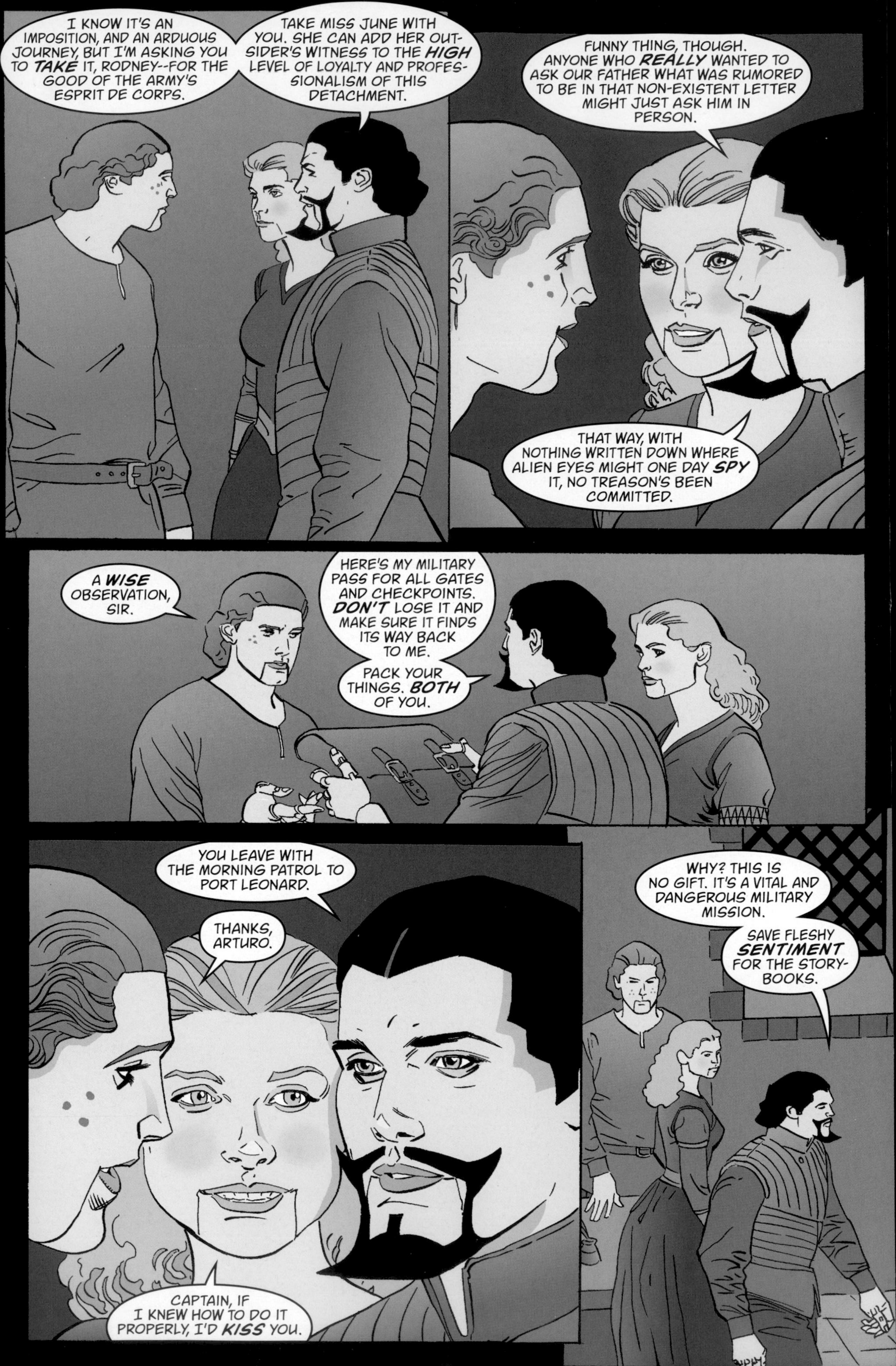
I KNOW IT'S AN IMPOSITION, AND AN ARDUOUS JOURNEY, BUT I'M ASKING YOU TO TAKE IT, RODNEY--FOR THE GOOD OF THE ARMY'S ESPRIT DE CORPS.
TAKE MISS JUNE WITH YOU. SHE CAN ADD HER OUTSIDER'S WITNESS TO THE HIGH LEVEL OF LOYALTY AND PROFESSIONALISM OF THIS DETACHMENT.
FUNNY THING, THOUGH. ANYONE WHO REALLY WANTED TO ASK OUR FATHER WHAT WAS RUMORED TO BE IN THAT NON-EXISTENT LETTER MIGHT JUST ASK HIM IN PERSON.
THAT WAY, WITH NOTHING WRITTEN DOWN WHERE ALIEN EYES MIGHT ONE DAY SPY IT, NO TREASON'S BEEN COMMITTED.
A WISE OBSERVATION, SIR.
HERE'S MY MILITARY PASS FOR ALL GATES AND CHECKPOINTS. DON'T LOSE IT AND MAKE SURE IT FINDS ITS WAY BACK TO ME.
PACK YOUR THINGS. BOTH OF YOU.
YOU LEAVE WITH THE MORNING PATROL TO PORT LEONARD.
THANKS, ARTURO.
CAPTAIN, IF I KNEW HOW TO DO IT PROPERLY, I'D KISS YOU.
WHY? THIS IS NO GIFT. IT'S A VITAL AND DANGEROUS MILITARY MISSION.
SAVE FLESHY SENTIMENT FOR THE STORYBOOKS.

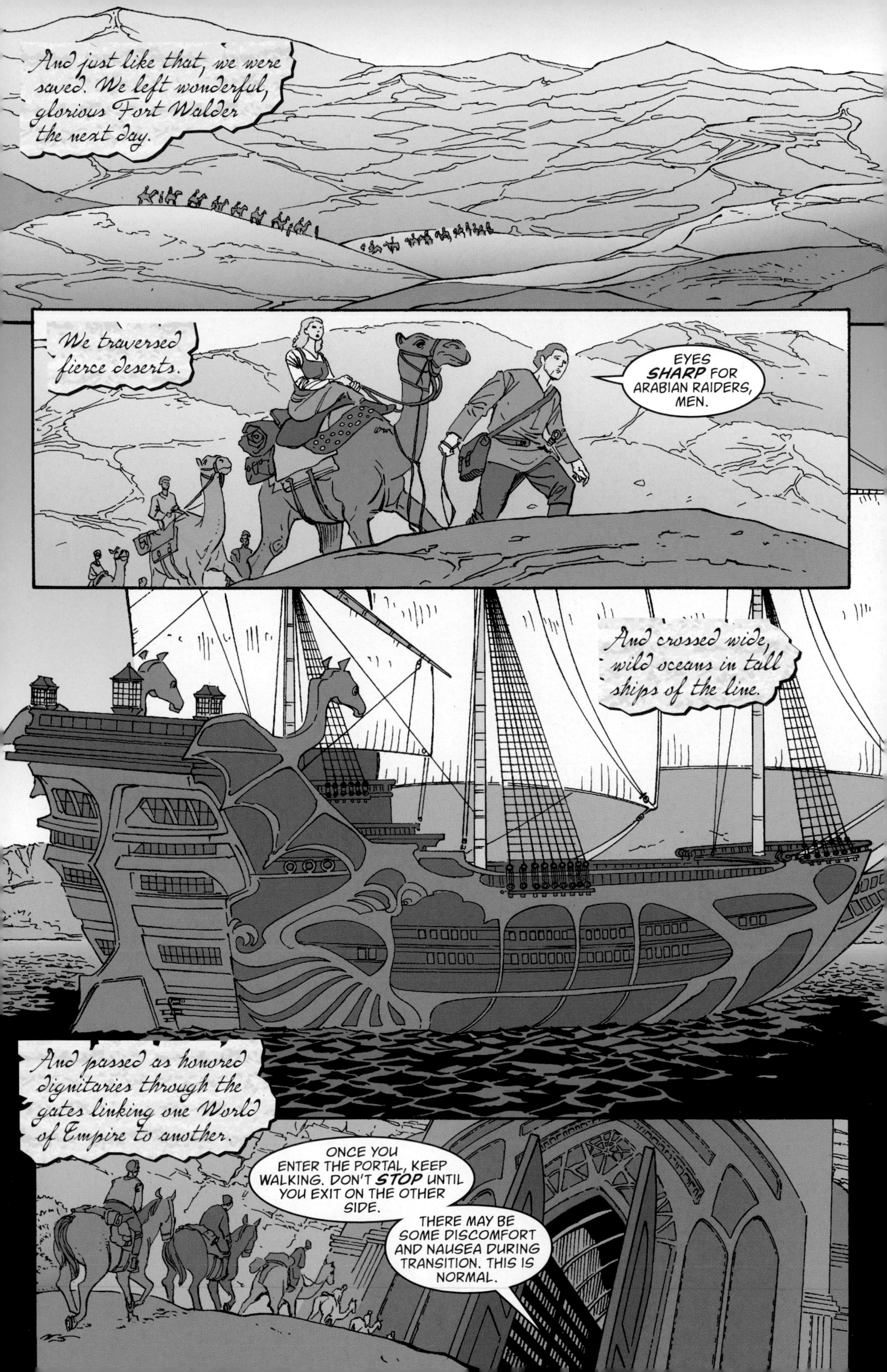

And just like that, we were saved. We left wonderful, glorious Fort Walder the next day.
We traversed fierce deserts.
EYES SHARP FOR ARABIAN RAIDERS, MEN.
And crossed wide, wild oceans in tall ships of the line.
And passed as honored dignitaries through the gates linking one World of Empire to another.
ONCE YOU ENTER THE PORTAL, KEEP WALKING. DON'T STOP UNTIL YOU EXIT ON THE OTHER SIDE.
THERE MAY BE SOME DISCOMFORT AND NAUSEA DURING TRANSITION. THIS IS NORMAL.

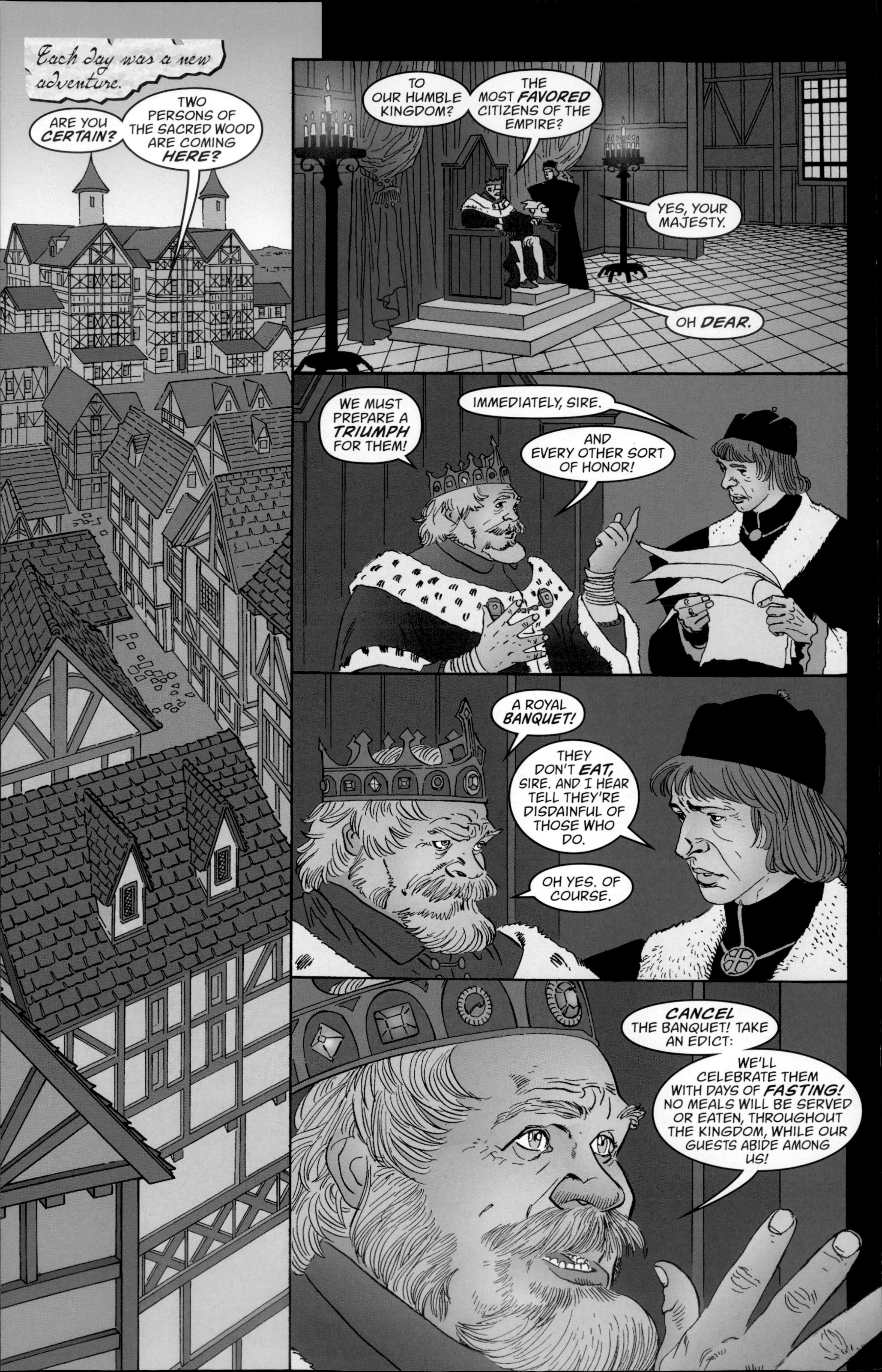
Each day was a new adventure.
ARE YOU CERTAIN?
TWO PERSONS OF THE SACRED WOOD ARE COMING HERE?
TO OUR HUMBLE KINGDOM?
THE MOST FAVORED CITIZENS OF THE EMPIRE?
YES, YOUR MAJESTY.
OH DEAR.
WE MUST PREPARE A TRIUMPH FOR THEM!
IMMEDIATELY, SIRE.
AND EVERY OTHER SORT OF HONOR!
A ROYAL BANQUET!
THEY DON'T EAT, SIRE. AND I HEAR TELL THEY'RE DISDAINFUL OF THOSE WHO DO.
OH YES. OF COURSE.
CANCEL THE BANQUET! TAKE AN EDICT:
WE'LL CELEBRATE THEM WITH DAYS OF FASTING! NO MEALS WILL BE SERVED OR EATEN, THROUGHOUT THE KINGDOM, WHILE OUR GUESTS ABIDE AMONG US!

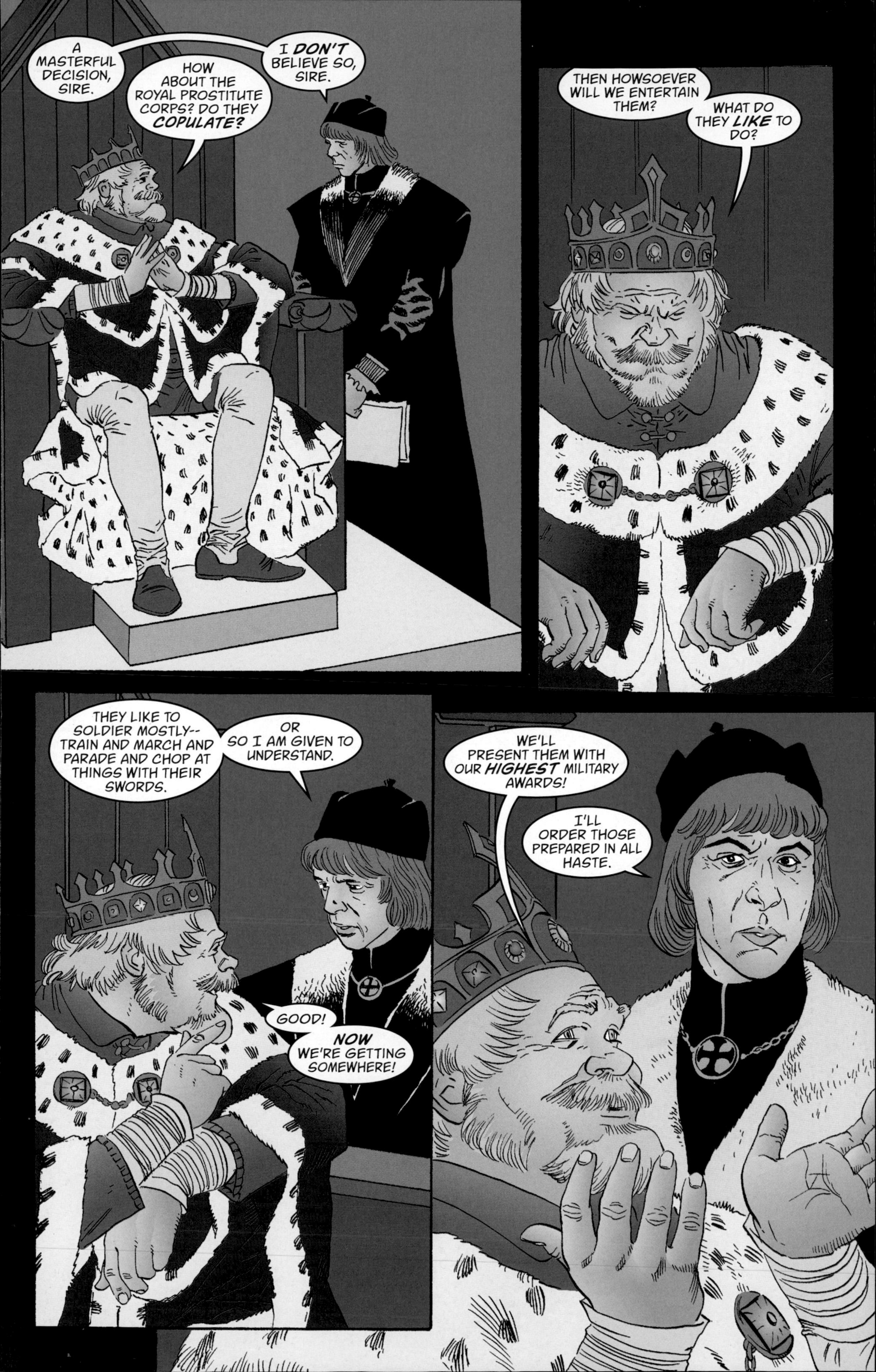
A MASTERFUL DECISION, SIRE.
HOW ABOUT THE ROYAL PROSTITUTE CORPS? DO THEY COPULATE?
I DON'T BELIEVE SO, SIRE.
THEN HOWSOEVER WILL WE ENTERTAIN THEM?
WHAT DO THEY LIKE TO DO?
THEY LIKE TO SOLDIER MOSTLY-- TRAIN AND MARCH AND PARADE AND CHOP AT THINGS WITH THEIR SWORDS.
OR SO I AM GIVEN TO UNDERSTAND.
GOOD!
NOW WE'RE GETTING SOMEWHERE!
WE'LL PRESENT THEM WITH OUR HIGHEST MILITARY AWARDS!
I'LL ORDER THOSE PREPARED IN ALL HASTE.

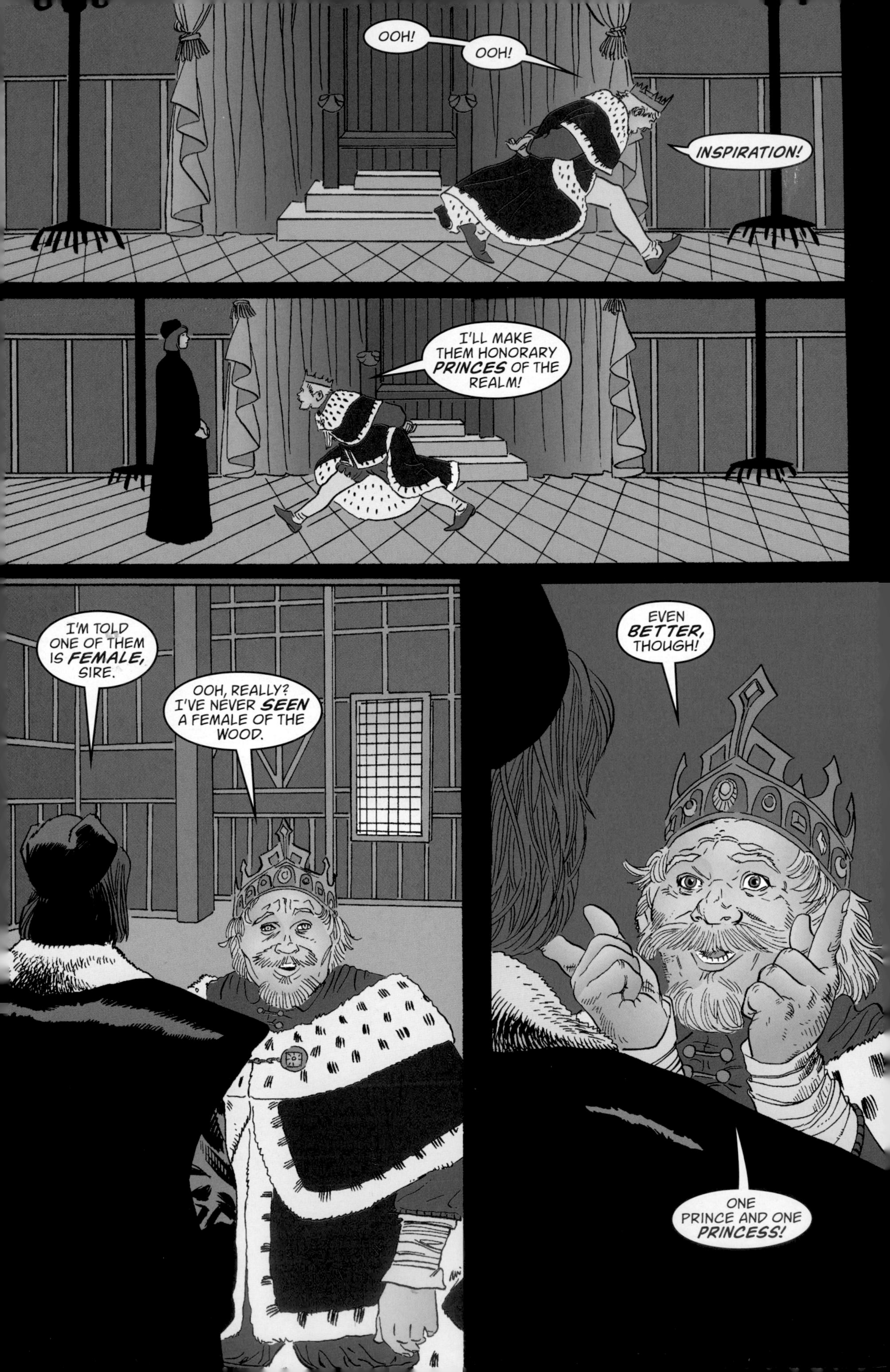
OOH!
OOH!
INSPIRATION!
I'LL MAKE THEM HONORARY PRINCES OF THE REALM!
I'M TOLD ONE OF THEM IS FEMALE, SIRE.
OOH, REALLY? I'VE NEVER SEEN A FEMALE OF THE WOOD.
EVEN BETTER, THOUGH!
ONE PRINCE AND ONE PRINCESS!

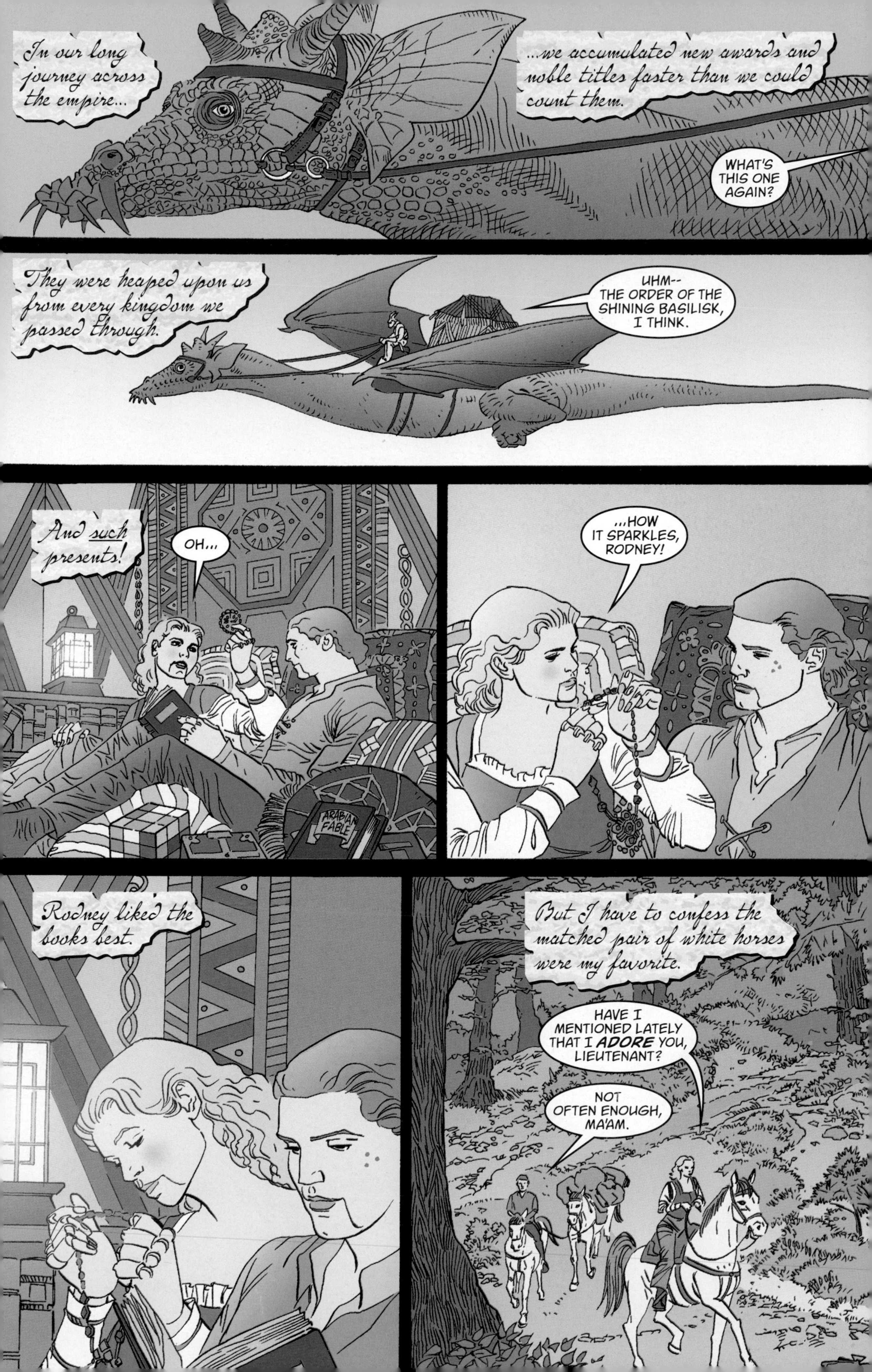

In our long journey across the empire...
...we accumulated new awards and noble titles faster than we could count them.
WHAT'S THIS ONE AGAIN?
They were heaped upon us from every kingdom we passed through.
UHM-- THE ORDER OF THE SHINING BASILISK, I THINK.
And such presents!
OH...
ARABIAN FABLE
...HOW IT SPARKLES, RODNEY!
Rodney liked the books best.
But I have to confess the matched pair of white horses were my favorite.
HAVE I MENTIONED LATELY THAT I ADORE YOU, LIEUTENANT?
NOT OFTEN ENOUGH, MA'AM.

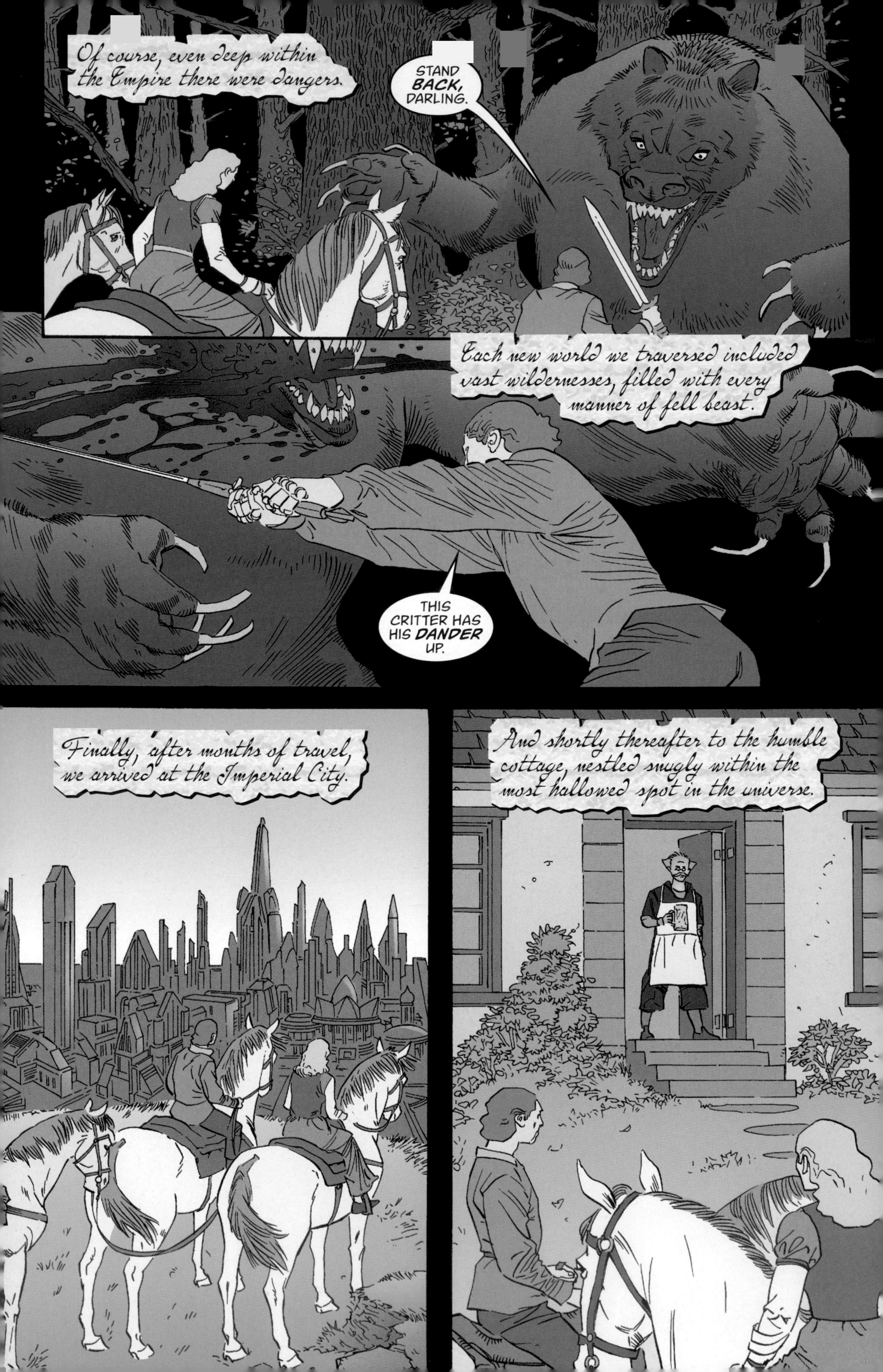
Of course, even deep within the Empire there were dangers.
STAND BACK, DARLING.
Each new world we traversed included vast wildernesses, filled with every manner of fell beast.
THIS CRITTER HAS HIS DANDER UP.
Finally, after months of travel, we arrived at the Imperial City.
And shortly thereafter to the humble cottage, nestled snugly within the most hallowed spot in the universe.

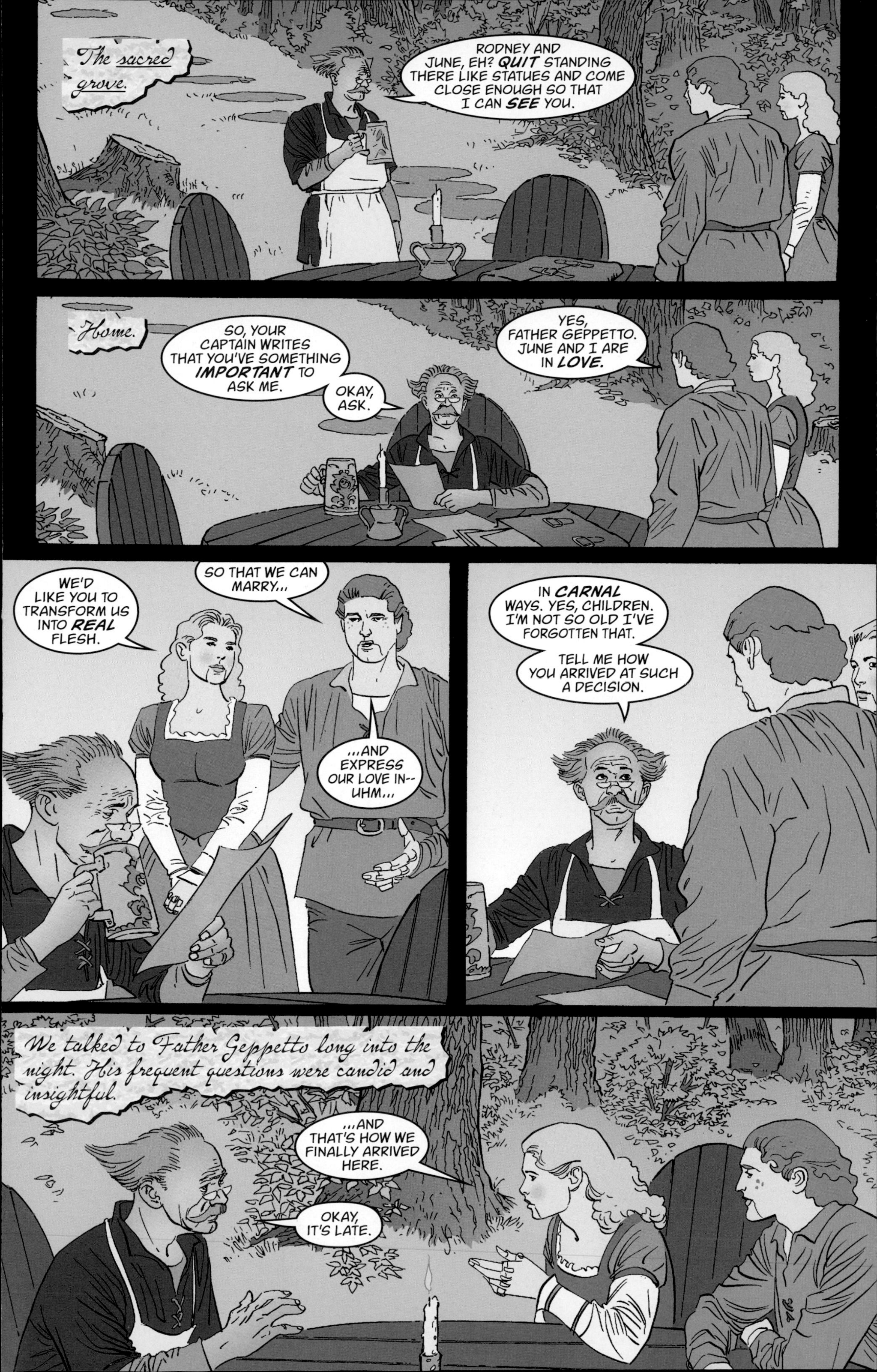
The sacred grove.
RODNEY AND JUNE, EH? QUIT STANDING THERE LIKE STATUES AND COME CLOSE ENOUGH SO THAT I CAN SEE YOU.
Home.
SO, YOUR CAPTAIN WRITES THAT YOU'VE SOMETHING IMPORTANT TO ASK ME.
OKAY, ASK.
YES, FATHER GEPPETTO. JUNE AND I ARE IN LOVE.
WE'D LIKE YOU TO TRANSFORM US INTO REAL FLESH.
SO THAT WE CAN MARRY...
...AND EXPRESS OUR LOVE IN--UHM...
IN CARNAL WAYS. YES, CHILDREN. I'M NOT SO OLD I'VE FORGOTTEN THAT.
TELL ME HOW YOU ARRIVED AT SUCH A DECISION.
We talked to Father Geppetto long into the night. His frequent questions were candid and insightful.
...AND THAT'S HOW WE FINALLY ARRIVED HERE.
OKAY, IT'S LATE.

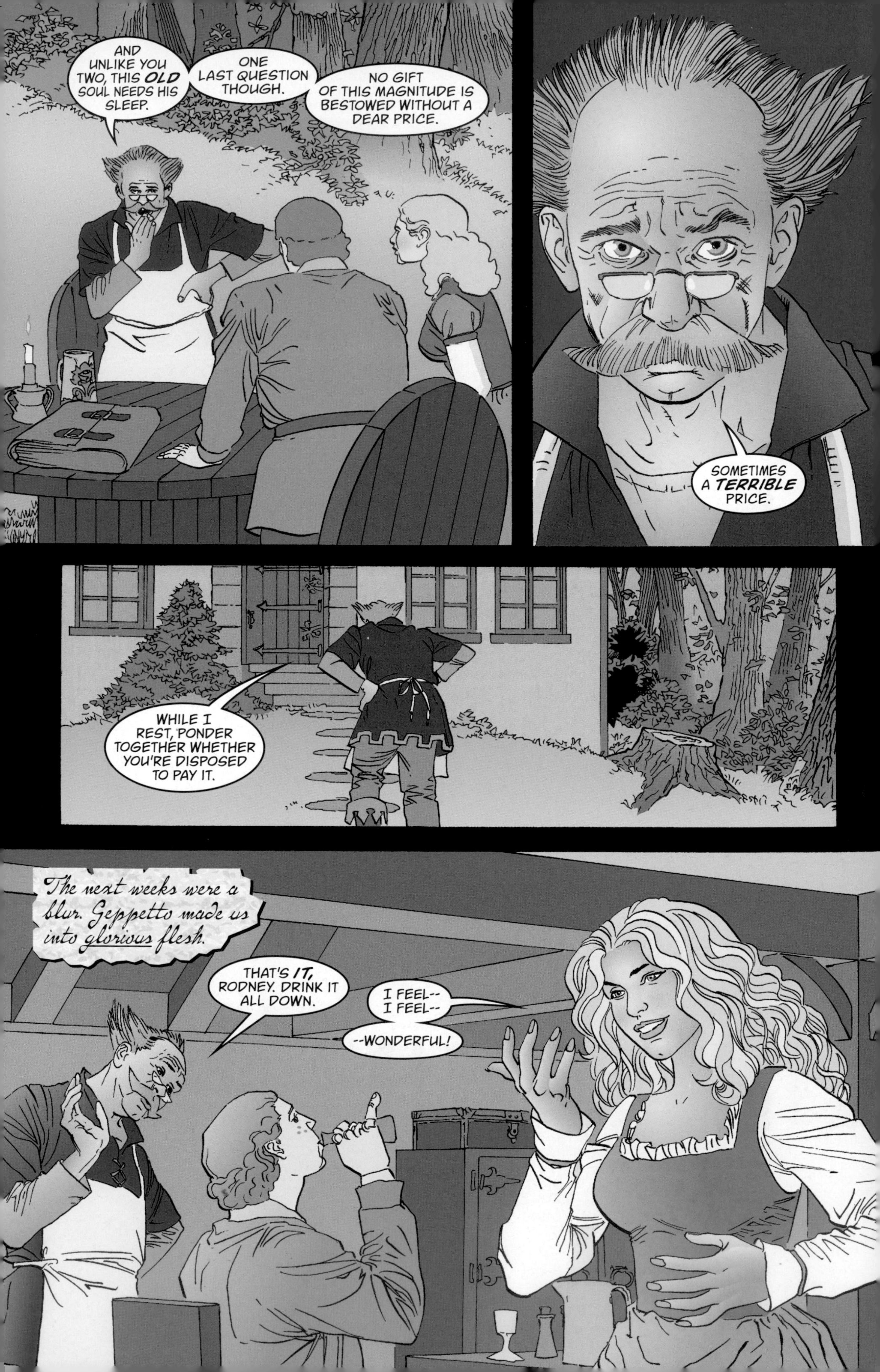
AND UNLIKE YOU TWO, THIS OLD SOUL NEEDS HIS SLEEP.
ONE LAST QUESTION THOUGH.
NO GIFT OF THIS MAGNITUDE IS BESTOWED WITHOUT A DEAR PRICE.
SOMETIMES A TERRIBLE PRICE.
WHILE I REST, PONDER TOGETHER WHETHER YOU'RE DISPOSED TO PAY IT.
The next weeks were a blur. Geppetto made us into glorious flesh.
THAT'S IT, RODNEY. DRINK IT ALL DOWN.
I FEEL-- I FEEL--
--WONDERFUL!

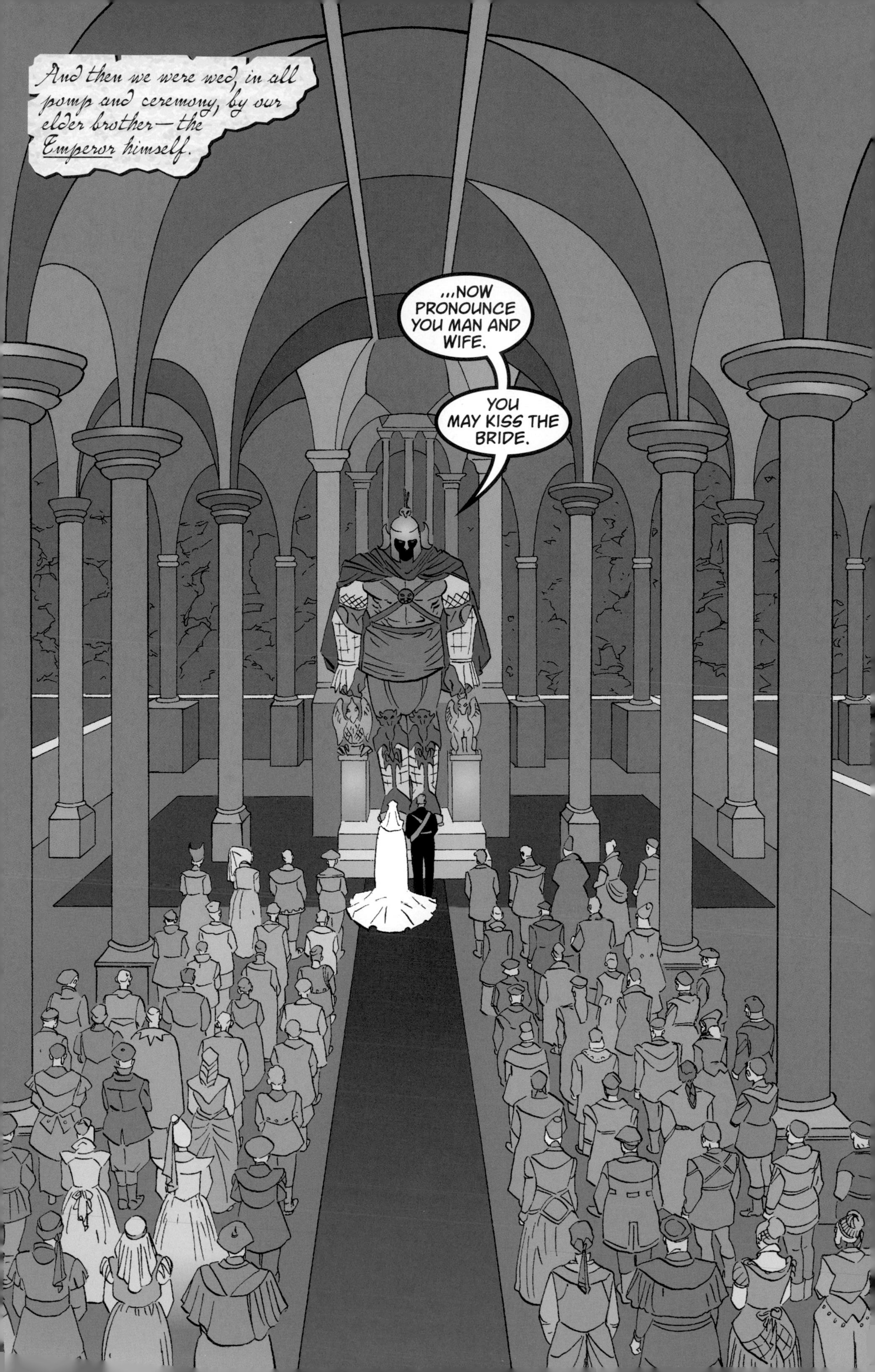
And then we were wed, in all pomp and ceremony, by our elder brother—the Emperor himself.
...NOW PRONOUNCE YOU MAN AND WIFE.
YOU MAY KISS THE BRIDE.

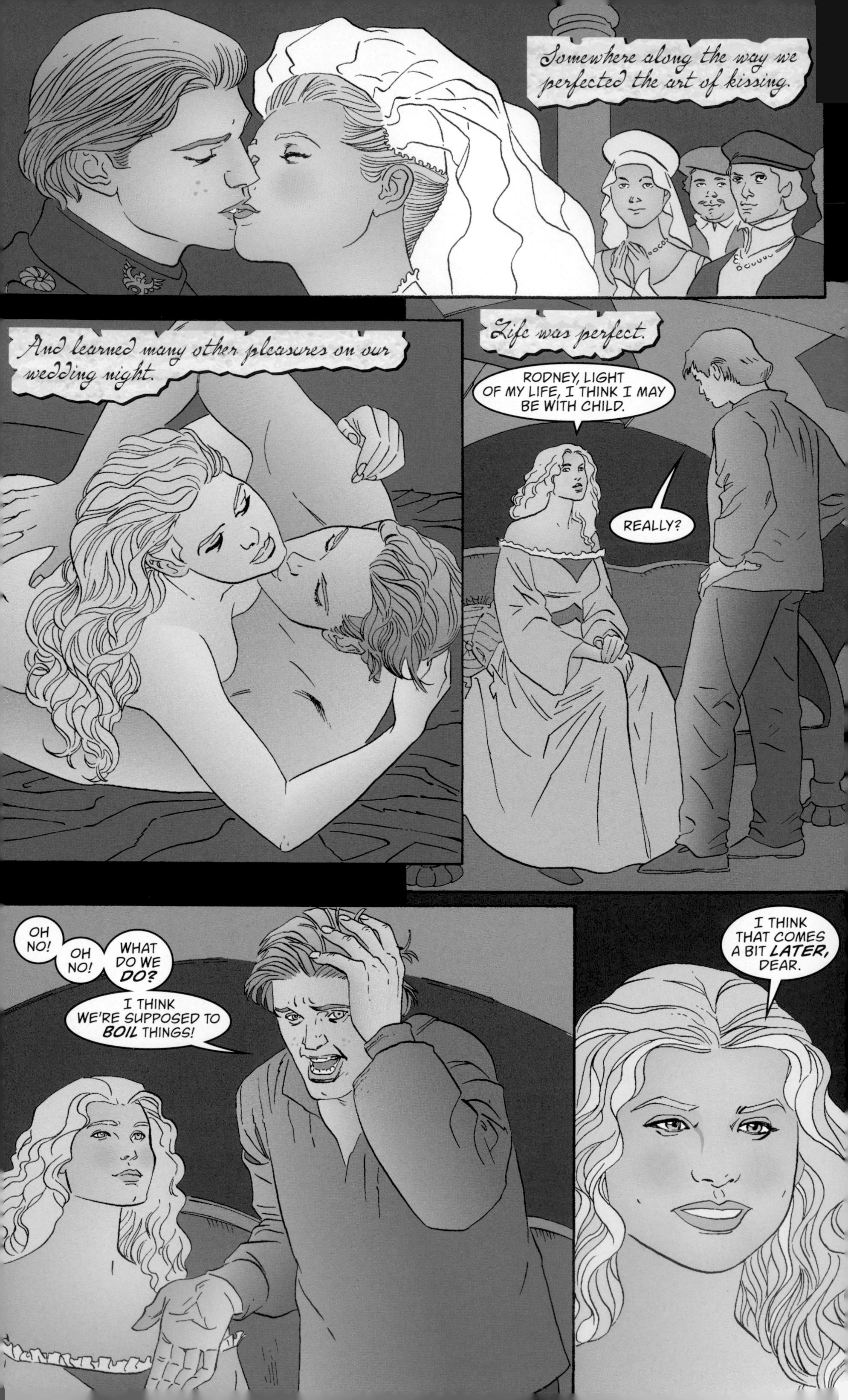
Somewhere along the way we perfected the art of kissing.
And learned many other pleasures on our wedding night.
Life was perfect.
RODNEY, LIGHT OF MY LIFE, I THINK I MAY BE WITH CHILD.
REALLY?
OH NO!
OH NO!
WHAT DO WE DO?
I THINK WE'RE SUPPOSED TO BOIL THINGS!
I THINK THAT COMES A BIT LATER, DEAR.

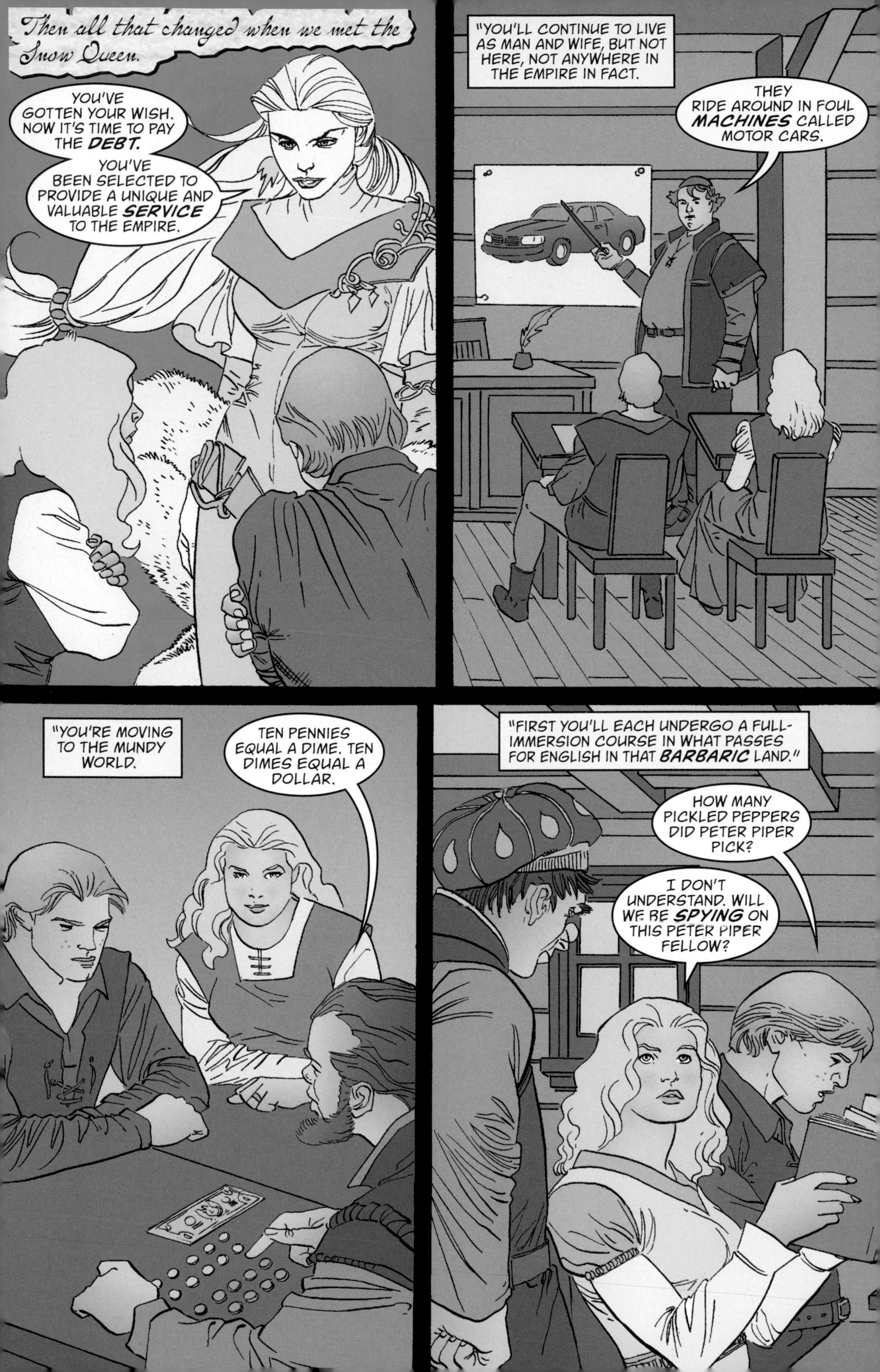
Then all that changed when we met the Snow Queen.
YOU'VE GOTTEN YOUR WISH. NOW IT'S TIME TO PAY THE DEBT.
YOU'VE BEEN SELECTED TO PROVIDE A UNIQUE AND VALUABLE SERVICE TO THE EMPIRE.
"YOU'LL CONTINUE TO LIVE AS MAN AND WIFE, BUT NOT HERE, NOT ANYWHERE IN THE EMPIRE IN FACT.
THEY RIDE AROUND IN FOUL MACHINES CALLED MOTOR CARS.
"YOU'RE MOVING TO THE MUNDY WORLD.
TEN PENNIES EQUAL A DIME. TEN DIMES EQUAL A DOLLAR.
"FIRST YOU'LL EACH UNDERGO A FULL-IMMERSION COURSE IN WHAT PASSES FOR ENGLISH IN THAT BARBARIC LAND."
HOW MANY PICKLED PEPPERS DID PETER PIPER PICK?
I DON'T UNDERSTAND. WILL WE BE SPYING ON THIS PETER PIPER FELLOW?

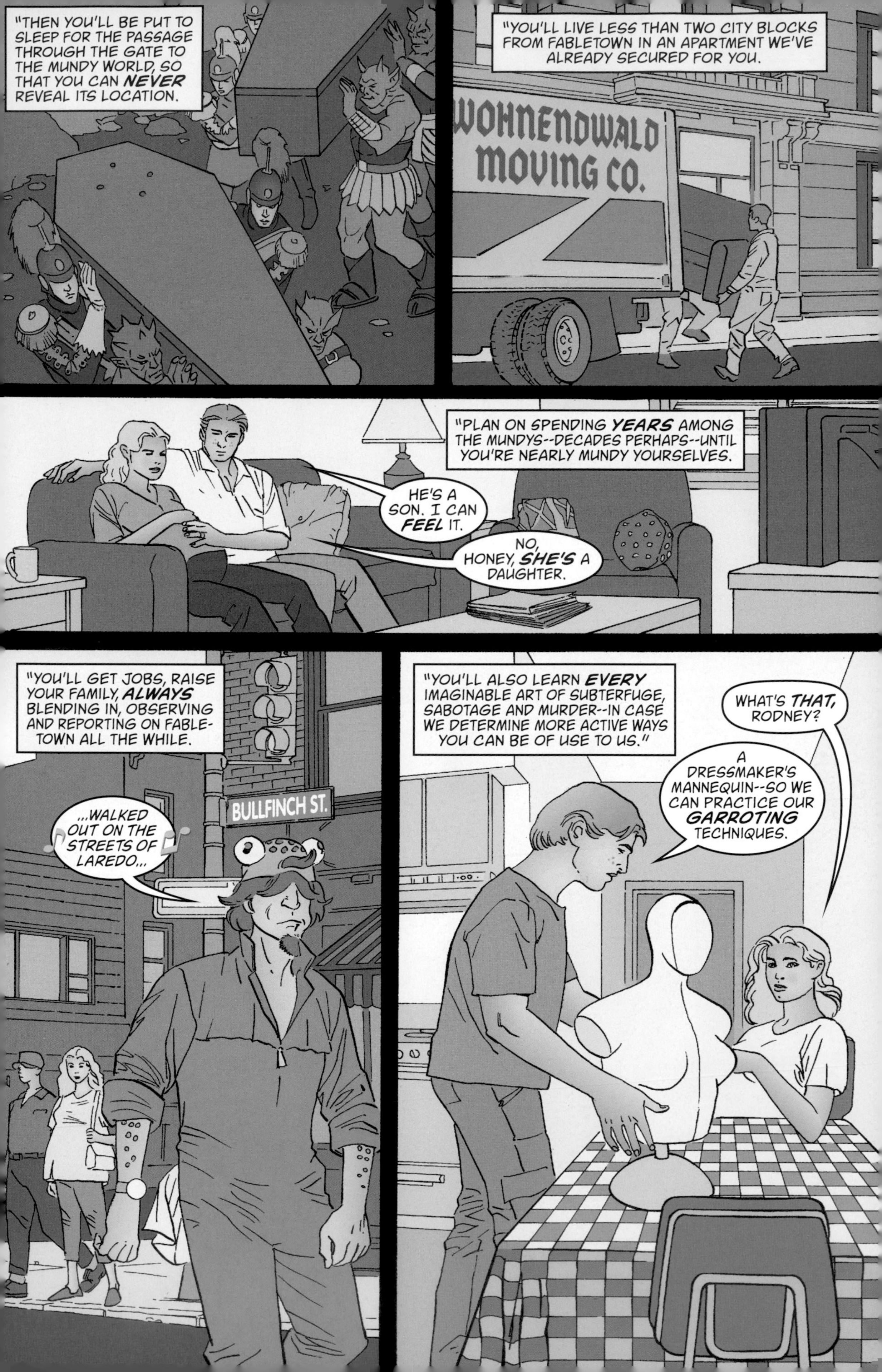
"THEN YOU'LL BE PUT TO SLEEP FOR THE PASSAGE THROUGH THE GATE TO THE MUNDY WORLD, SO THAT YOU CAN NEVER REVEAL ITS LOCATION.
"YOU'LL LIVE LESS THAN TWO CITY BLOCKS FROM FABLETOWN IN AN APARTMENT WE'VE ALREADY SECURED FOR YOU.
WOHNENDWALD MOVING CO.
"PLAN ON SPENDING YEARS AMONG THE MUNDYS--DECADES PERHAPS--UNTIL YOU'RE NEARLY MUNDY YOURSELVES.
HE'S A SON. I CAN FEEL IT.
NO, HONEY, SHE'S A DAUGHTER.
"YOU'LL GET JOBS, RAISE YOUR FAMILY, ALWAYS BLENDING IN, OBSERVING AND REPORTING ON FABLE-TOWN ALL THE WHILE.
BULLFINCH ST.
...WALKED OUT ON THE STREETS OF LAREDO...
"YOU'LL ALSO LEARN EVERY IMAGINABLE ART OF SUBTERFUGE, SABOTAGE AND MURDER--IN CASE WE DETERMINE MORE ACTIVE WAYS YOU CAN BE OF USE TO US."
WHAT'S THAT, RODNEY?
A DRESSMAKER'S MANNEQUIN--SO WE CAN PRACTICE OUR GARROTING TECHNIQUES.

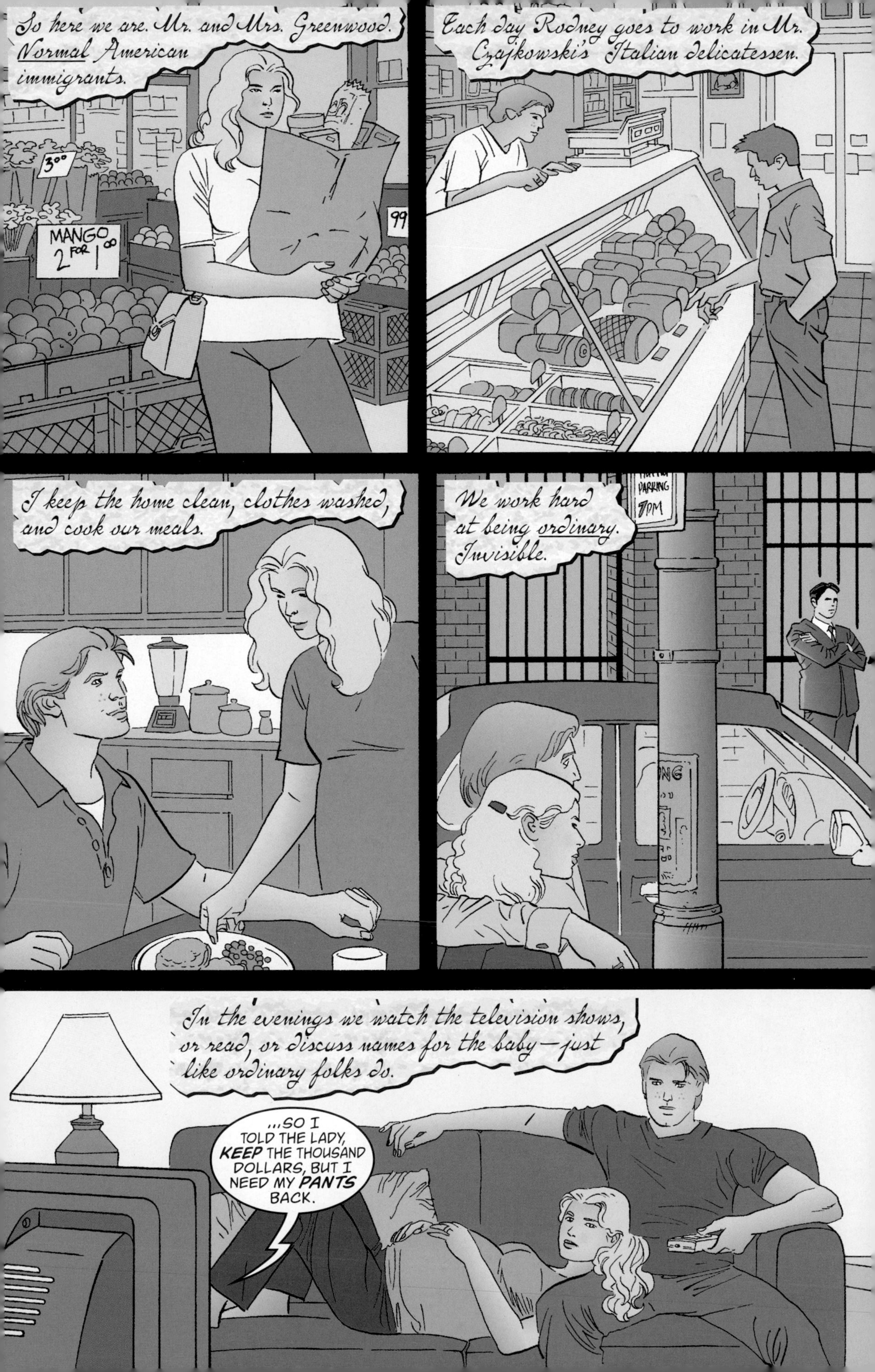
So here we are. Mr. and Mrs. Greenwood. Normal American immigrants.
3.00
MANGO 2 FOR 1.00
99
Each day Rodney goes to work in Mr. Czajkowski's Italian delicatessen.
I keep the home clean, clothes washed, and cook our meals.
We work hard at being ordinary. Invisible.
PARKING 7PM
In the evenings we watch the television shows, or read, or discuss names for the baby—just like ordinary folks do.
...SO I TOLD THE LADY, KEEP THE THOUSAND DOLLARS, BUT I NEED MY PANTS BACK.

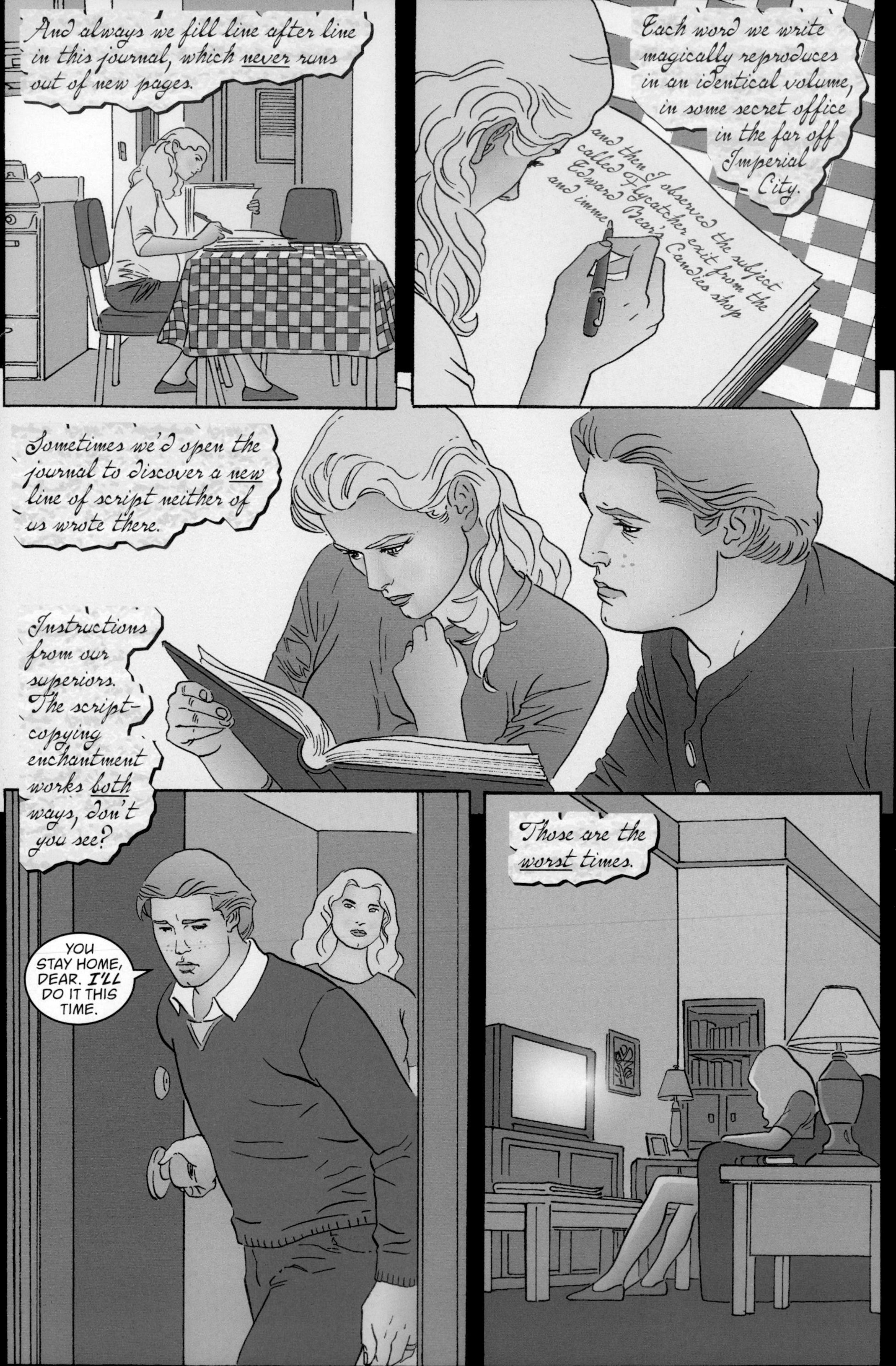
And always we fill line after line in this journal, which never runs out of new pages.
Each word we write magically reproduces in an identical volume, in some secret office in the far off Imperial City.
and then I observed the subject called Flycatcher exit from the Edward Bear's Candies shop and imme
Sometimes we'd open the journal to discover a new line of script neither of us wrote there.
Instructions from our superiors. The script-copying enchantment works both ways, don't you see?
YOU STAY HOME, DEAR. I'LL DO IT THIS TIME.
Those are the worst times.

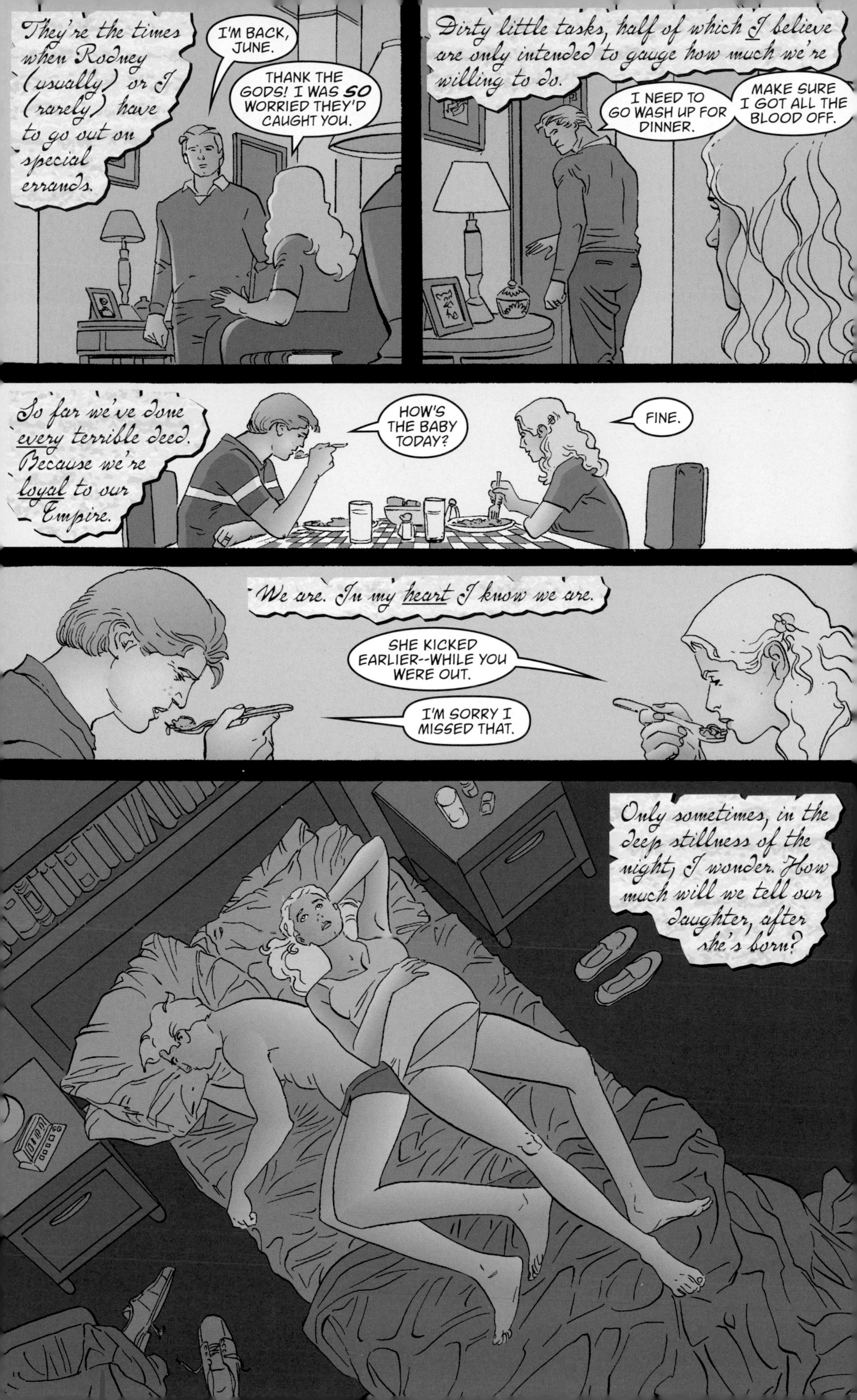
They're the times when Rodney (usually) or I (rarely) have to go out on special errands.
I'M BACK, JUNE.
THANK THE GODS! I WAS SO WORRIED THEY'D CAUGHT YOU.
Dirty little tasks, half of which I believe are only intended to gauge how much we're willing to do.
I NEED TO GO WASH UP FOR DINNER.
MAKE SURE I GOT ALL THE BLOOD OFF.
So far we've done every terrible deed. Because we're loyal to our Empire.
HOW'S THE BABY TODAY?
FINE.
We are. In my heart I know we are.
SHE KICKED EARLIER--WHILE YOU WERE OUT.
I'M SORRY I MISSED THAT.
Only sometimes, in the deep stillness of the night, I wonder. How much will we tell our daughter, after she's born?

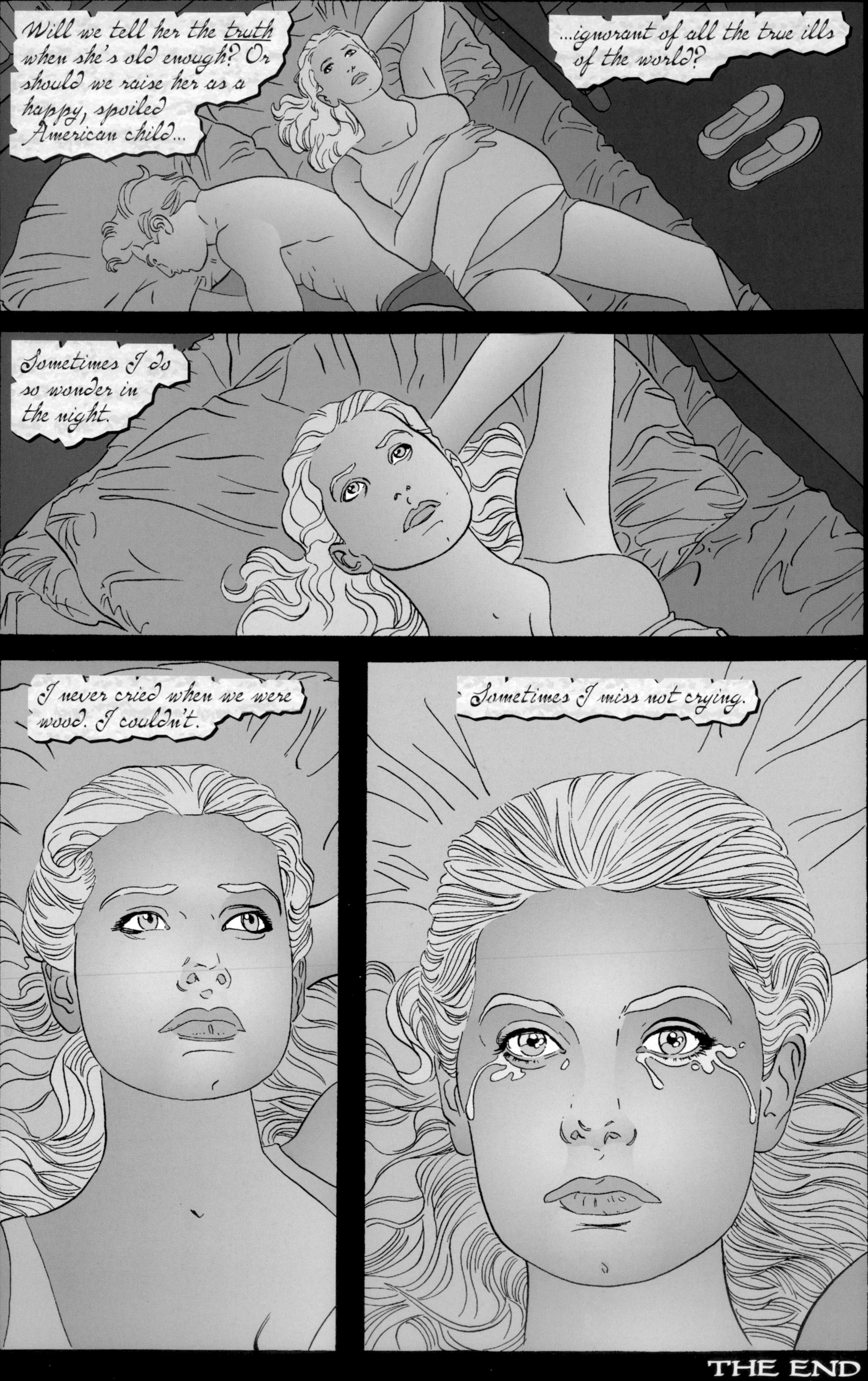
Will we tell her the truth when she's old enough? Or should we raise her as a happy, spoiled American child...
...ignorant of all the true ills of the world?
Sometimes I do so wonder in the night.
I never cried when we were wood. I couldn't.
Sometimes I miss not crying.
THE END

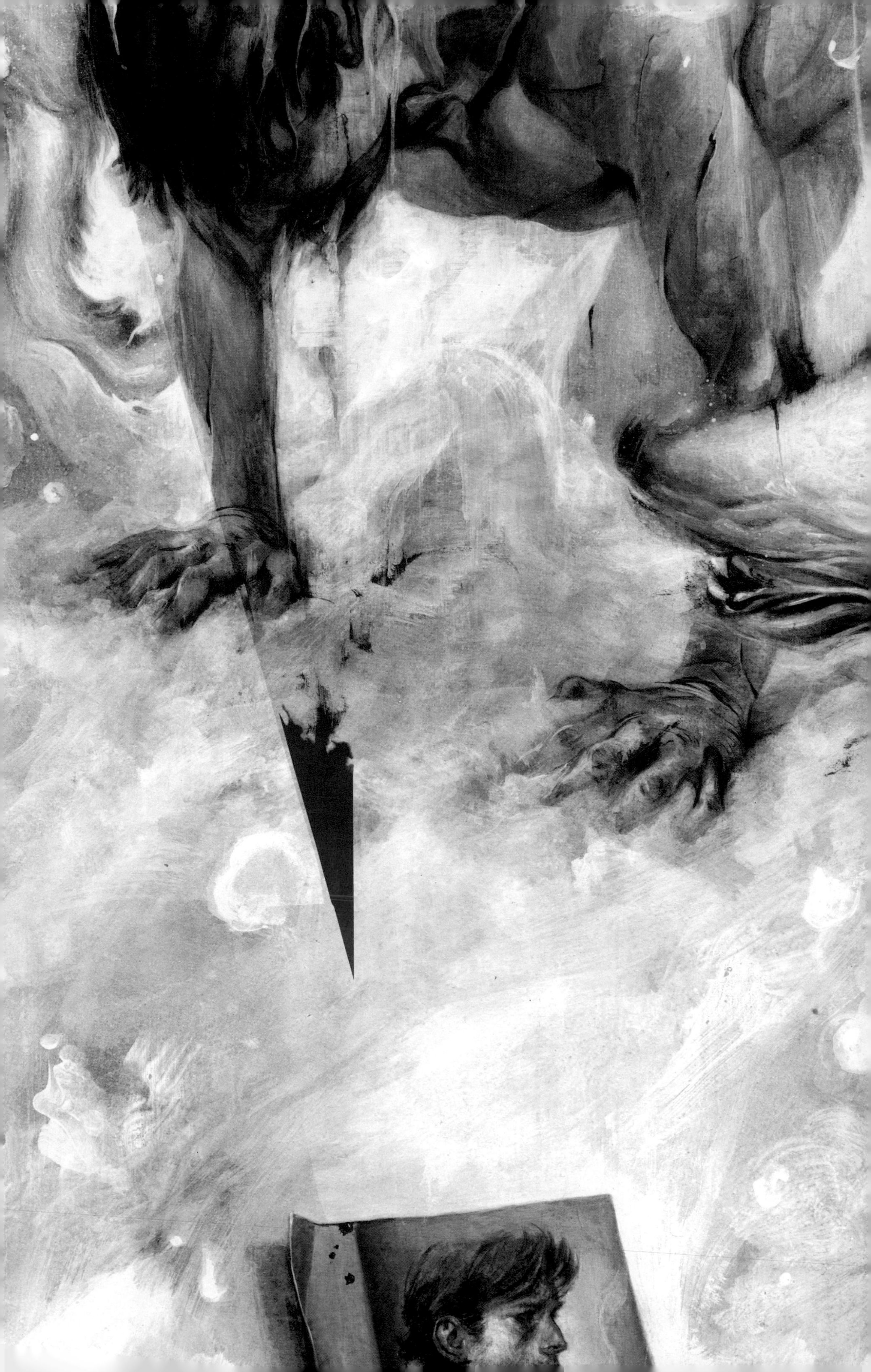

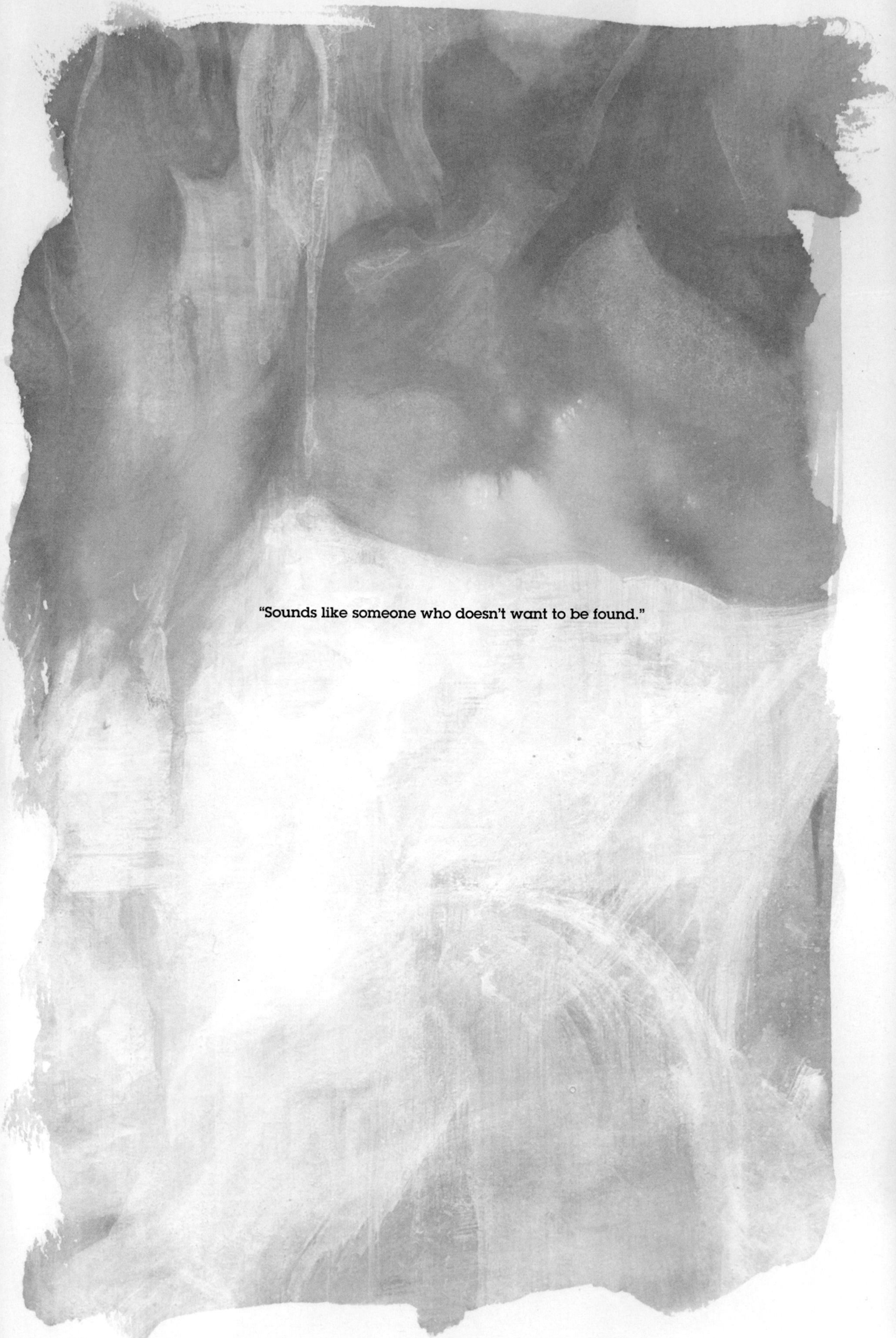
"Sounds like someone who doesn't want to be found."

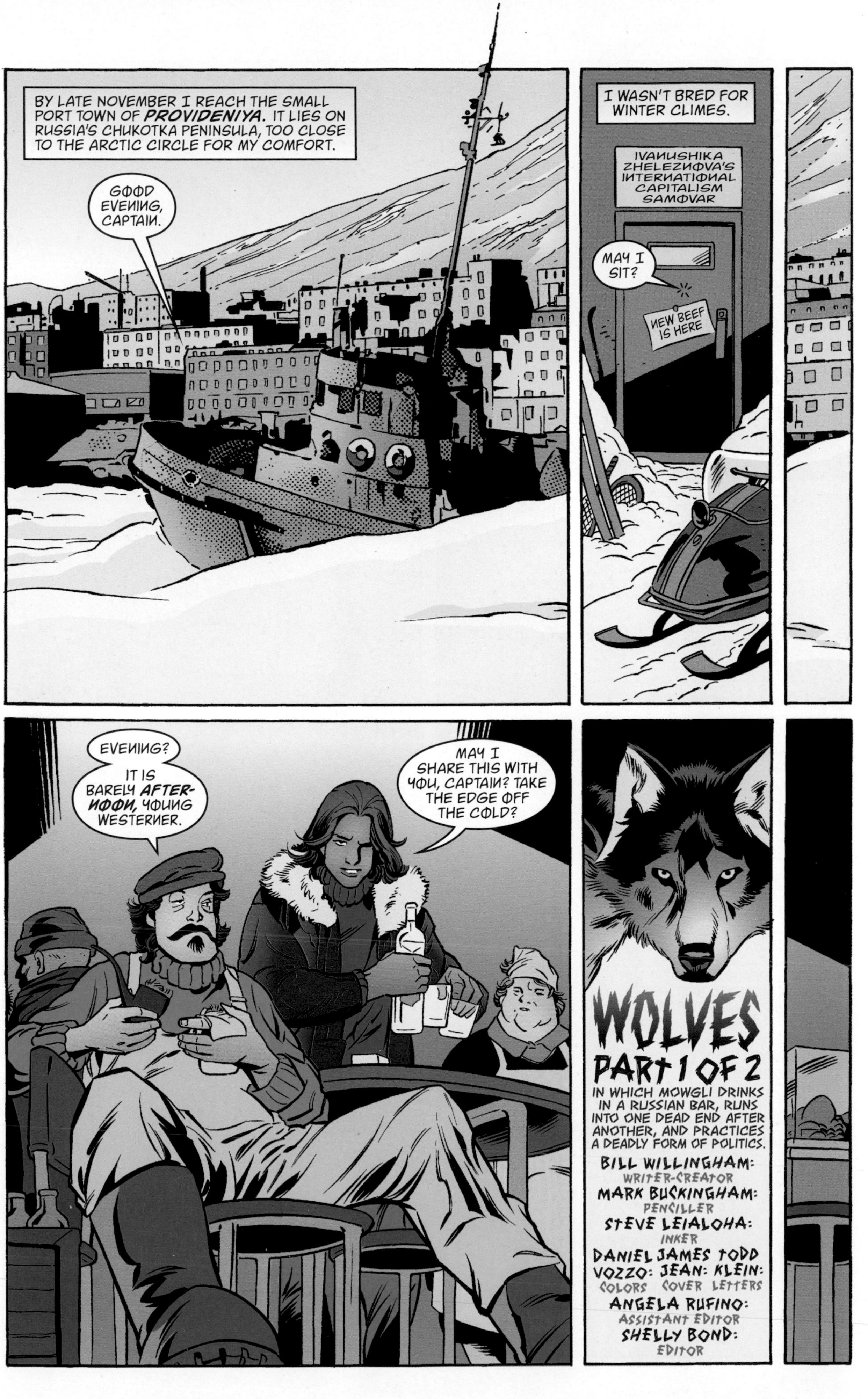
BY LATE NOVEMBER I REACH THE SMALL PORT TOWN OF PROVIDENIYA. IT LIES ON RUSSIA'S CHUKOTKA PENINSULA, TOO CLOSE TO THE ARCTIC CIRCLE FOR MY COMFORT.
GOOD EVENING, CAPTAIN.
I WASN'T BRED FOR WINTER CLIMES.
IVANUSHIKA ZHELEZNOVA'S INTERNATIONAL CAPITALISM SAMOVAR
MAY I SIT?
NEW BEEF IS HERE
EVENING? IT IS BARELY AFTERNOON, YOUNG WESTERNER.
MAY I SHARE THIS WITH YOU, CAPTAIN? TAKE THE EDGE OFF THE COLD?
WOLVES
PART 1 OF 2
IN WHICH MOWGLI DRINKS IN A RUSSIAN BAR, RUNS INTO ONE DEAD END AFTER ANOTHER, AND PRACTICES A DEADLY FORM OF POLITICS.
BILL WILLINGHAM: WRITER-CREATOR
MARK BUCKINGHAM: PENCILLER
STEVE LEIALOHA: INKER
DANIEL VOZZO: COLORS
JAMES JEAN: COVER
TODD KLEIN: LETTERS
ANGELA RUFINO: ASSISTANT EDITOR
SHELLY BOND: EDITOR

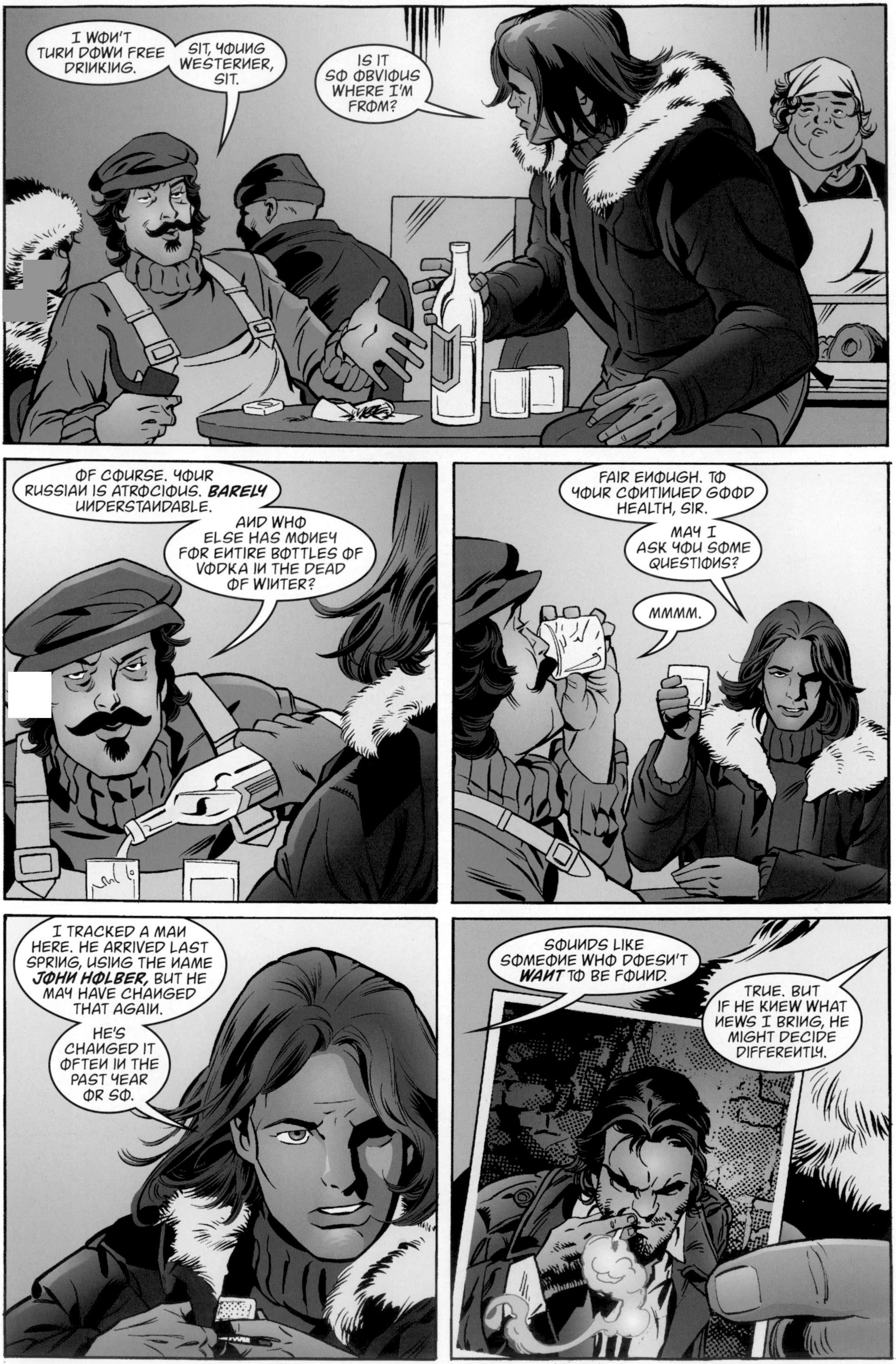
I WON'T TURN DOWN FREE DRINKING.
SIT, YOUNG WESTERNER, SIT.
IS IT SO OBVIOUS WHERE I'M FROM?
OF COURSE. YOUR RUSSIAN IS ATROCIOUS. **BARELY** UNDERSTANDABLE.
AND WHO ELSE HAS MONEY FOR ENTIRE BOTTLES OF VODKA IN THE DEAD OF WINTER?
FAIR ENOUGH. TO YOUR CONTINUED GOOD HEALTH, SIR.
MAY I ASK YOU SOME QUESTIONS?
MMMM.
I TRACKED A MAN HERE. HE ARRIVED LAST SPRING, USING THE NAME **JOHN HOLBER,** BUT HE MAY HAVE CHANGED THAT AGAIN.
HE'S CHANGED IT OFTEN IN THE PAST YEAR OR SO.
SOUNDS LIKE SOMEONE WHO DOESN'T **WANT** TO BE FOUND.
TRUE. BUT IF HE KNEW WHAT NEWS I BRING, HE MIGHT DECIDE DIFFERENTLY.

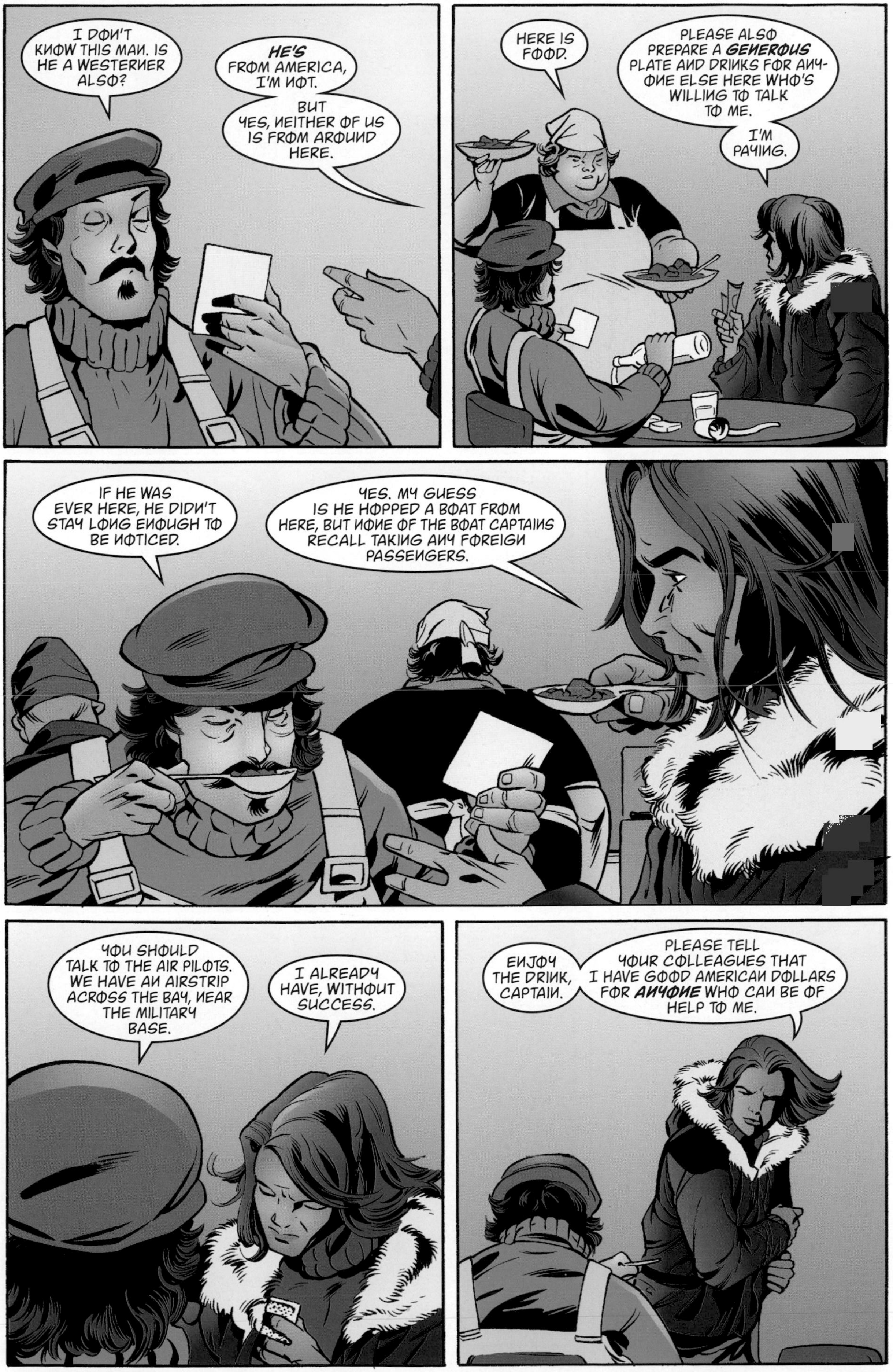

I DON'T KNOW THIS MAN. IS HE A WESTERNER ALSO?
HE'S FROM AMERICA, I'M NOT.
BUT YES, NEITHER OF US IS FROM AROUND HERE.
HERE IS FOOD.
PLEASE ALSO PREPARE A GENEROUS PLATE AND DRINKS FOR ANY-ONE ELSE HERE WHO'S WILLING TO TALK TO ME.
I'M PAYING.
IF HE WAS EVER HERE, HE DIDN'T STAY LONG ENOUGH TO BE NOTICED.
YES. MY GUESS IS HE HOPPED A BOAT FROM HERE, BUT NONE OF THE BOAT CAPTAINS RECALL TAKING ANY FOREIGN PASSENGERS.
YOU SHOULD TALK TO THE AIR PILOTS. WE HAVE AN AIRSTRIP ACROSS THE BAY, NEAR THE MILITARY BASE.
I ALREADY HAVE, WITHOUT SUCCESS.
ENJOY THE DRINK, CAPTAIN.
PLEASE TELL YOUR COLLEAGUES THAT I HAVE GOOD AMERICAN DOLLARS FOR ANYONE WHO CAN BE OF HELP TO ME.

FABLETOWN'S FARM ANNEX IN UPSTATE NEW YORK.

SIT **STILL**, YOU HOOLIGANS.

WHY DO WE ALWAYS HAVE TO GET PICTURES TAKEN ALL THE TIME?

BECAUSE, WHEN YOU FINALLY MEET YOUR FATHER, HE'LL WANT TO SEE HOW EACH OF YOU **LOOKED** WHILE GROWING UP.

MERRY CHRISTMAS DADDY from:

DARIEN
DARE

BUT IT'S NOT CHRISTMAS YET, MOMMY.

IT'S CLOSE ENOUGH.

MERRY CHRISTMAS DADDY from:

BloSSom

SO WILL WE GET PRESENTS **EARLY** TOO?

NO.

MERRY CHRISTMAS DADDY from:

AMBROSE

DOES **DADDY** GET THE GIFTS WE SEND HIM?

OF COURSE.

MERRY CHRISTMAS DADDY from:

Winter

MR. SUNNYFLOWER SAYS DADDY **GOBBLES** PEOPLE UP.

MR. SUNFLOWER HAS ANGER ISSUES.

MERRY CHRISTMAS DADDY from:

CONNER

WILL HE **EVER** COME HOME?

SOMEDAY.

MERRY CHRISTMAS DADDY from:

Therese

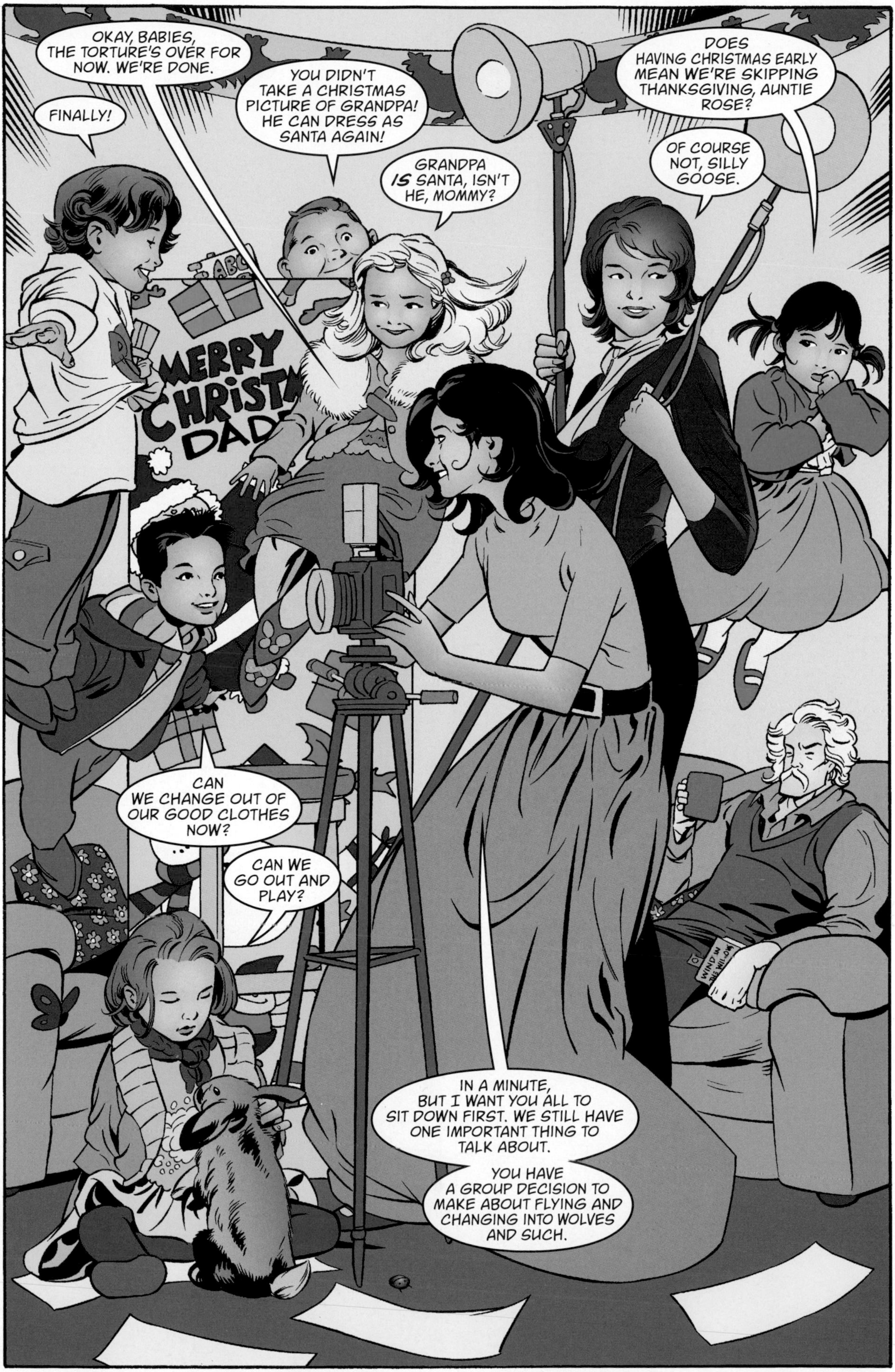
OKAY, BABIES, THE TORTURE'S OVER FOR NOW. WE'RE DONE.
FINALLY!
YOU DIDN'T TAKE A CHRISTMAS PICTURE OF GRANDPA! HE CAN DRESS AS SANTA AGAIN!
GRANDPA *IS* SANTA, ISN'T HE, MOMMY?
DOES HAVING CHRISTMAS EARLY MEAN **WE'RE** SKIPPING THANKSGIVING, AUNTIE ROSE?
OF COURSE NOT, SILLY GOOSE.
CAN WE CHANGE OUT OF OUR GOOD CLOTHES NOW?
CAN WE GO OUT AND PLAY?
IN A MINUTE, BUT I WANT YOU ALL TO SIT DOWN FIRST. WE STILL HAVE ONE IMPORTANT THING TO TALK ABOUT.
YOU HAVE A GROUP DECISION TO MAKE ABOUT FLYING AND CHANGING INTO WOLVES AND SUCH.

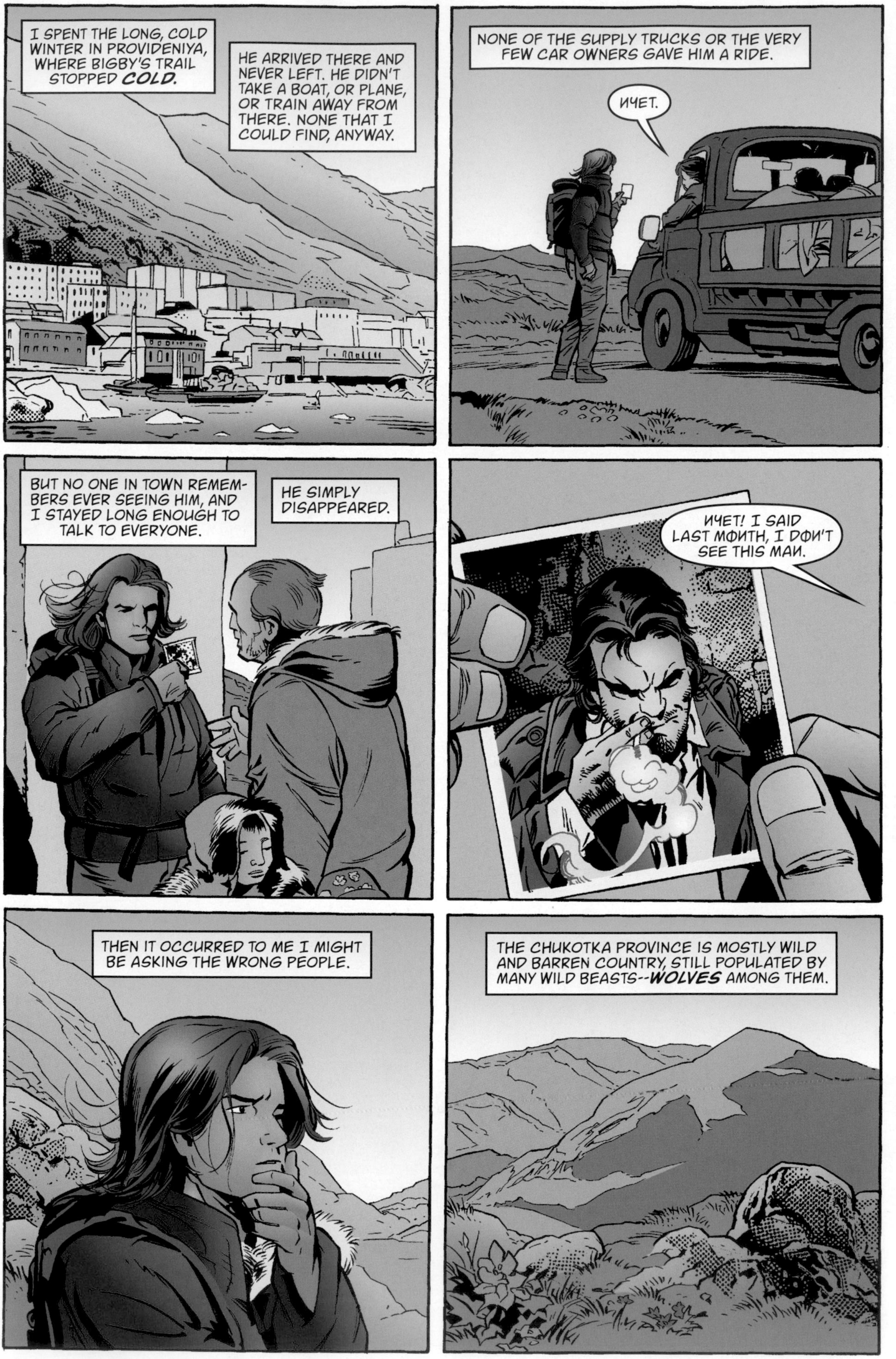
I SPENT THE LONG, COLD WINTER IN PROVIDENIYA, WHERE BIGBY'S TRAIL STOPPED **COLD.**
HE ARRIVED THERE AND NEVER LEFT. HE DIDN'T TAKE A BOAT, OR PLANE, OR TRAIN AWAY FROM THERE. NONE THAT I COULD FIND, ANYWAY.
NONE OF THE SUPPLY TRUCKS OR THE VERY FEW CAR OWNERS GAVE HIM A RIDE.
ИЧЕТ.
BUT NO ONE IN TOWN REMEMBERS EVER SEEING HIM, AND I STAYED LONG ENOUGH TO TALK TO EVERYONE.
HE SIMPLY DISAPPEARED.
ИЧЕТ! I SAID LAST МФИТН, I DФИ'T SEE THIS МАИ.
THEN IT OCCURRED TO ME I MIGHT BE ASKING THE WRONG PEOPLE.
THE CHUKOTKA PROVINCE IS MOSTLY WILD AND BARREN COUNTRY, STILL POPULATED BY MANY WILD BEASTS--**WOLVES** AMONG THEM.

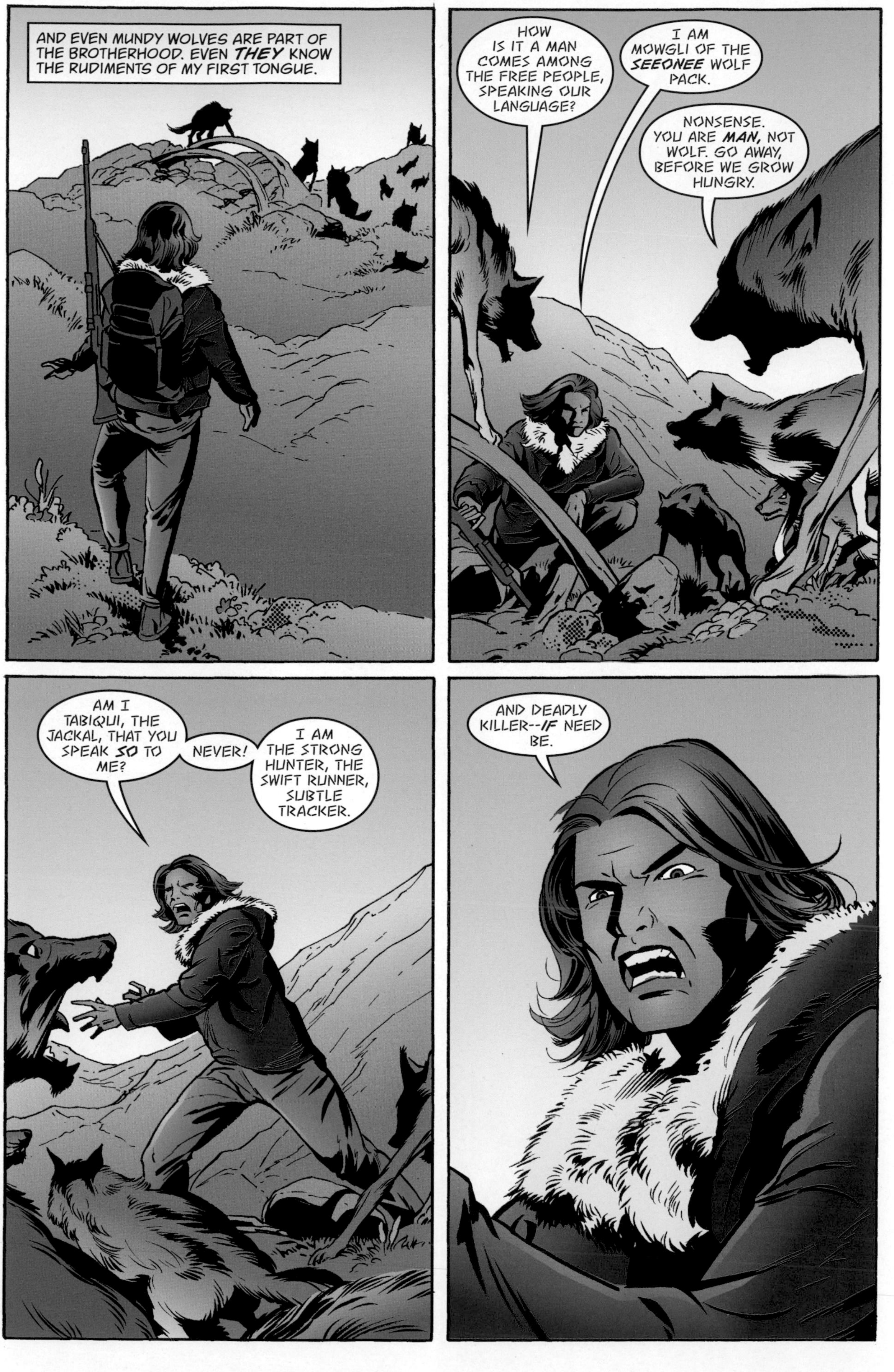
AND EVEN MUNDY WOLVES ARE PART OF THE BROTHERHOOD. EVEN THEY KNOW THE RUDIMENTS OF MY FIRST TONGUE.
HOW IS IT A MAN COMES AMONG THE FREE PEOPLE, SPEAKING OUR LANGUAGE?
I AM MOWGLI OF THE SEEONEE WOLF PACK.
NONSENSE. YOU ARE MAN, NOT WOLF. GO AWAY, BEFORE WE GROW HUNGRY.
AM I TABIQUI, THE JACKAL, THAT YOU SPEAK SO TO ME?
NEVER!
I AM THE STRONG HUNTER, THE SWIFT RUNNER, SUBTLE TRACKER.
AND DEADLY KILLER--IF NEED BE.

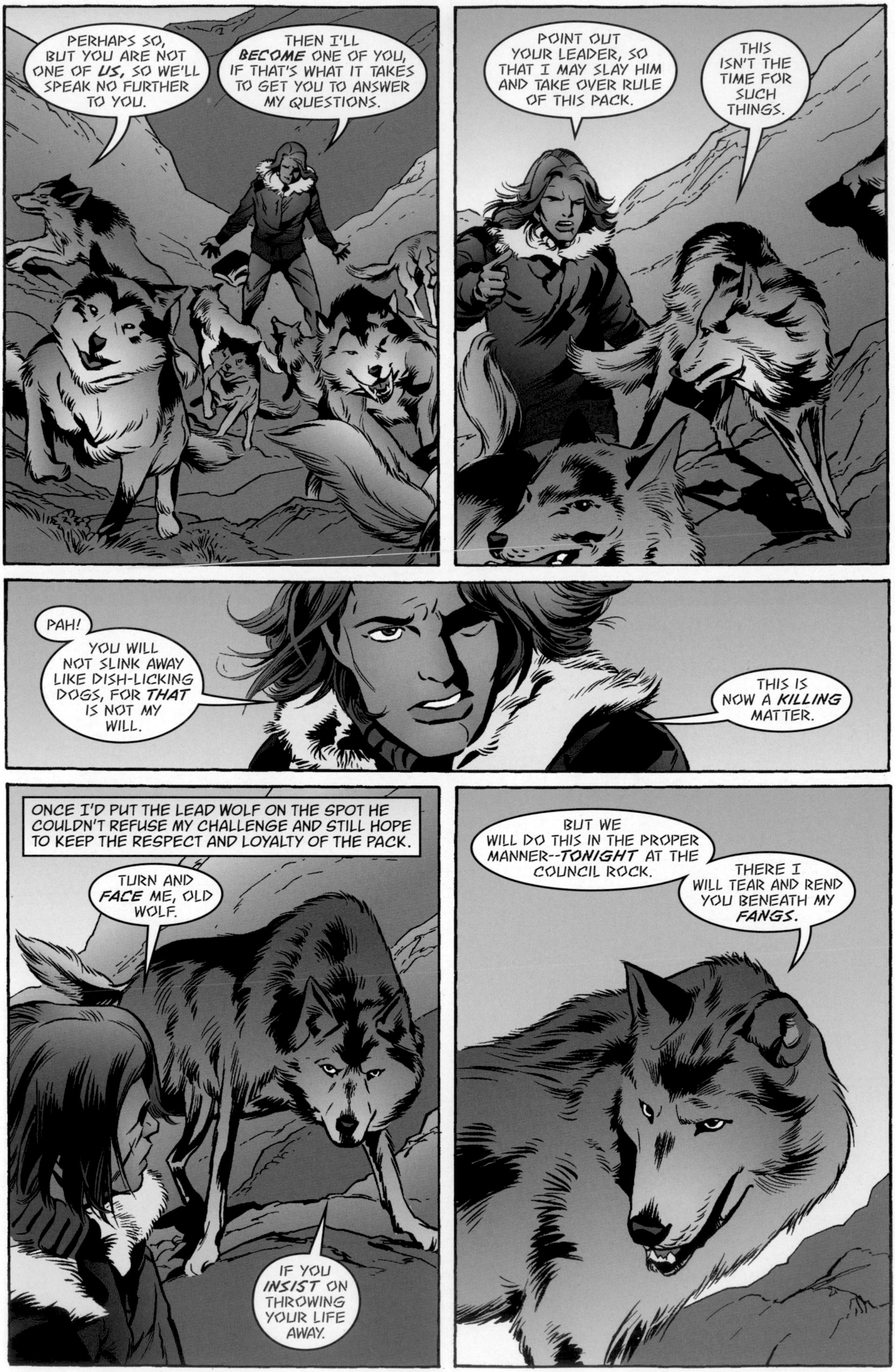
PERHAPS SO, BUT YOU ARE NOT ONE OF US, SO WE'LL SPEAK NO FURTHER TO YOU.
THEN I'LL BECOME ONE OF YOU, IF THAT'S WHAT IT TAKES TO GET YOU TO ANSWER MY QUESTIONS.
POINT OUT YOUR LEADER, SO THAT I MAY SLAY HIM AND TAKE OVER RULE OF THIS PACK.
THIS ISN'T THE TIME FOR SUCH THINGS.
PAH!
YOU WILL NOT SLINK AWAY LIKE DISH-LICKING DOGS, FOR THAT IS NOT MY WILL.
THIS IS NOW A KILLING MATTER.
ONCE I'D PUT THE LEAD WOLF ON THE SPOT HE COULDN'T REFUSE MY CHALLENGE AND STILL HOPE TO KEEP THE RESPECT AND LOYALTY OF THE PACK.
TURN AND FACE ME, OLD WOLF.
IF YOU INSIST ON THROWING YOUR LIFE AWAY.
BUT WE WILL DO THIS IN THE PROPER MANNER--TONIGHT AT THE COUNCIL ROCK.
THERE I WILL TEAR AND REND YOU BENEATH MY FANGS.

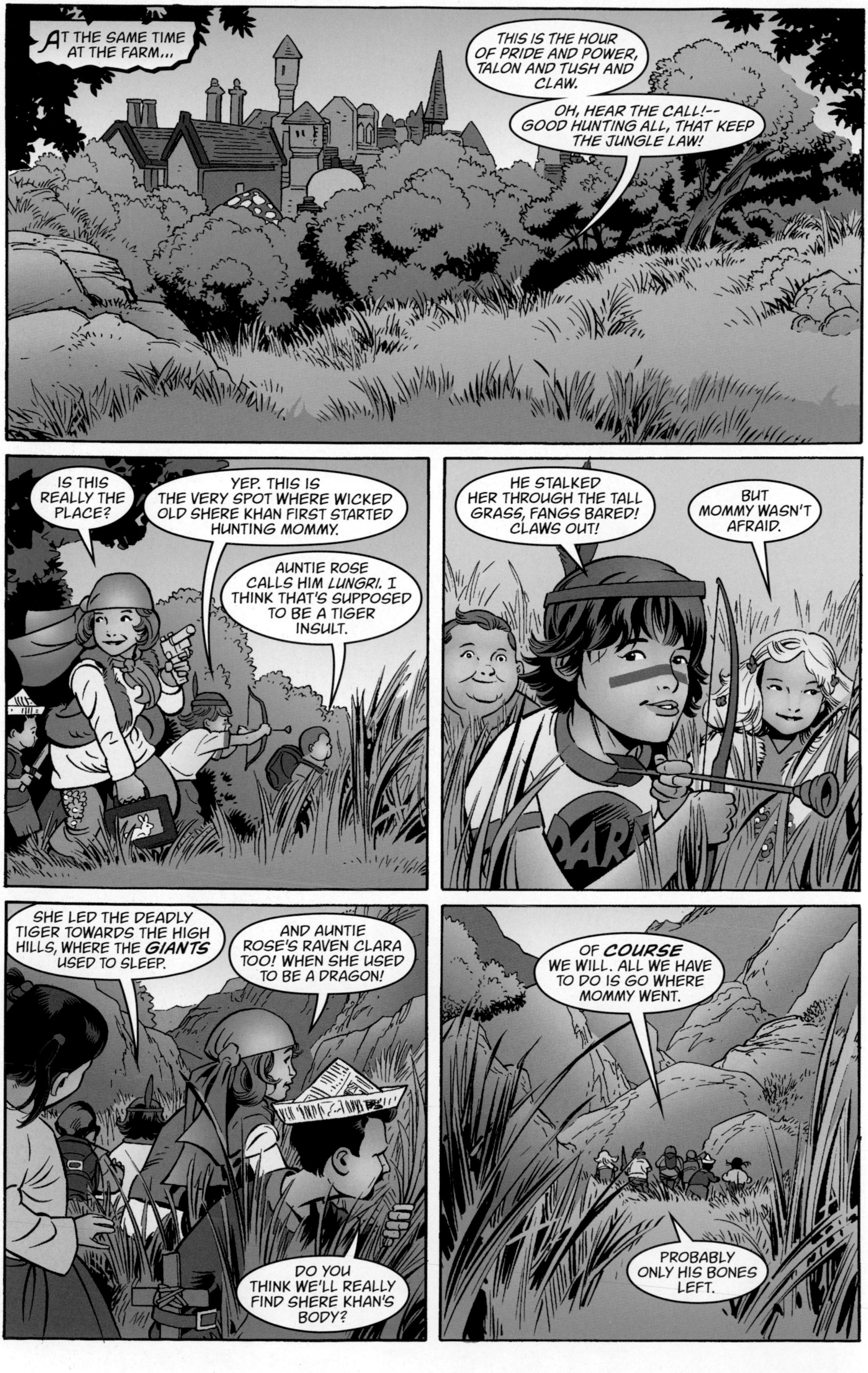
AT THE SAME TIME AT THE FARM...
THIS IS THE HOUR OF PRIDE AND POWER, TALON AND TUSH AND CLAW.
OH, HEAR THE CALL!-- GOOD HUNTING ALL, THAT KEEP THE JUNGLE LAW!
IS THIS REALLY THE PLACE?
YEP. THIS IS THE VERY SPOT WHERE WICKED OLD SHERE KHAN FIRST STARTED HUNTING MOMMY.
AUNTIE ROSE CALLS HIM *LUNGRI*. I THINK THAT'S SUPPOSED TO BE A TIGER INSULT.
HE STALKED HER THROUGH THE TALL GRASS, FANGS BARED! CLAWS OUT!
BUT MOMMY WASN'T AFRAID.
SHE LED THE DEADLY TIGER TOWARDS THE HIGH HILLS, WHERE THE ***GIANTS*** USED TO SLEEP.
AND AUNTIE ROSE'S RAVEN CLARA TOO! WHEN SHE USED TO BE A DRAGON!
DO YOU THINK WE'LL REALLY FIND SHERE KHAN'S BODY?
OF ***COURSE*** WE WILL. ALL WE HAVE TO DO IS GO WHERE MOMMY WENT.
PROBABLY ONLY HIS BONES LEFT.

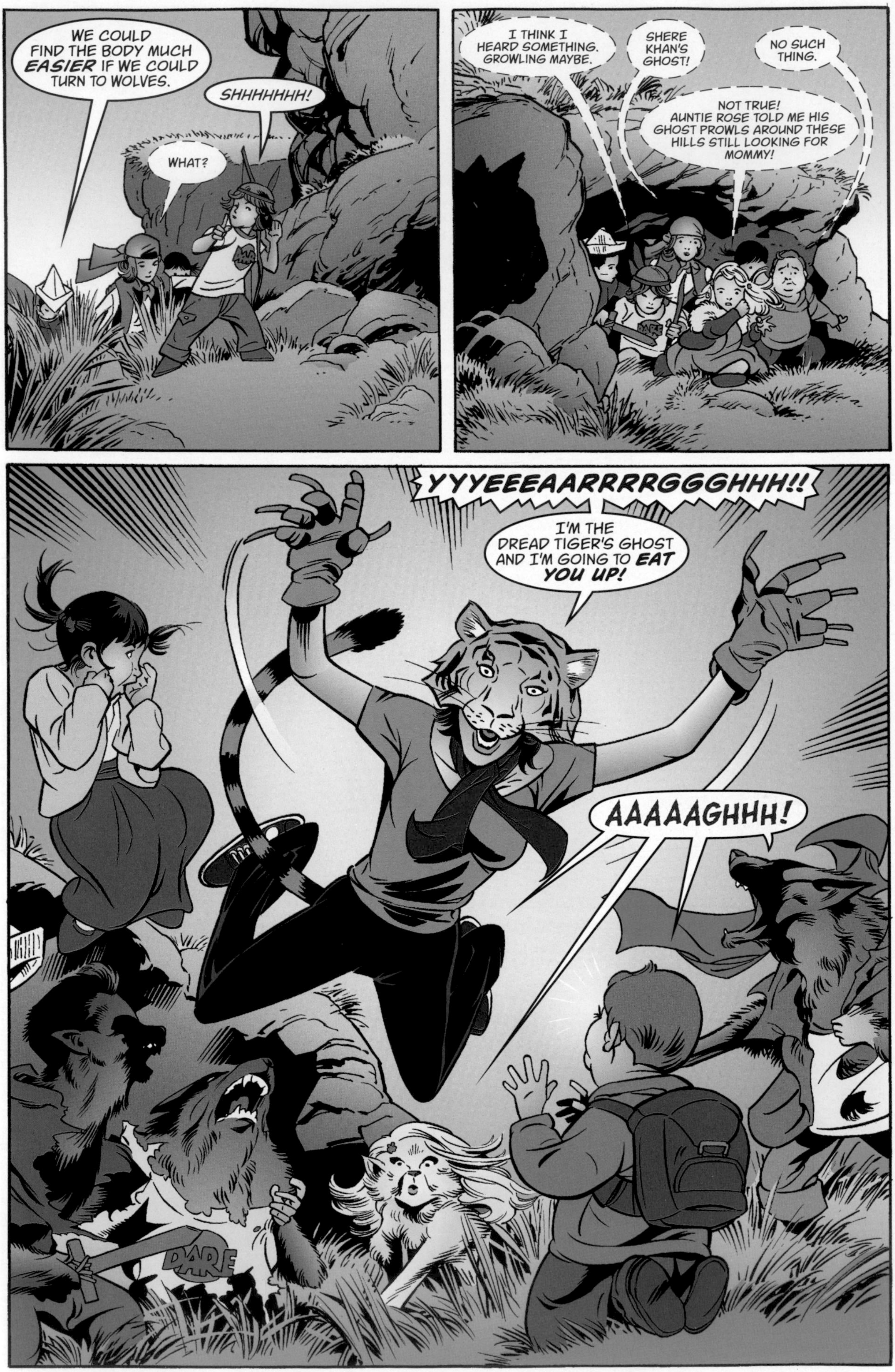
WE COULD FIND THE BODY MUCH EASIER IF WE COULD TURN TO WOLVES.
SHHHHHHH!
WHAT?
I THINK I HEARD SOMETHING. GROWLING MAYBE.
SHERE KHAN'S GHOST!
NO SUCH THING.
NOT TRUE! AUNTIE ROSE TOLD ME HIS GHOST PROWLS AROUND THESE HILLS STILL LOOKING FOR MOMMY!
YYYEEEAARRRRGGGHHH!!
I'M THE DREAD TIGER'S GHOST AND I'M GOING TO EAT YOU UP!
AAAAAGHHH!

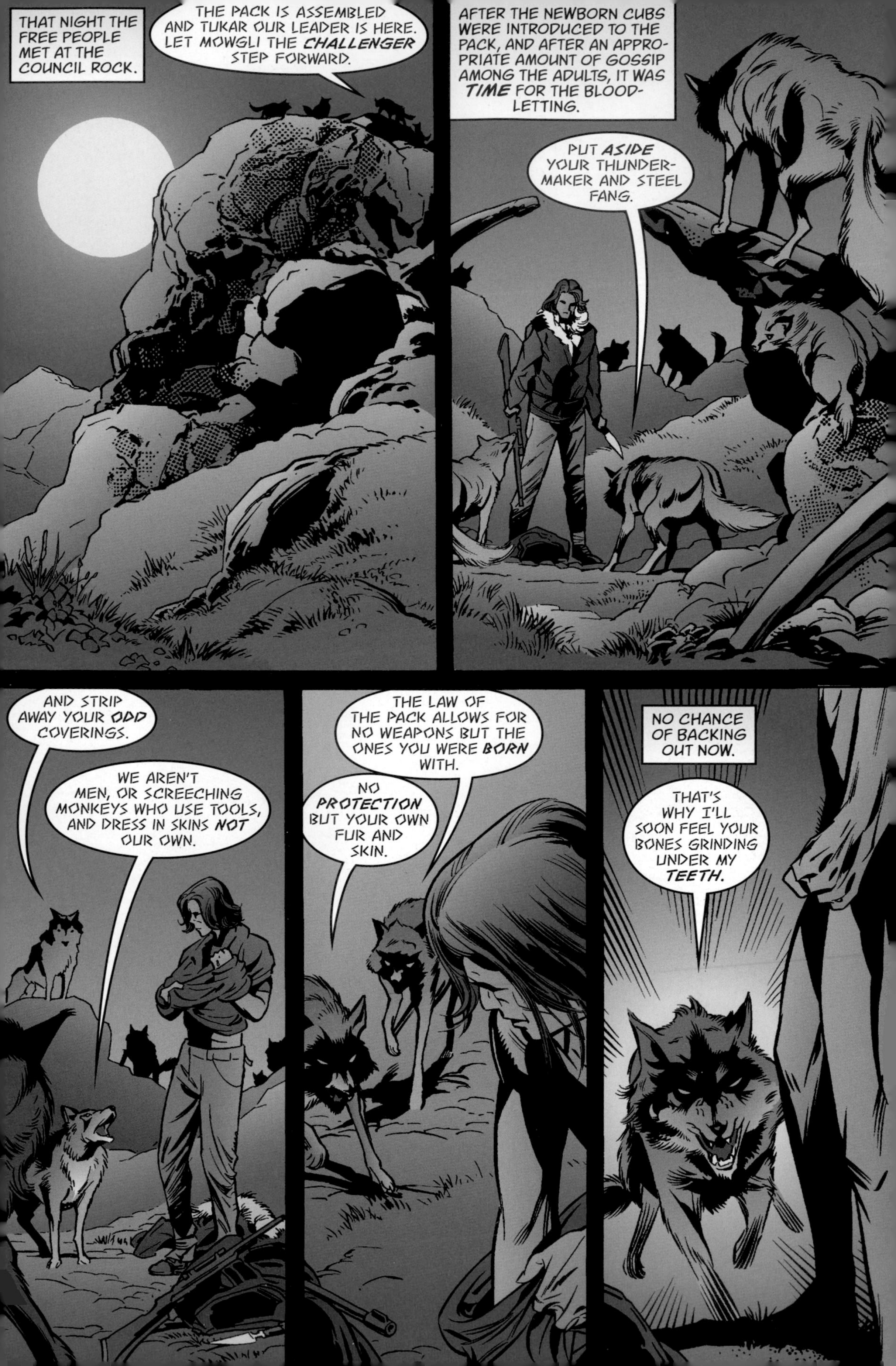
THAT NIGHT THE FREE PEOPLE MET AT THE COUNCIL ROCK.
THE PACK IS ASSEMBLED AND TUKAR OUR LEADER IS HERE. LET MOWGLI THE *CHALLENGER* STEP FORWARD.
AFTER THE NEWBORN CUBS WERE INTRODUCED TO THE PACK, AND AFTER AN APPROPRIATE AMOUNT OF GOSSIP AMONG THE ADULTS, IT WAS *TIME* FOR THE BLOOD-LETTING.
PUT *ASIDE* YOUR THUNDER-MAKER AND STEEL FANG.
AND STRIP AWAY YOUR *ODD* COVERINGS.
WE AREN'T MEN, OR SCREECHING MONKEYS WHO USE TOOLS, AND DRESS IN SKINS *NOT* OUR OWN.
THE LAW OF THE PACK ALLOWS FOR NO WEAPONS BUT THE ONES YOU WERE *BORN* WITH.
NO *PROTECTION* BUT YOUR OWN FUR AND SKIN.
NO CHANCE OF BACKING OUT NOW.
THAT'S WHY I'LL SOON FEEL YOUR BONES GRINDING UNDER MY *TEETH*.

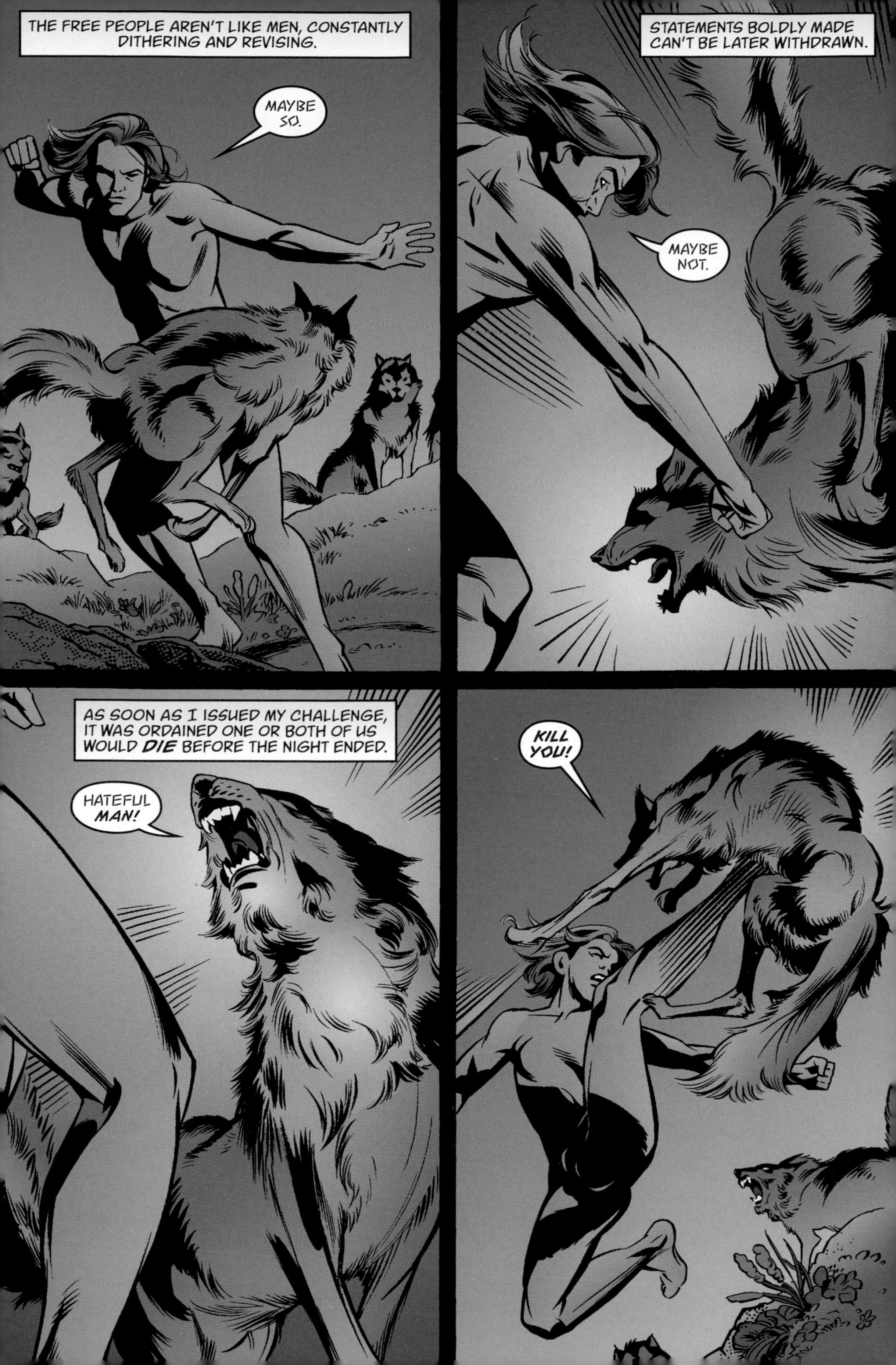
THE FREE PEOPLE AREN'T LIKE MEN, CONSTANTLY DITHERING AND REVISING.
MAYBE SO.
STATEMENTS BOLDLY MADE CAN'T BE LATER WITHDRAWN.
MAYBE NOT.
AS SOON AS I ISSUED MY CHALLENGE, IT WAS ORDAINED ONE OR BOTH OF US WOULD DIE BEFORE THE NIGHT ENDED.
HATEFUL MAN!
KILL YOU!

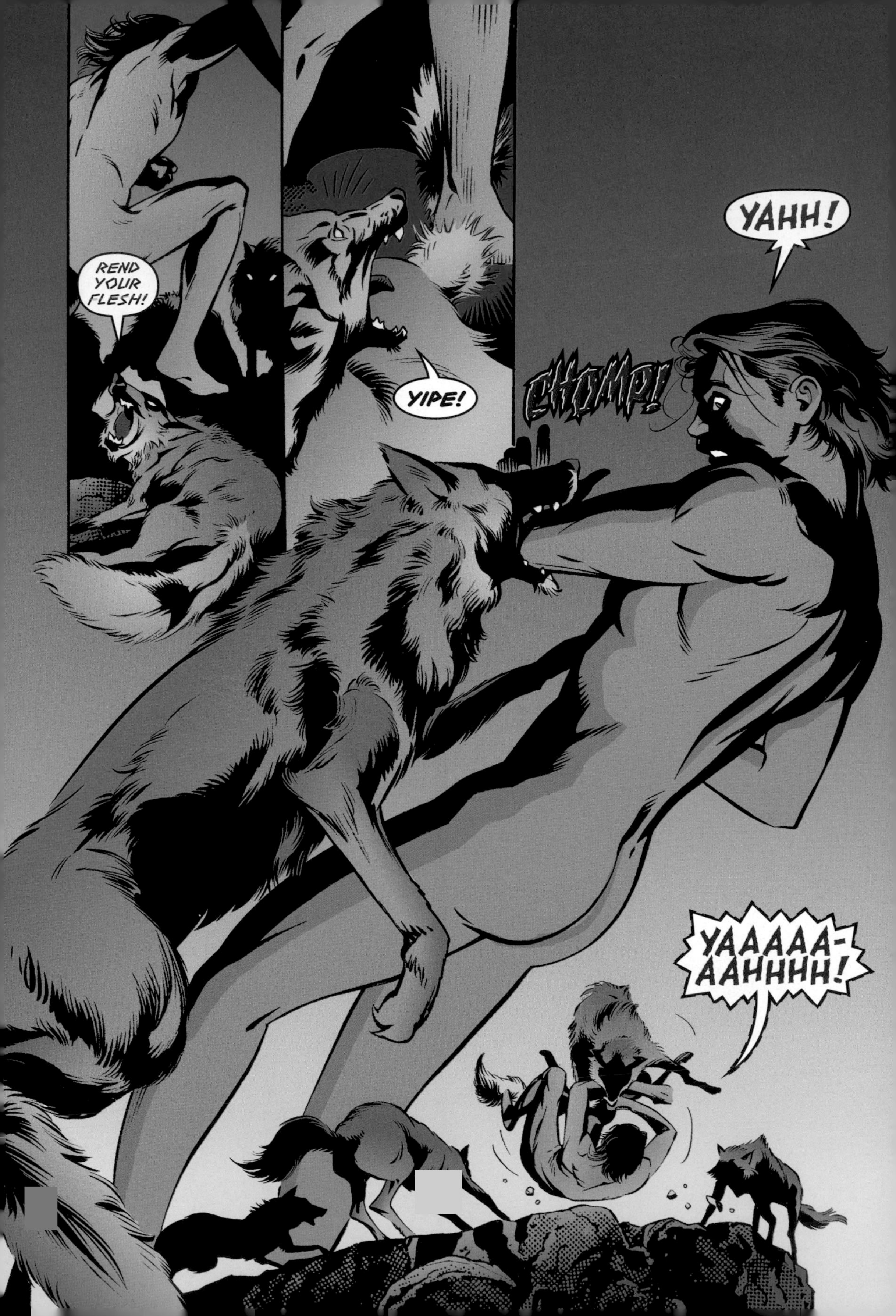
REND YOUR FLESH!
YIPE!
YAHH!
CHOMP!
YAAAAA-AAHHHH!

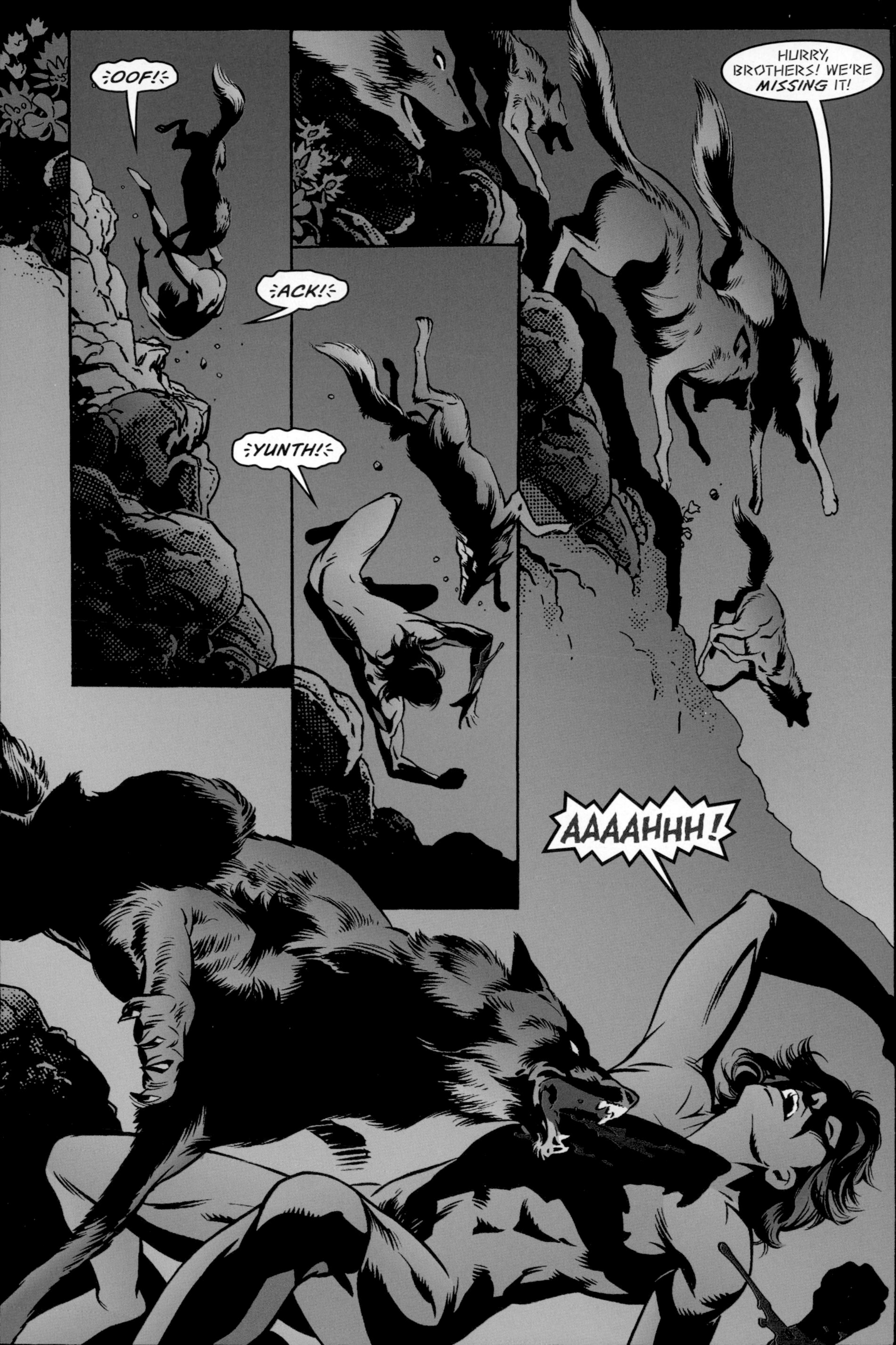

OOF!
ACK!
YUNTH!
HURRY, BROTHERS! WE'RE MISSING IT!
AAAAHHH!

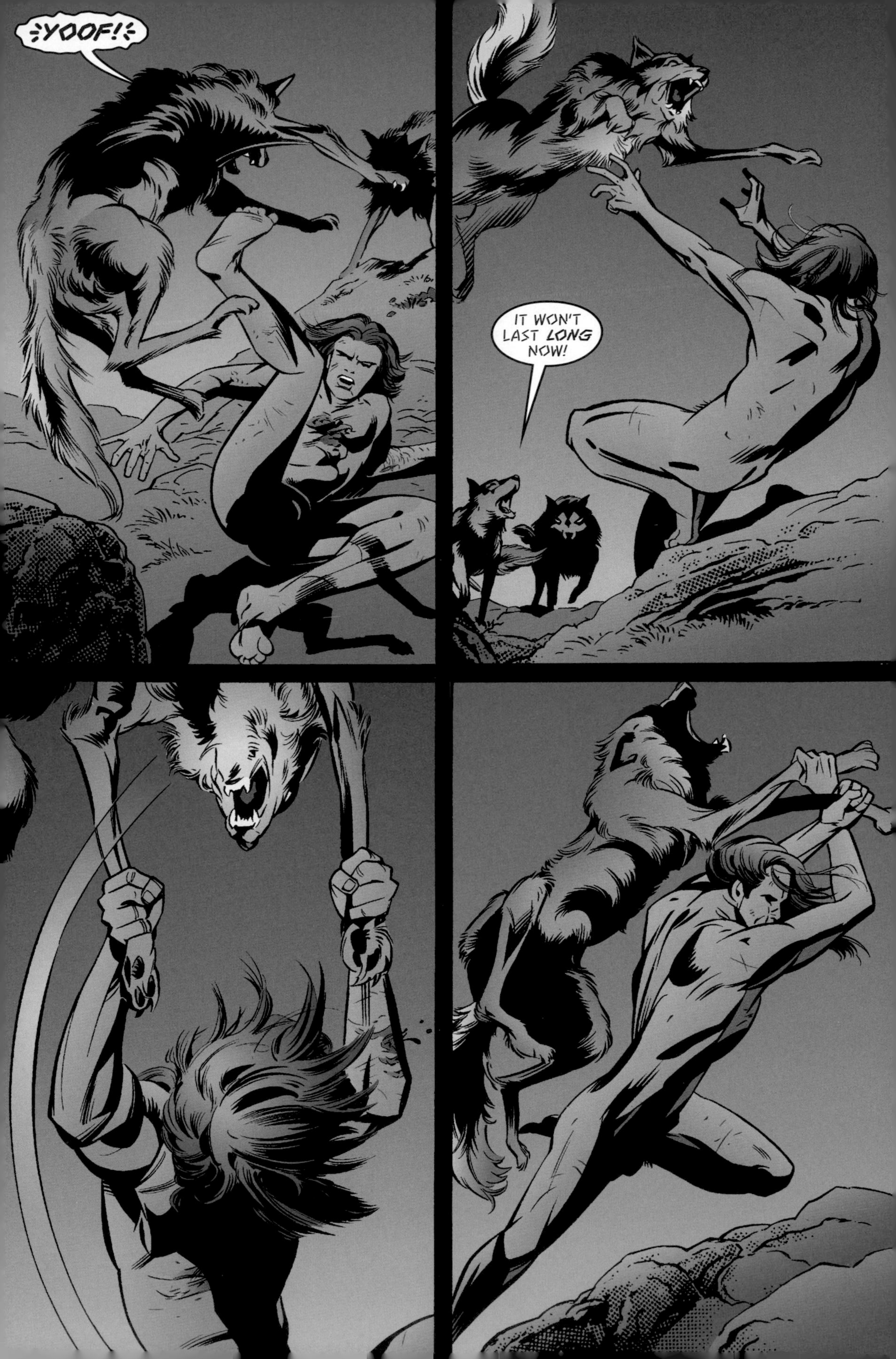
YOOF!
IT WON'T LAST LONG NOW!

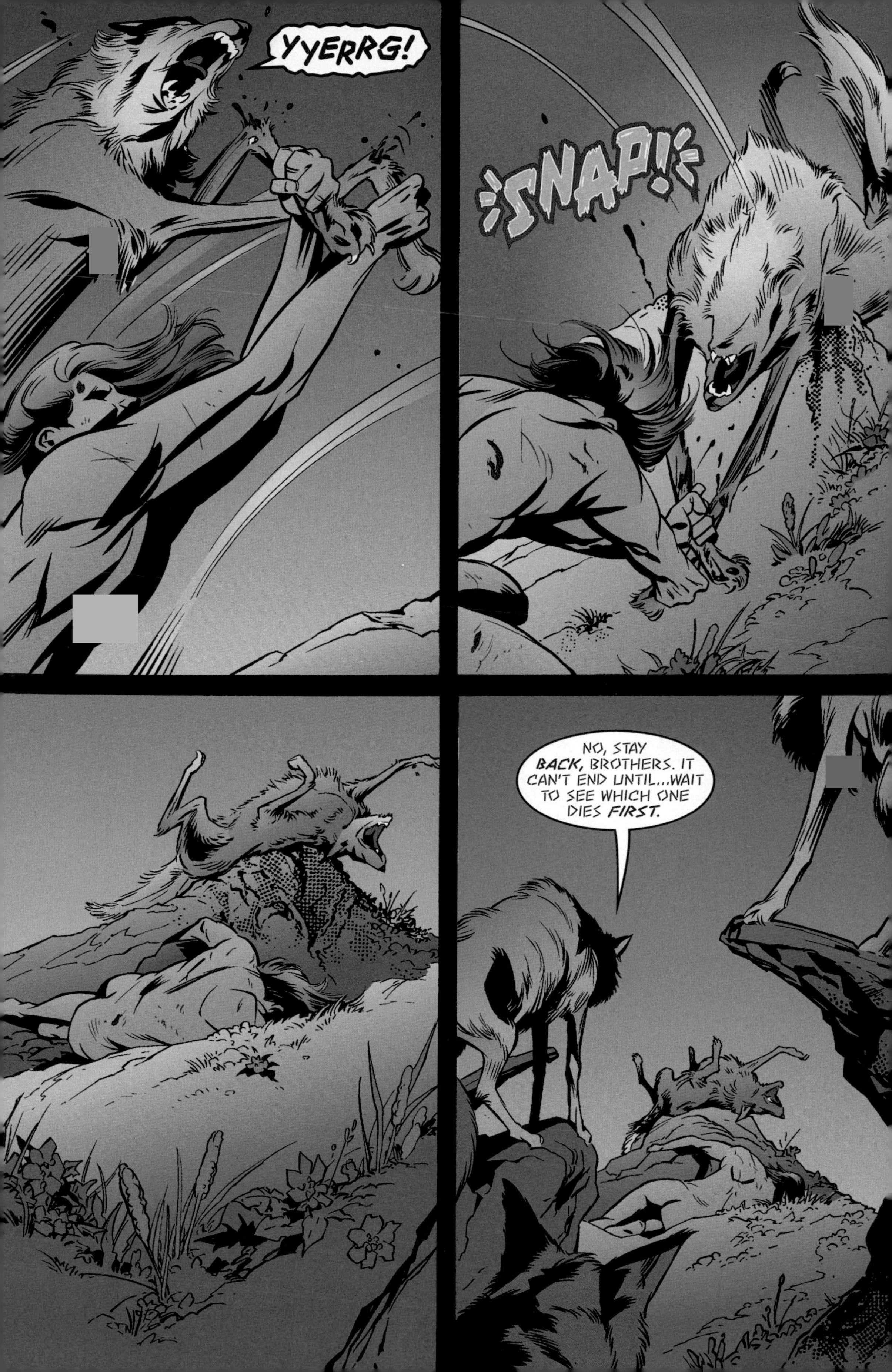
YYERRG!
SNAP!
NO, STAY BACK, BROTHERS. IT CAN'T END UNTIL...WAIT TO SEE WHICH ONE DIES FIRST.

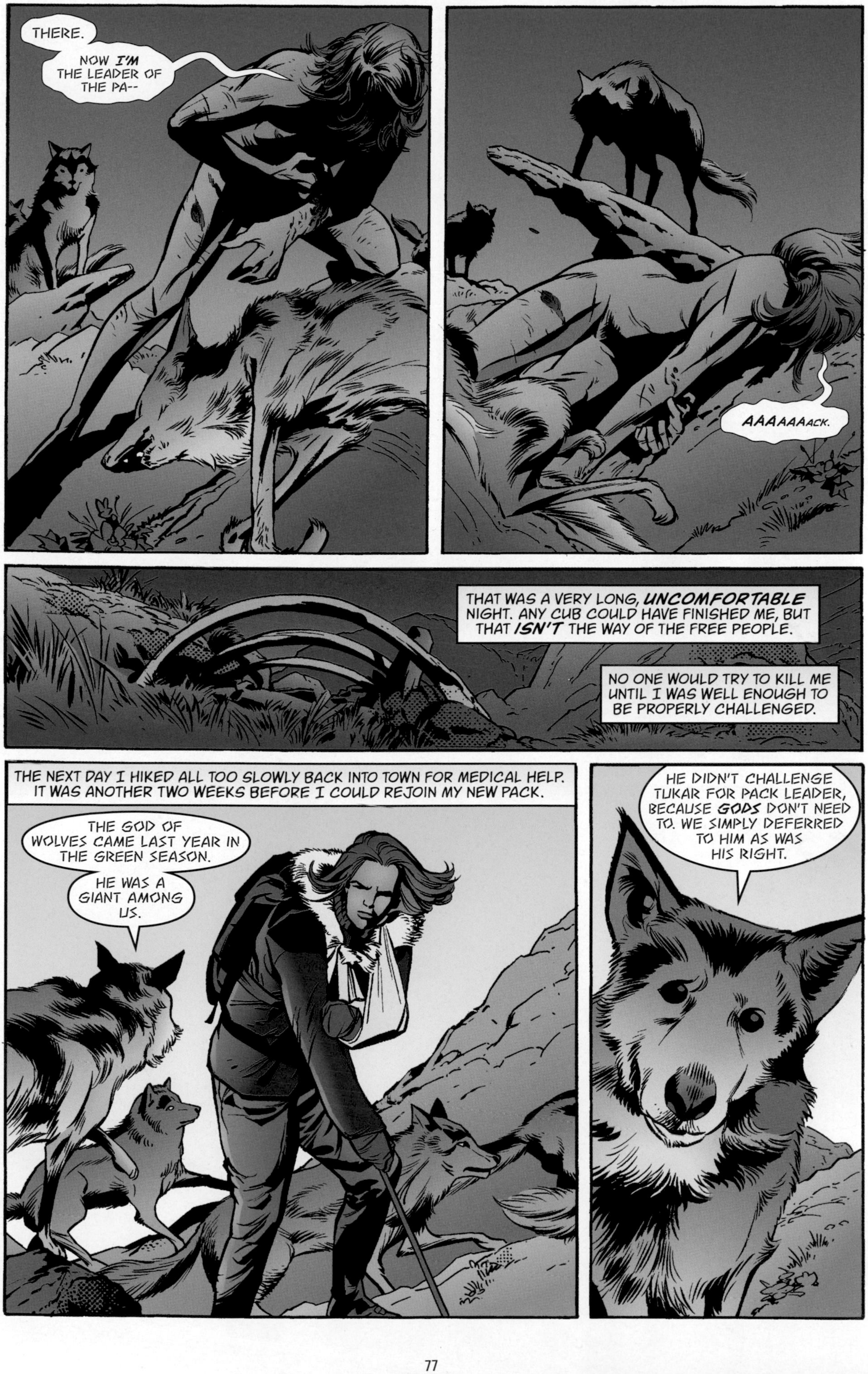
THERE.
NOW I'M THE LEADER OF THE PA--
AAAAAAACK.
THAT WAS A VERY LONG, UNCOMFORTABLE NIGHT. ANY CUB COULD HAVE FINISHED ME, BUT THAT ISN'T THE WAY OF THE FREE PEOPLE.
NO ONE WOULD TRY TO KILL ME UNTIL I WAS WELL ENOUGH TO BE PROPERLY CHALLENGED.
THE NEXT DAY I HIKED ALL TOO SLOWLY BACK INTO TOWN FOR MEDICAL HELP. IT WAS ANOTHER TWO WEEKS BEFORE I COULD REJOIN MY NEW PACK.
THE GOD OF WOLVES CAME LAST YEAR IN THE GREEN SEASON.
HE WAS A GIANT AMONG US.
HE DIDN'T CHALLENGE TUKAR FOR PACK LEADER, BECAUSE GODS DON'T NEED TO. WE SIMPLY DEFERRED TO HIM AS WAS HIS RIGHT.

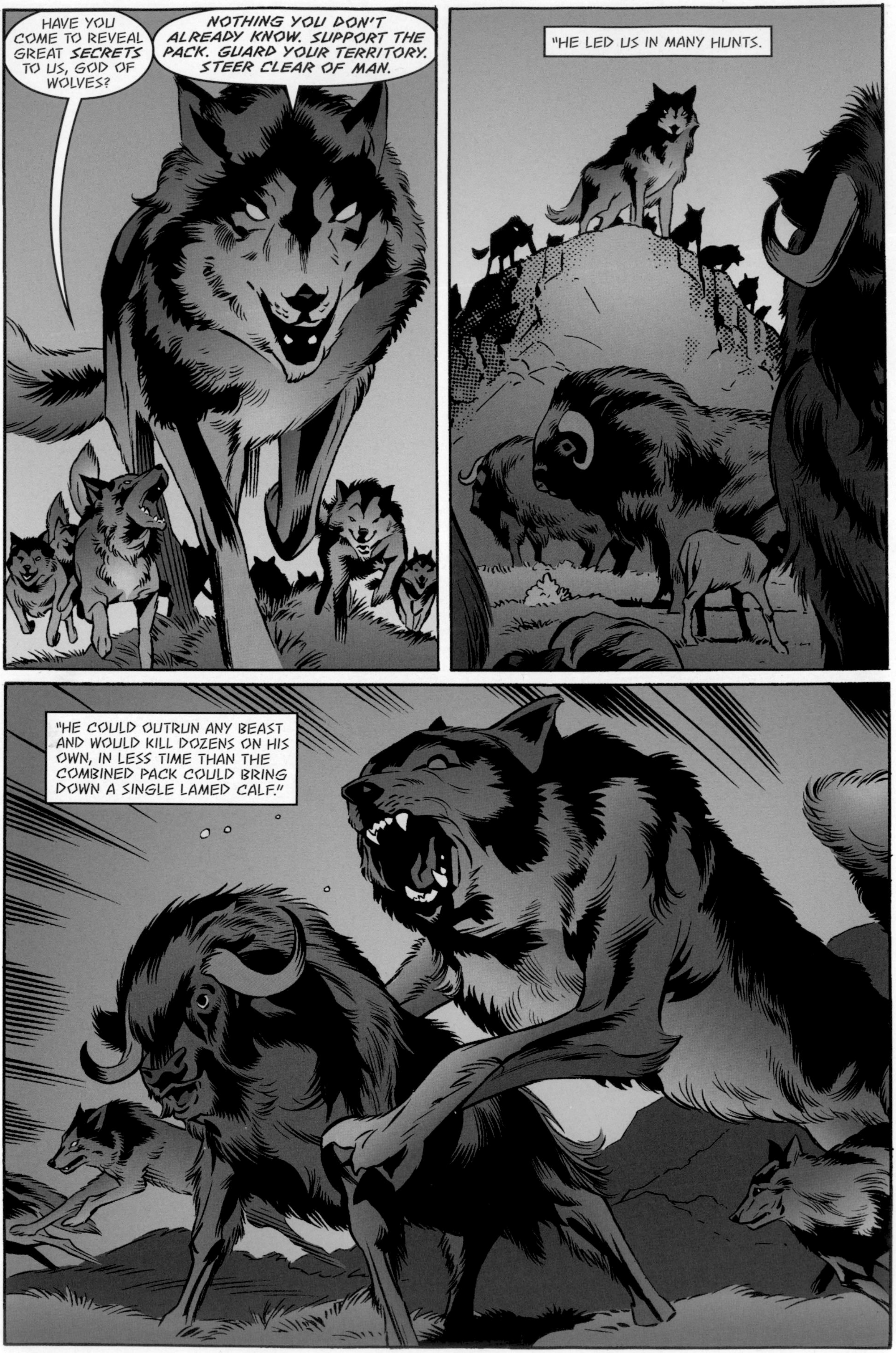
HAVE YOU COME TO REVEAL GREAT SECRETS TO US, GOD OF WOLVES?
NOTHING YOU DON'T ALREADY KNOW. SUPPORT THE PACK. GUARD YOUR TERRITORY. STEER CLEAR OF MAN.
"HE LED US IN MANY HUNTS.
"HE COULD OUTRUN ANY BEAST AND WOULD KILL DOZENS ON HIS OWN, IN LESS TIME THAN THE COMBINED PACK COULD BRING DOWN A SINGLE LAMED CALF."

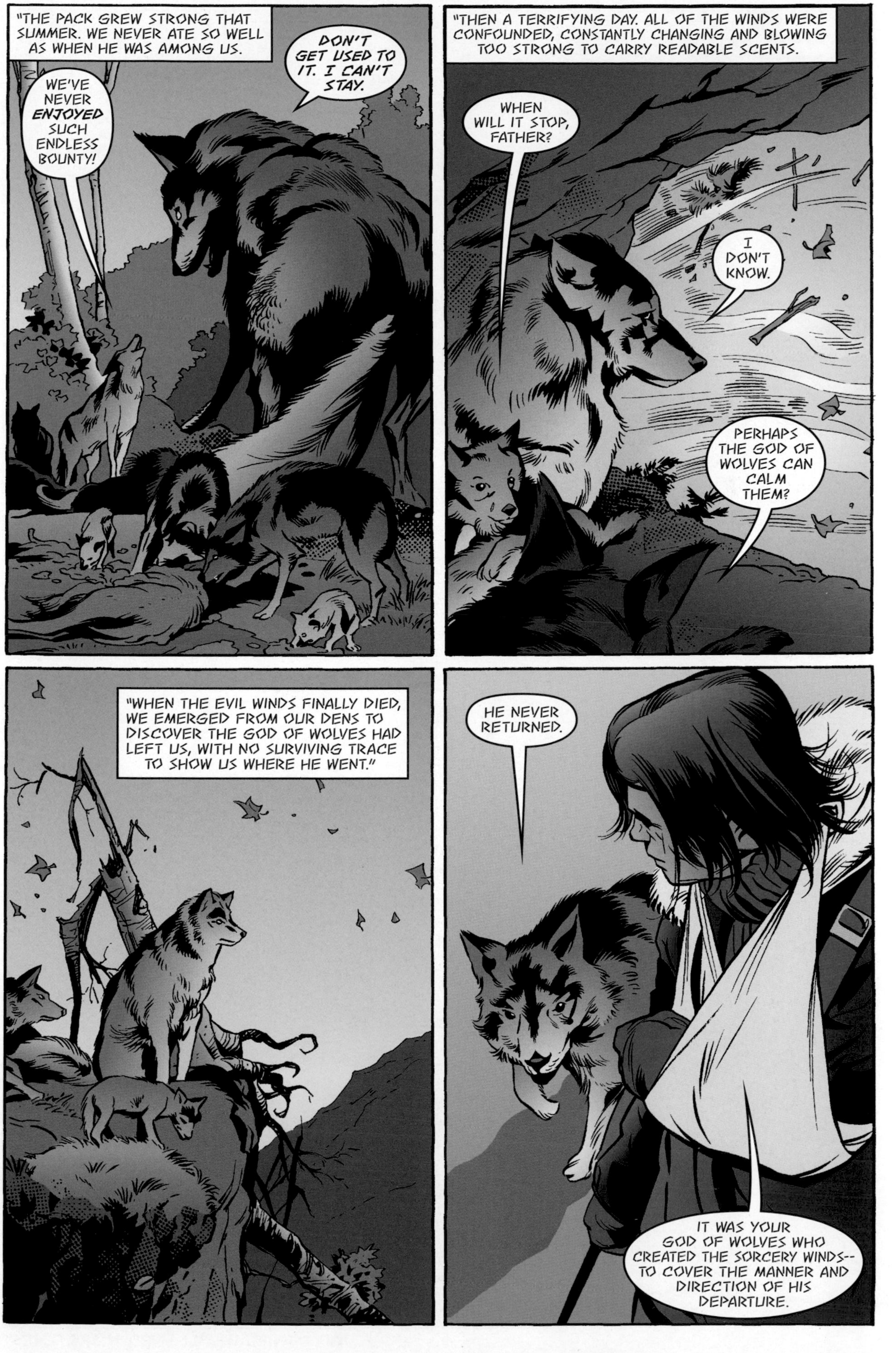

"THE PACK GREW STRONG THAT SUMMER. WE NEVER ATE SO WELL AS WHEN HE WAS AMONG US.
WE'VE NEVER ENJOYED SUCH ENDLESS BOUNTY!
DON'T GET USED TO IT. I CAN'T STAY.
"THEN A TERRIFYING DAY. ALL OF THE WINDS WERE CONFOUNDED, CONSTANTLY CHANGING AND BLOWING TOO STRONG TO CARRY READABLE SCENTS.
WHEN WILL IT STOP, FATHER?
I DON'T KNOW.
PERHAPS THE GOD OF WOLVES CAN CALM THEM?
"WHEN THE EVIL WINDS FINALLY DIED, WE EMERGED FROM OUR DENS TO DISCOVER THE GOD OF WOLVES HAD LEFT US, WITH NO SURVIVING TRACE TO SHOW US WHERE HE WENT."
HE NEVER RETURNED.
IT WAS YOUR GOD OF WOLVES WHO CREATED THE SORCERY WINDS-- TO COVER THE MANNER AND DIRECTION OF HIS DEPARTURE.

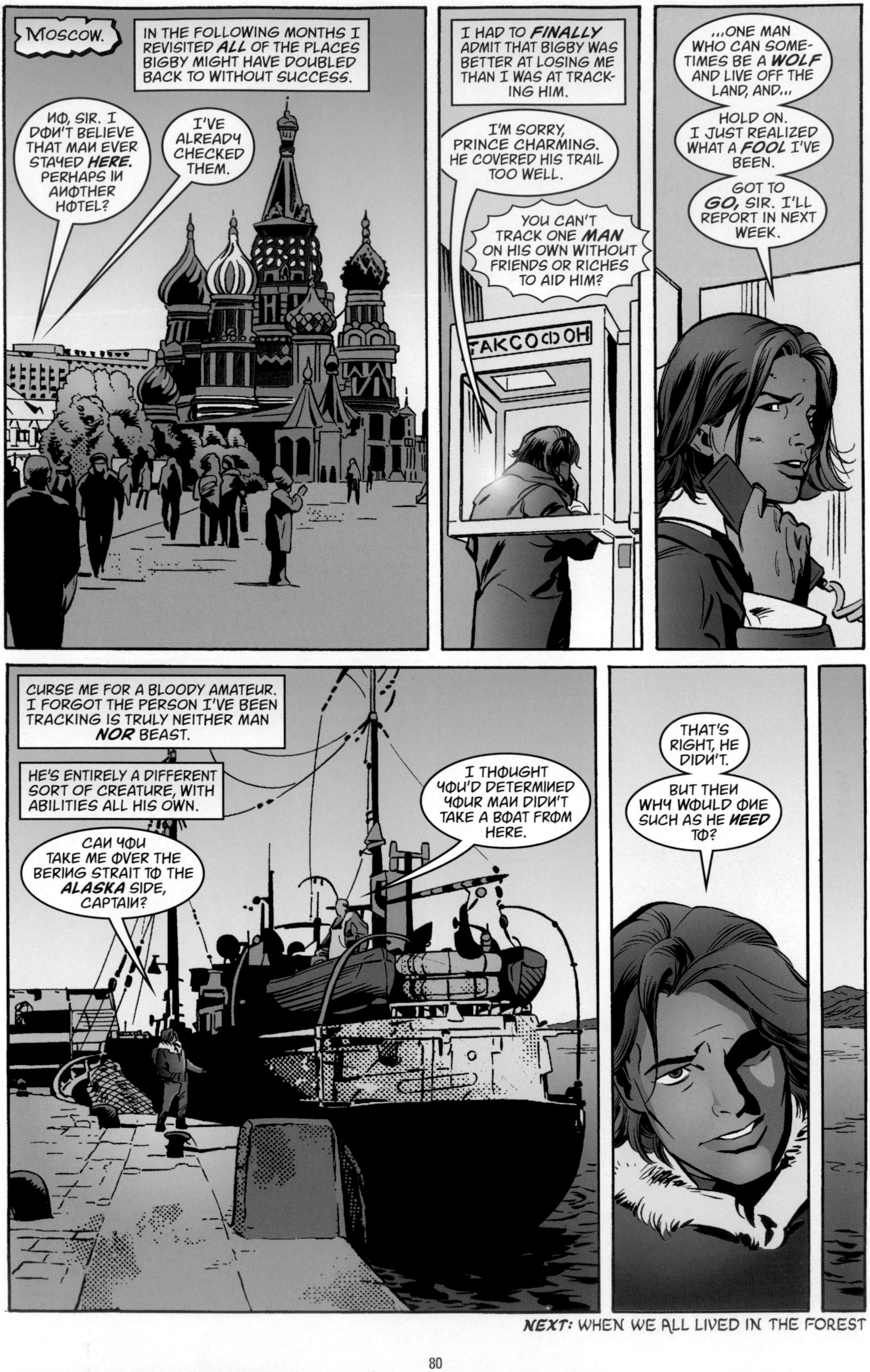
MOSCOW.
IN THE FOLLOWING MONTHS I REVISITED ALL OF THE PLACES BIGBY MIGHT HAVE DOUBLED BACK TO WITHOUT SUCCESS.
NO, SIR. I DON'T BELIEVE THAT MAN EVER STAYED HERE. PERHAPS IN ANOTHER HOTEL?
I'VE ALREADY CHECKED THEM.
I HAD TO FINALLY ADMIT THAT BIGBY WAS BETTER AT LOSING ME THAN I WAS AT TRACKING HIM.
I'M SORRY, PRINCE CHARMING. HE COVERED HIS TRAIL TOO WELL.
YOU CAN'T TRACK ONE MAN ON HIS OWN WITHOUT FRIENDS OR RICHES TO AID HIM?
ТАКСОФОН
...ONE MAN WHO CAN SOMETIMES BE A WOLF AND LIVE OFF THE LAND, AND...
HOLD ON. I JUST REALIZED WHAT A FOOL I'VE BEEN.
GOT TO GO, SIR. I'LL REPORT IN NEXT WEEK.
CURSE ME FOR A BLOODY AMATEUR. I FORGOT THE PERSON I'VE BEEN TRACKING IS TRULY NEITHER MAN NOR BEAST.
HE'S ENTIRELY A DIFFERENT SORT OF CREATURE, WITH ABILITIES ALL HIS OWN.
CAN YOU TAKE ME OVER THE BERING STRAIT TO THE ALASKA SIDE, CAPTAIN?
I THOUGHT YOU'D DETERMINED YOUR MAN DIDN'T TAKE A BOAT FROM HERE.
THAT'S RIGHT, HE DIDN'T.
BUT THEN WHY WOULD ONE SUCH AS HE NEED TO?
NEXT: WHEN WE ALL LIVED IN THE FOREST

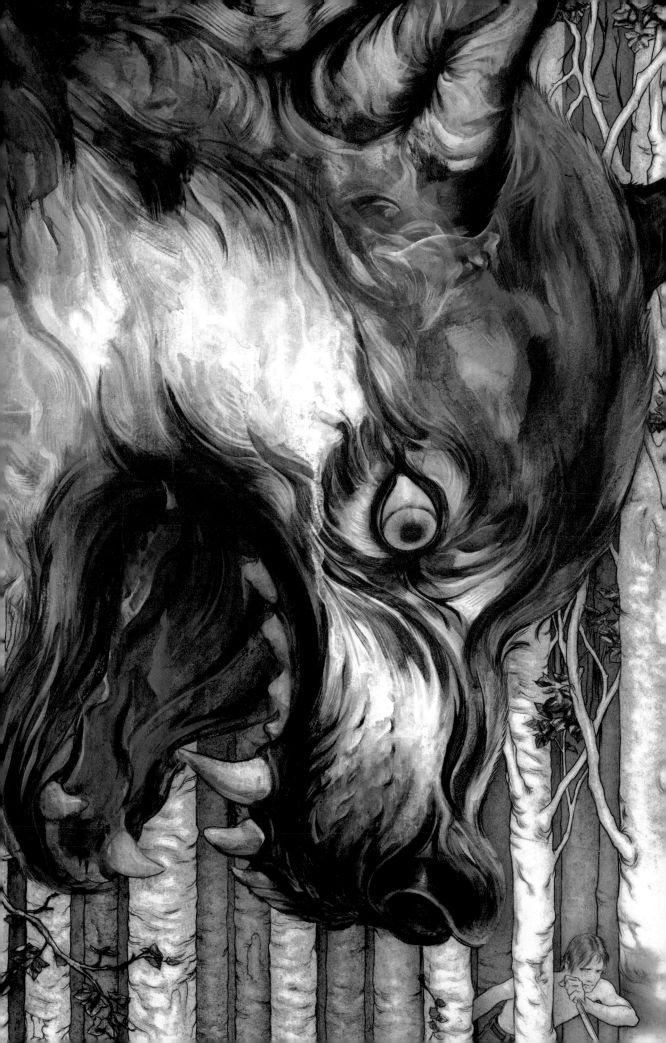

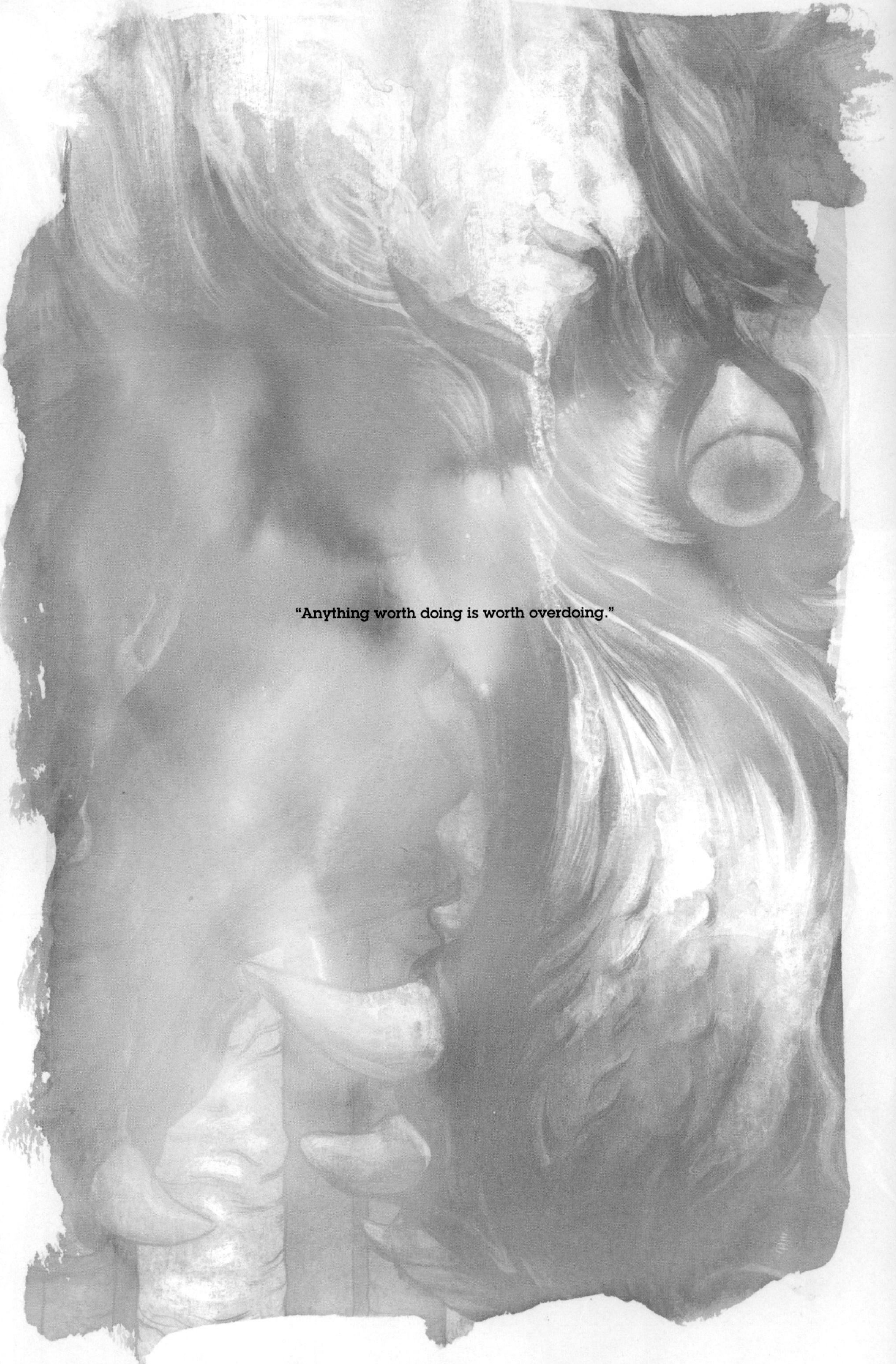

"Anything worth doing is worth overdoing."

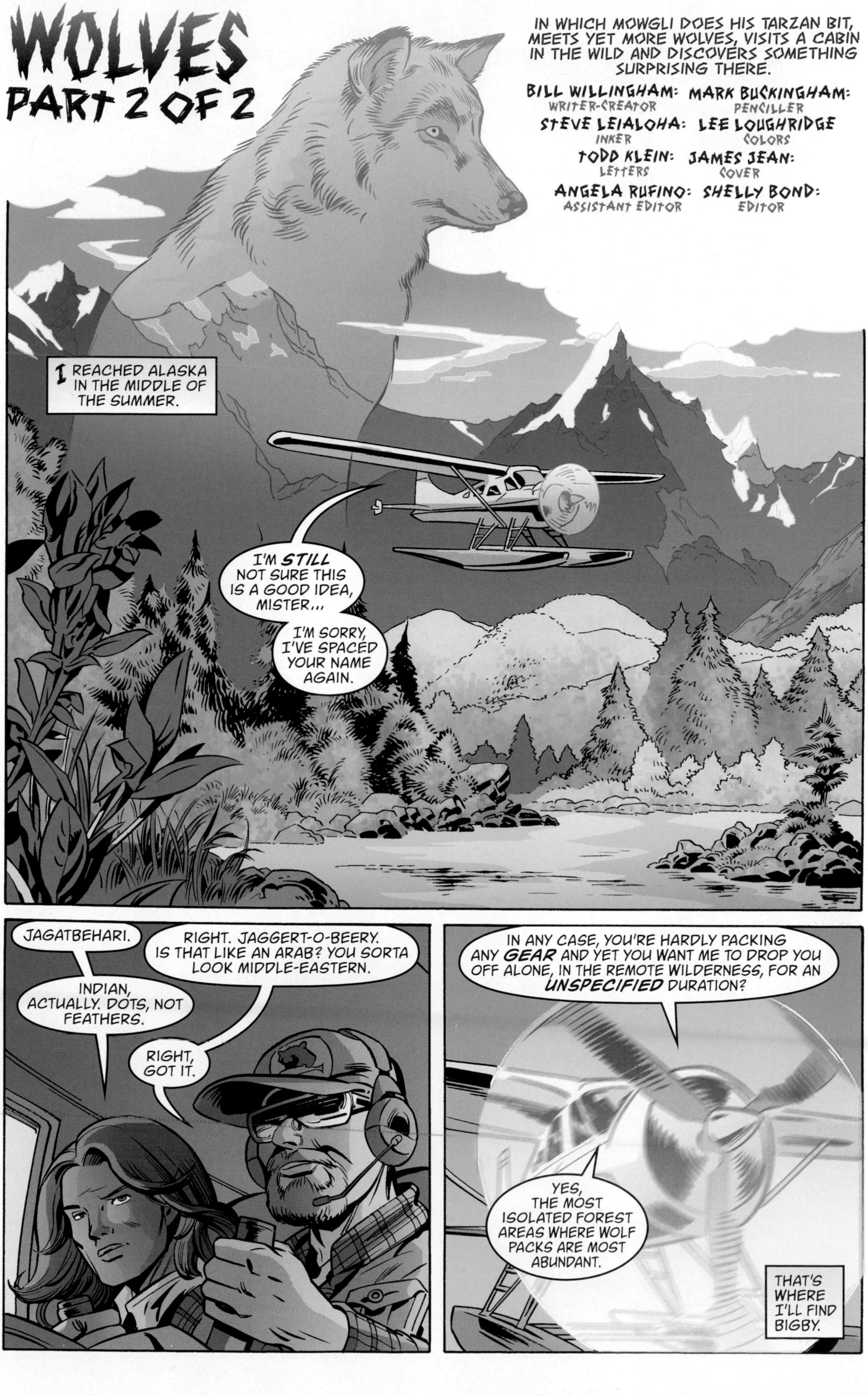

WOLVES
PART 2 OF 2
IN WHICH MOWGLI DOES HIS TARZAN BIT, MEETS YET MORE WOLVES, VISITS A CABIN IN THE WILD AND DISCOVERS SOMETHING SURPRISING THERE.
BILL WILLINGHAM: WRITER-CREATOR
MARK BUCKINGHAM: PENCILLER
STEVE LEIALOHA: INKER
LEE LOUGHRIDGE COLORS
TODD KLEIN: LETTERS
JAMES JEAN: COVER
ANGELA RUFINO: ASSISTANT EDITOR
SHELLY BOND: EDITOR
I REACHED ALASKA IN THE MIDDLE OF THE SUMMER.
I'M STILL NOT SURE THIS IS A GOOD IDEA, MISTER...
I'M SORRY, I'VE SPACED YOUR NAME AGAIN.
JAGATBEHARI.
RIGHT. JAGGERT-O-BEERY. IS THAT LIKE AN ARAB? YOU SORTA LOOK MIDDLE-EASTERN.
INDIAN, ACTUALLY. DOTS, NOT FEATHERS.
RIGHT, GOT IT.
IN ANY CASE, YOU'RE HARDLY PACKING ANY GEAR AND YET YOU WANT ME TO DROP YOU OFF ALONE, IN THE REMOTE WILDERNESS, FOR AN UNSPECIFIED DURATION?
YES, THE MOST ISOLATED FOREST AREAS WHERE WOLF PACKS ARE MOST ABUNDANT.
THAT'S WHERE I'LL FIND BIGBY.

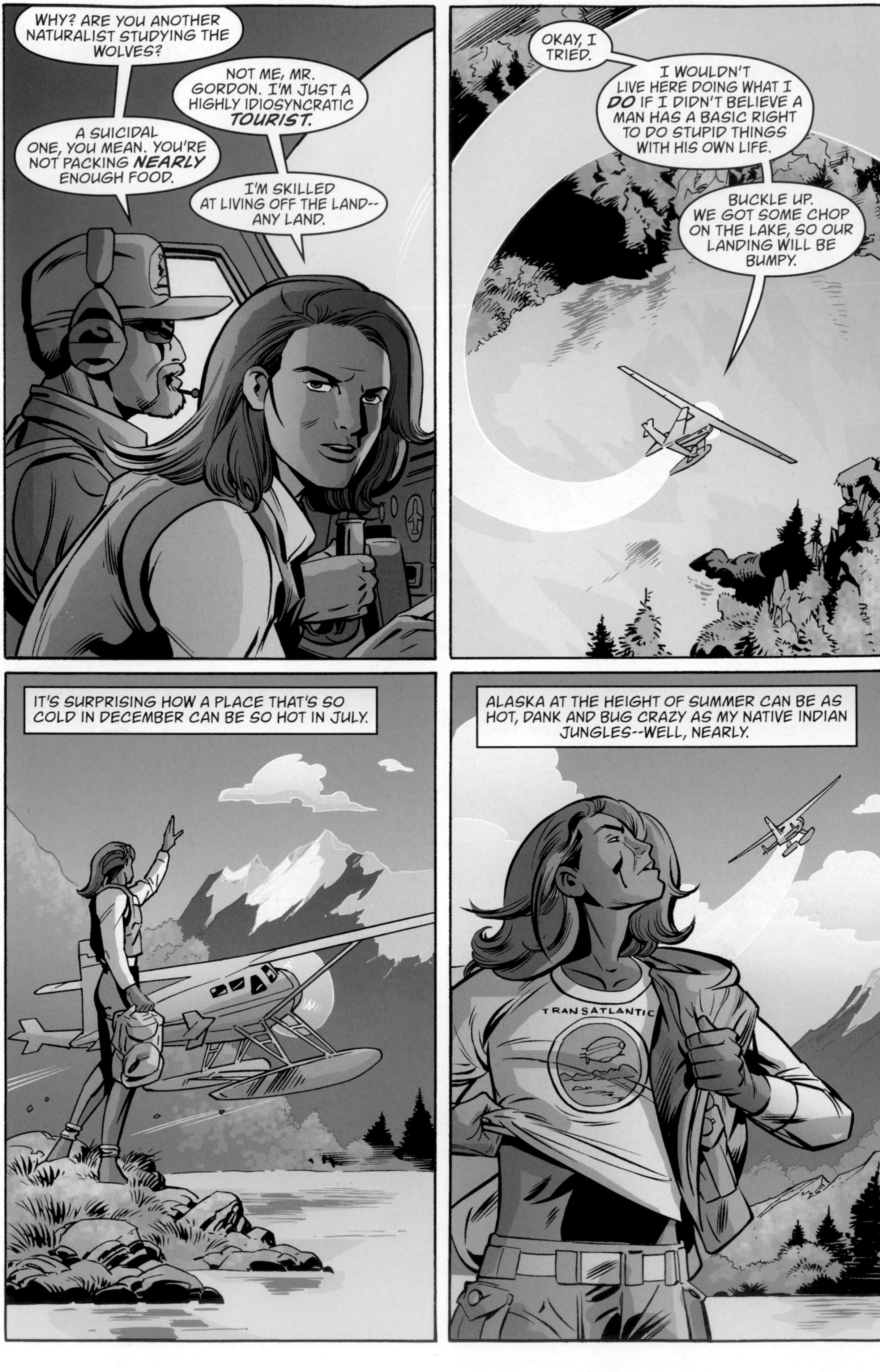
WHY? ARE YOU ANOTHER NATURALIST STUDYING THE WOLVES?
NOT ME, MR. GORDON. I'M JUST A HIGHLY IDIOSYNCRATIC TOURIST.
A SUICIDAL ONE, YOU MEAN. YOU'RE NOT PACKING NEARLY ENOUGH FOOD.
I'M SKILLED AT LIVING OFF THE LAND-- ANY LAND.
OKAY, I TRIED.
I WOULDN'T LIVE HERE DOING WHAT I DO IF I DIDN'T BELIEVE A MAN HAS A BASIC RIGHT TO DO STUPID THINGS WITH HIS OWN LIFE.
BUCKLE UP. WE GOT SOME CHOP ON THE LAKE, SO OUR LANDING WILL BE BUMPY.
IT'S SURPRISING HOW A PLACE THAT'S SO COLD IN DECEMBER CAN BE SO HOT IN JULY.
ALASKA AT THE HEIGHT OF SUMMER CAN BE AS HOT, DANK AND BUG CRAZY AS MY NATIVE INDIAN JUNGLES--WELL, NEARLY.
TRANSATLANTIC

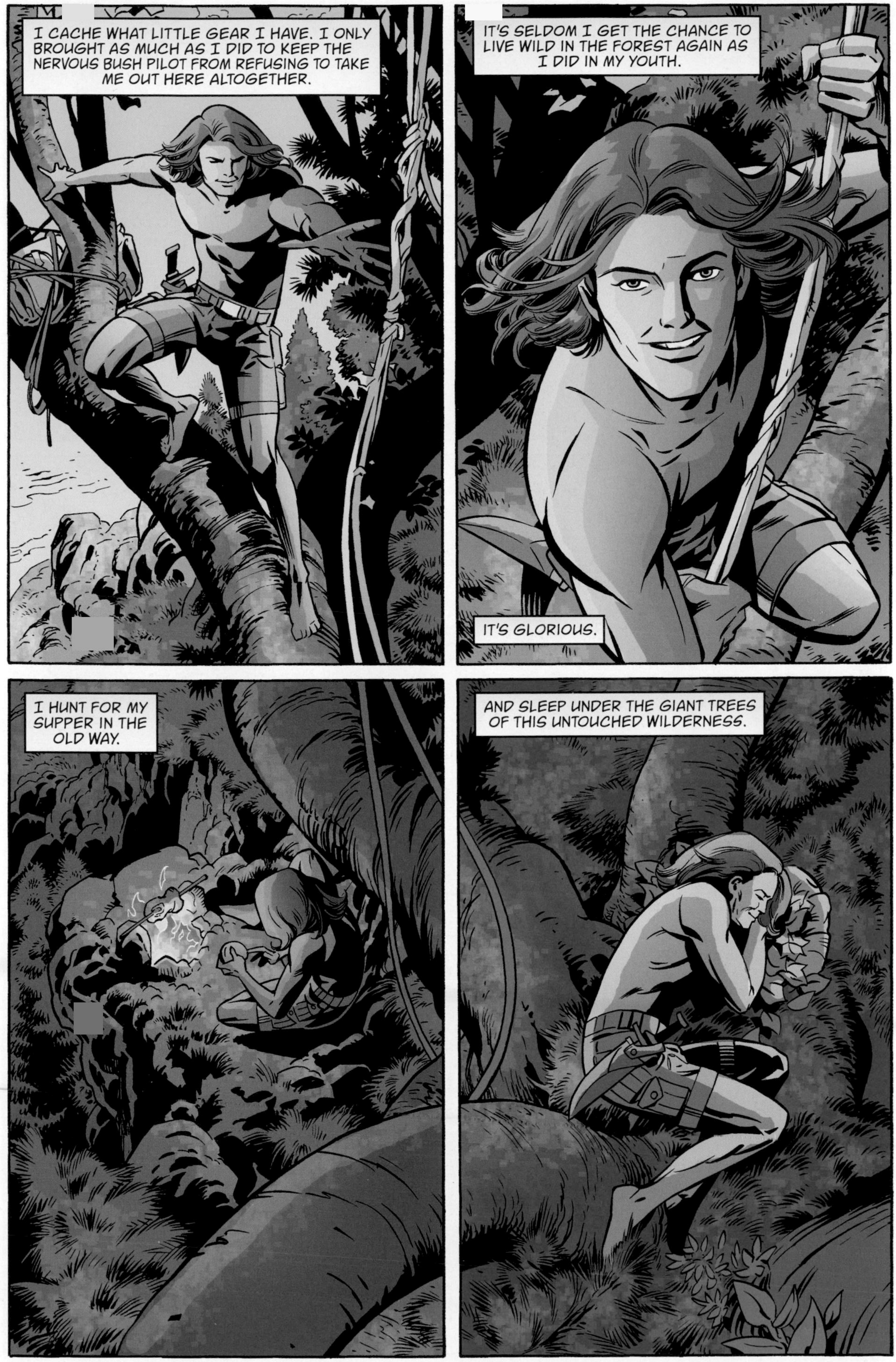
I CACHE WHAT LITTLE GEAR I HAVE. I ONLY BROUGHT AS MUCH AS I DID TO KEEP THE NERVOUS BUSH PILOT FROM REFUSING TO TAKE ME OUT HERE ALTOGETHER.
IT'S SELDOM I GET THE CHANCE TO LIVE WILD IN THE FOREST AGAIN AS I DID IN MY YOUTH.
IT'S GLORIOUS.
I HUNT FOR MY SUPPER IN THE OLD WAY.
AND SLEEP UNDER THE GIANT TREES OF THIS UNTOUCHED WILDERNESS.

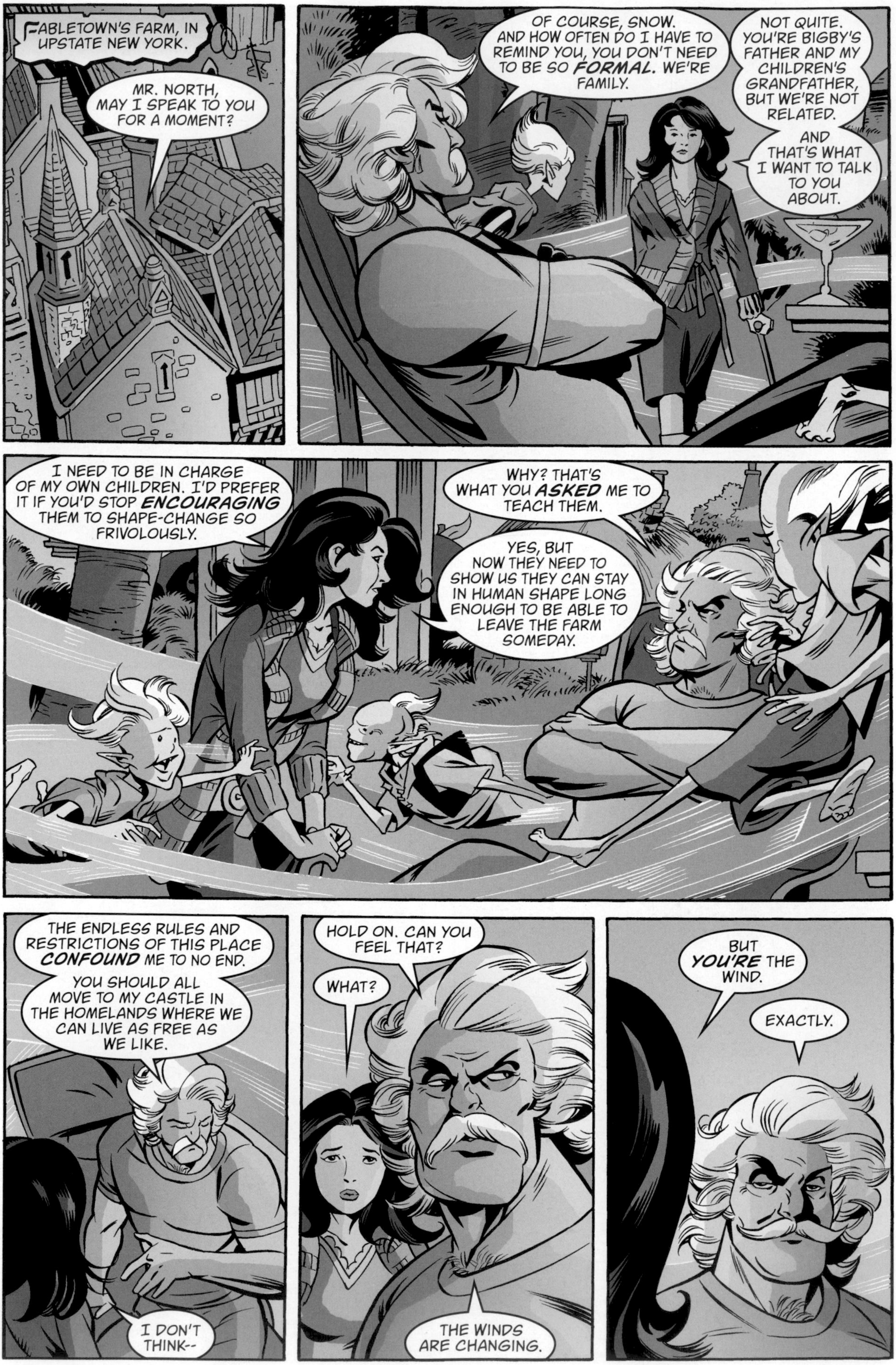
FABLETOWN'S FARM, IN UPSTATE NEW YORK.
MR. NORTH, MAY I SPEAK TO YOU FOR A MOMENT?
OF COURSE, SNOW. AND HOW OFTEN DO I HAVE TO REMIND YOU, YOU DON'T NEED TO BE SO FORMAL. WE'RE FAMILY.
NOT QUITE. YOU'RE BIGBY'S FATHER AND MY CHILDREN'S GRANDFATHER, BUT WE'RE NOT RELATED.
AND THAT'S WHAT I WANT TO TALK TO YOU ABOUT.
I NEED TO BE IN CHARGE OF MY OWN CHILDREN. I'D PREFER IT IF YOU'D STOP ENCOURAGING THEM TO SHAPE-CHANGE SO FRIVOLOUSLY.
WHY? THAT'S WHAT YOU ASKED ME TO TEACH THEM.
YES, BUT NOW THEY NEED TO SHOW US THEY CAN STAY IN HUMAN SHAPE LONG ENOUGH TO BE ABLE TO LEAVE THE FARM SOMEDAY.
THE ENDLESS RULES AND RESTRICTIONS OF THIS PLACE CONFOUND ME TO NO END.
YOU SHOULD ALL MOVE TO MY CASTLE IN THE HOMELANDS WHERE WE CAN LIVE AS FREE AS WE LIKE.
I DON'T THINK--
HOLD ON. CAN YOU FEEL THAT?
WHAT?
THE WINDS ARE CHANGING.
BUT YOU'RE THE WIND.
EXACTLY.

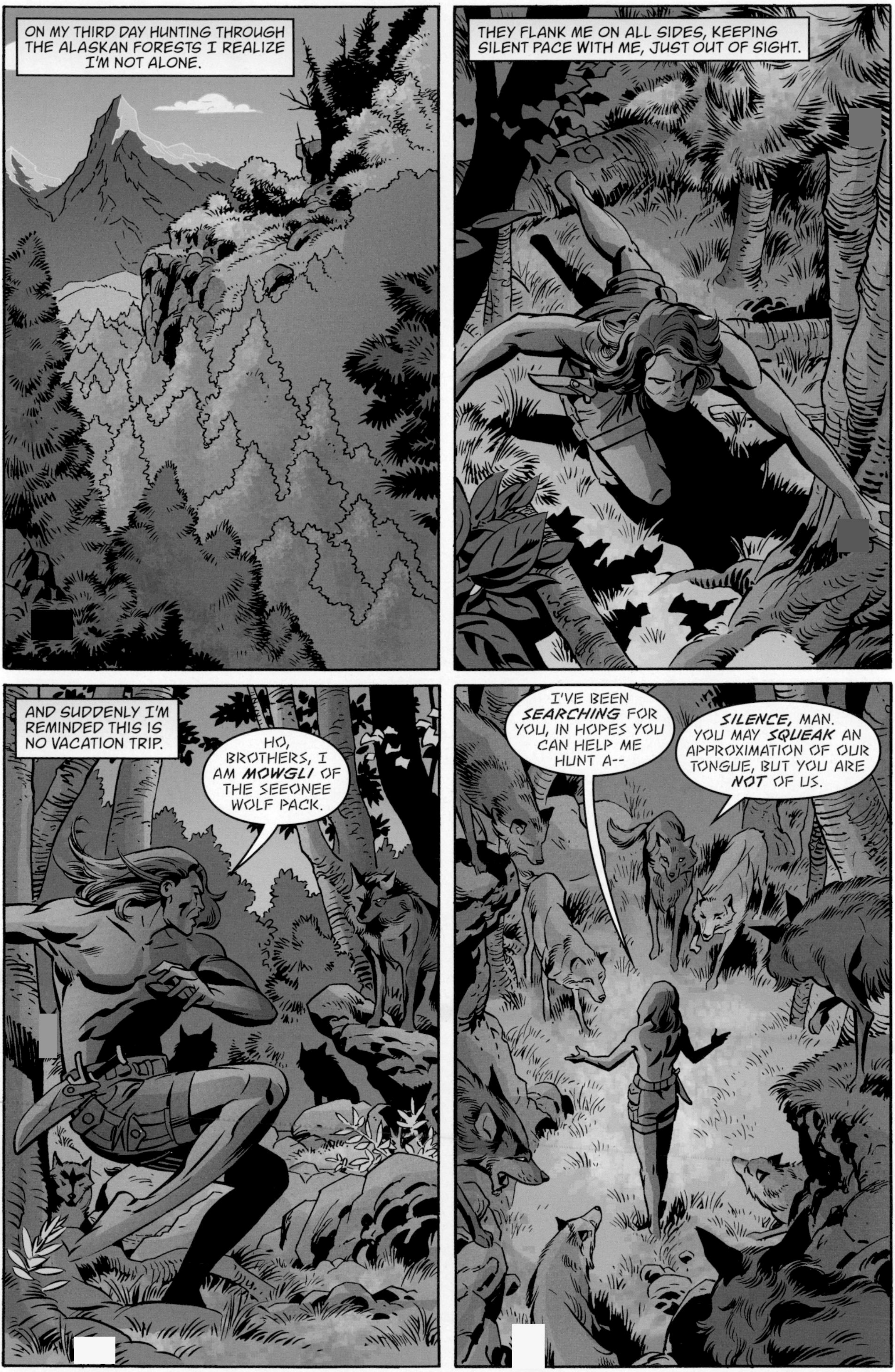
ON MY THIRD DAY HUNTING THROUGH THE ALASKAN FORESTS I REALIZE I'M NOT ALONE.
THEY FLANK ME ON ALL SIDES, KEEPING SILENT PACE WITH ME, JUST OUT OF SIGHT.
AND SUDDENLY I'M REMINDED THIS IS NO VACATION TRIP.
HO, BROTHERS, I AM MOWGLI OF THE SEEONEE WOLF PACK.
I'VE BEEN SEARCHING FOR YOU, IN HOPES YOU CAN HELP ME HUNT A--
SILENCE, MAN. YOU MAY SQUEAK AN APPROXIMATION OF OUR TONGUE, BUT YOU ARE NOT OF US.

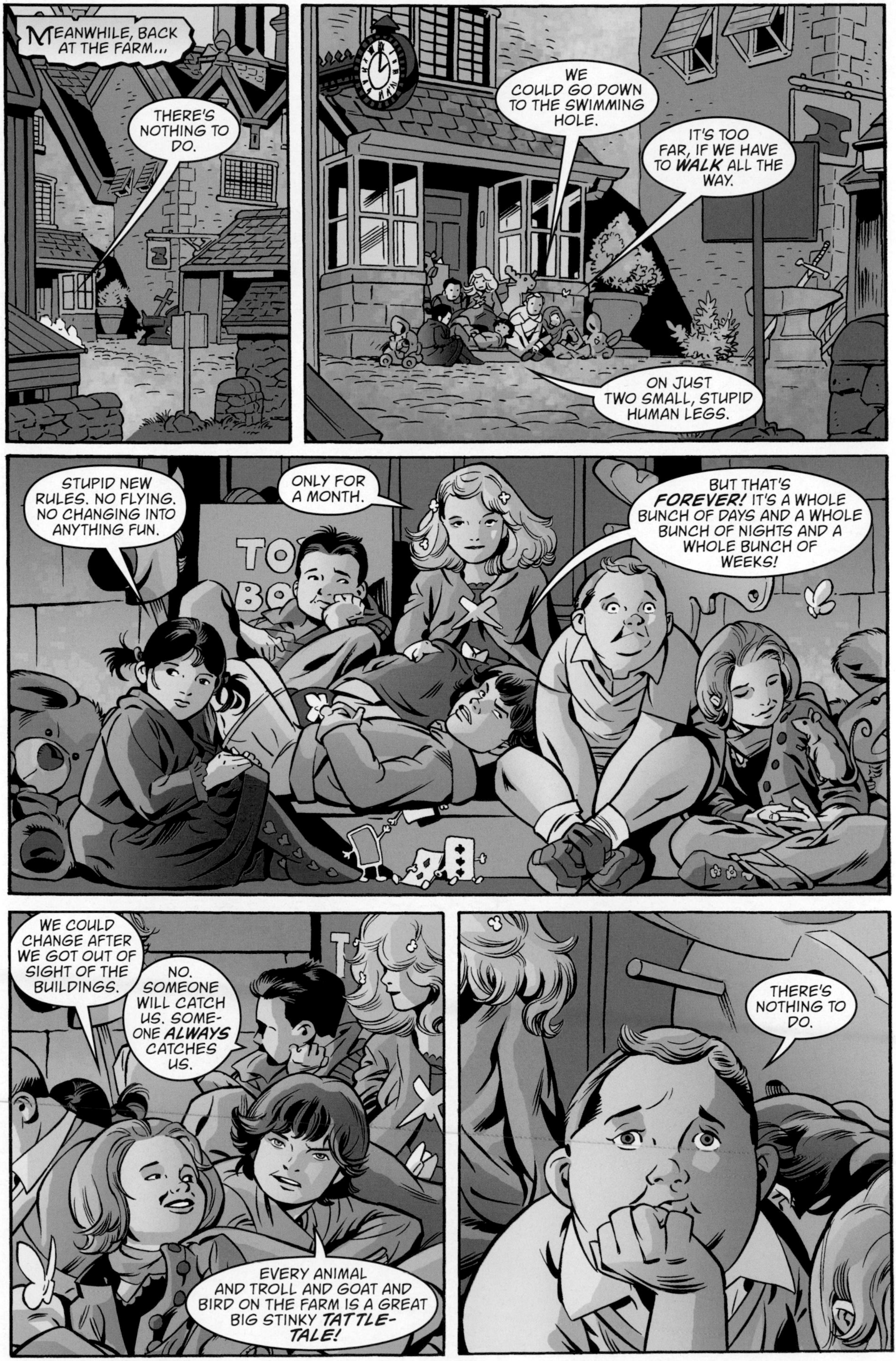
MEANWHILE, BACK AT THE FARM...
THERE'S NOTHING TO DO.
WE COULD GO DOWN TO THE SWIMMING HOLE.
IT'S TOO FAR, IF WE HAVE TO WALK ALL THE WAY.
ON JUST TWO SMALL, STUPID HUMAN LEGS.
STUPID NEW RULES. NO FLYING. NO CHANGING INTO ANYTHING FUN.
ONLY FOR A MONTH.
BUT THAT'S FOREVER! IT'S A WHOLE BUNCH OF DAYS AND A WHOLE BUNCH OF NIGHTS AND A WHOLE BUNCH OF WEEKS!
WE COULD CHANGE AFTER WE GOT OUT OF SIGHT OF THE BUILDINGS.
NO. SOMEONE WILL CATCH US. SOME-ONE ALWAYS CATCHES US.
EVERY ANIMAL AND TROLL AND GOAT AND BIRD ON THE FARM IS A GREAT BIG STINKY TATTLE-TALE!
THERE'S NOTHING TO DO.

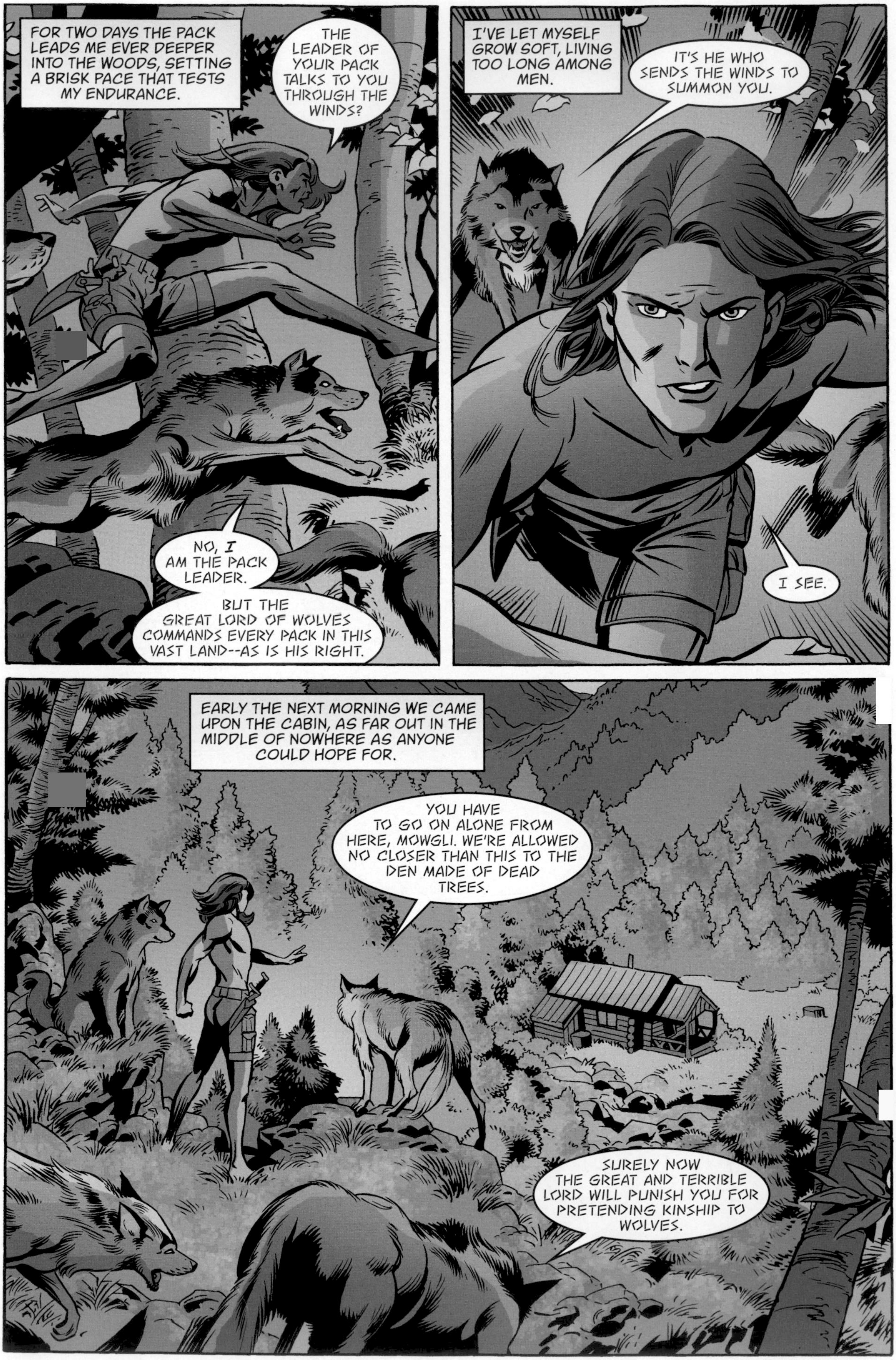
FOR TWO DAYS THE PACK LEADS ME EVER DEEPER INTO THE WOODS, SETTING A BRISK PACE THAT TESTS MY ENDURANCE.
THE LEADER OF YOUR PACK TALKS TO YOU THROUGH THE WINDS?
NO, *I* AM THE PACK LEADER.
BUT THE GREAT LORD OF WOLVES COMMANDS EVERY PACK IN THIS VAST LAND--AS IS HIS RIGHT.
I'VE LET MYSELF GROW SOFT, LIVING TOO LONG AMONG MEN.
IT'S HE WHO SENDS THE WINDS TO SUMMON YOU.
I SEE.
EARLY THE NEXT MORNING WE CAME UPON THE CABIN, AS FAR OUT IN THE MIDDLE OF NOWHERE AS ANYONE COULD HOPE FOR.
YOU HAVE TO GO ON ALONE FROM HERE, MOWGLI. WE'RE ALLOWED NO CLOSER THAN THIS TO THE DEN MADE OF DEAD TREES.
SURELY NOW THE GREAT AND TERRIBLE LORD WILL PUNISH YOU FOR PRETENDING KINSHIP TO WOLVES.

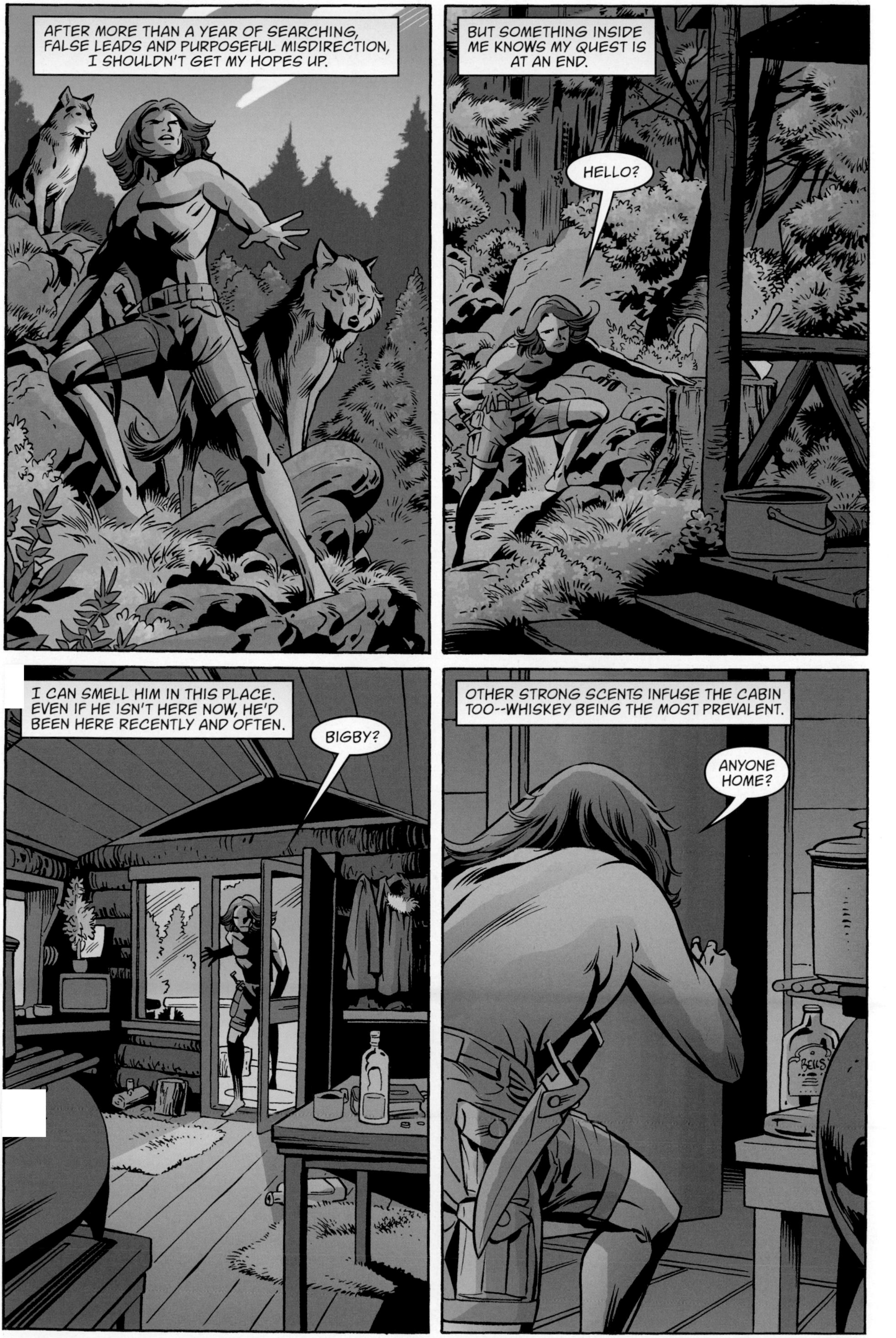
AFTER MORE THAN A YEAR OF SEARCHING, FALSE LEADS AND PURPOSEFUL MISDIRECTION, I SHOULDN'T GET MY HOPES UP.
BUT SOMETHING INSIDE ME KNOWS MY QUEST IS AT AN END.
HELLO?
I CAN SMELL HIM IN THIS PLACE. EVEN IF HE ISN'T HERE NOW, HE'D BEEN HERE RECENTLY AND OFTEN.
BIGBY?
OTHER STRONG SCENTS INFUSE THE CABIN TOO--WHISKEY BEING THE MOST PREVALENT.
ANYONE HOME?

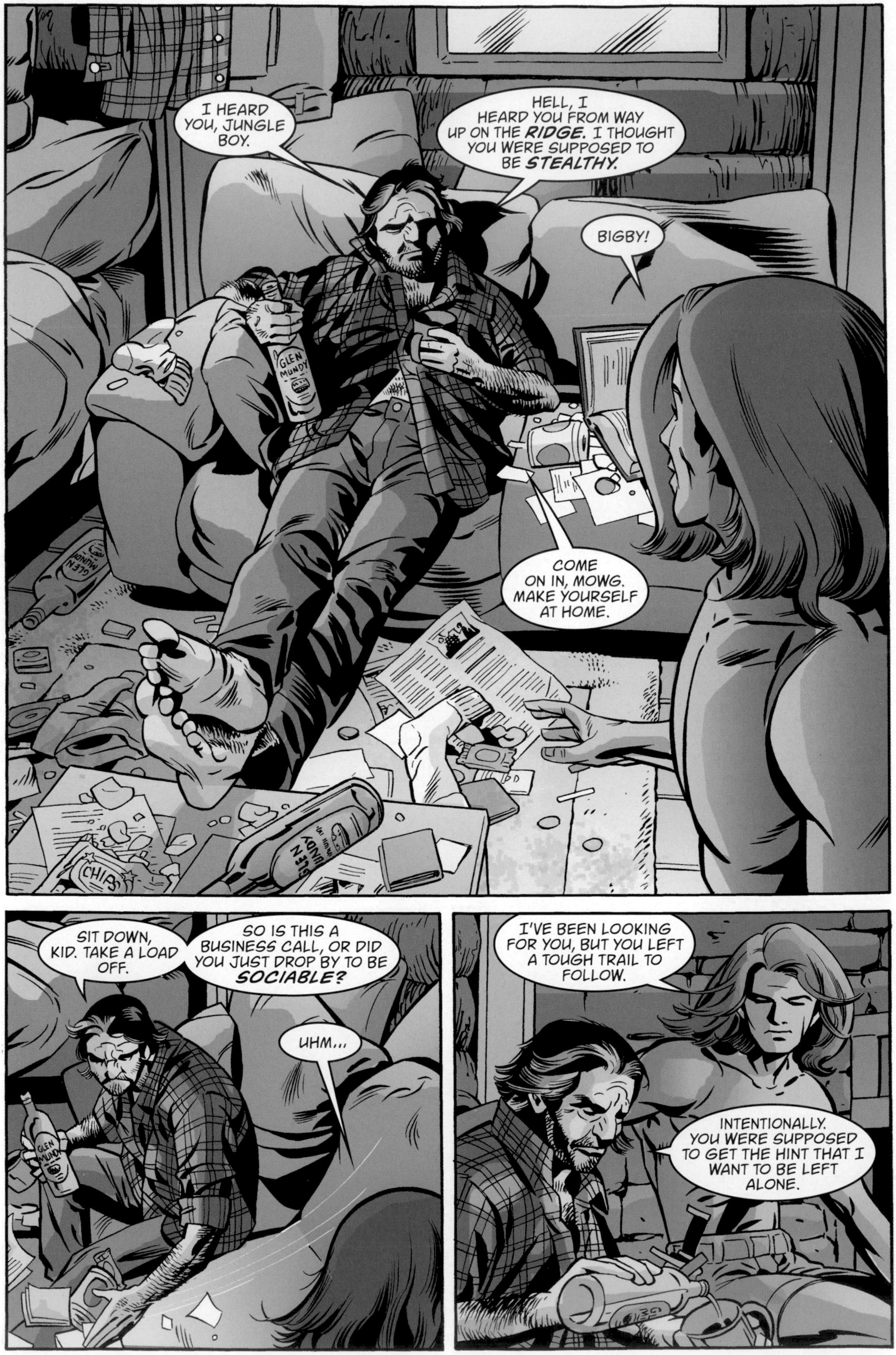
I HEARD YOU, JUNGLE BOY.
HELL, I HEARD YOU FROM WAY UP ON THE RIDGE. I THOUGHT YOU WERE SUPPOSED TO BE STEALTHY.
BIGBY!
COME ON IN, MOWG. MAKE YOURSELF AT HOME.
GLEN MUNDY
CHIPS
SIT DOWN, KID. TAKE A LOAD OFF.
SO IS THIS A BUSINESS CALL, OR DID YOU JUST DROP BY TO BE SOCIABLE?
UHM...
I'VE BEEN LOOKING FOR YOU, BUT YOU LEFT A TOUGH TRAIL TO FOLLOW.
INTENTIONALLY. YOU WERE SUPPOSED TO GET THE HINT THAT I WANT TO BE LEFT ALONE.

WANT A SNORT TO TAKE THE **EDGE** OFF?

OR IF YOU'RE PARTICULAR ABOUT HOW YOU TAKE YOUR BOOZE, YOU CAN USE THE CUP AND I'LL DRINK FROM THE BOTTLE. NO DIFFERENCE TO ME.

NO, I'M FINE.

MORE FOR **ME**, THEN.

ISN'T IT A BIT TOO EARLY IN THE DAY?

NONSENSE. ANYTHING WORTH DOING IS WORTH **OVERDOING**.

NOW, DID YOU DROP BY SIMPLY TO QUESTION MY **DRINKING** HABITS, OR IS THERE SOMETHING ON YOUR MIND THAT'S ACTUALLY ANY OF YOUR DAMNED **BUSINESS**?

FABLETOWN NEEDS YOU BACK, BIGBY.

TOO BAD. I'M ALL DONE WITH THAT.

I HAD THE WOLVES LET YOU COME THROUGH BECAUSE IT'S PART OF YOUR JOB AS ONE OF THE TOURISTS TO CHECK UP ON FABLES LIVING OUTSIDE THE COMMUNITY.

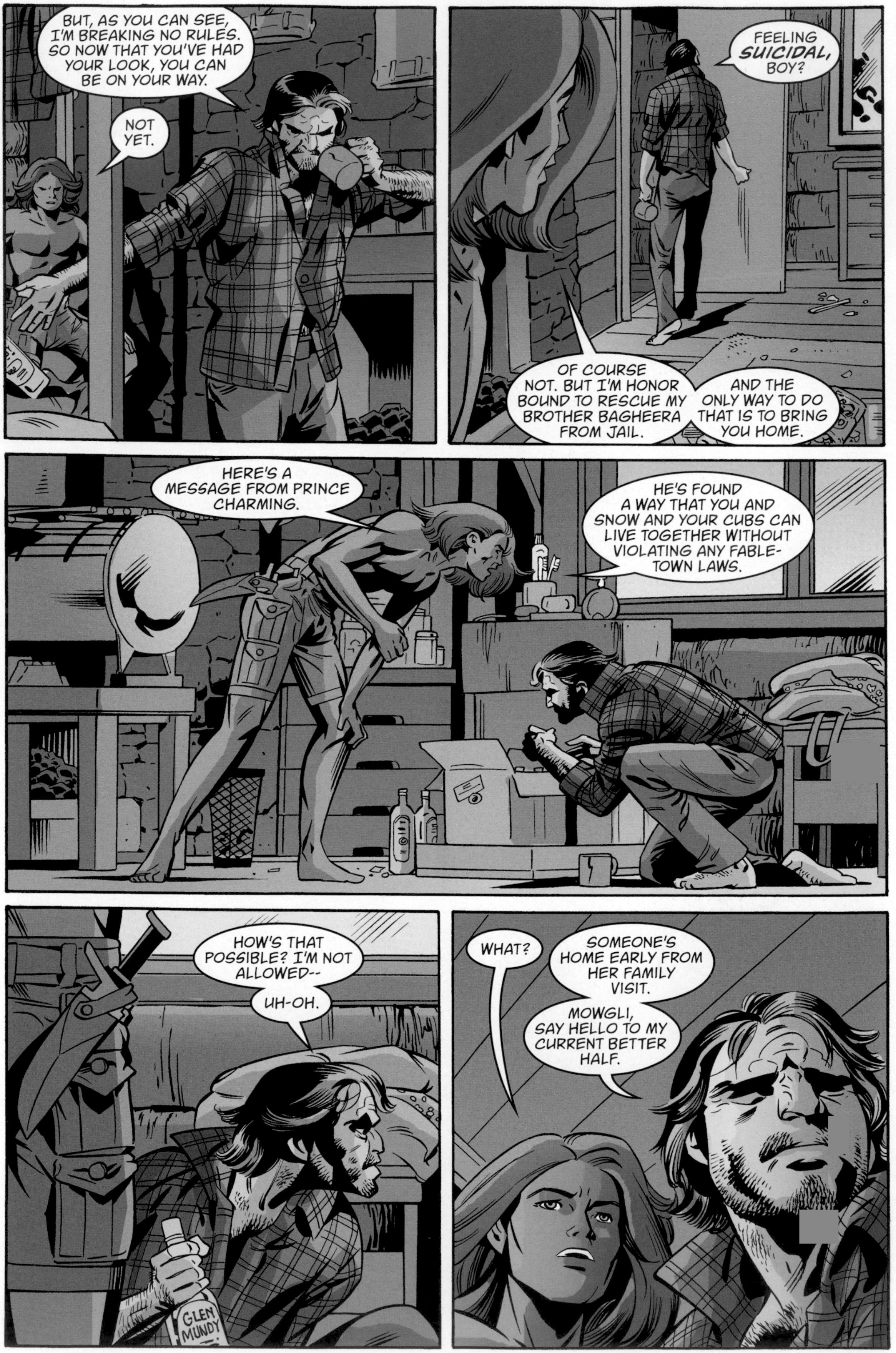
BUT, AS YOU CAN SEE, I'M BREAKING NO RULES. SO NOW THAT YOU'VE HAD YOUR LOOK, YOU CAN BE ON YOUR WAY.
NOT YET.
FEELING SUICIDAL, BOY?
OF COURSE NOT. BUT I'M HONOR BOUND TO RESCUE MY BROTHER BAGHEERA FROM JAIL.
AND THE ONLY WAY TO DO THAT IS TO BRING YOU HOME.
HERE'S A MESSAGE FROM PRINCE CHARMING.
HE'S FOUND A WAY THAT YOU AND SNOW AND YOUR CUBS CAN LIVE TOGETHER WITHOUT VIOLATING ANY FABLE-TOWN LAWS.
HOW'S THAT POSSIBLE? I'M NOT ALLOWED--
UH-OH.
GLEN MUNDY
WHAT?
SOMEONE'S HOME EARLY FROM HER FAMILY VISIT.
MOWGLI, SAY HELLO TO MY CURRENT BETTER HALF.

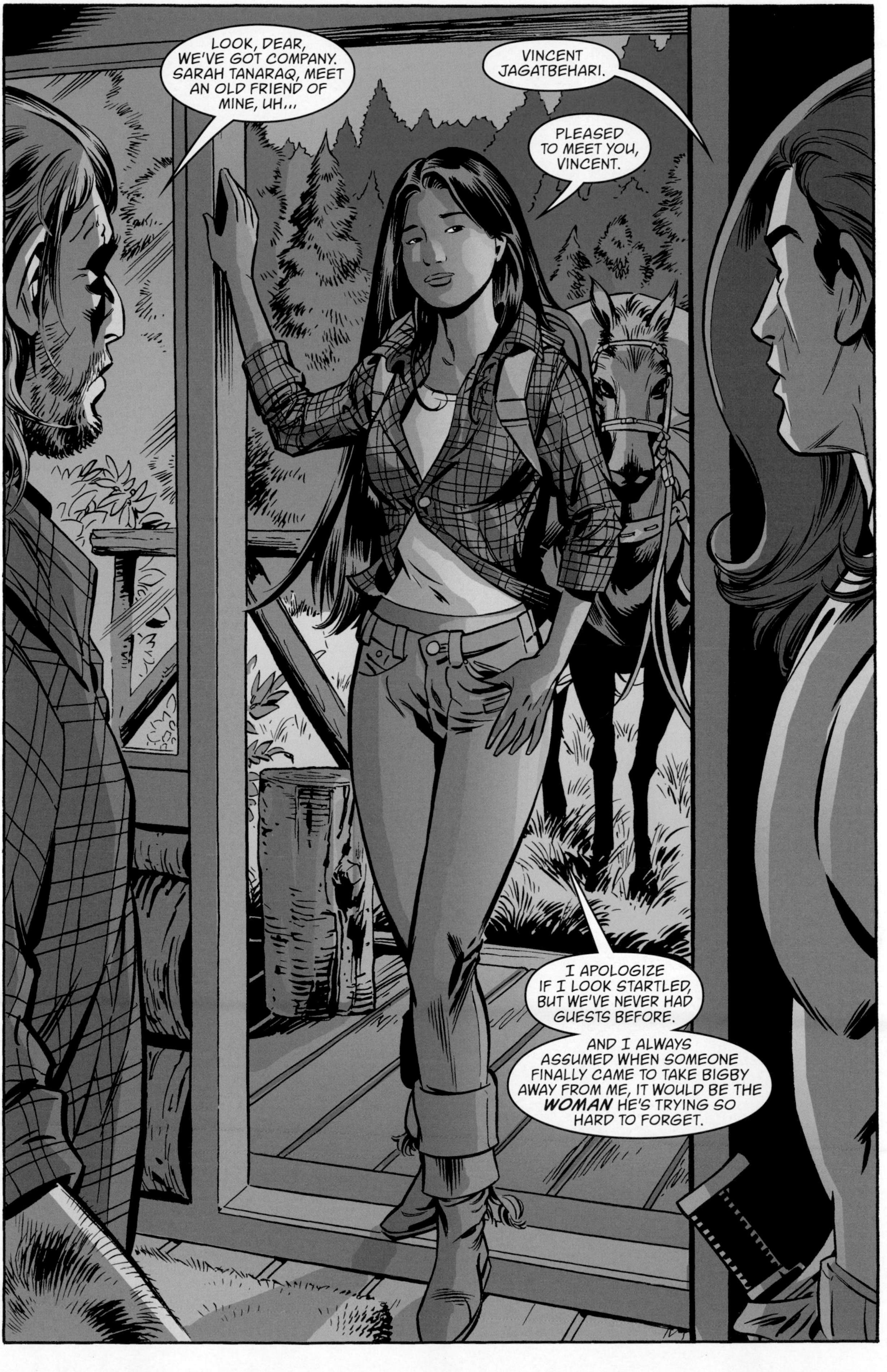
LOOK, DEAR, WE'VE GOT COMPANY. SARAH TANARAQ, MEET AN OLD FRIEND OF MINE, UH...
VINCENT JAGATBEHARI.
PLEASED TO MEET YOU, VINCENT.
I APOLOGIZE IF I LOOK STARTLED, BUT WE'VE NEVER HAD GUESTS BEFORE.
AND I ALWAYS ASSUMED WHEN SOMEONE FINALLY CAME TO TAKE BIGBY AWAY FROM ME, IT WOULD BE THE WOMAN HE'S TRYING SO HARD TO FORGET.

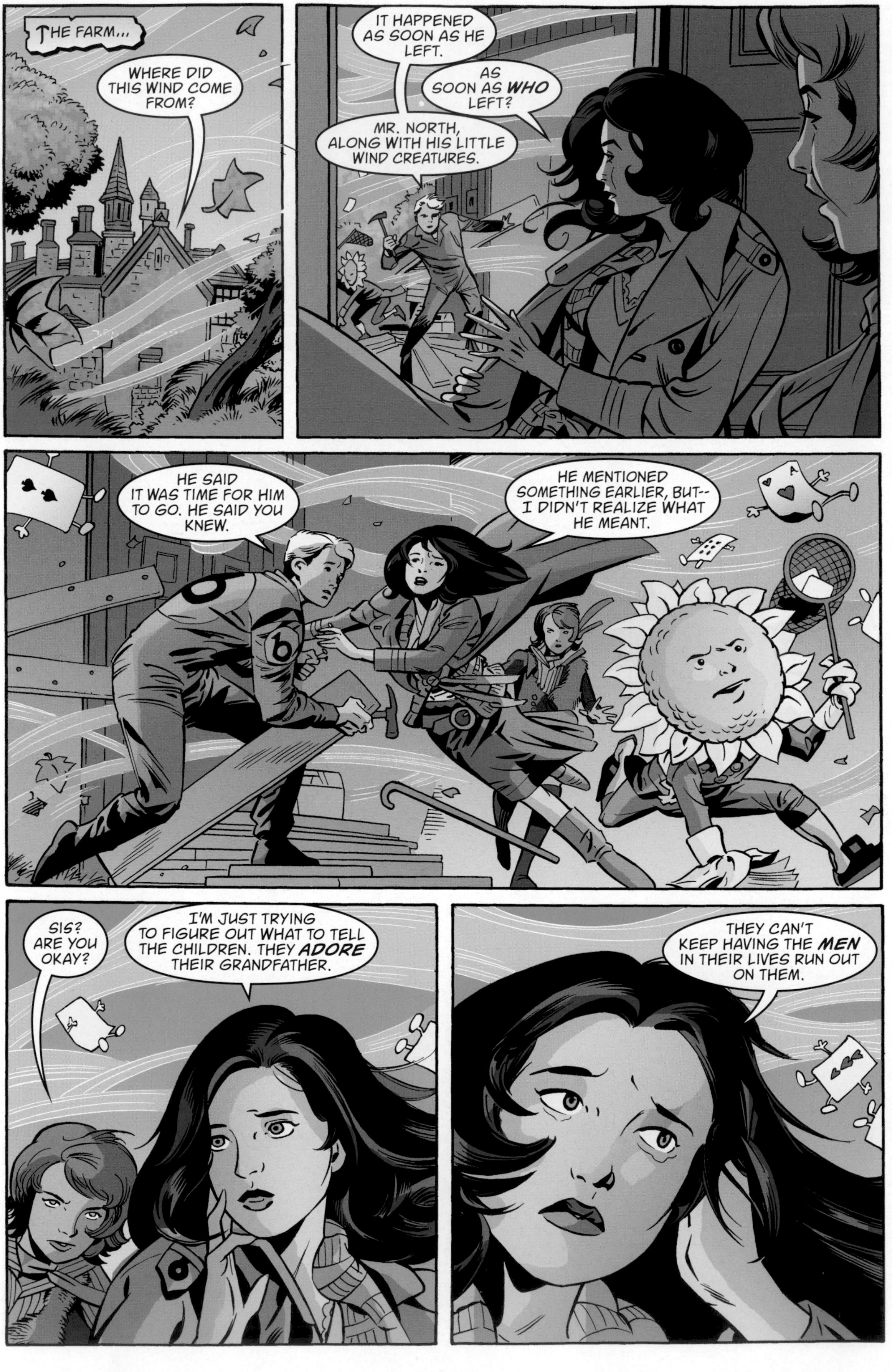
THE FARM...
WHERE DID THIS WIND COME FROM?
IT HAPPENED AS SOON AS HE LEFT.
AS SOON AS WHO LEFT?
MR. NORTH, ALONG WITH HIS LITTLE WIND CREATURES.
HE SAID IT WAS TIME FOR HIM TO GO. HE SAID YOU KNEW.
HE MENTIONED SOMETHING EARLIER, BUT-- I DIDN'T REALIZE WHAT HE MEANT.
SIS? ARE YOU OKAY?
I'M JUST TRYING TO FIGURE OUT WHAT TO TELL THE CHILDREN. THEY ADORE THEIR GRANDFATHER.
THEY CAN'T KEEP HAVING THE MEN IN THEIR LIVES RUN OUT ON THEM.

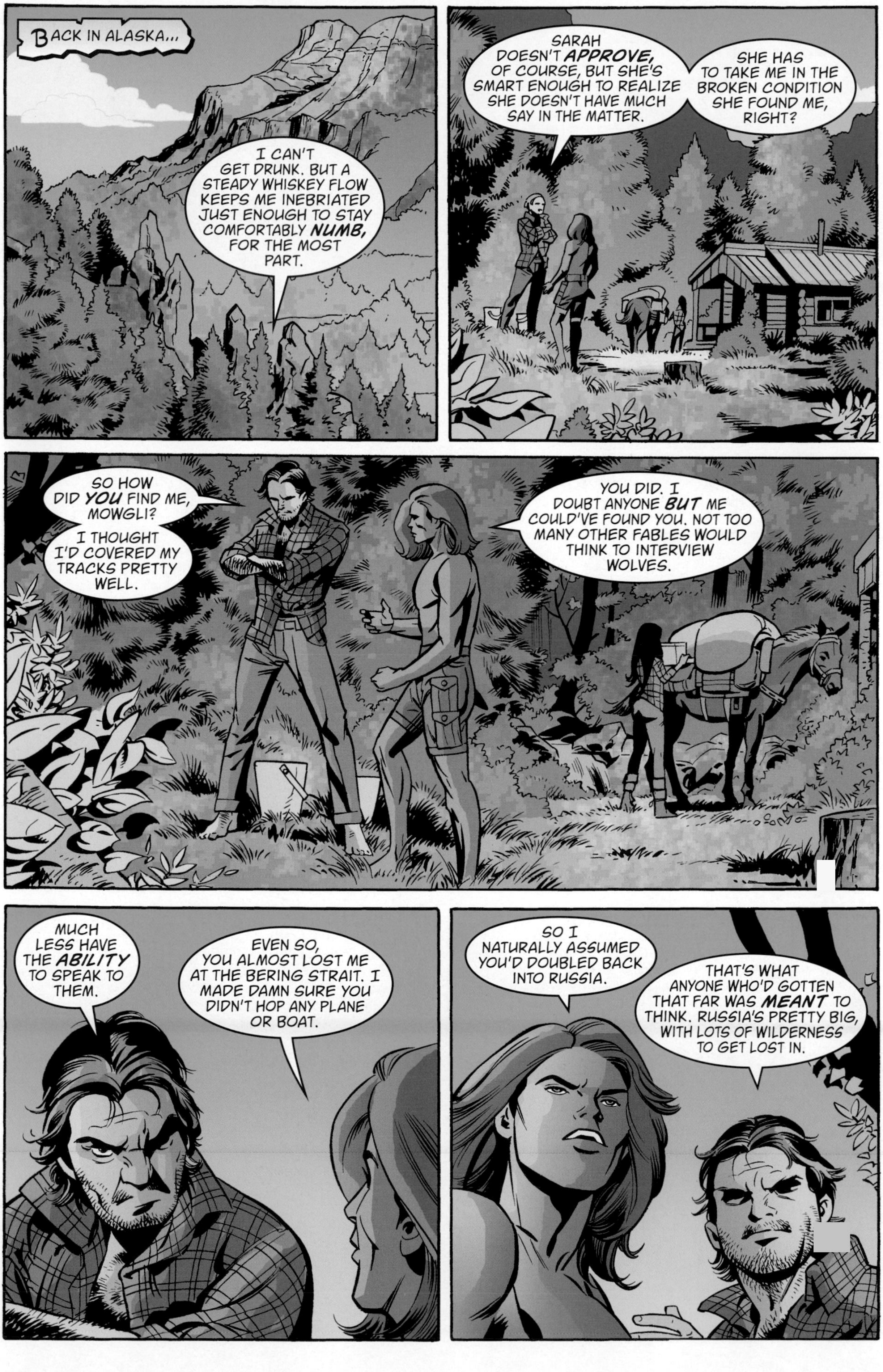
BACK IN ALASKA...
I CAN'T GET DRUNK. BUT A STEADY WHISKEY FLOW KEEPS ME INEBRIATED JUST ENOUGH TO STAY COMFORTABLY NUMB, FOR THE MOST PART.
SARAH DOESN'T APPROVE, OF COURSE, BUT SHE'S SMART ENOUGH TO REALIZE SHE DOESN'T HAVE MUCH SAY IN THE MATTER.
SHE HAS TO TAKE ME IN THE BROKEN CONDITION SHE FOUND ME, RIGHT?
SO HOW DID YOU FIND ME, MOWGLI?
I THOUGHT I'D COVERED MY TRACKS PRETTY WELL.
YOU DID. I DOUBT ANYONE BUT ME COULD'VE FOUND YOU. NOT TOO MANY OTHER FABLES WOULD THINK TO INTERVIEW WOLVES.
MUCH LESS HAVE THE ABILITY TO SPEAK TO THEM.
EVEN SO, YOU ALMOST LOST ME AT THE BERING STRAIT. I MADE DAMN SURE YOU DIDN'T HOP ANY PLANE OR BOAT.
SO I NATURALLY ASSUMED YOU'D DOUBLED BACK INTO RUSSIA.
THAT'S WHAT ANYONE WHO'D GOTTEN THAT FAR WAS MEANT TO THINK. RUSSIA'S PRETTY BIG, WITH LOTS OF WILDERNESS TO GET LOST IN.

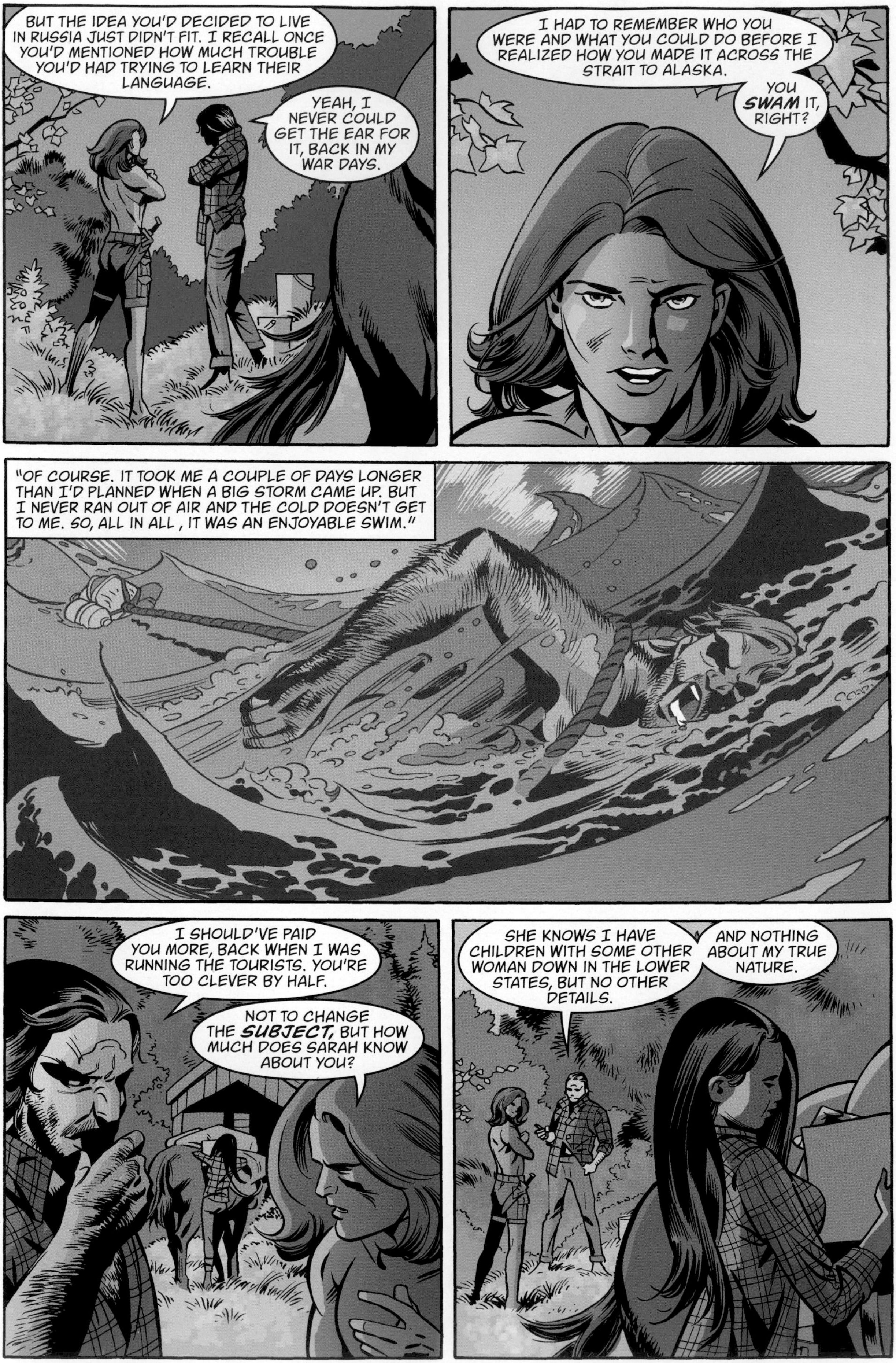

BUT THE IDEA YOU'D DECIDED TO LIVE IN RUSSIA JUST DIDN'T FIT. I RECALL ONCE YOU'D MENTIONED HOW MUCH TROUBLE YOU'D HAD TRYING TO LEARN THEIR LANGUAGE.
YEAH, I NEVER COULD GET THE EAR FOR IT, BACK IN MY WAR DAYS.
I HAD TO REMEMBER WHO YOU WERE AND WHAT YOU COULD DO BEFORE I REALIZED HOW YOU MADE IT ACROSS THE STRAIT TO ALASKA.
YOU **SWAM** IT, RIGHT?
"OF COURSE. IT TOOK ME A COUPLE OF DAYS LONGER THAN I'D PLANNED WHEN A BIG STORM CAME UP. BUT I NEVER RAN OUT OF AIR AND THE COLD DOESN'T GET TO ME. SO, ALL IN ALL, IT WAS AN ENJOYABLE SWIM."
I SHOULD'VE PAID YOU MORE, BACK WHEN I WAS RUNNING THE TOURISTS. YOU'RE TOO CLEVER BY HALF.
NOT TO CHANGE THE **SUBJECT,** BUT HOW MUCH DOES SARAH KNOW ABOUT YOU?
SHE KNOWS I HAVE CHILDREN WITH SOME OTHER WOMAN DOWN IN THE LOWER STATES, BUT NO OTHER DETAILS.
AND NOTHING ABOUT MY TRUE NATURE.

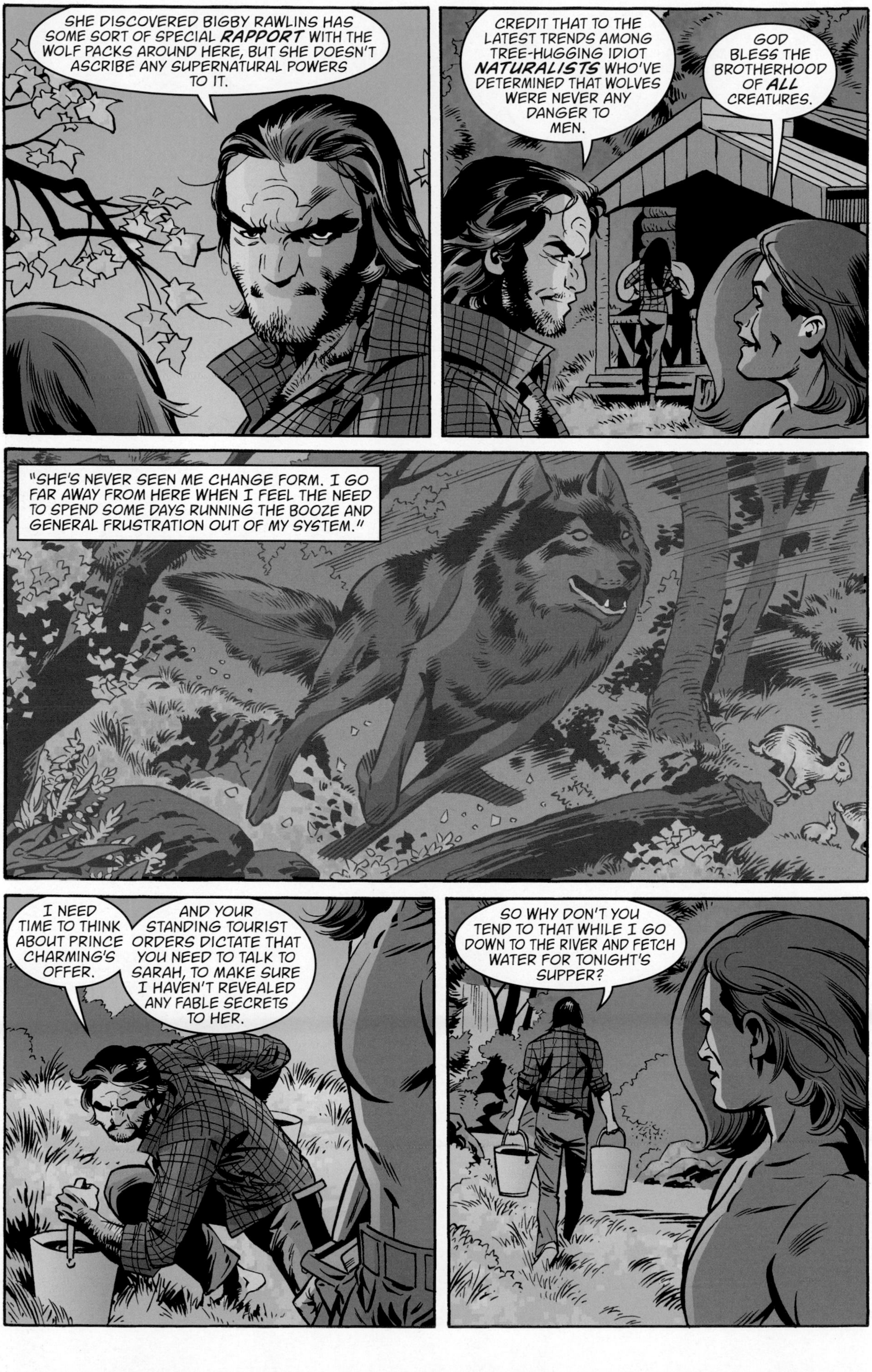

SHE DISCOVERED BIGBY RAWLINS HAS SOME SORT OF SPECIAL RAPPORT WITH THE WOLF PACKS AROUND HERE, BUT SHE DOESN'T ASCRIBE ANY SUPERNATURAL POWERS TO IT.
CREDIT THAT TO THE LATEST TRENDS AMONG TREE-HUGGING IDIOT NATURALISTS WHO'VE DETERMINED THAT WOLVES WERE NEVER ANY DANGER TO MEN.
GOD BLESS THE BROTHERHOOD OF ALL CREATURES.
"SHE'S NEVER SEEN ME CHANGE FORM. I GO FAR AWAY FROM HERE WHEN I FEEL THE NEED TO SPEND SOME DAYS RUNNING THE BOOZE AND GENERAL FRUSTRATION OUT OF MY SYSTEM."
I NEED TIME TO THINK ABOUT PRINCE CHARMING'S OFFER.
AND YOUR STANDING TOURIST ORDERS DICTATE THAT YOU NEED TO TALK TO SARAH, TO MAKE SURE I HAVEN'T REVEALED ANY FABLE SECRETS TO HER.
SO WHY DON'T YOU TEND TO THAT WHILE I GO DOWN TO THE RIVER AND FETCH WATER FOR TONIGHT'S SUPPER?

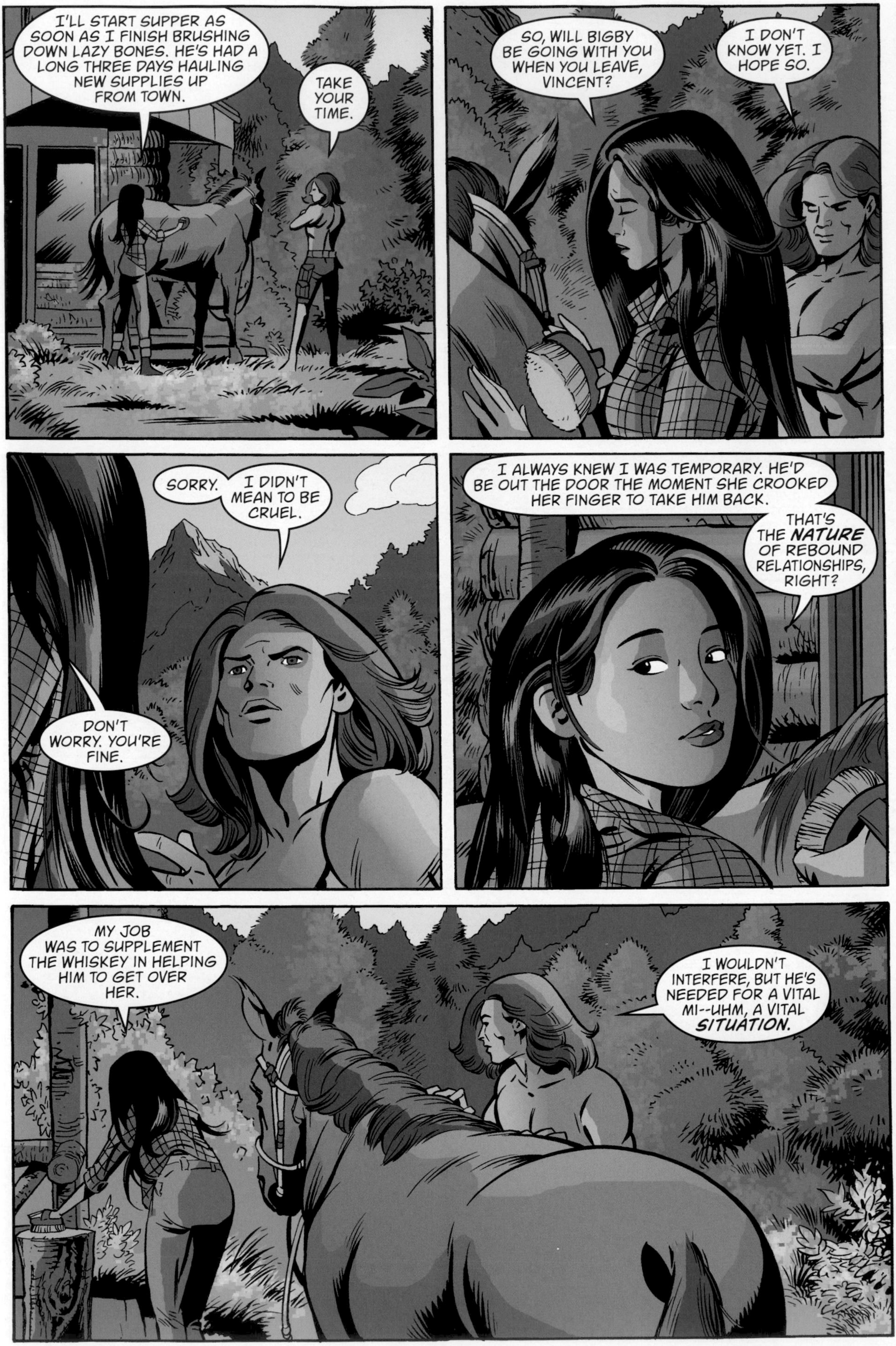

I'LL START SUPPER AS SOON AS I FINISH BRUSHING DOWN LAZY BONES. HE'S HAD A LONG THREE DAYS HAULING NEW SUPPLIES UP FROM TOWN.
TAKE YOUR TIME.
SO, WILL BIGBY BE GOING WITH YOU WHEN YOU LEAVE, VINCENT?
I DON'T KNOW YET. I HOPE SO.
SORRY.
I DIDN'T MEAN TO BE CRUEL.
DON'T WORRY. YOU'RE FINE.
I ALWAYS KNEW I WAS TEMPORARY. HE'D BE OUT THE DOOR THE MOMENT SHE CROOKED HER FINGER TO TAKE HIM BACK.
THAT'S THE NATURE OF REBOUND RELATIONSHIPS, RIGHT?
MY JOB WAS TO SUPPLEMENT THE WHISKEY IN HELPING HIM TO GET OVER HER.
I WOULDN'T INTERFERE, BUT HE'S NEEDED FOR A VITAL MI--UHM, A VITAL SITUATION.

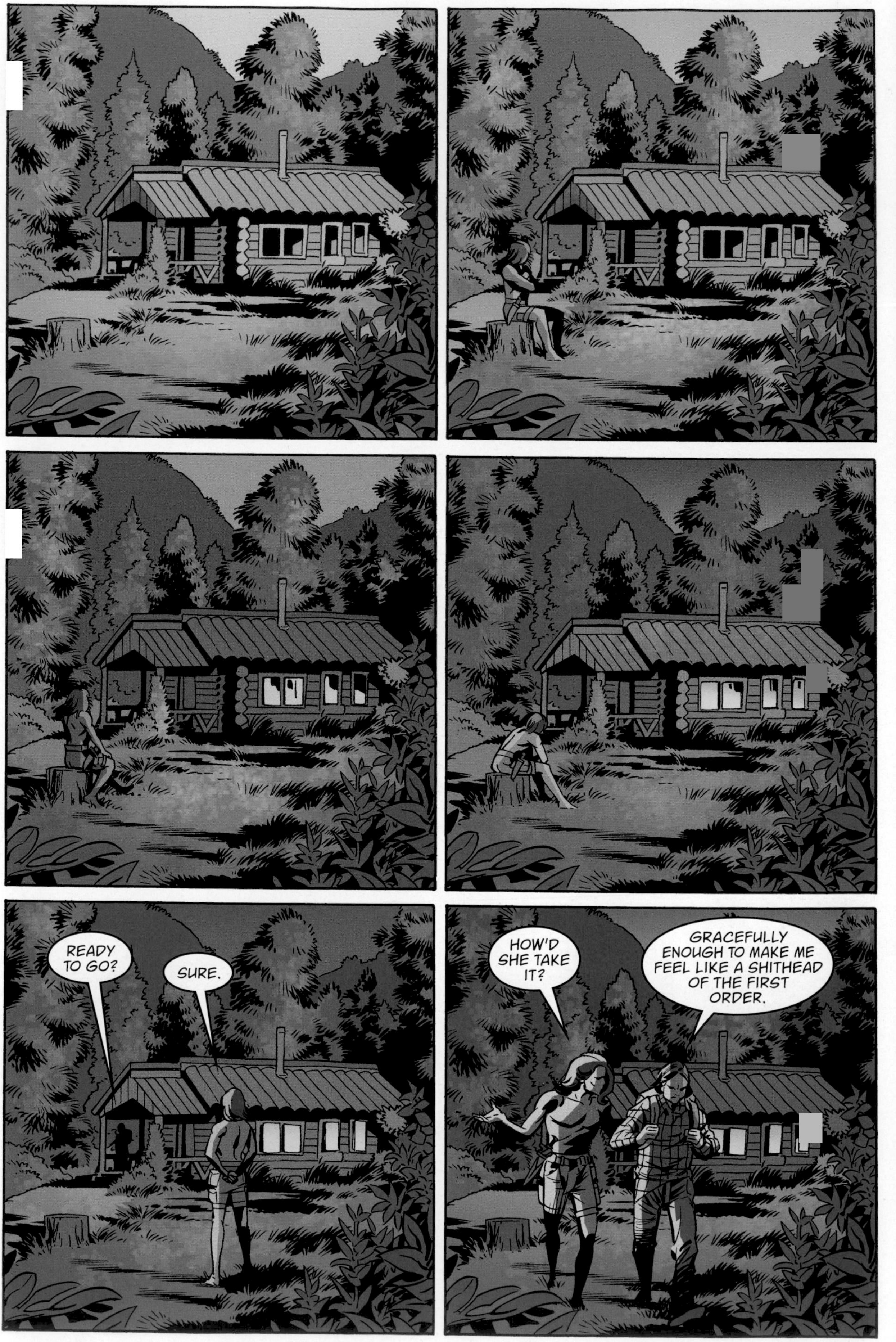
READY TO GO?
SURE.
HOW'D SHE TAKE IT?
GRACEFULLY ENOUGH TO MAKE ME FEEL LIKE A SHITHEAD OF THE FIRST ORDER.

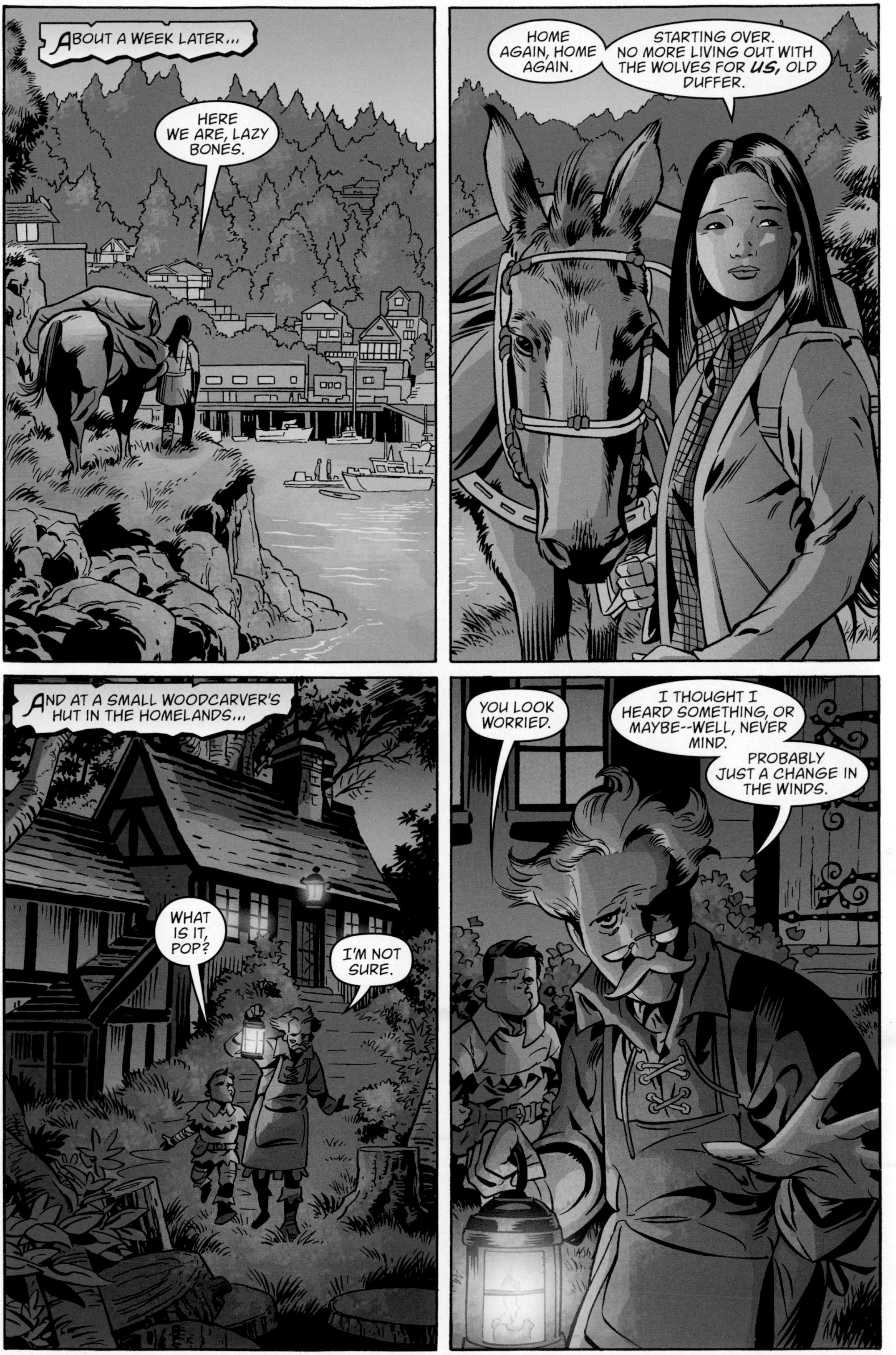
About a week later...
Here we are, lazy bones.
Home again, home again.
Starting over. No more living out with the wolves for us, old duffer.
And at a small woodcarver's hut in the Homelands...
What is it, Pop?
I'm not sure.
You look worried.
I thought I heard something, or maybe--well, never mind.
Probably just a change in the winds.

LATE AT NIGHT AT THE FARM...

HELLO? IS SOMEONE *DOWN* THERE?

THERE BETTER NOT BE ANY CUBS WHO SHOULD BE IN BED RAIDING THE *ICEBOX*.

NO, SNOW, IT'S JUST *ME*.

COLIN! WHY ARE YOU HERE AGAIN? IS THERE MORE TROUBLE COMING?

NO. AT LEAST I DON'T *THINK* SO.

THEN WHY--

IT'S HARD TO BE SURE, SNOW, BUT I THINK I'M HERE TO SAY GOODBYE. I DON'T THINK YOU NEED ME ANYMORE.

WHY? HOW?

IF I HAD TO GUESS, IT'S BECAUSE THINGS GET BETTER NOW--FOR *YOU*, I MEAN.

AND FOR ME, I THINK IT'S FINALLY TIME FOR ME TO MOVE ALONG TO WHATEVER HAPPENS NEXT.

NEXT: BETTER DAYS?

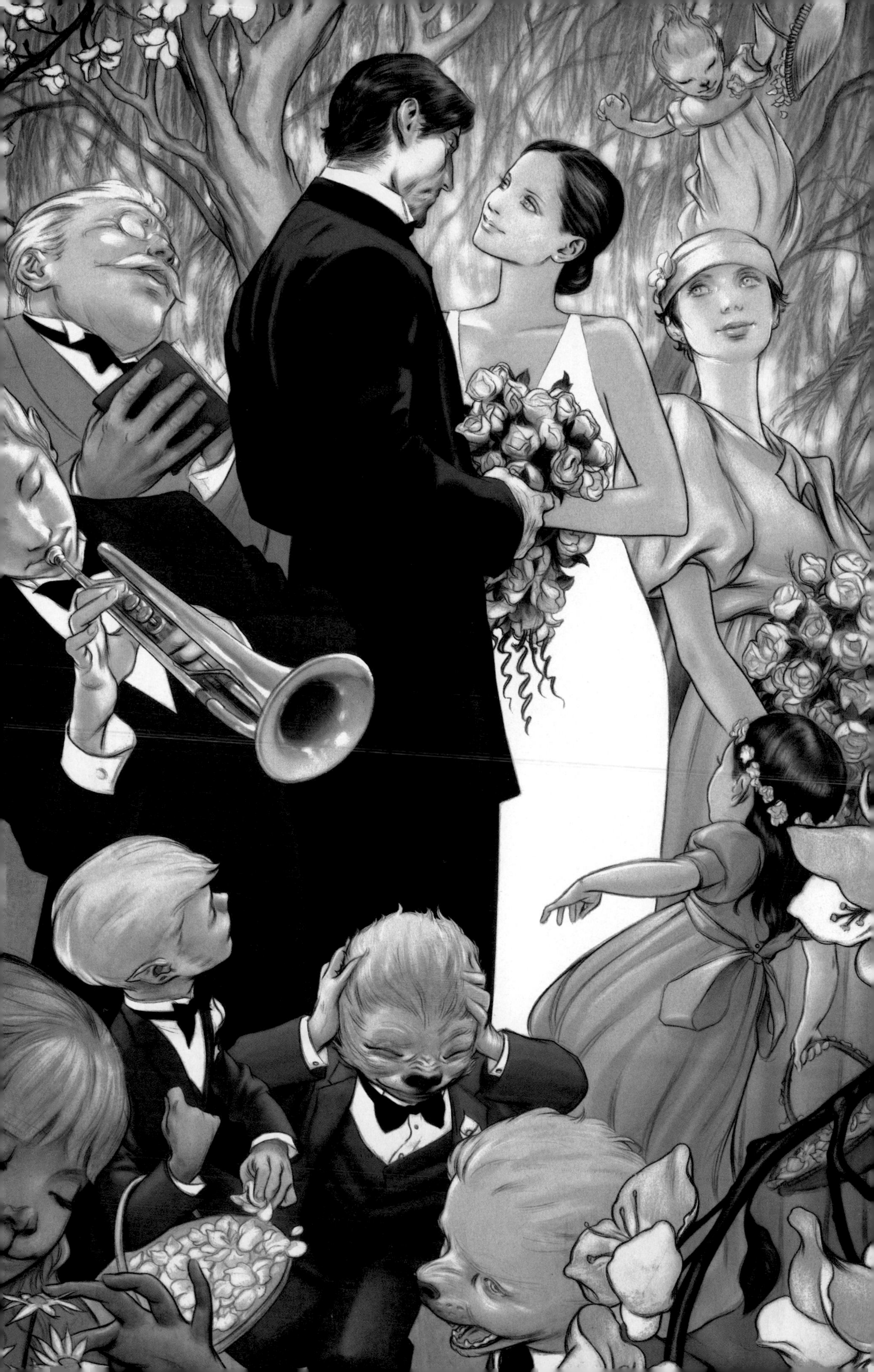

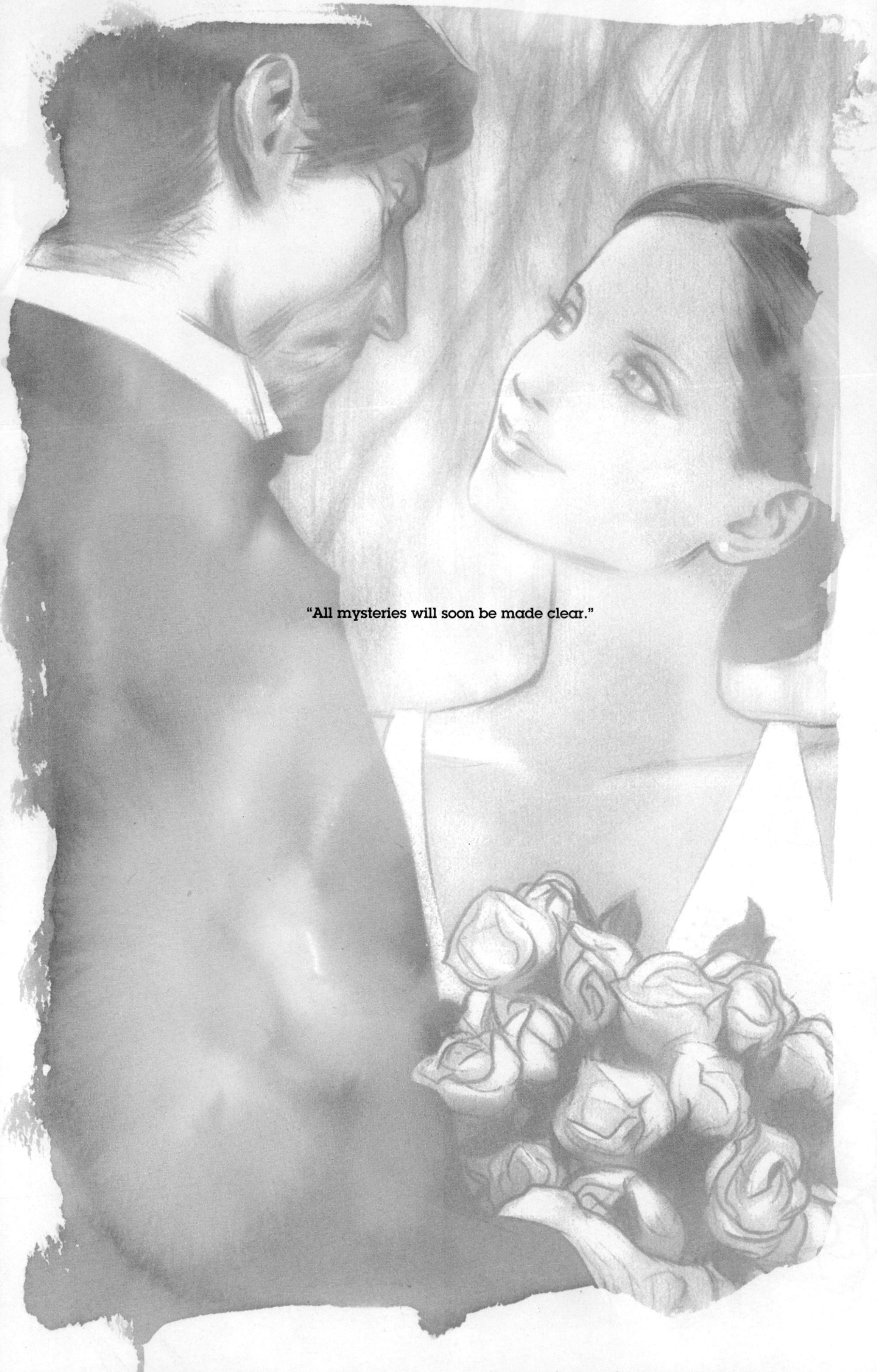
"All mysteries will soon be made clear."

CHAPTER ONE: SECRET AGENT MAN

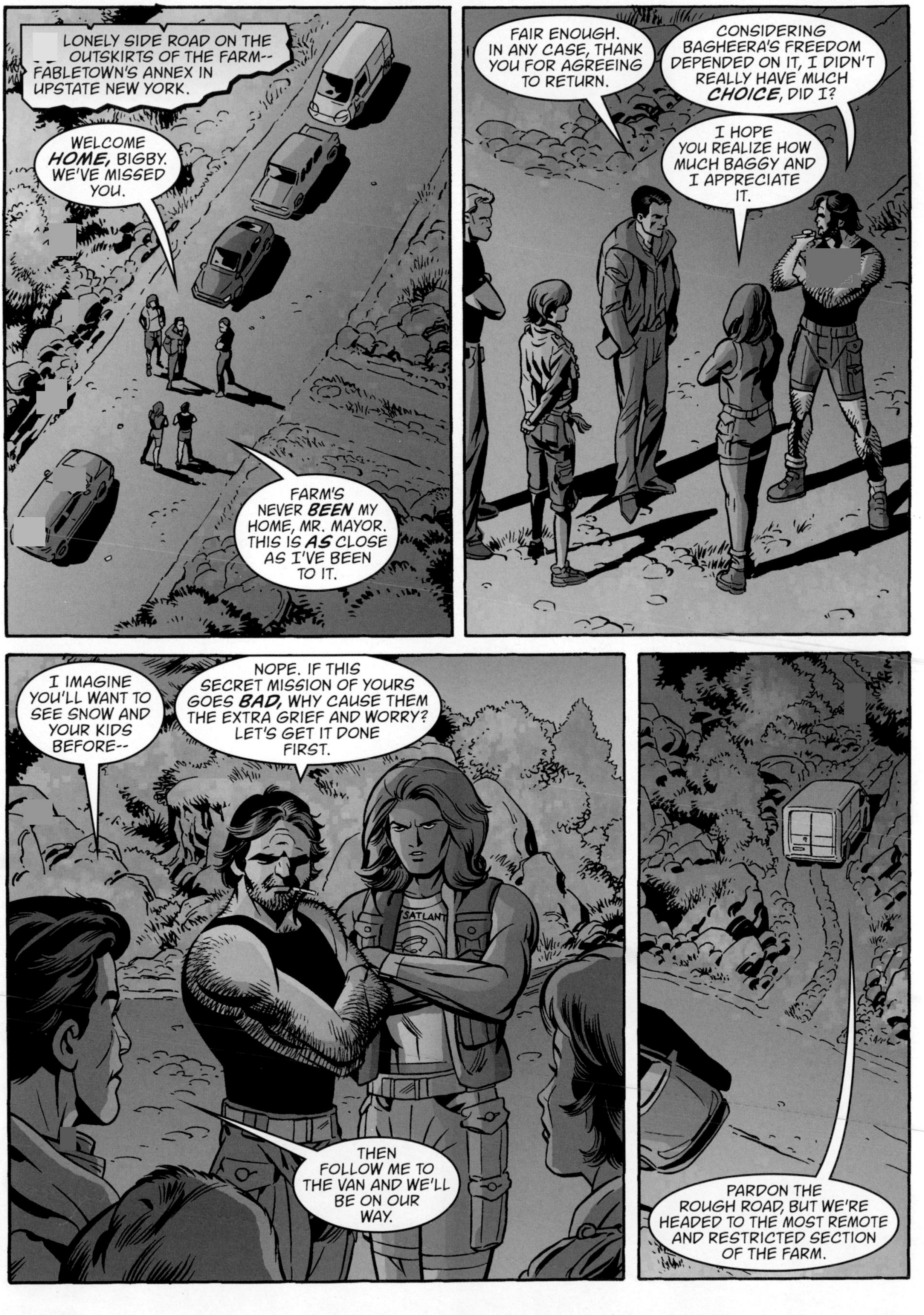
LONELY SIDE ROAD ON THE OUTSKIRTS OF THE FARM-- FABLETOWN'S ANNEX IN UPSTATE NEW YORK.
WELCOME HOME, BIGBY. WE'VE MISSED YOU.
FARM'S NEVER BEEN MY HOME, MR. MAYOR. THIS IS AS CLOSE AS I'VE BEEN TO IT.
FAIR ENOUGH. IN ANY CASE, THANK YOU FOR AGREEING TO RETURN.
CONSIDERING BAGHEERA'S FREEDOM DEPENDED ON IT, I DIDN'T REALLY HAVE MUCH CHOICE, DID I?
I HOPE YOU REALIZE HOW MUCH BAGGY AND I APPRECIATE IT.
I IMAGINE YOU'LL WANT TO SEE SNOW AND YOUR KIDS BEFORE--
NOPE. IF THIS SECRET MISSION OF YOURS GOES BAD, WHY CAUSE THEM THE EXTRA GRIEF AND WORRY? LET'S GET IT DONE FIRST.
THEN FOLLOW ME TO THE VAN AND WE'LL BE ON OUR WAY.
PARDON THE ROUGH ROAD, BUT WE'RE HEADED TO THE MOST REMOTE AND RESTRICTED SECTION OF THE FARM.

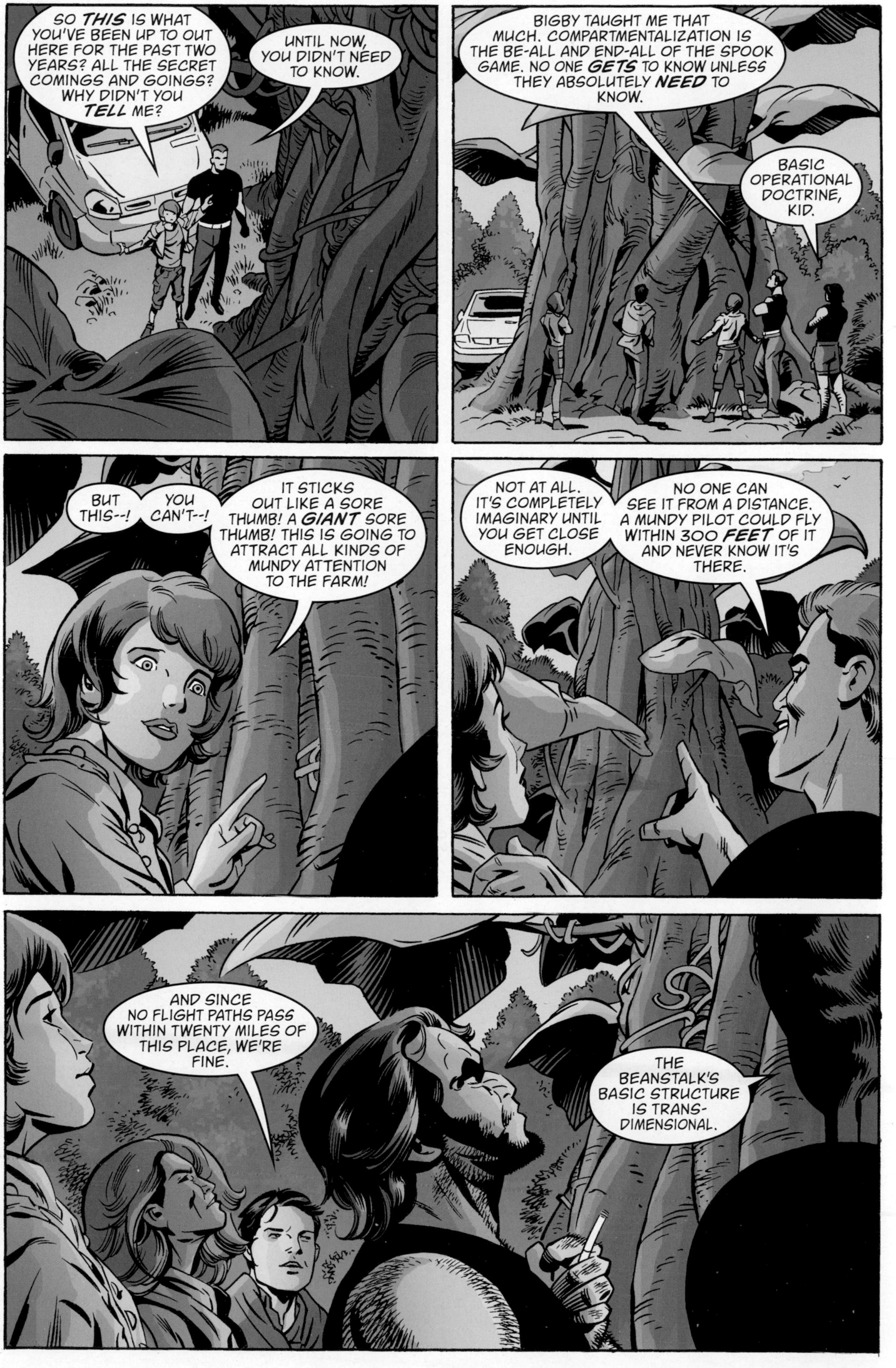
SO THIS IS WHAT YOU'VE BEEN UP TO OUT HERE FOR THE PAST TWO YEARS? ALL THE SECRET COMINGS AND GOINGS? WHY DIDN'T YOU TELL ME?
UNTIL NOW, YOU DIDN'T NEED TO KNOW.
BIGBY TAUGHT ME THAT MUCH. COMPARTMENTALIZATION IS THE BE-ALL AND END-ALL OF THE SPOOK GAME. NO ONE GETS TO KNOW UNLESS THEY ABSOLUTELY NEED TO KNOW.
BASIC OPERATIONAL DOCTRINE, KID.
BUT THIS--!
YOU CAN'T--!
IT STICKS OUT LIKE A SORE THUMB! A GIANT SORE THUMB! THIS IS GOING TO ATTRACT ALL KINDS OF MUNDY ATTENTION TO THE FARM!
NOT AT ALL. IT'S COMPLETELY IMAGINARY UNTIL YOU GET CLOSE ENOUGH.
NO ONE CAN SEE IT FROM A DISTANCE. A MUNDY PILOT COULD FLY WITHIN 300 FEET OF IT AND NEVER KNOW IT'S THERE.
AND SINCE NO FLIGHT PATHS PASS WITHIN TWENTY MILES OF THIS PLACE, WE'RE FINE.
THE BEANSTALK'S BASIC STRUCTURE IS TRANS-DIMENSIONAL.

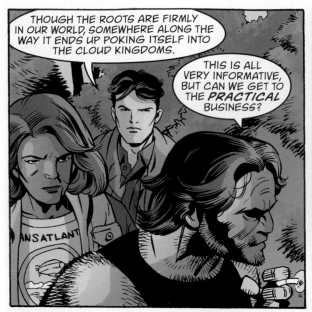

THOUGH THE ROOTS ARE FIRMLY IN OUR WORLD, SOMEWHERE ALONG THE WAY IT ENDS UP POKING ITSELF INTO THE CLOUD KINGDOMS.

THIS IS ALL VERY INFORMATIVE, BUT CAN WE GET TO THE *PRACTICAL* BUSINESS?

I ASSUME I'M GOING TO *CLIMB* THIS THING?

EXACTLY.

WHERE'S MY GEAR?

IT'S WAITING FOR YOU UPSTAIRS, ALONG WITH YOUR *SPECIFIC* INSTRUCTIONS. WE THOUGHT IT BETTER THAT WAY, TO FURTHER GUARD AGAINST ANYTHING LEAKING OUT.

YOUR CONTACT WILL MEET YOU AT THE TOP.

THEN I MIGHT AS WELL GET STARTED.

ARE YOU SURE THERE ISN'T *ANYTHING* YOU WANT ME TO TELL SNOW?

I'M SURE, ROSE.

IF I *DON'T* RETURN, I WAS NEVER HERE IN THE FIRST PLACE.

IF I DO, I CAN TELL HER MYSELF.

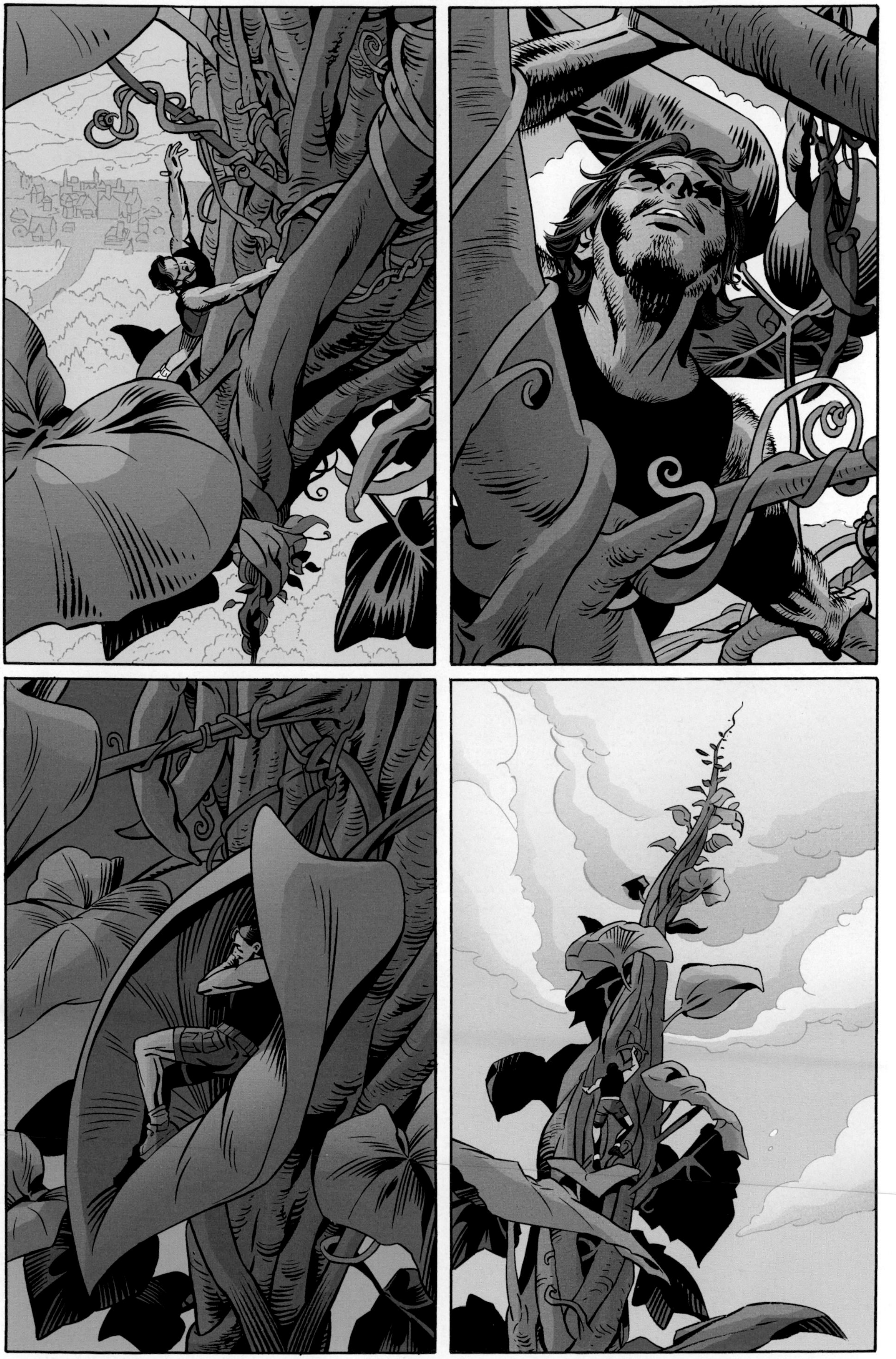

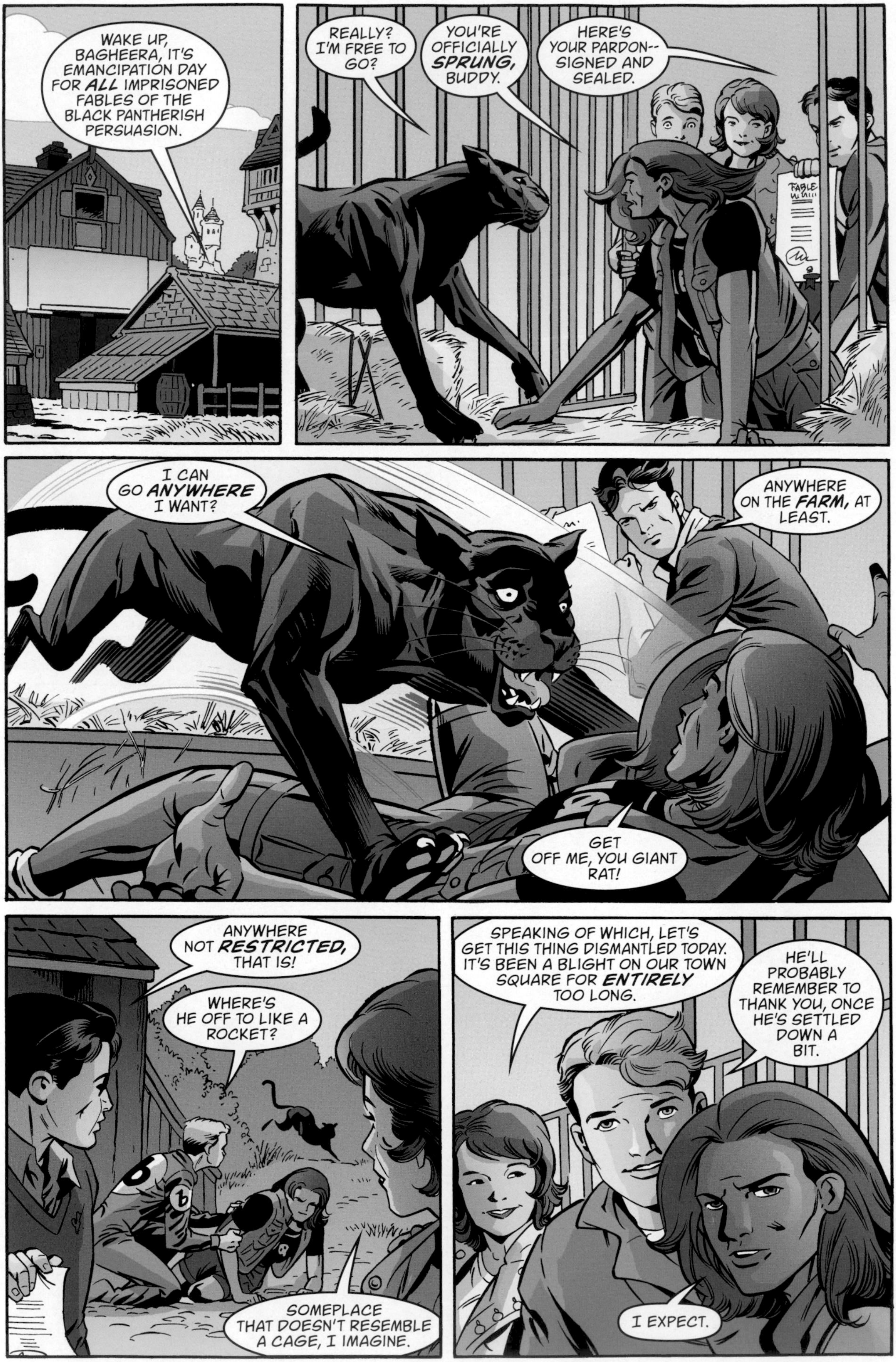
WAKE UP, BAGHEERA, IT'S EMANCIPATION DAY FOR ALL IMPRISONED FABLES OF THE BLACK PANTHERISH PERSUASION.
REALLY? I'M FREE TO GO?
YOU'RE OFFICIALLY SPRUNG, BUDDY.
HERE'S YOUR PARDON-- SIGNED AND SEALED.
I CAN GO ANYWHERE I WANT?
ANYWHERE ON THE FARM, AT LEAST.
GET OFF ME, YOU GIANT RAT!
ANYWHERE NOT RESTRICTED, THAT IS!
WHERE'S HE OFF TO LIKE A ROCKET?
SOMEPLACE THAT DOESN'T RESEMBLE A CAGE, I IMAGINE.
SPEAKING OF WHICH, LET'S GET THIS THING DISMANTLED TODAY. IT'S BEEN A BLIGHT ON OUR TOWN SQUARE FOR ENTIRELY TOO LONG.
HE'LL PROBABLY REMEMBER TO THANK YOU, ONCE HE'S SETTLED DOWN A BIT.
I EXPECT.

CHAPTER TWO: CASTLES IN THE SKY

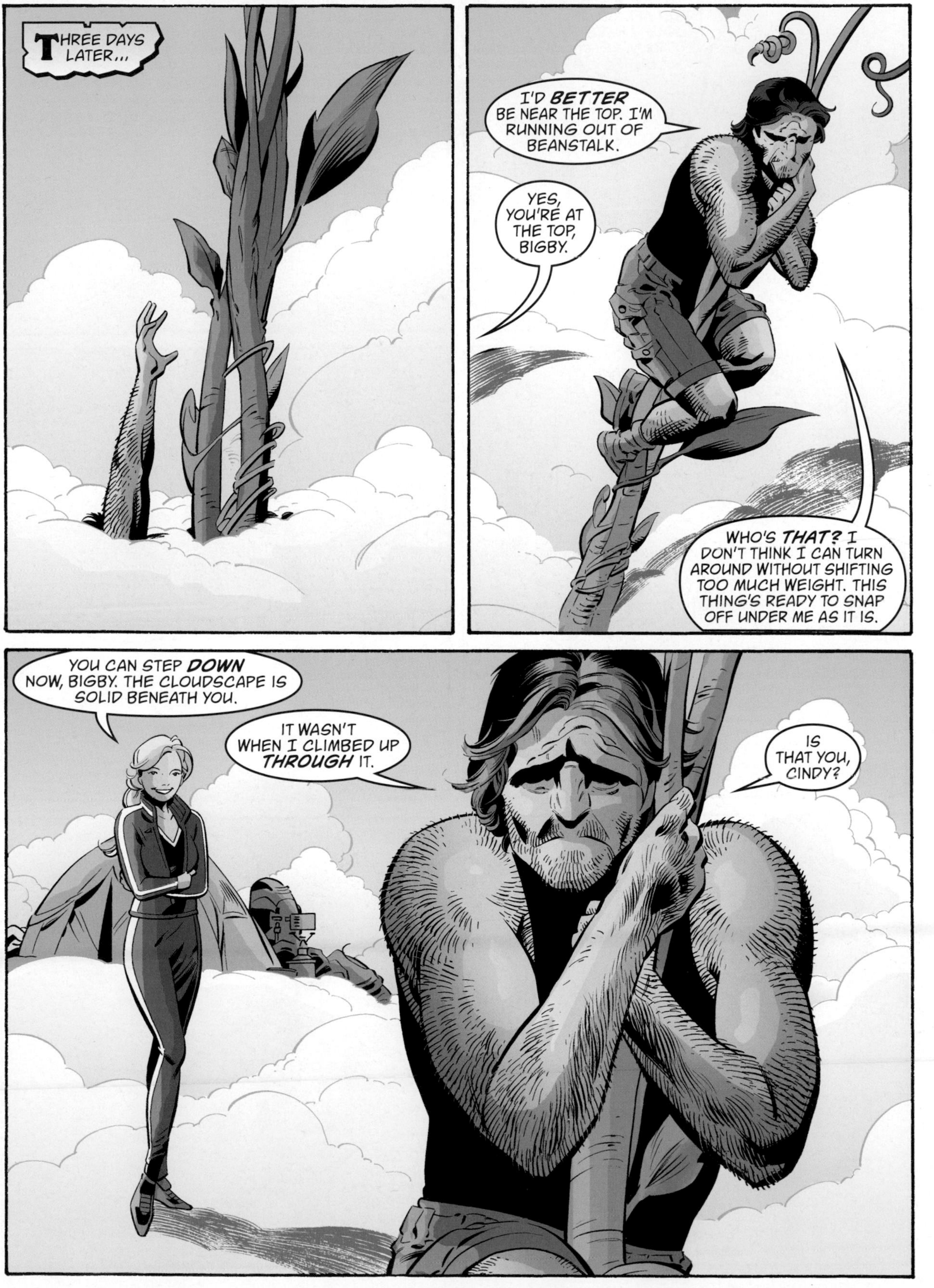
THREE DAYS LATER...
I'D BETTER BE NEAR THE TOP. I'M RUNNING OUT OF BEANSTALK.
YES, YOU'RE AT THE TOP, BIGBY.
WHO'S THAT? I DON'T THINK I CAN TURN AROUND WITHOUT SHIFTING TOO MUCH WEIGHT. THIS THING'S READY TO SNAP OFF UNDER ME AS IT IS.
YOU CAN STEP DOWN NOW, BIGBY. THE CLOUDSCAPE IS SOLID BENEATH YOU.
IT WASN'T WHEN I CLIMBED UP THROUGH IT.
IS THAT YOU, CINDY?

YES, IT'S ME, AND YOU REALLY CAN GET DOWN. IT'S SOLID FROM THE TOP, EVEN THOUGH YOU COULD PASS THROUGH FROM BELOW. THAT'S THE WAY THE ENCHANTMENT WORKS.

HONESTLY, I DON'T THINK I'VE EVER SEEN YOU AFRAID OF *ANYTHING* BEFORE, BIGBY.

AND YOU STILL HAVEN'T. *NERVOUS* ISN'T THE SAME AS SCARED.

REMEMBER, ME AND MINE DIDN'T EVOLVE FROM MONKEYS LIKE YOU AND YOURS. I DON'T HAVE CLIMBING HARD-WIRED INTO ME FROM A MILLION GENERATIONS PAST.

POINT TAKEN, BUT YOU REALLY *CAN* STEP DOWN. SEE? I'M JUMPING UP AND DOWN RIGHT NEXT TO YOU AND I'M NOT FALLING THROUGH.

TRUST ME. I'VE BEEN LIVING UP HERE FOR MONTHS, PREPARING THE WAY FOR YOU WITH THE LOCALS.

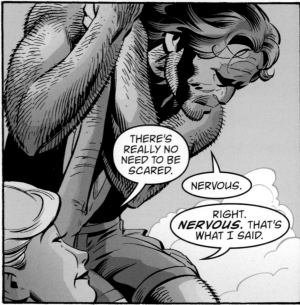

THERE'S REALLY NO NEED TO BE SCARED.

NERVOUS.

RIGHT. *NERVOUS.* THAT'S WHAT I SAID.

OKAY, HERE GOES NOTHING.

IF YOU *DO* FALL THROUGH, YOU'LL HAVE A LONG TIME TO REGRET LISTENING TO ME ON THE WAY DOWN.

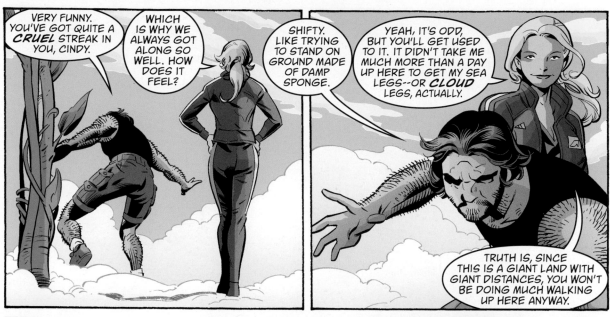

VERY FUNNY. YOU'VE GOT QUITE A *CRUEL* STREAK IN YOU, CINDY.

WHICH IS WHY WE ALWAYS GOT ALONG SO WELL. HOW DOES IT FEEL?

SHIFTY. LIKE TRYING TO STAND ON GROUND MADE OF DAMP SPONGE.

YEAH, IT'S ODD, BUT YOU'LL GET USED TO IT. IT DIDN'T TAKE ME MUCH MORE THAN A DAY UP HERE TO GET MY SEA LEGS--OR *CLOUD* LEGS, ACTUALLY.

TRUTH IS, SINCE THIS IS A GIANT LAND WITH GIANT DISTANCES, YOU WON'T BE DOING MUCH WALKING UP HERE ANYWAY.

RADISKOP!

YES, CINDERELLA?

CAN YOU INFORM OUR HOST THAT THE GUEST OF HONOR HAS ARRIVED?

YOU BETCHA!

HE SEEMS ENTHUSIASTIC.

RADY'S A BIG SWEETHEART.

BIG IS RIGHT--BIG ENOUGH TO SWALLOW US *BOTH* IN TWO OR THREE BITES.

HELP ME BREAK CAMP WHILE WE WAIT FOR OUR TRANSPORT TO ARRIVE.

WE WON'T BE COMING BACK THIS WAY.

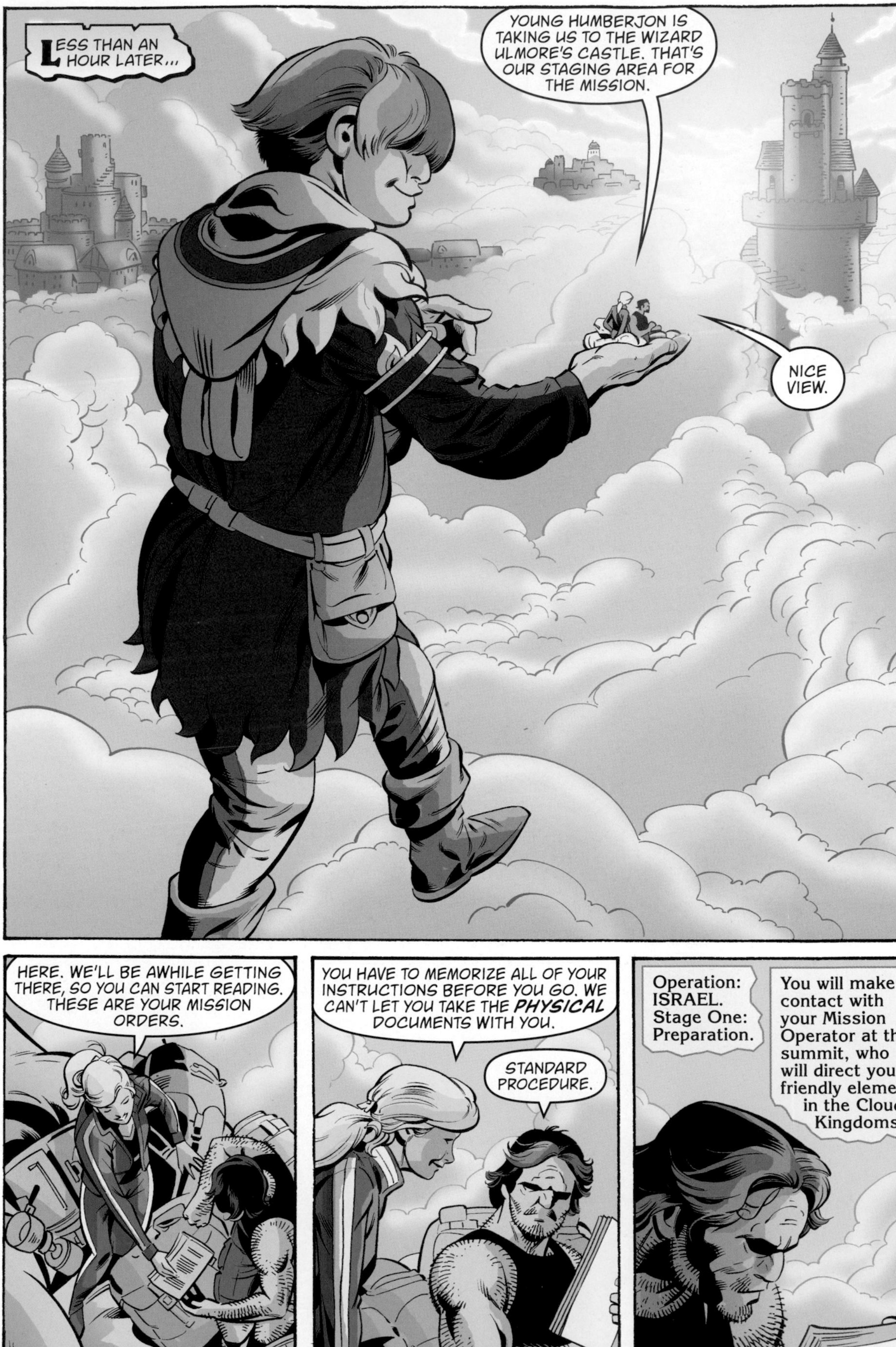
LESS THAN AN HOUR LATER...
YOUNG HUMBERJON IS TAKING US TO THE WIZARD ULMORE'S CASTLE. THAT'S OUR STAGING AREA FOR THE MISSION.
NICE VIEW.
HERE. WE'LL BE AWHILE GETTING THERE, SO YOU CAN START READING. THESE ARE YOUR MISSION ORDERS.
YOU HAVE TO MEMORIZE ALL OF YOUR INSTRUCTIONS BEFORE YOU GO. WE CAN'T LET YOU TAKE THE PHYSICAL DOCUMENTS WITH YOU.
STANDARD PROCEDURE.
Operation: ISRAEL. Stage One: Preparation.
You will make contact with your Mission Operator at the summit, who will direct you to friendly elements in the Cloud Kingdoms.

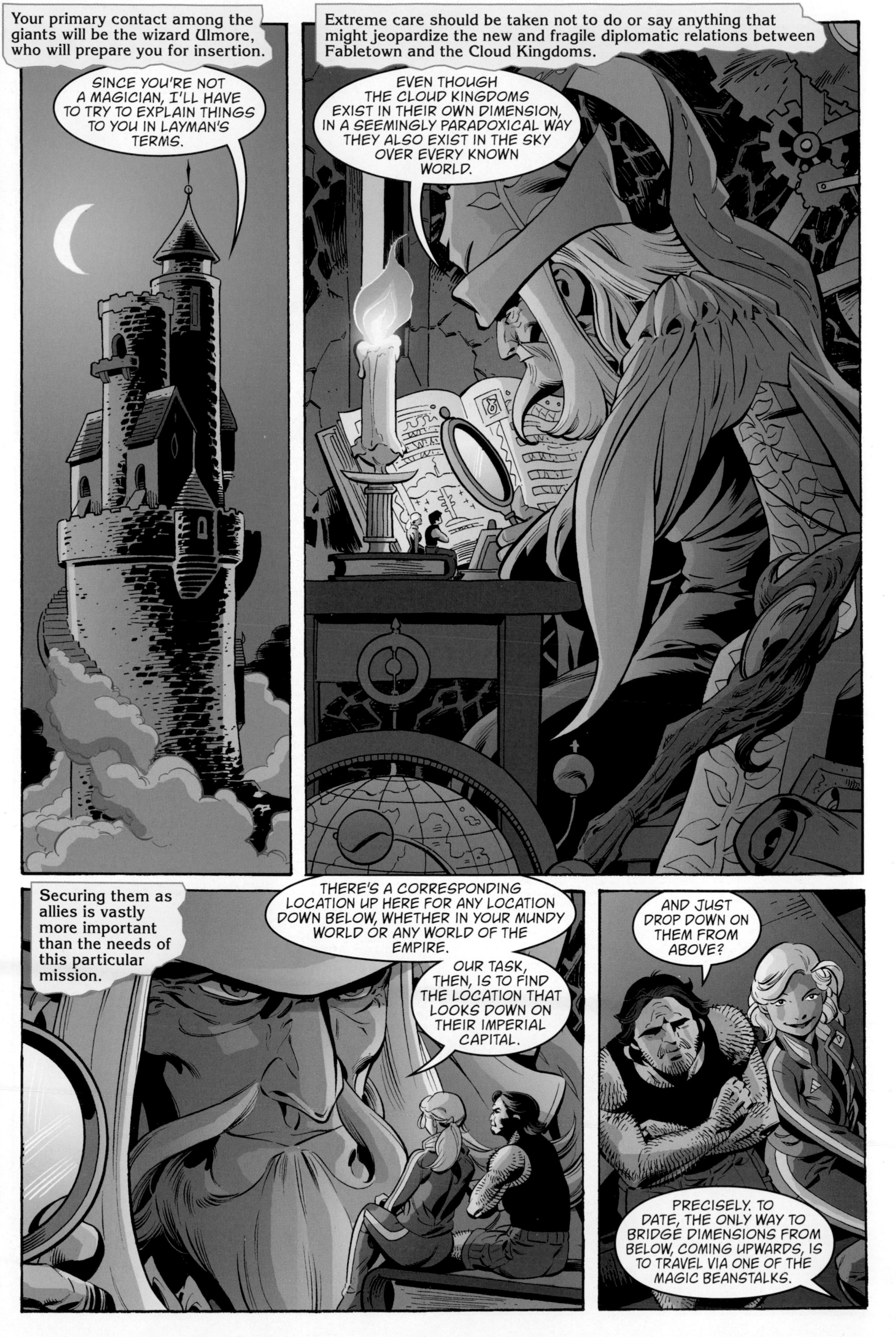
Your primary contact among the giants will be the wizard Ulmore, who will prepare you for insertion.
SINCE YOU'RE NOT A MAGICIAN, I'LL HAVE TO TRY TO EXPLAIN THINGS TO YOU IN LAYMAN'S TERMS.
Extreme care should be taken not to do or say anything that might jeopardize the new and fragile diplomatic relations between Fabletown and the Cloud Kingdoms.
EVEN THOUGH THE CLOUD KINGDOMS EXIST IN THEIR OWN DIMENSION, IN A SEEMINGLY PARADOXICAL WAY THEY ALSO EXIST IN THE SKY OVER EVERY KNOWN WORLD.
Securing them as allies is vastly more important than the needs of this particular mission.
THERE'S A CORRESPONDING LOCATION UP HERE FOR ANY LOCATION DOWN BELOW, WHETHER IN YOUR MUNDY WORLD OR ANY WORLD OF THE EMPIRE.
OUR TASK, THEN, IS TO FIND THE LOCATION THAT LOOKS DOWN ON THEIR IMPERIAL CAPITAL.
AND JUST DROP DOWN ON THEM FROM ABOVE?
PRECISELY. TO DATE, THE ONLY WAY TO BRIDGE DIMENSIONS FROM BELOW, COMING UPWARDS, IS TO TRAVEL VIA ONE OF THE MAGIC BEANSTALKS.

THAT'S KEPT US **SAFE** SO FAR FROM THE ADVERSARY'S ARMIES.

BUT THE DIMENSIONAL DOORWAYS ARE **ALWAYS** OPEN GOING IN THE OTHER DIRECTION.

THREE DAYS LATER...

WE SHOULDN'T NEED ANYTHING BUT **GRAVITY** TO DO THE TRICK.

ARE YOU READY TO GO, BIGBY? GOT ALL YOUR EQUIPMENT?

THE HOLE'S DUG, SIR.

I ALMOST SLIPPED THROUGH IT MYSELF.

I HOPE SO. THERE'S NO ROOM FOR ANYTHING ELSE.

BETTER HOLD YOUR HAND DIRECTLY OVER THE HOLE, ULMORE. I CAN'T JUMP VERY **FAR** UNDER ALL THIS WEIGHT.

BE CARELESS DOWN THERE!

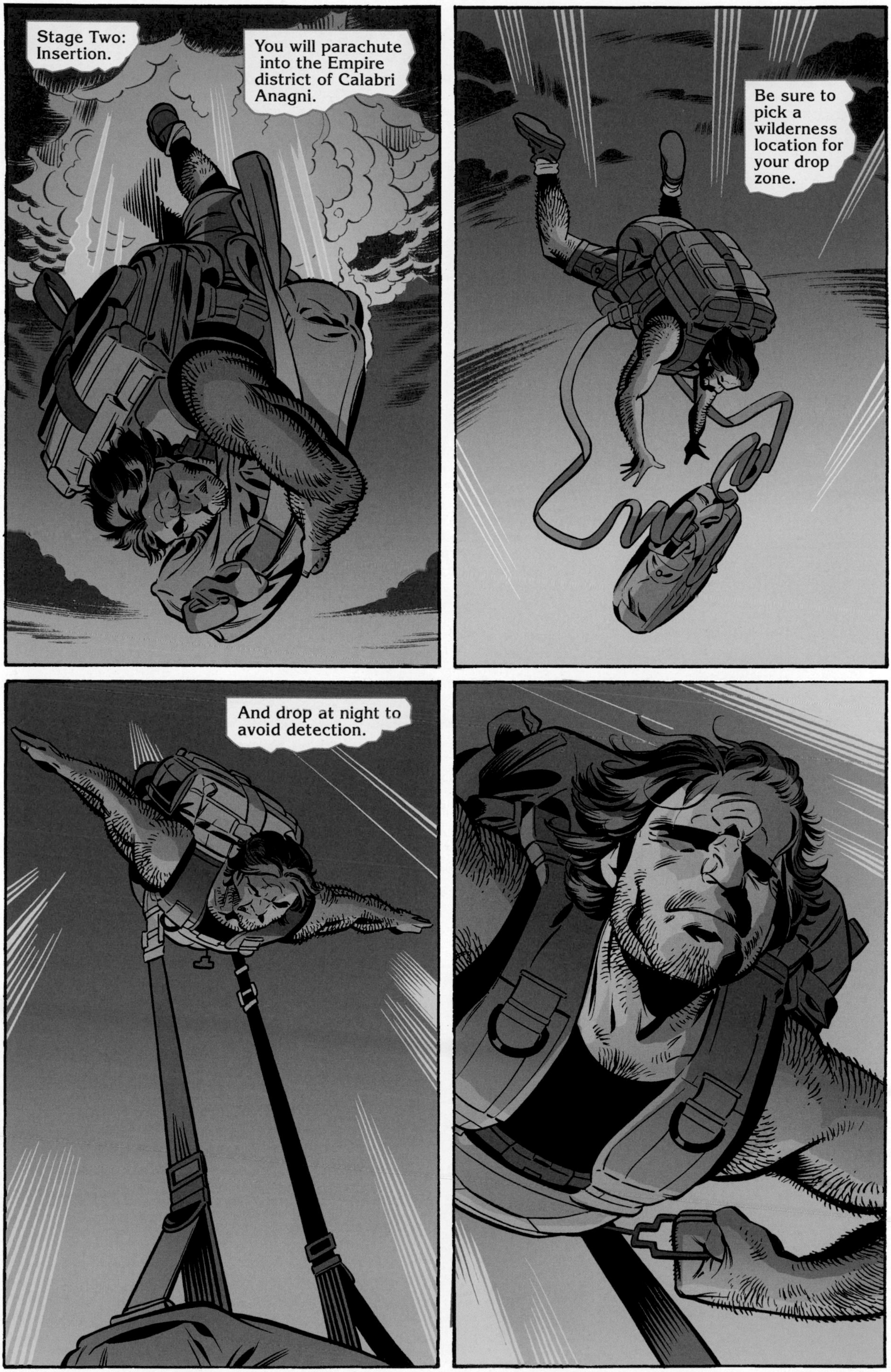
Stage Two: Insertion.
You will parachute into the Empire district of Calabri Anagni.
Be sure to pick a wilderness location for your drop zone.
And drop at night to avoid detection.

CHAPTER THREE: BEHIND ENEMY LINES

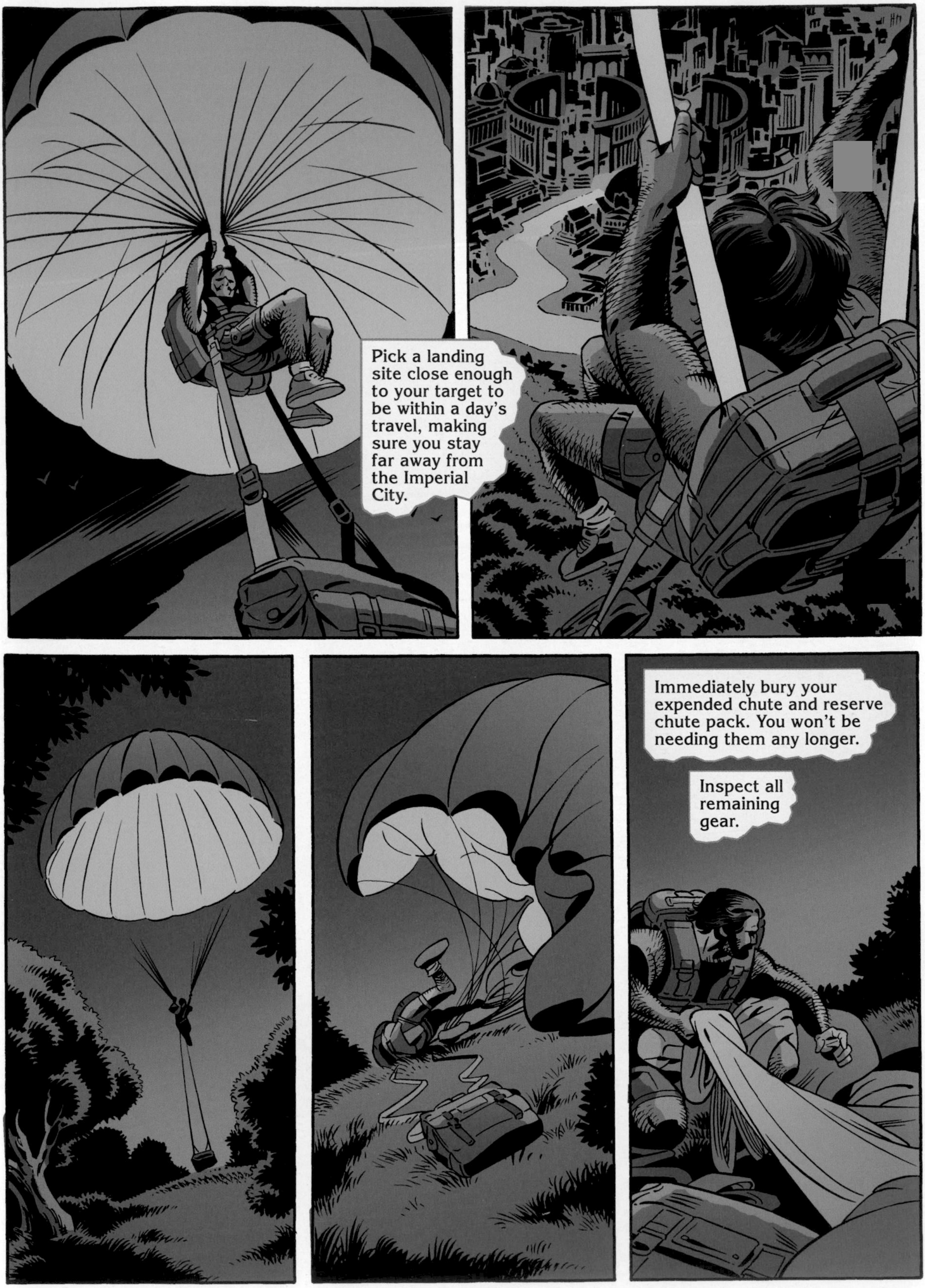
Pick a landing site close enough to your target to be within a day's travel, making sure you stay far away from the Imperial City.
Immediately bury your expended chute and reserve chute pack. You won't be needing them any longer.
Inspect all remaining gear.

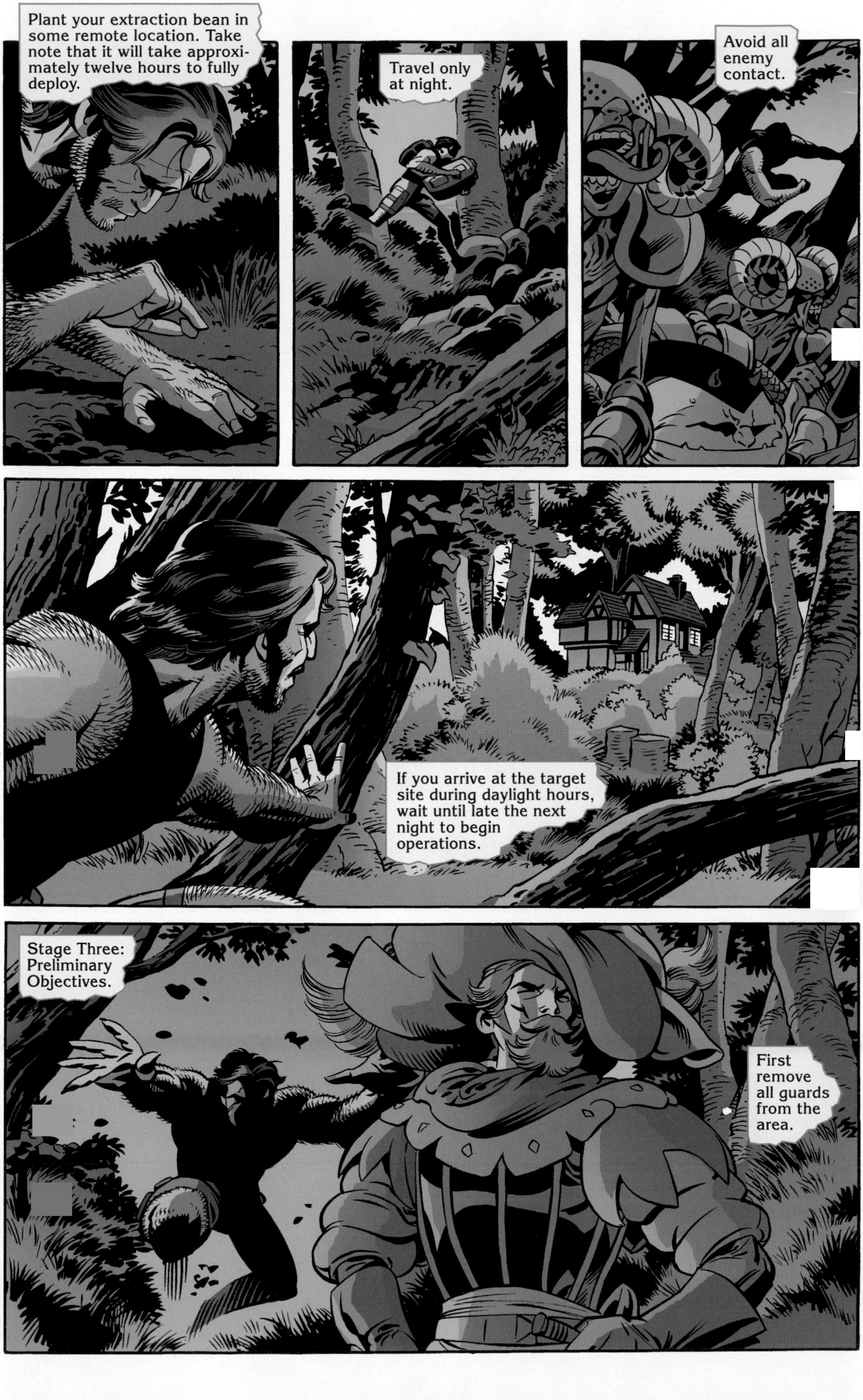
Plant your extraction bean in some remote location. Take note that it will take approximately twelve hours to fully deploy.
Travel only at night.
Avoid all enemy contact.
If you arrive at the target site during daylight hours, wait until late the next night to begin operations.
Stage Three: Preliminary Objectives.
First remove all guards from the area.

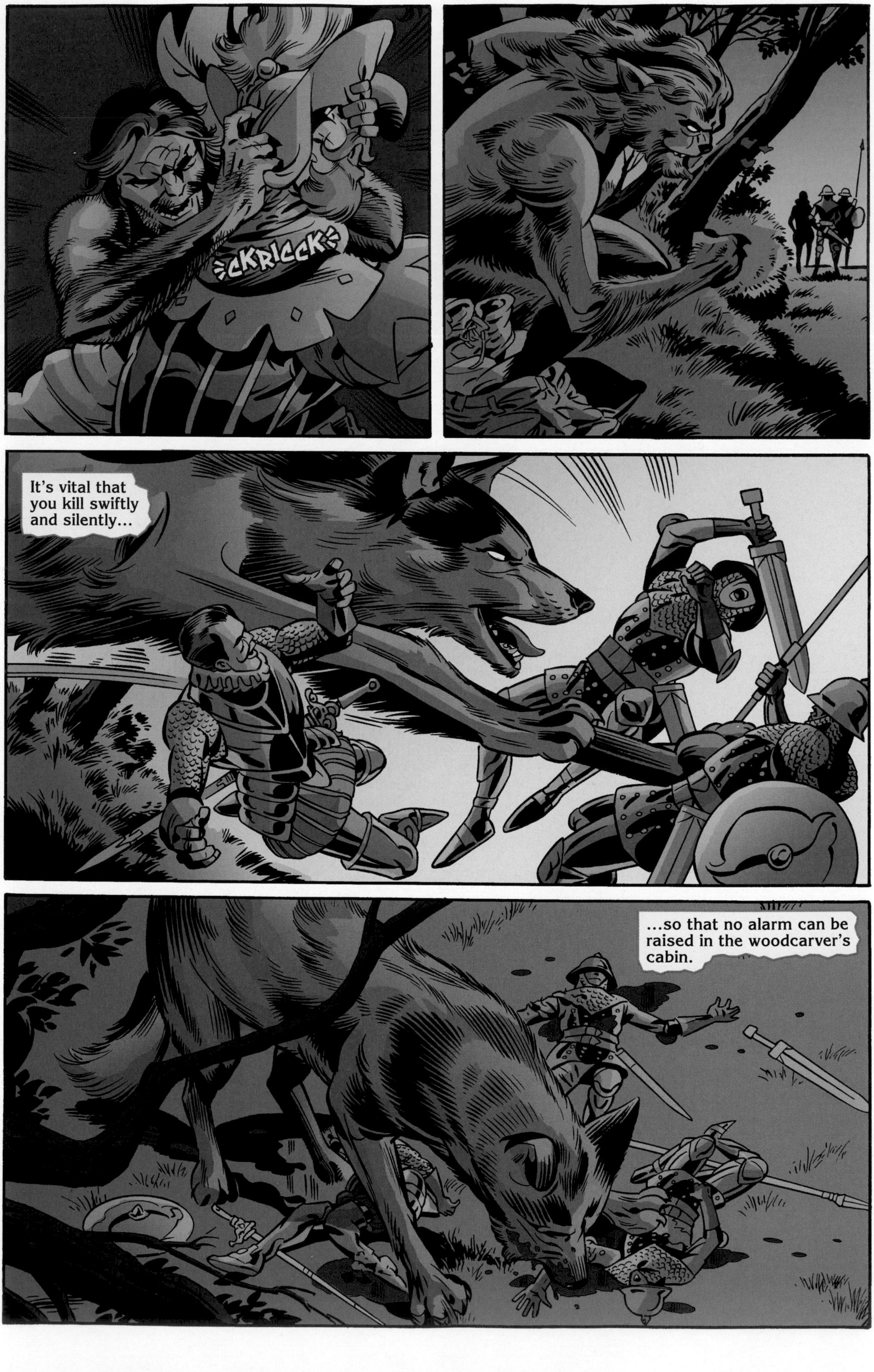
CKRICCK
It's vital that you kill swiftly and silently...
...so that no alarm can be raised in the woodcarver's cabin.

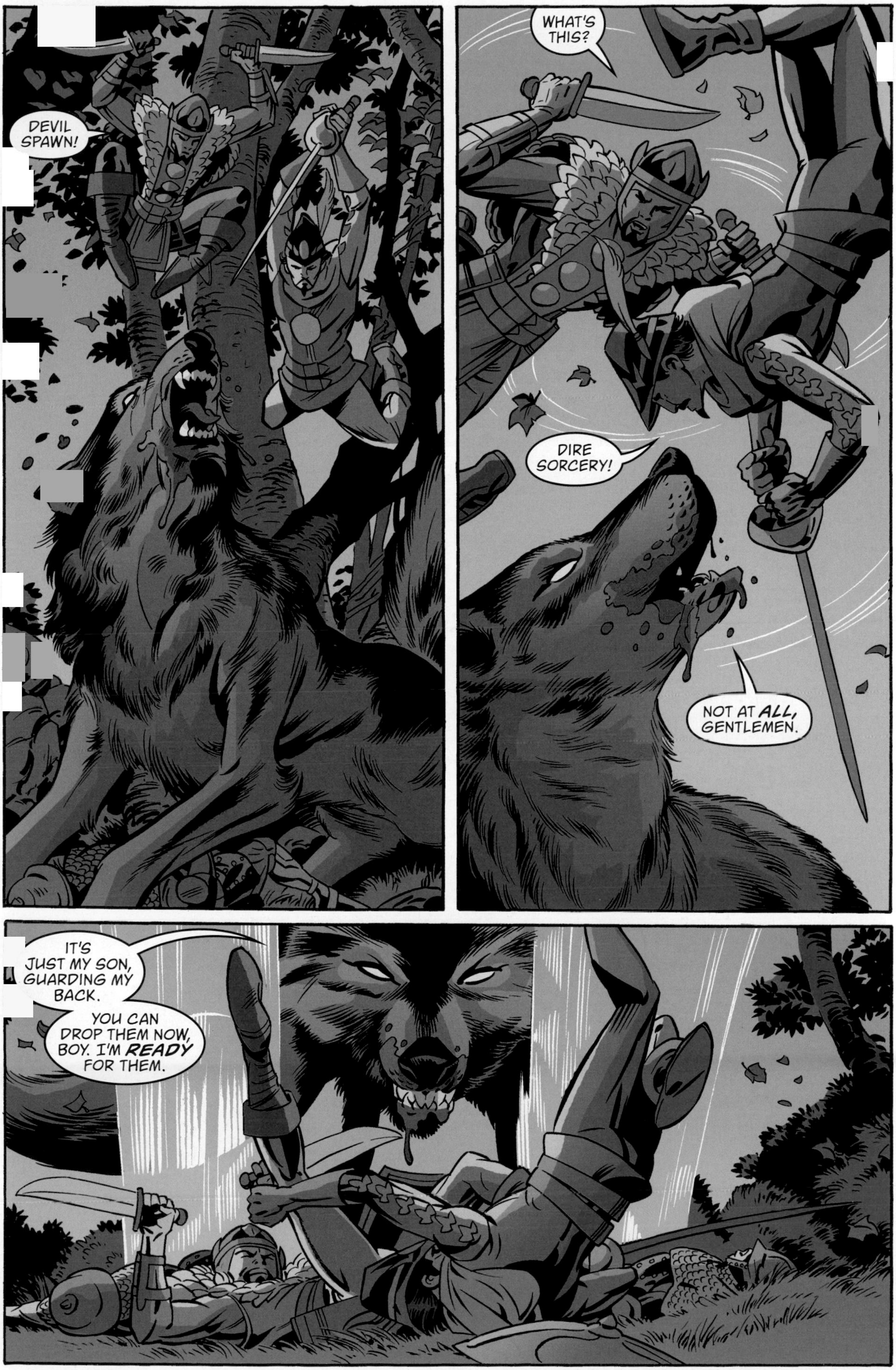

DEVIL SPAWN!
WHAT'S THIS?
DIRE SORCERY!
NOT AT ALL, GENTLEMEN.
IT'S JUST MY SON, GUARDING MY BACK.
YOU CAN DROP THEM NOW, BOY. I'M READY FOR THEM.

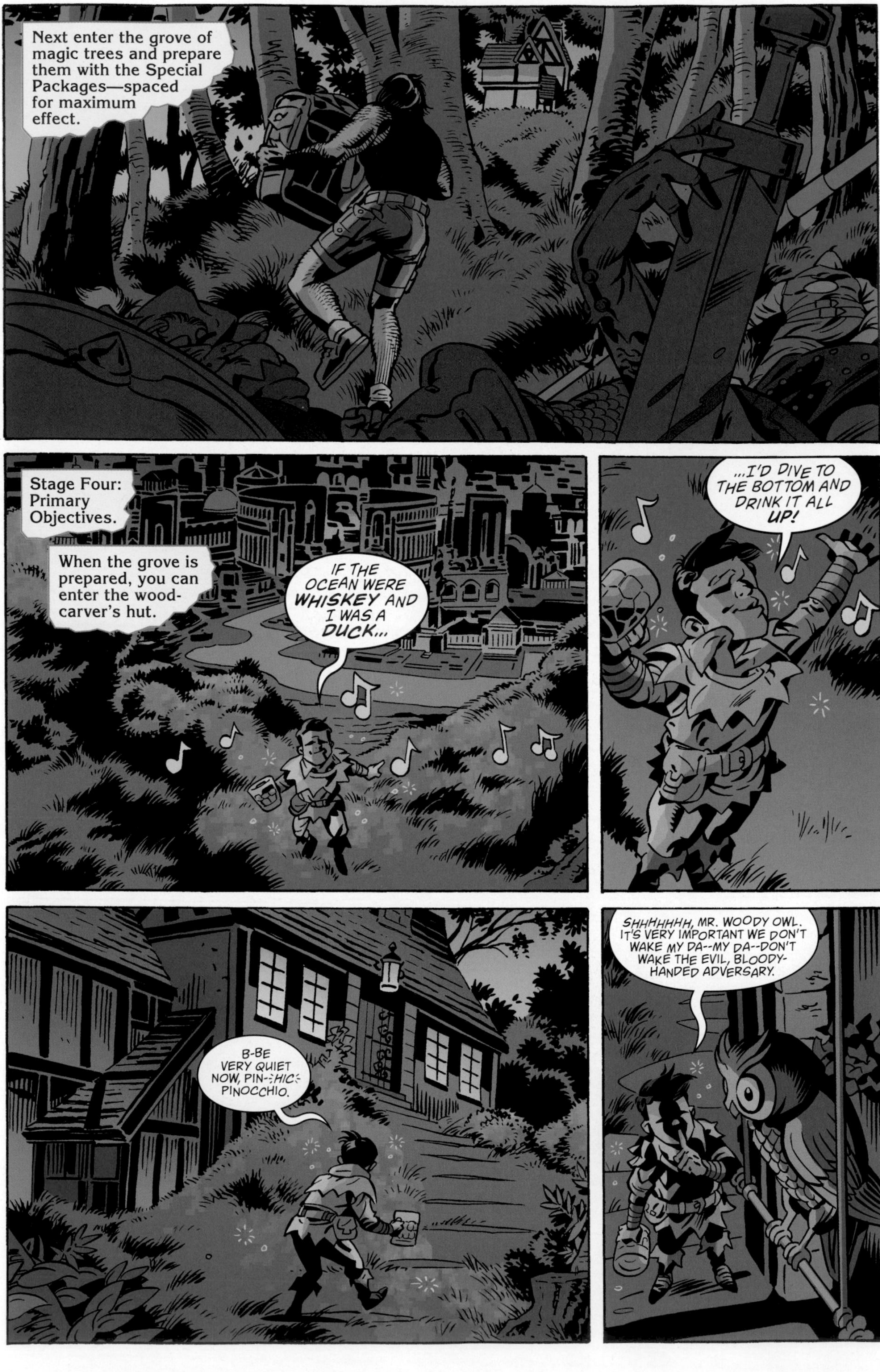
Next enter the grove of magic trees and prepare them with the Special Packages—spaced for maximum effect.
Stage Four: Primary Objectives.
When the grove is prepared, you can enter the wood-carver's hut.
IF THE OCEAN WERE WHISKEY AND I WAS A DUCK...
...I'D DIVE TO THE BOTTOM AND DRINK IT ALL UP!
B-BE VERY QUIET NOW, PIN--HIC--PINOCCHIO.
SHHHHHHH, MR. WOODY OWL. IT'S VERY IMPORTANT WE DON'T WAKE MY DA--MY DA--DON'T WAKE THE EVIL, BLOODY-HANDED ADVERSARY.

KINDLY OLD CONQUERORS NEED THEIR *SLEEP*.

If possible, try to free the Blue Fairy from her imprisonment. If that fails, try to destroy her.

BIGBY?

SHHHHHHH, PINOCCHIO. GEPPETTO'S SLEEPING ONLY TWO ROOMS AWAY, AND WE DON'T WANT TO WAKE HIM.

WHAT ARE YOU *DOING* HERE, BIGBY?

TRYING TO MURDER YOUR DAD'S *POWER SOURCE*. DIDN'T WORK, THOUGH.

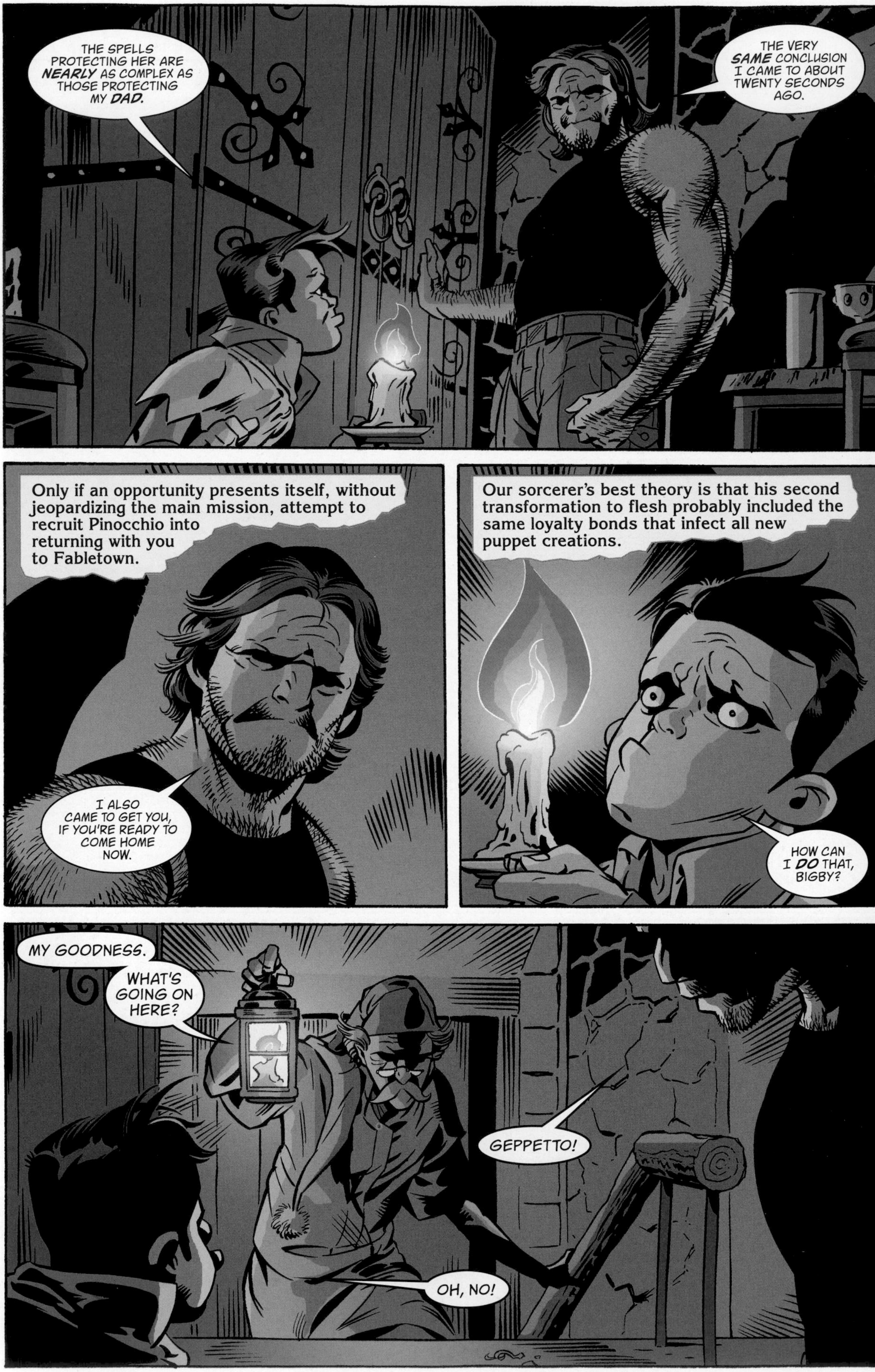
THE SPELLS PROTECTING HER ARE NEARLY AS COMPLEX AS THOSE PROTECTING MY DAD.
THE VERY SAME CONCLUSION I CAME TO ABOUT TWENTY SECONDS AGO.
Only if an opportunity presents itself, without jeopardizing the main mission, attempt to recruit Pinocchio into returning with you to Fabletown.
I ALSO CAME TO GET YOU, IF YOU'RE READY TO COME HOME NOW.
Our sorcerer's best theory is that his second transformation to flesh probably included the same loyalty bonds that infect all new puppet creations.
HOW CAN I DO THAT, BIGBY?
MY GOODNESS.
WHAT'S GOING ON HERE?
GEPPETTO!
OH, NO!

CHAPTER FOUR: THE ISRAEL ANALOG

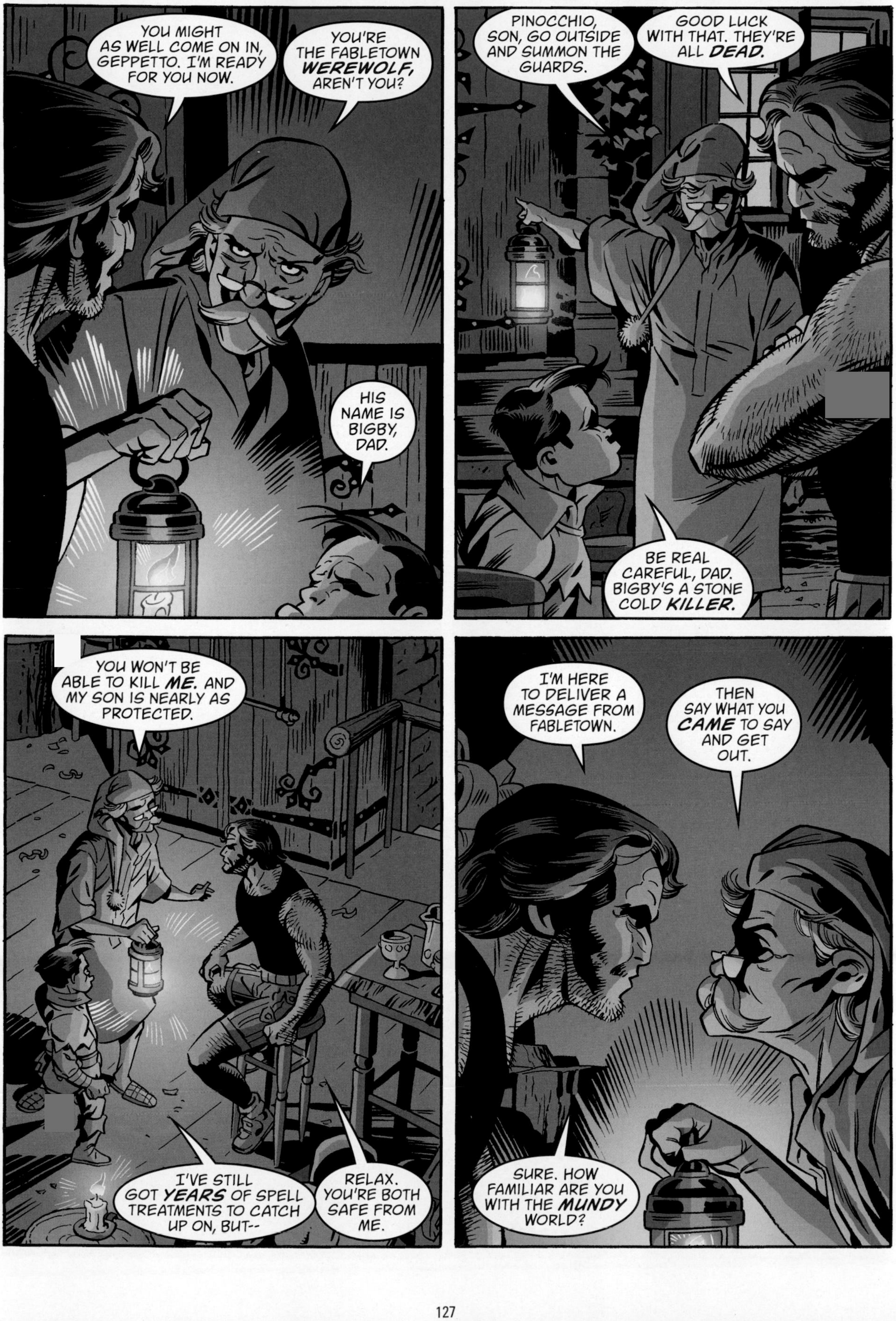
YOU MIGHT AS WELL COME ON IN, GEPPETTO. I'M READY FOR YOU NOW.
YOU'RE THE FABLETOWN WEREWOLF, AREN'T YOU?
HIS NAME IS BIGBY, DAD.
PINOCCHIO, SON, GO OUTSIDE AND SUMMON THE GUARDS.
GOOD LUCK WITH THAT. THEY'RE ALL DEAD.
BE REAL CAREFUL, DAD. BIGBY'S A STONE COLD KILLER.
YOU WON'T BE ABLE TO KILL ME. AND MY SON IS NEARLY AS PROTECTED.
I'VE STILL GOT YEARS OF SPELL TREATMENTS TO CATCH UP ON, BUT--
RELAX. YOU'RE BOTH SAFE FROM ME.
I'M HERE TO DELIVER A MESSAGE FROM FABLETOWN.
THEN SAY WHAT YOU CAME TO SAY AND GET OUT.
SURE. HOW FAMILIAR ARE YOU WITH THE MUNDY WORLD?

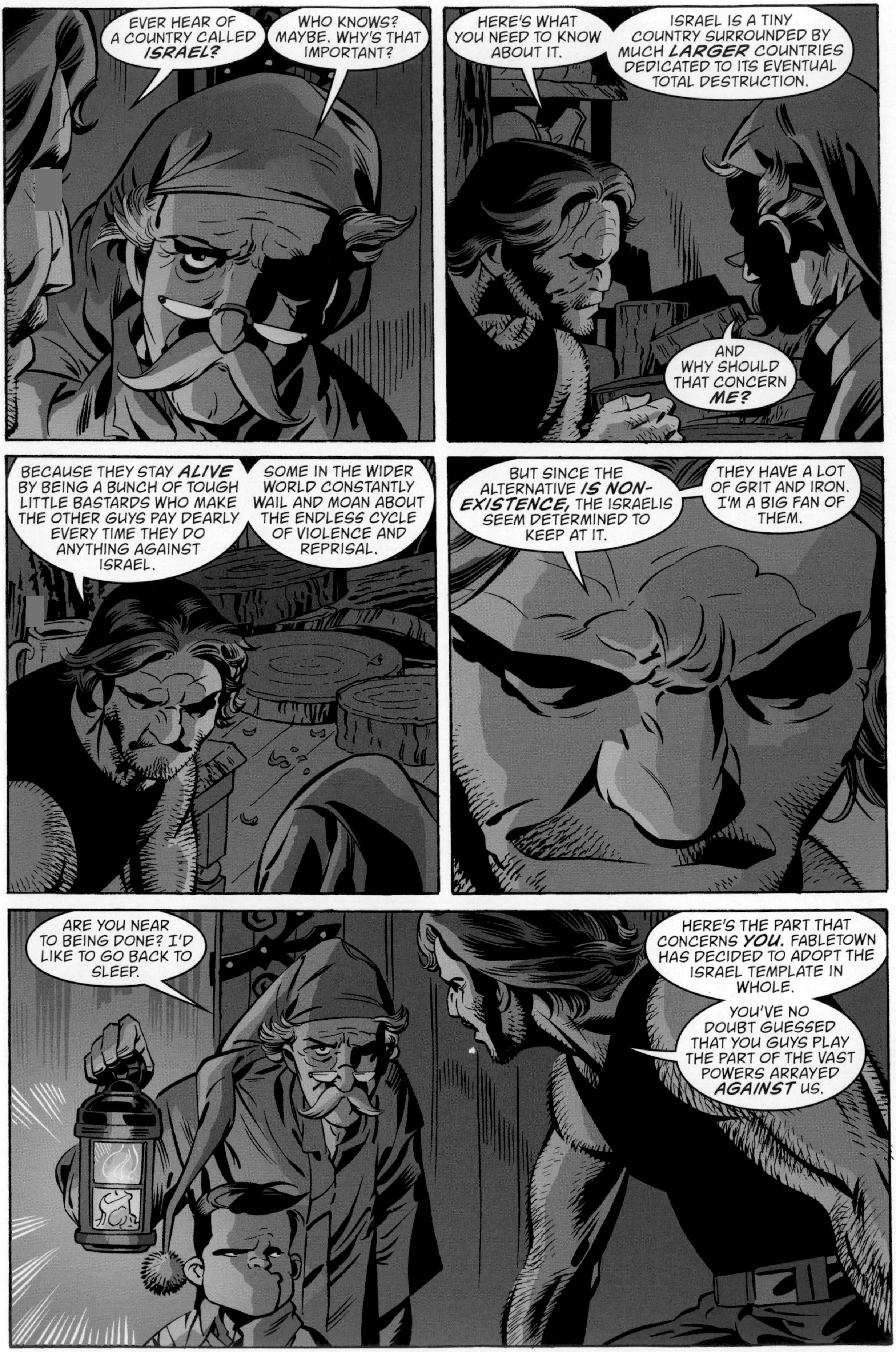
EVER HEAR OF A COUNTRY CALLED ISRAEL?
WHO KNOWS? MAYBE. WHY'S THAT IMPORTANT?
HERE'S WHAT YOU NEED TO KNOW ABOUT IT.
ISRAEL IS A TINY COUNTRY SURROUNDED BY MUCH LARGER COUNTRIES DEDICATED TO ITS EVENTUAL TOTAL DESTRUCTION.
AND WHY SHOULD THAT CONCERN ME?
BECAUSE THEY STAY ALIVE BY BEING A BUNCH OF TOUGH LITTLE BASTARDS WHO MAKE THE OTHER GUYS PAY DEARLY EVERY TIME THEY DO ANYTHING AGAINST ISRAEL.
SOME IN THE WIDER WORLD CONSTANTLY WAIL AND MOAN ABOUT THE ENDLESS CYCLE OF VIOLENCE AND REPRISAL.
BUT SINCE THE ALTERNATIVE IS NON-EXISTENCE, THE ISRAELIS SEEM DETERMINED TO KEEP AT IT.
THEY HAVE A LOT OF GRIT AND IRON. I'M A BIG FAN OF THEM.
ARE YOU NEAR TO BEING DONE? I'D LIKE TO GO BACK TO SLEEP.
HERE'S THE PART THAT CONCERNS YOU. FABLETOWN HAS DECIDED TO ADOPT THE ISRAEL TEMPLATE IN WHOLE.
YOU'VE NO DOUBT GUESSED THAT YOU GUYS PLAY THE PART OF THE VAST POWERS ARRAYED AGAINST US.

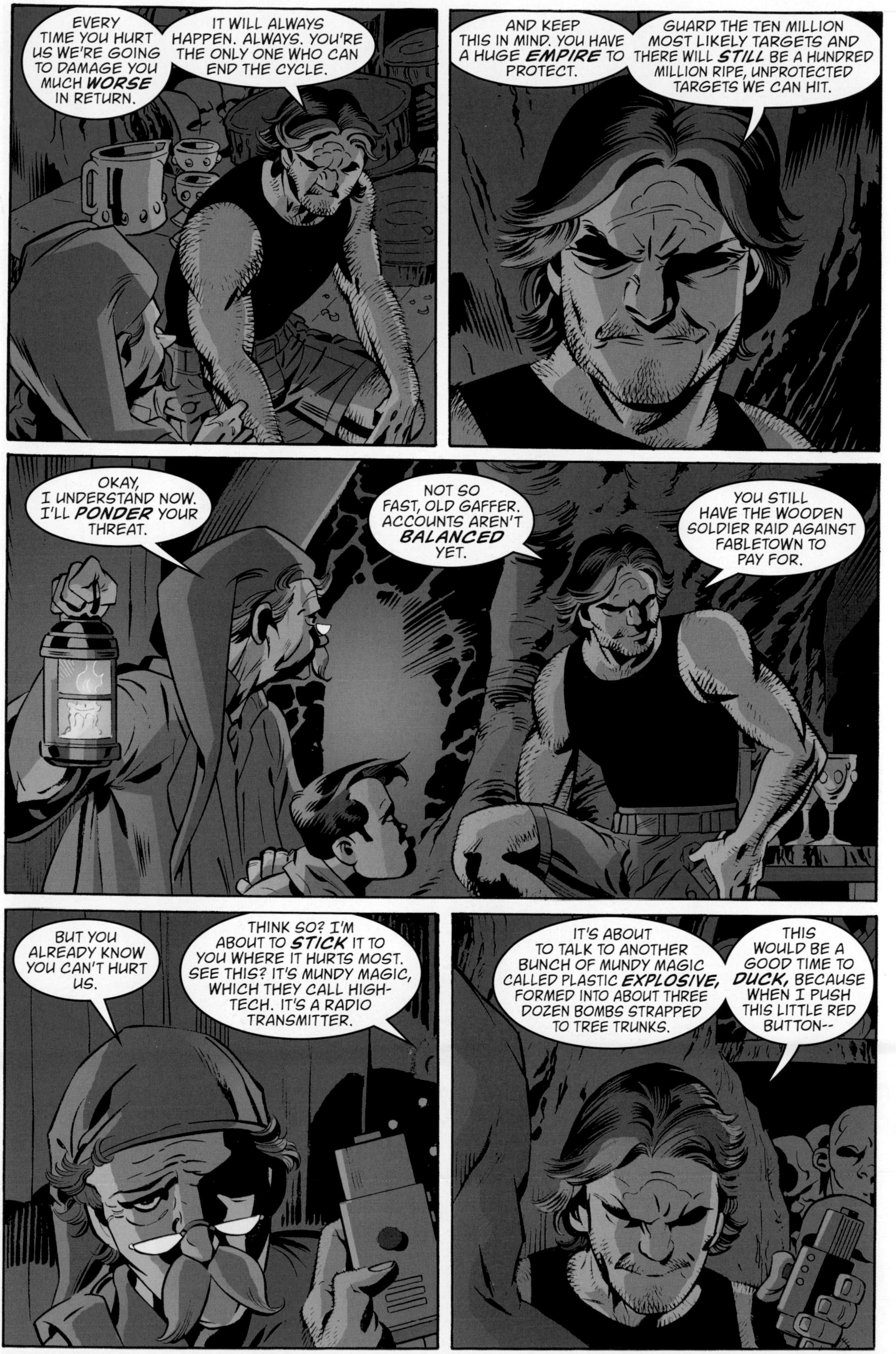
EVERY TIME YOU HURT US WE'RE GOING TO DAMAGE YOU MUCH WORSE IN RETURN.
IT WILL ALWAYS HAPPEN. ALWAYS. YOU'RE THE ONLY ONE WHO CAN END THE CYCLE.
AND KEEP THIS IN MIND. YOU HAVE A HUGE EMPIRE TO PROTECT.
GUARD THE TEN MILLION MOST LIKELY TARGETS AND THERE WILL STILL BE A HUNDRED MILLION RIPE, UNPROTECTED TARGETS WE CAN HIT.
OKAY, I UNDERSTAND NOW. I'LL PONDER YOUR THREAT.
NOT SO FAST, OLD GAFFER. ACCOUNTS AREN'T BALANCED YET.
YOU STILL HAVE THE WOODEN SOLDIER RAID AGAINST FABLETOWN TO PAY FOR.
BUT YOU ALREADY KNOW YOU CAN'T HURT US.
THINK SO? I'M ABOUT TO STICK IT TO YOU WHERE IT HURTS MOST. SEE THIS? IT'S MUNDY MAGIC, WHICH THEY CALL HIGH-TECH. IT'S A RADIO TRANSMITTER.
IT'S ABOUT TO TALK TO ANOTHER BUNCH OF MUNDY MAGIC CALLED PLASTIC EXPLOSIVE, FORMED INTO ABOUT THREE DOZEN BOMBS STRAPPED TO TREE TRUNKS.
THIS WOULD BE A GOOD TIME TO DUCK, BECAUSE WHEN I PUSH THIS LITTLE RED BUTTON--

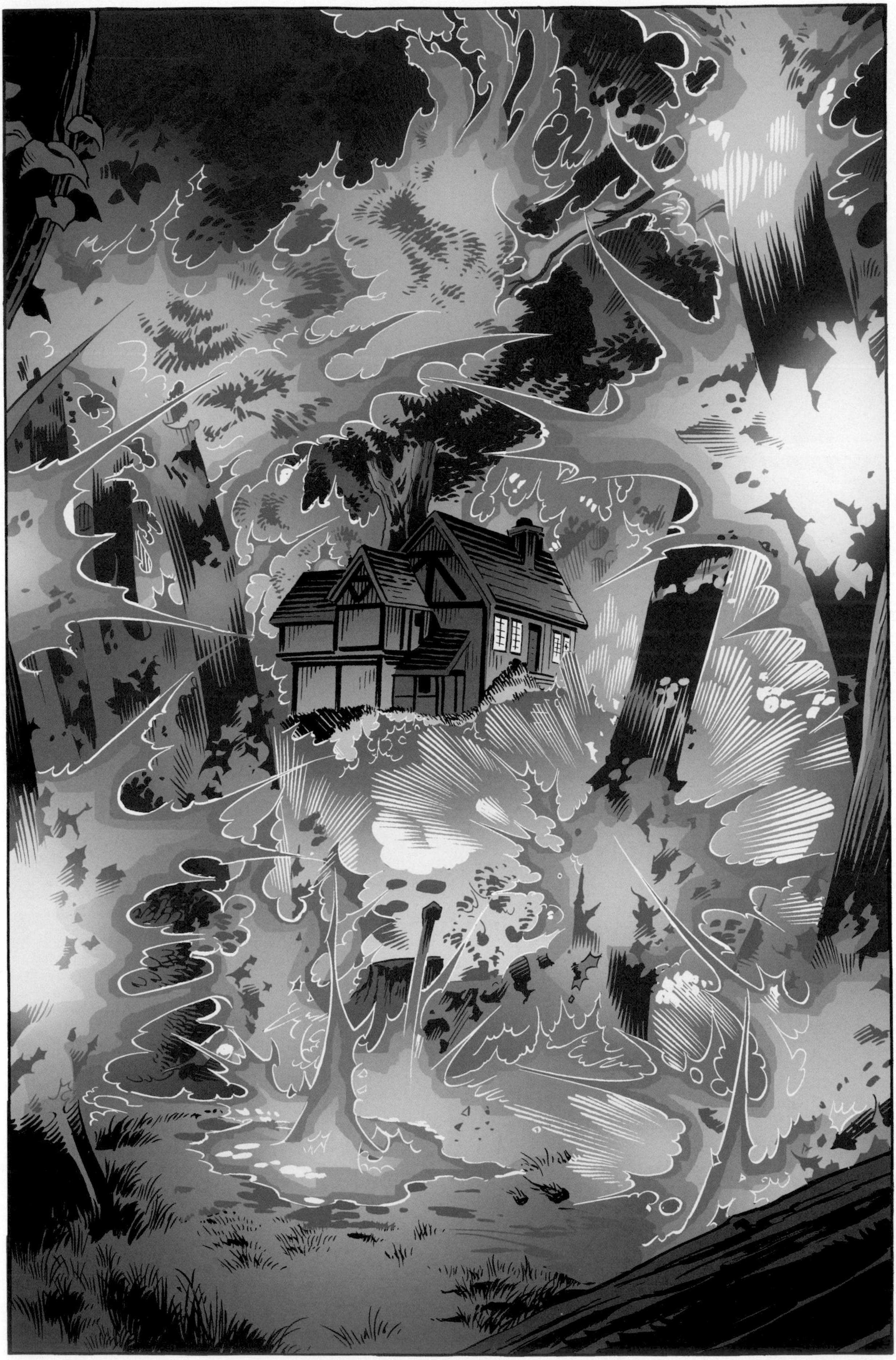

SOMETIME LATER...

COME ON, OLD MAN. YOUR CABIN'S STARTED TO BURN.

AND EVEN IF THOSE SPELLS PROTECT YOU FROM BURNING UP WITH IT, I *DOUBT* YOU'LL WANT TO WAIT FOR THEM TO FIND YOU TWO UNDER THE SCORCHED REMAINS.

:COUGH- COUGH!:

I'VE JUST TAKEN YOUR MAGIC GROVE AWAY FROM YOU.

YEAH, I KNOW IT'LL GROW BACK--EVENTUALLY--BUT I SUSPECT IT'LL BE AT LEAST A GENERATION BEFORE YOU CAN PRODUCE NEW WOODEN CHILDREN FROM IT.

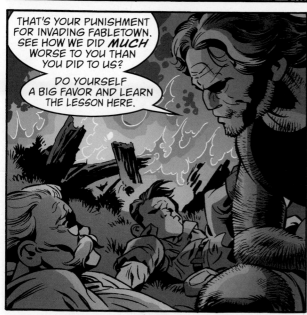

THAT'S YOUR PUNISHMENT FOR INVADING FABLETOWN. SEE HOW WE DID *MUCH* WORSE TO YOU THAN YOU DID TO US?

DO YOURSELF A BIG FAVOR AND LEARN THE LESSON HERE.

THAT WAS THE STICK, NOW HERE'S THE CARROT. MOST OF THE HEADS FROM YOUR INVASION FORCE ARE STILL ALIVE.

WE MIGHT BE WILLING TO EXCHANGE THEM FOR THINGS WE WANT--IF YOU CAN CONVINCE US YOU'RE INCLINED TO BE *NICE* FROM NOW ON.

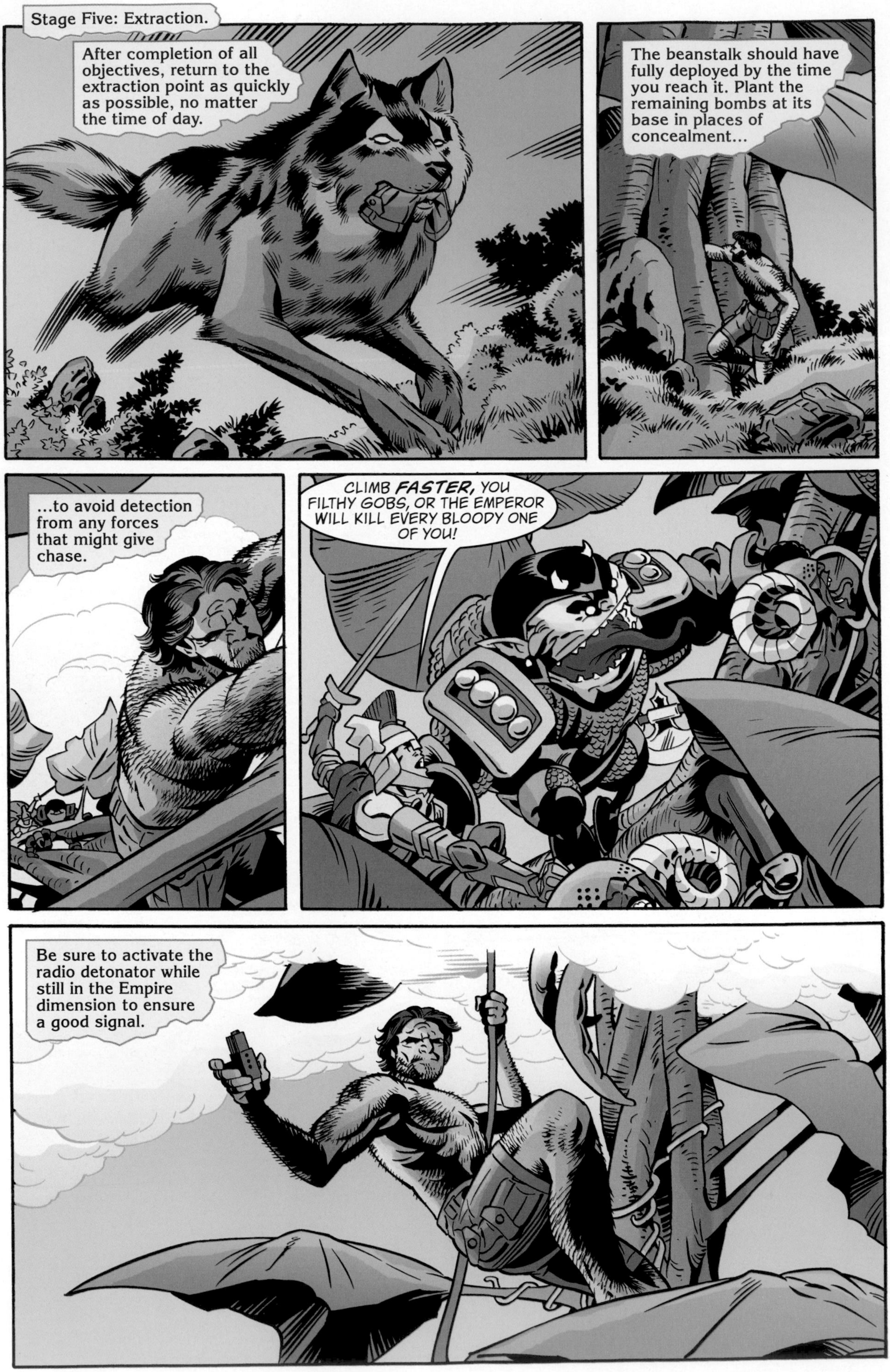
Stage Five: Extraction.
After completion of all objectives, return to the extraction point as quickly as possible, no matter the time of day.
The beanstalk should have fully deployed by the time you reach it. Plant the remaining bombs at its base in places of concealment...
...to avoid detection from any forces that might give chase.
CLIMB FASTER, YOU FILTHY GOBS, OR THE EMPEROR WILL KILL EVERY BLOODY ONE OF YOU!
Be sure to activate the radio detonator while still in the Empire dimension to ensure a good signal.

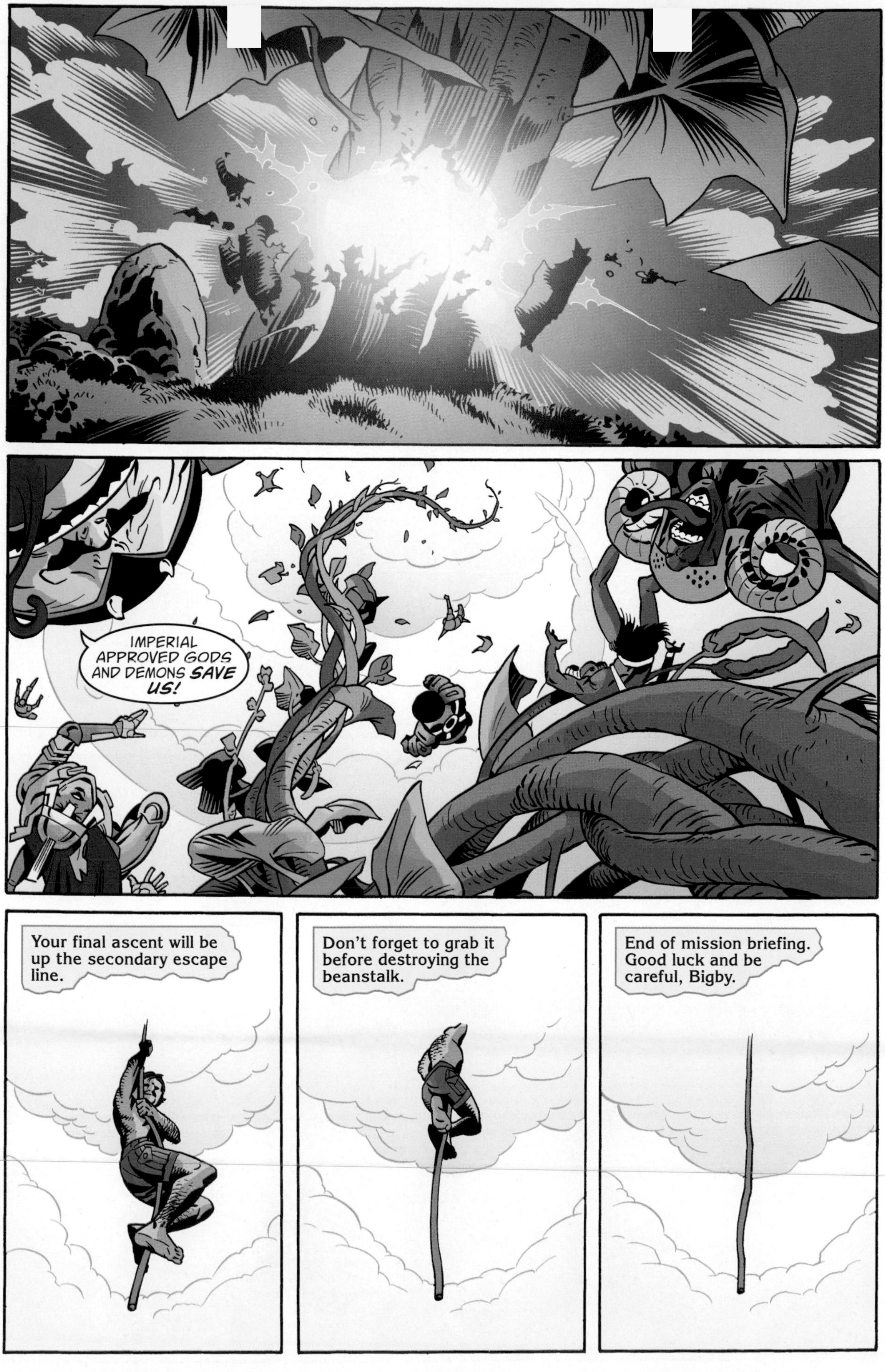
IMPERIAL APPROVED GODS AND DEMONS *SAVE US!*
Your final ascent will be up the secondary escape line.
Don't forget to grab it before destroying the beanstalk.
End of mission briefing. Good luck and be careful, Bigby.

CHAPTER FIVE: HOME IS THE HUNTER

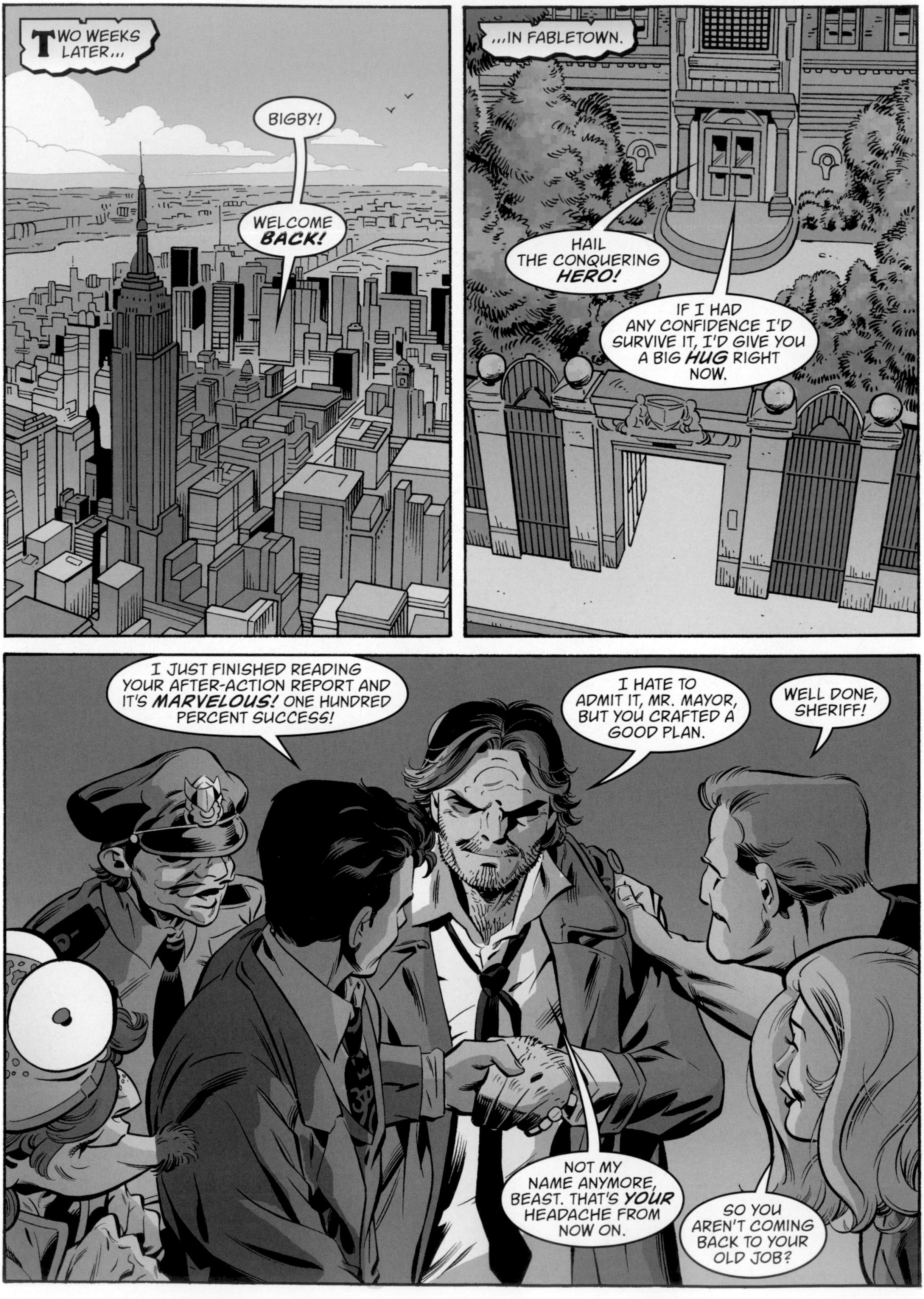

TWO WEEKS LATER...
BIGBY!
WELCOME BACK!
...IN FABLETOWN.
HAIL THE CONQUERING HERO!
IF I HAD ANY CONFIDENCE I'D SURVIVE IT, I'D GIVE YOU A BIG HUG RIGHT NOW.
I JUST FINISHED READING YOUR AFTER-ACTION REPORT AND IT'S MARVELOUS! ONE HUNDRED PERCENT SUCCESS!
I HATE TO ADMIT IT, MR. MAYOR, BUT YOU CRAFTED A GOOD PLAN.
WELL DONE, SHERIFF!
NOT MY NAME ANYMORE, BEAST. THAT'S YOUR HEADACHE FROM NOW ON.
SO YOU AREN'T COMING BACK TO YOUR OLD JOB?

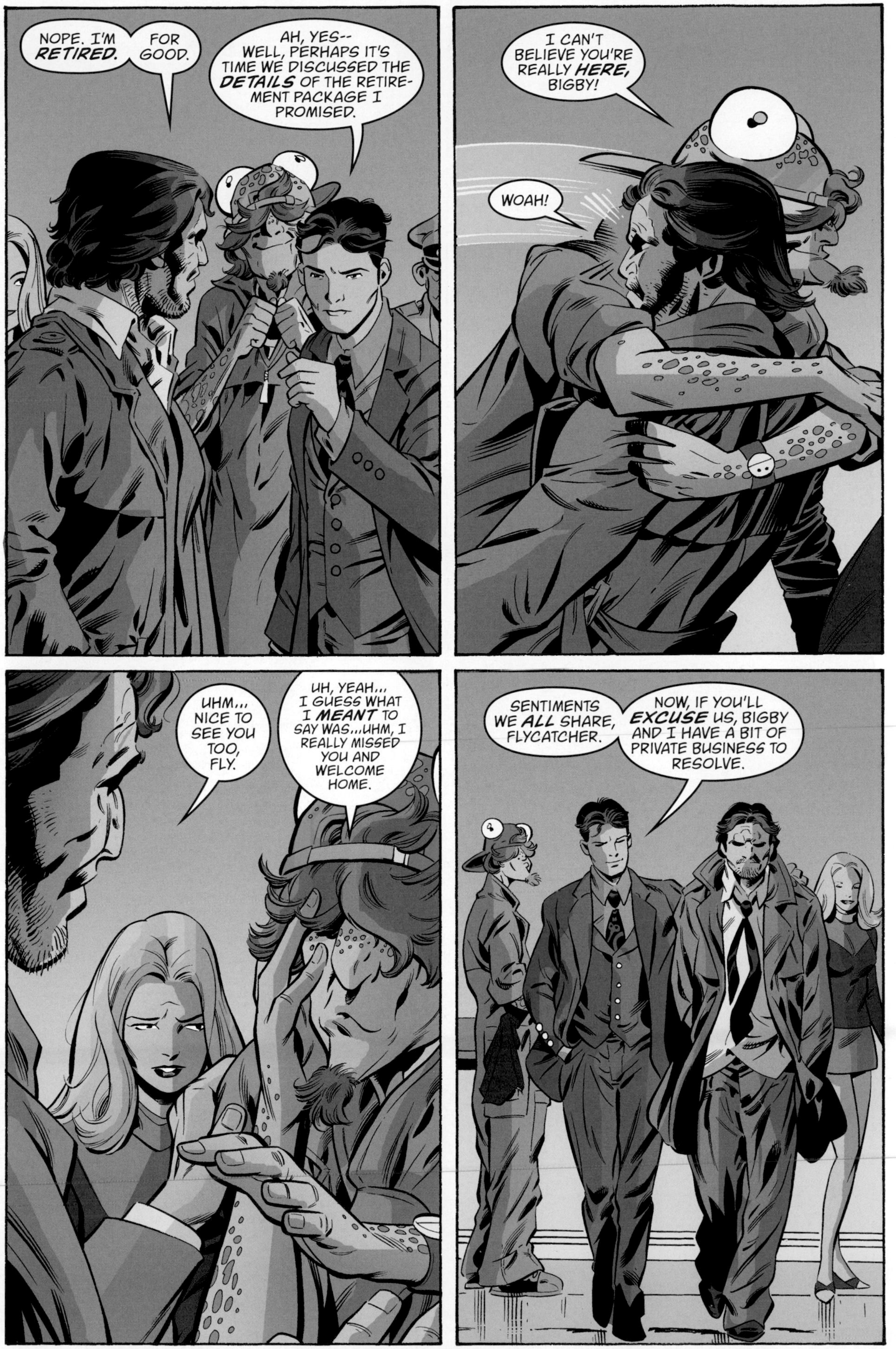
NOPE. I'M RETIRED.
FOR GOOD.
AH, YES-- WELL, PERHAPS IT'S TIME WE DISCUSSED THE DETAILS OF THE RETIREMENT PACKAGE I PROMISED.
I CAN'T BELIEVE YOU'RE REALLY HERE, BIGBY!
WOAH!
UHM... NICE TO SEE YOU TOO, FLY.
UH, YEAH... I GUESS WHAT I MEANT TO SAY WAS...UHM, I REALLY MISSED YOU AND WELCOME HOME.
SENTIMENTS WE ALL SHARE, FLYCATCHER.
NOW, IF YOU'LL EXCUSE US, BIGBY AND I HAVE A BIT OF PRIVATE BUSINESS TO RESOLVE.

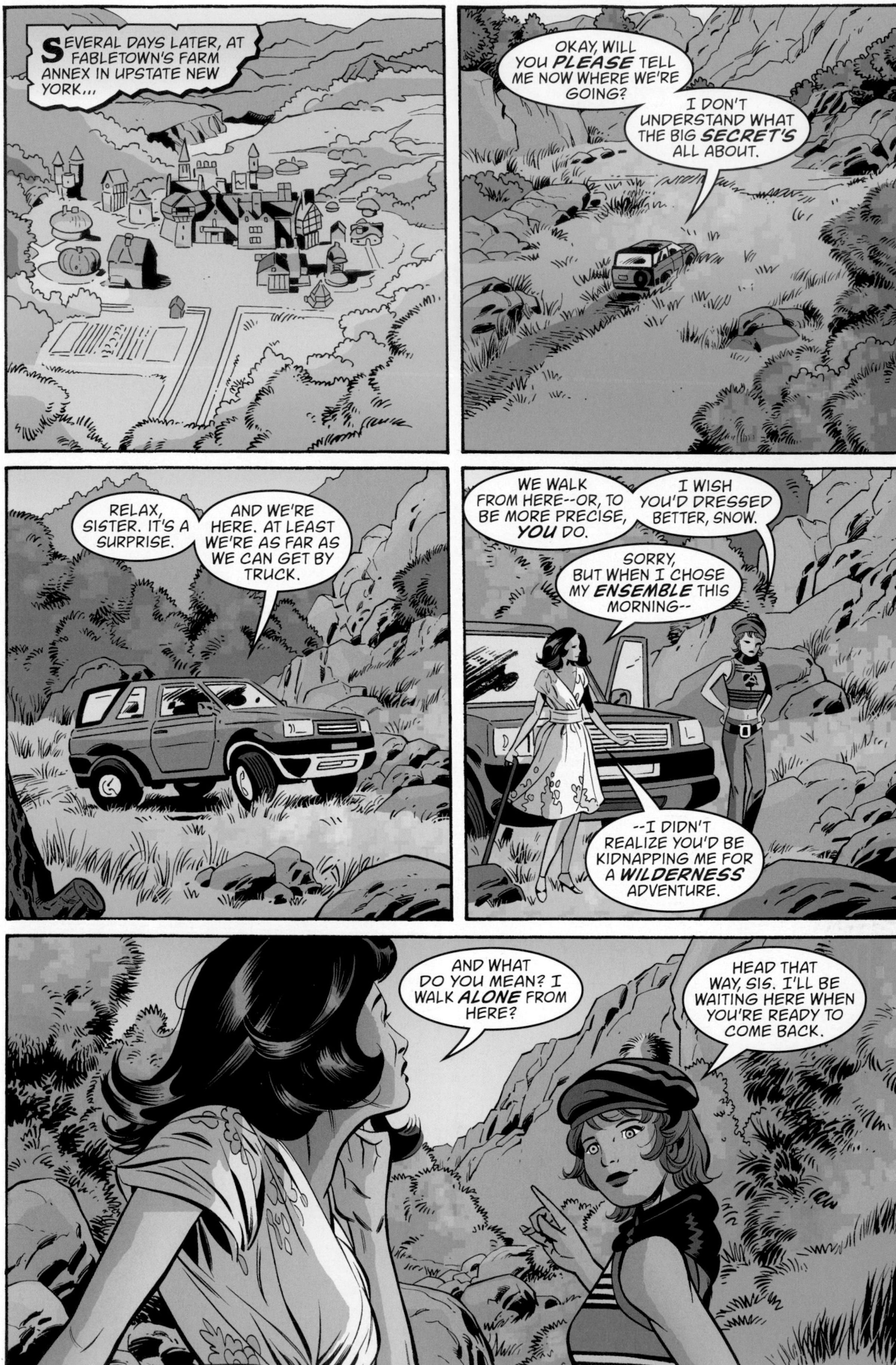
SEVERAL DAYS LATER, AT FABLETOWN'S FARM ANNEX IN UPSTATE NEW YORK...
OKAY, WILL YOU PLEASE TELL ME NOW WHERE WE'RE GOING?
I DON'T UNDERSTAND WHAT THE BIG SECRET'S ALL ABOUT.
RELAX, SISTER. IT'S A SURPRISE.
AND WE'RE HERE. AT LEAST WE'RE AS FAR AS WE CAN GET BY TRUCK.
WE WALK FROM HERE--OR, TO BE MORE PRECISE, YOU DO.
I WISH YOU'D DRESSED BETTER, SNOW.
SORRY, BUT WHEN I CHOSE MY ENSEMBLE THIS MORNING--
--I DIDN'T REALIZE YOU'D BE KIDNAPPING ME FOR A WILDERNESS ADVENTURE.
AND WHAT DO YOU MEAN? I WALK ALONE FROM HERE?
HEAD THAT WAY, SIS. I'LL BE WAITING HERE WHEN YOU'RE READY TO COME BACK.

CHAPTER SIX: RESTORATION

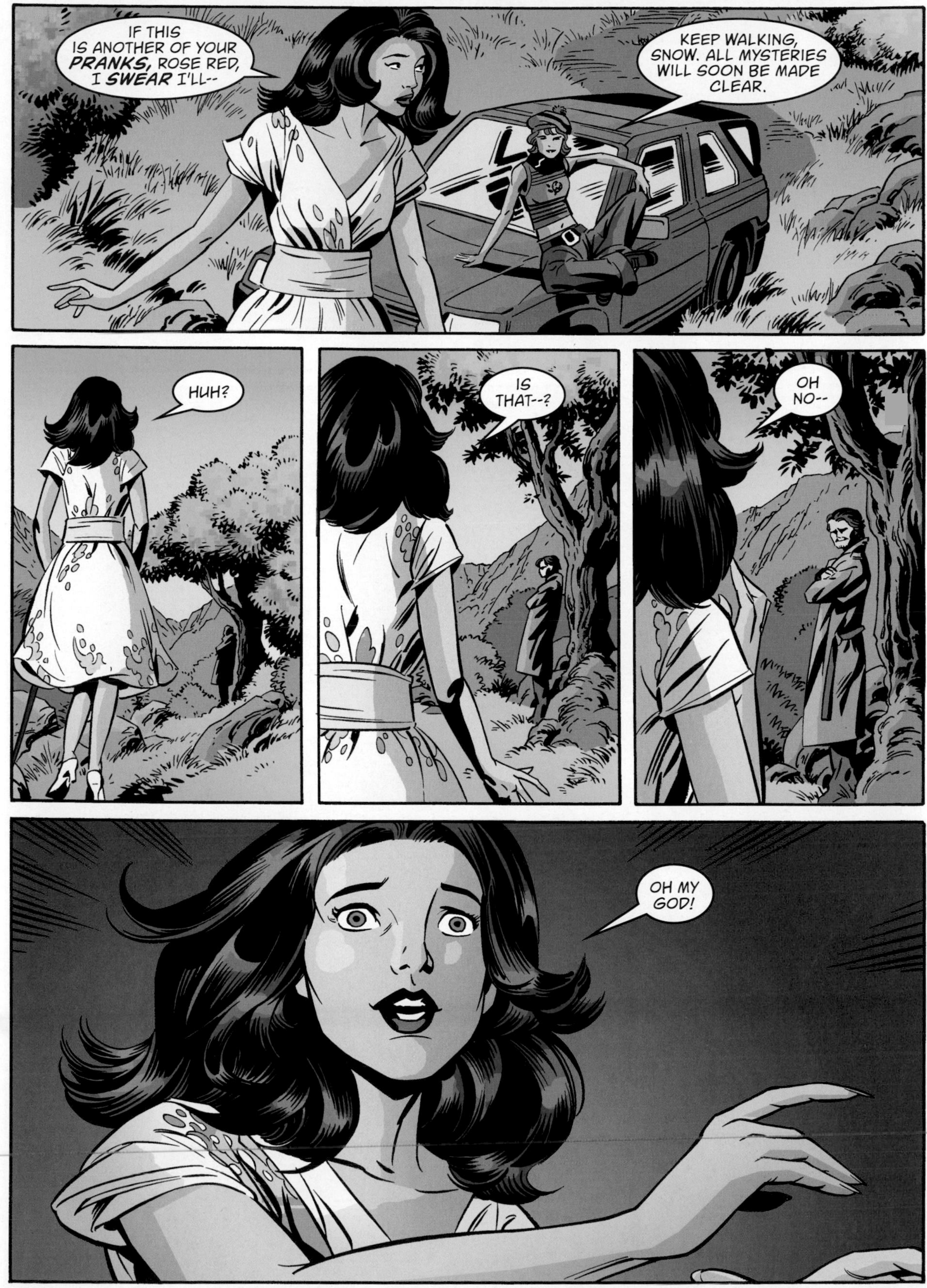
IF THIS IS ANOTHER OF YOUR *PRANKS,* ROSE RED, I *SWEAR* I'LL--
KEEP WALKING, SNOW. ALL MYSTERIES WILL SOON BE MADE CLEAR.
HUH?
IS THAT--?
OH NO--
OH MY GOD!

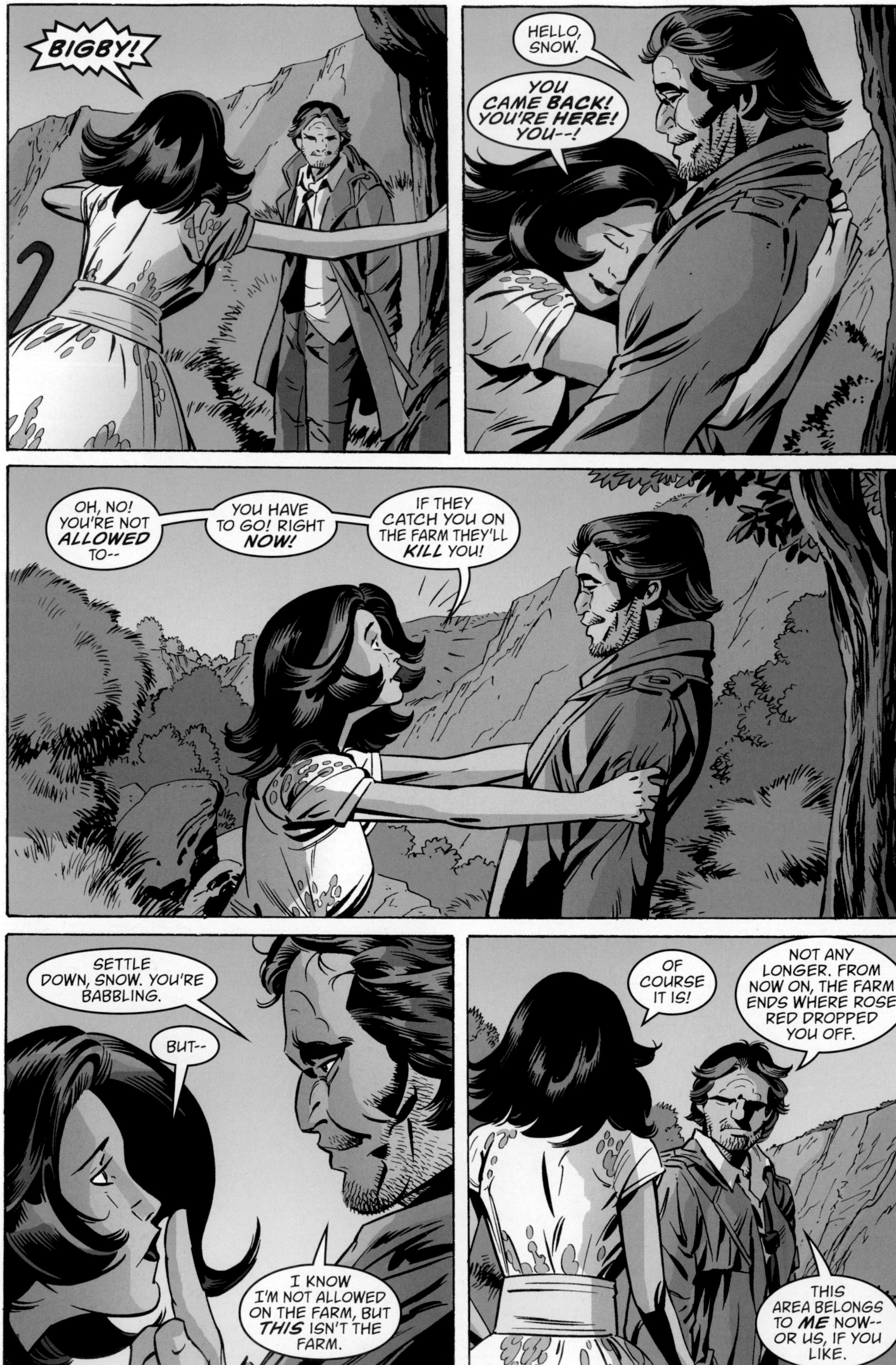

BIGBY!
HELLO, SNOW.
YOU CAME BACK! YOU'RE HERE! YOU--!
OH, NO! YOU'RE NOT ALLOWED TO--
YOU HAVE TO GO! RIGHT NOW!
IF THEY CATCH YOU ON THE FARM THEY'LL KILL YOU!
SETTLE DOWN, SNOW. YOU'RE BABBLING.
BUT--
I KNOW I'M NOT ALLOWED ON THE FARM, BUT THIS ISN'T THE FARM.
OF COURSE IT IS!
NOT ANY LONGER. FROM NOW ON, THE FARM ENDS WHERE ROSE RED DROPPED YOU OFF.
THIS AREA BELONGS TO ME NOW--OR US, IF YOU LIKE.

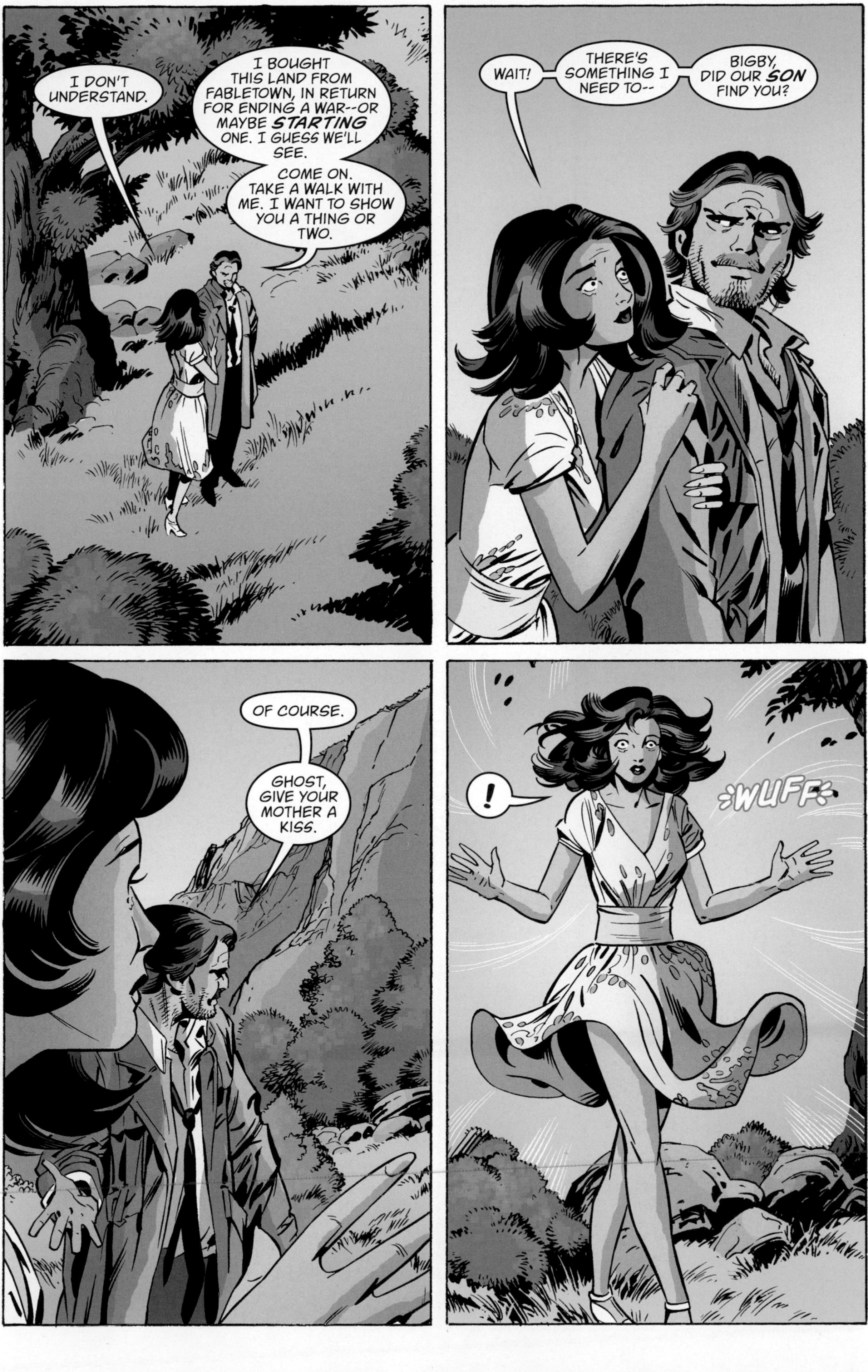
I DON'T UNDERSTAND.
I BOUGHT THIS LAND FROM FABLETOWN, IN RETURN FOR ENDING A WAR--OR MAYBE STARTING ONE. I GUESS WE'LL SEE.
COME ON. TAKE A WALK WITH ME. I WANT TO SHOW YOU A THING OR TWO.
WAIT!
THERE'S SOMETHING I NEED TO--
BIGBY, DID OUR SON FIND YOU?
OF COURSE.
GHOST, GIVE YOUR MOTHER A KISS.
!
WUFF

CHAPTER SEVEN: THE BIG VALLEY

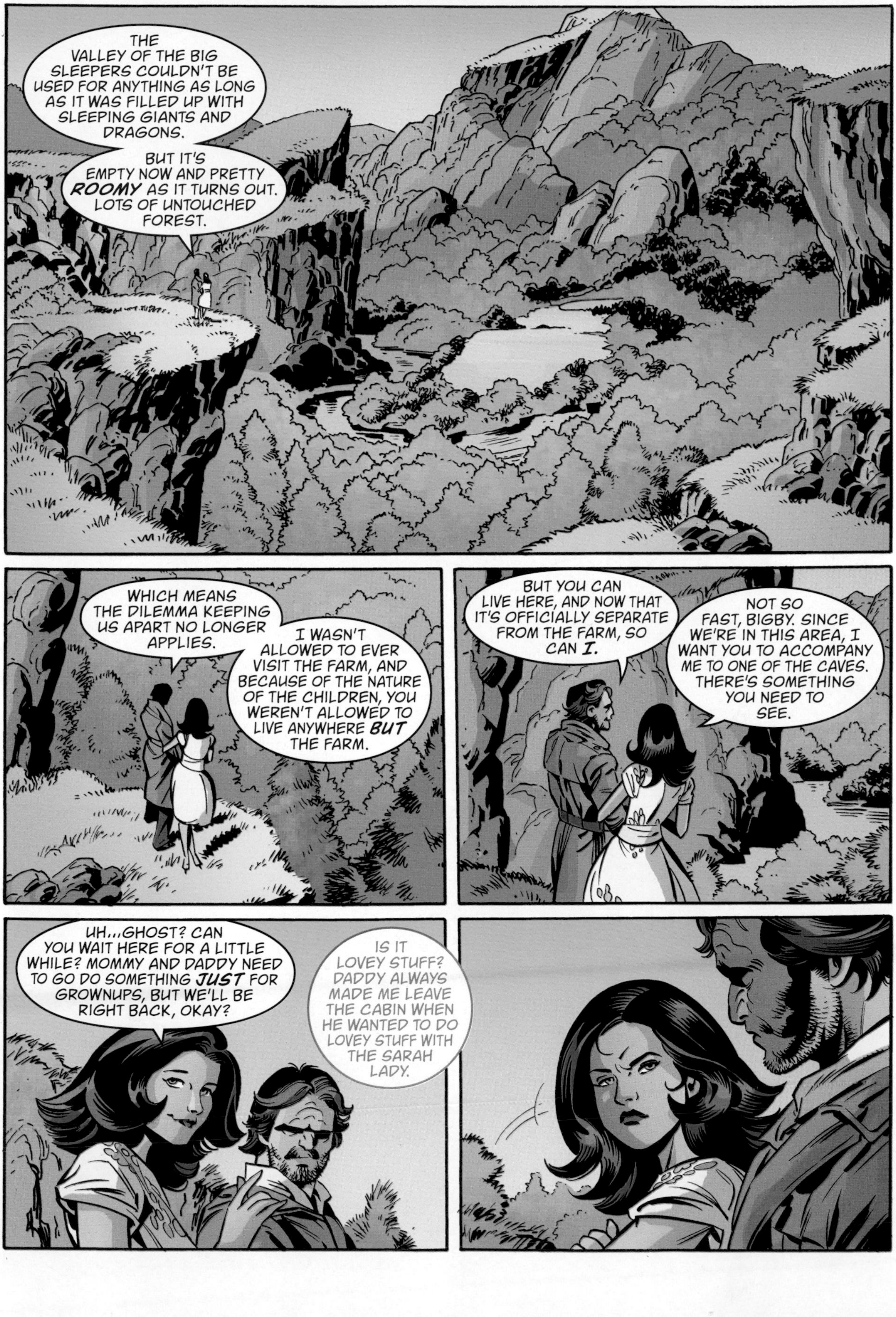

THE VALLEY OF THE BIG SLEEPERS COULDN'T BE USED FOR ANYTHING AS LONG AS IT WAS FILLED UP WITH SLEEPING GIANTS AND DRAGONS.
BUT IT'S EMPTY NOW AND PRETTY ROOMY AS IT TURNS OUT. LOTS OF UNTOUCHED FOREST.
WHICH MEANS THE DILEMMA KEEPING US APART NO LONGER APPLIES.
I WASN'T ALLOWED TO EVER VISIT THE FARM, AND BECAUSE OF THE NATURE OF THE CHILDREN, YOU WEREN'T ALLOWED TO LIVE ANYWHERE BUT THE FARM.
BUT YOU CAN LIVE HERE, AND NOW THAT IT'S OFFICIALLY SEPARATE FROM THE FARM, SO CAN I.
NOT SO FAST, BIGBY. SINCE WE'RE IN THIS AREA, I WANT YOU TO ACCOMPANY ME TO ONE OF THE CAVES. THERE'S SOMETHING YOU NEED TO SEE.
UH...GHOST? CAN YOU WAIT HERE FOR A LITTLE WHILE? MOMMY AND DADDY NEED TO GO DO SOMETHING JUST FOR GROWNUPS, BUT WE'LL BE RIGHT BACK, OKAY?
IS IT LOVEY STUFF? DADDY ALWAYS MADE ME LEAVE THE CABIN WHEN HE WANTED TO DO LOVEY STUFF WITH THE SARAH LADY.

OKAY, *THAT'S* A CONVERSATION WE NEED TO HAVE REAL SOON.

BUT FIRST THINGS FIRST.

SINCE THERE ARE SO MANY NATURAL CAVES IN THESE HILLS, I DECIDED TO USE ONE TO KEEP CERTAIN THINGS HIDDEN.

YOU HAVE SOME WORK TO DO BEFORE I CAN LET YOU SEE THE KIDS--OUR *OTHER* KIDS.

FIRST SOME READING. THIS BOX IS FULL OF ALL THE LETTERS THEY WROTE YOU. EACH ONE HAS A COPY OF YOUR REPLY PAPER-CLIPPED TO IT.

THEN YOU CAN UNWRAP ALL THE GIFTS THEY SENT YOU FOR CHRISTMAS, BIRTHDAYS, AND FATHER'S DAY.

MAKE *DAMN* SURE YOU MEMORIZE WHO GAVE YOU WHAT.

AND FINALLY WE'LL GO OVER THE GIFTS YOU SENT THEM, SO IT DOESN'T COME AS A *COMPLETE* SURPRISE TO YOU WHEN THEY MENTION THEM.

GOT IT.

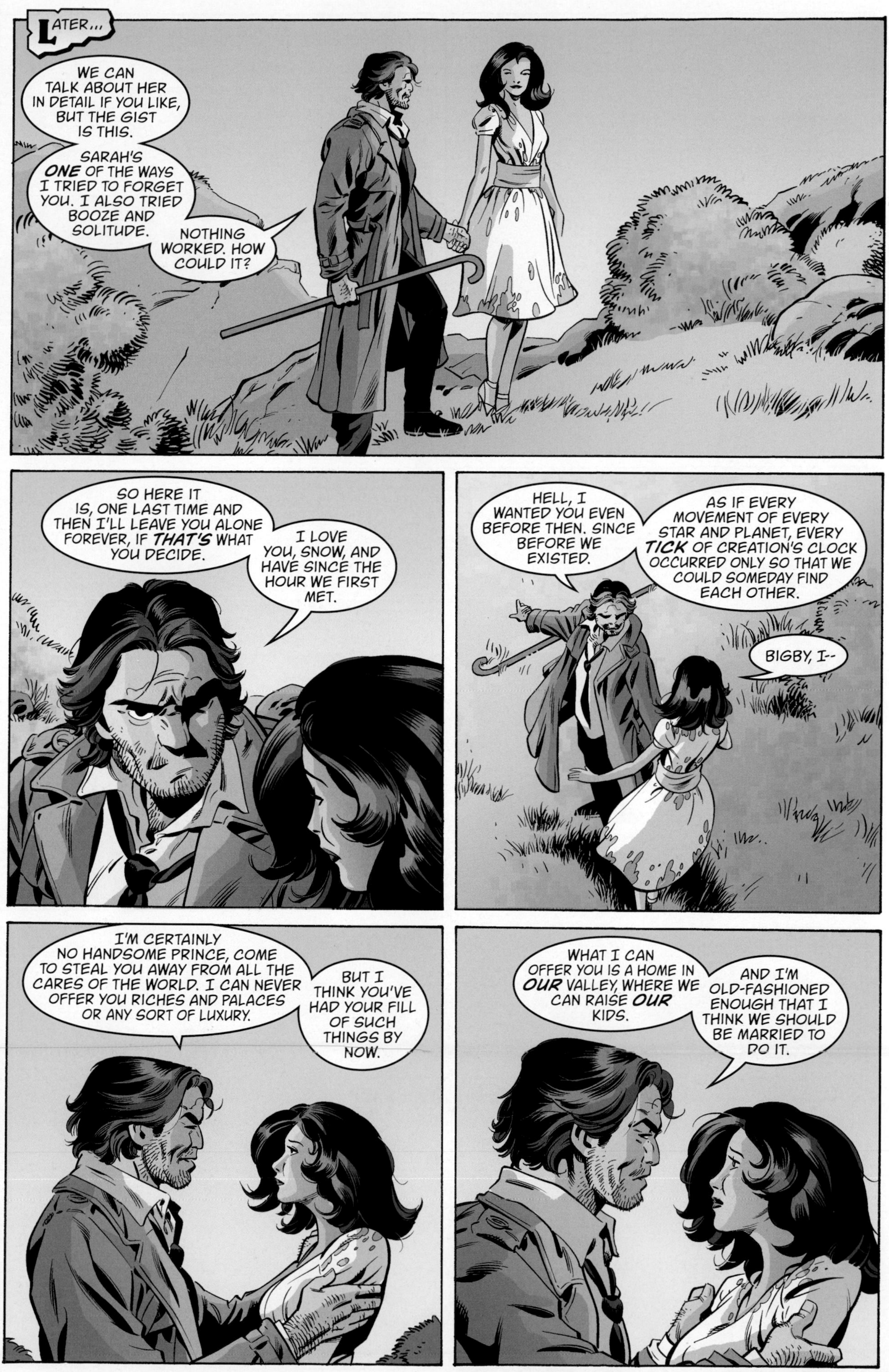
LATER...
WE CAN TALK ABOUT HER IN DETAIL IF YOU LIKE, BUT THE GIST IS THIS.
SARAH'S ONE OF THE WAYS I TRIED TO FORGET YOU. I ALSO TRIED BOOZE AND SOLITUDE.
NOTHING WORKED. HOW COULD IT?
SO HERE IT IS, ONE LAST TIME AND THEN I'LL LEAVE YOU ALONE FOREVER, IF THAT'S WHAT YOU DECIDE.
I LOVE YOU, SNOW, AND HAVE SINCE THE HOUR WE FIRST MET.
HELL, I WANTED YOU EVEN BEFORE THEN. SINCE BEFORE WE EXISTED.
AS IF EVERY MOVEMENT OF EVERY STAR AND PLANET, EVERY TICK OF CREATION'S CLOCK OCCURRED ONLY SO THAT WE COULD SOMEDAY FIND EACH OTHER.
BIGBY, I--
I'M CERTAINLY NO HANDSOME PRINCE, COME TO STEAL YOU AWAY FROM ALL THE CARES OF THE WORLD. I CAN NEVER OFFER YOU RICHES AND PALACES OR ANY SORT OF LUXURY.
BUT I THINK YOU'VE HAD YOUR FILL OF SUCH THINGS BY NOW.
WHAT I CAN OFFER YOU IS A HOME IN OUR VALLEY, WHERE WE CAN RAISE OUR KIDS.
AND I'M OLD-FASHIONED ENOUGH THAT I THINK WE SHOULD BE MARRIED TO DO IT.

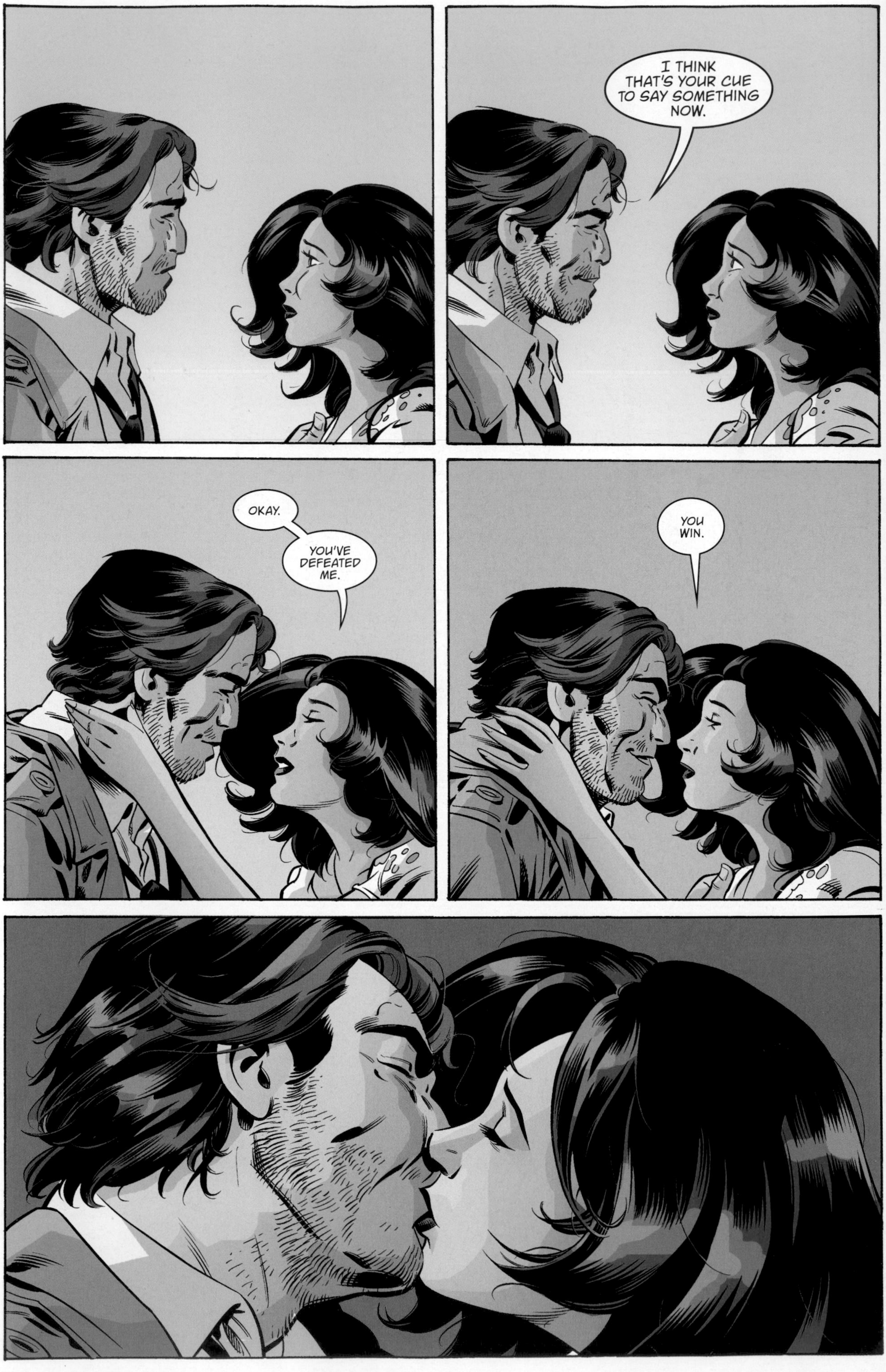
I THINK THAT'S YOUR CUE TO SAY SOMETHING NOW.
OKAY.
YOU'VE DEFEATED ME.
YOU WIN.

CHAPTER EIGHT: THE WEDDING

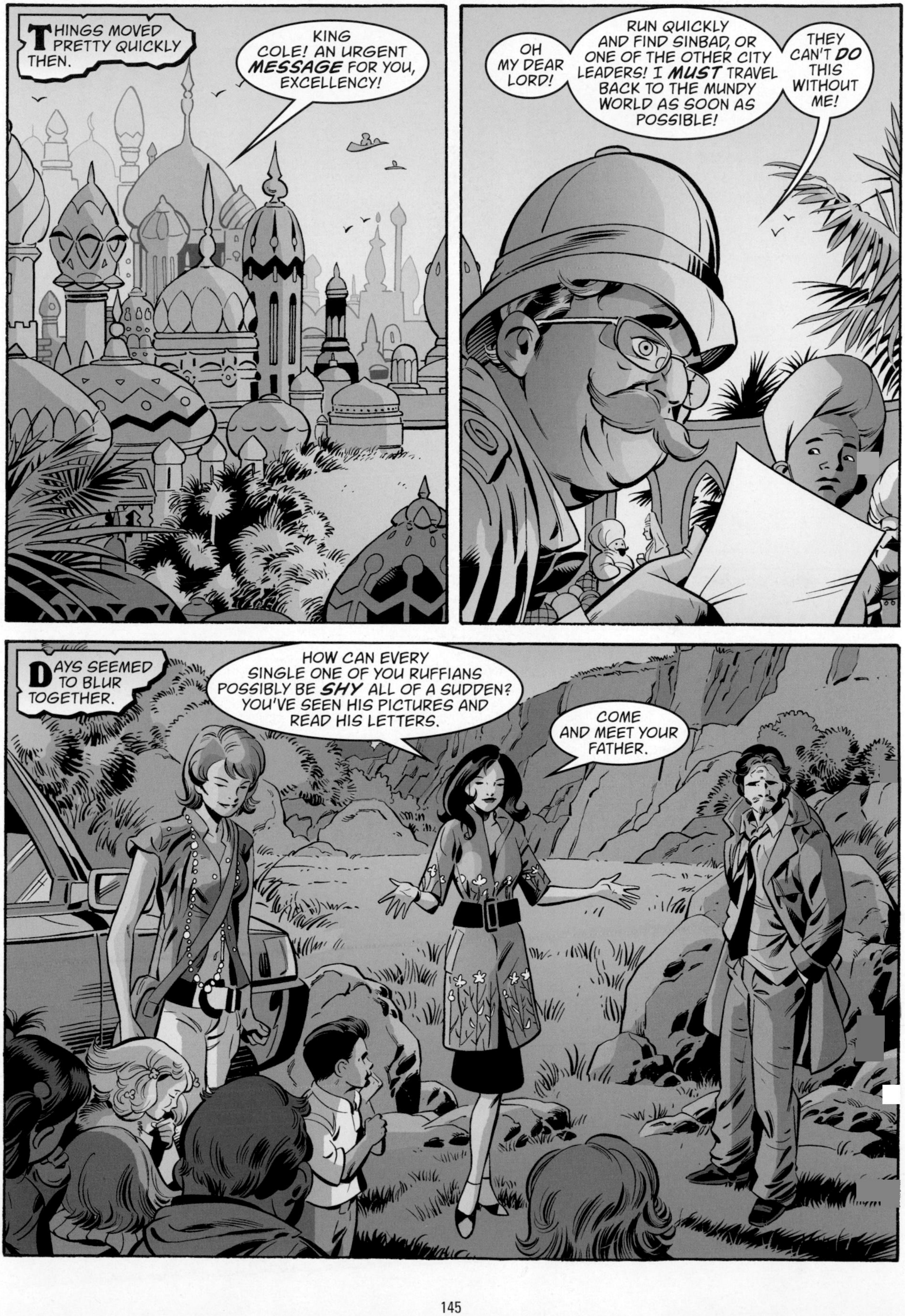
THINGS MOVED PRETTY QUICKLY THEN.
KING COLE! AN URGENT MESSAGE FOR YOU, EXCELLENCY!
OH MY DEAR LORD!
RUN QUICKLY AND FIND SINBAD, OR ONE OF THE OTHER CITY LEADERS! I MUST TRAVEL BACK TO THE MUNDY WORLD AS SOON AS POSSIBLE!
THEY CAN'T DO THIS WITHOUT ME!
DAYS SEEMED TO BLUR TOGETHER.
HOW CAN EVERY SINGLE ONE OF YOU RUFFIANS POSSIBLY BE SHY ALL OF A SUDDEN? YOU'VE SEEN HIS PICTURES AND READ HIS LETTERS.
COME AND MEET YOUR FATHER.

PLANS WERE MADE.

WHAT I HAVE TO SAY IS SIMPLY THIS.

IF YOU PICK ANYONE ELSE AS YOUR MAID OF HONOR, *FORGET* FREE BABYSITTING FOREVER.

REYNARD! *FINALLY!* WHERE ARE THE TROLLS?

RELAX, BOY BLUE. THEY'RE ON THE WAY. THEY DON'T MOVE AS FAST AS *I* DO. BUT THEY'RE STURDY. EACH ONE CAN PACK A TON.

GOOD, BECAUSE THIS IS AS FAR AS THE TRUCKS WILL GO, AND WE NEED TO GET ALL OF THIS HEAVY STUFF OVER THOSE HILLS.

I'VE PUT UP NOTICES FOR EVERY CARPENTER, PLUMBER, BRICK-LAYER AND STONE MASON IN FABLE-TOWN.

GET THEM ALL OUT HERE BY *YESTERDAY,* FLY.

I'M DETERMINED TO HAVE THEIR HOUSE FINISHED BY THE TIME THEY GET BACK FROM THEIR HONEY-MOON.

I'M IN THE AIR NOW, MAYBE SIX HOURS OUT. WHATEVER YOU DO, DON'T LET THEM START *WITHOUT* ME!

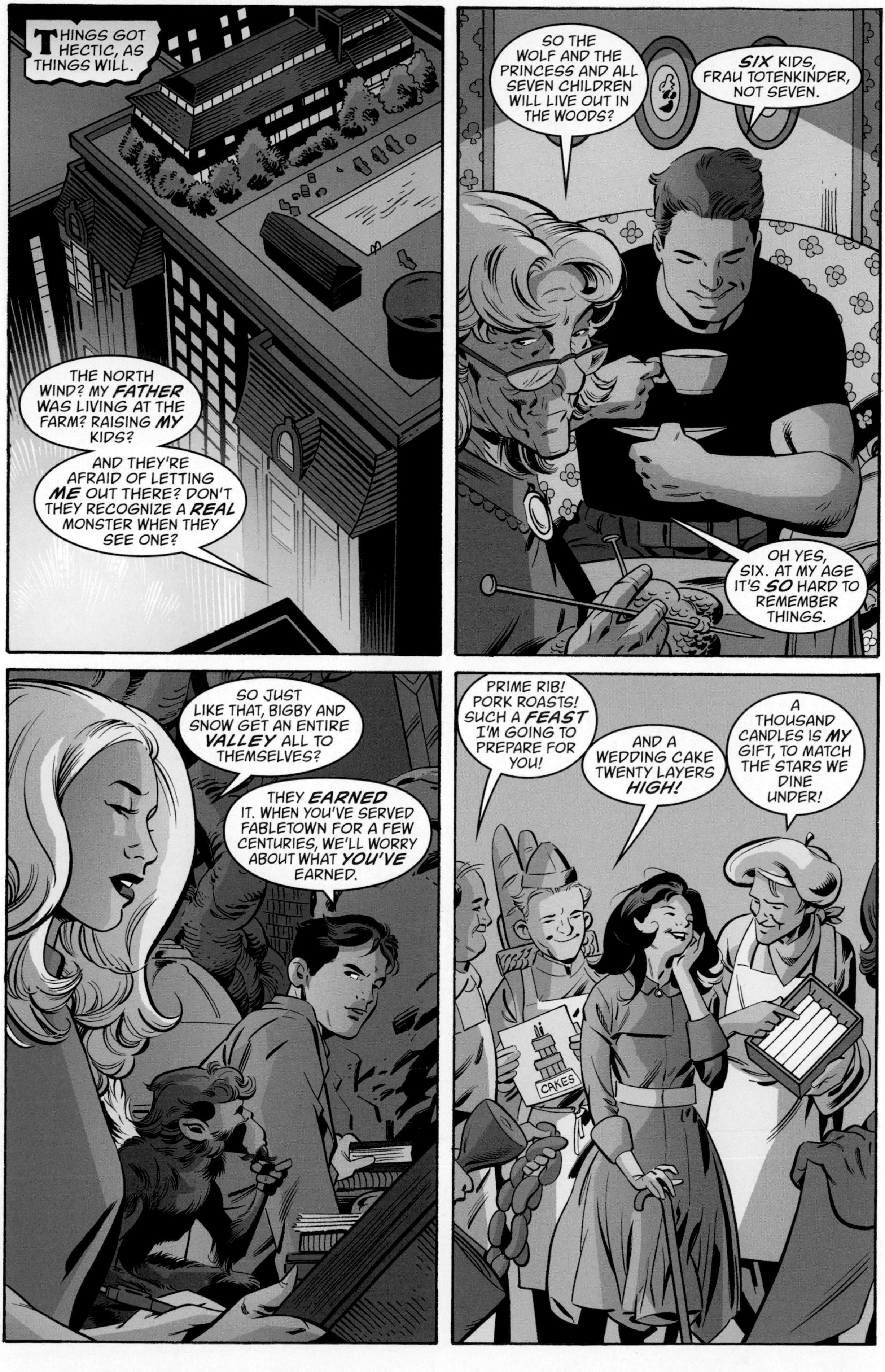
THINGS GOT HECTIC, AS THINGS WILL.
SO THE WOLF AND THE PRINCESS AND ALL SEVEN CHILDREN WILL LIVE OUT IN THE WOODS?
SIX KIDS, FRAU TOTENKINDER, NOT SEVEN.
THE NORTH WIND? MY FATHER WAS LIVING AT THE FARM? RAISING MY KIDS?
AND THEY'RE AFRAID OF LETTING ME OUT THERE? DON'T THEY RECOGNIZE A REAL MONSTER WHEN THEY SEE ONE?
OH YES, SIX. AT MY AGE IT'S SO HARD TO REMEMBER THINGS.
SO JUST LIKE THAT, BIGBY AND SNOW GET AN ENTIRE VALLEY ALL TO THEMSELVES?
THEY EARNED IT. WHEN YOU'VE SERVED FABLETOWN FOR A FEW CENTURIES, WE'LL WORRY ABOUT WHAT YOU'VE EARNED.
PRIME RIB! PORK ROASTS! SUCH A FEAST I'M GOING TO PREPARE FOR YOU!
AND A WEDDING CAKE TWENTY LAYERS HIGH!
A THOUSAND CANDLES IS MY GIFT, TO MATCH THE STARS WE DINE UNDER!
CAKES

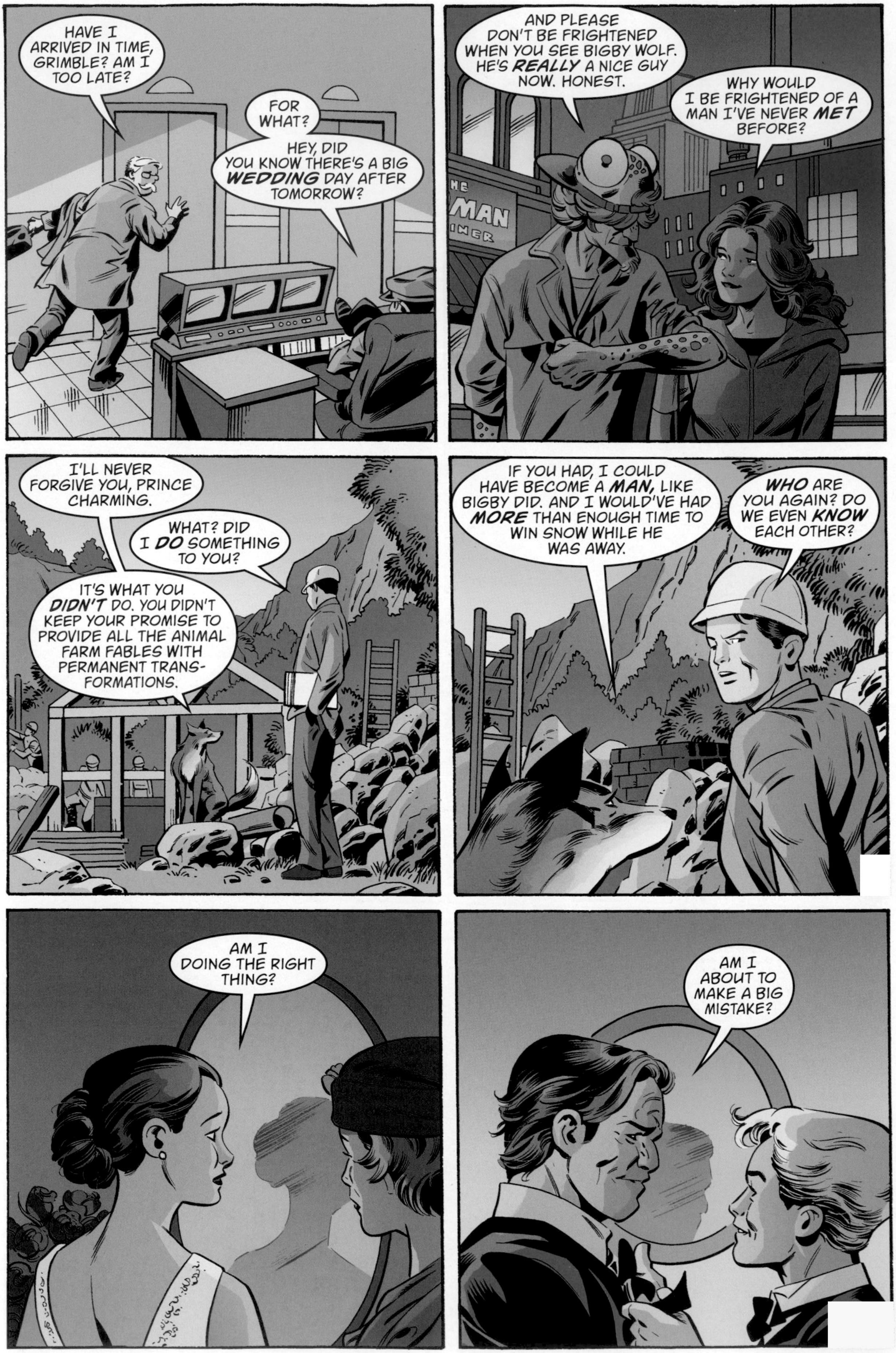
HAVE I ARRIVED IN TIME, GRIMBLE? AM I TOO LATE?
FOR WHAT?
HEY, DID YOU KNOW THERE'S A BIG WEDDING DAY AFTER TOMORROW?
AND PLEASE DON'T BE FRIGHTENED WHEN YOU SEE BIGBY WOLF. HE'S REALLY A NICE GUY NOW. HONEST.
WHY WOULD I BE FRIGHTENED OF A MAN I'VE NEVER MET BEFORE?
I'LL NEVER FORGIVE YOU, PRINCE CHARMING.
WHAT? DID I DO SOMETHING TO YOU?
IT'S WHAT YOU DIDN'T DO. YOU DIDN'T KEEP YOUR PROMISE TO PROVIDE ALL THE ANIMAL FARM FABLES WITH PERMANENT TRANS-FORMATIONS.
IF YOU HAD, I COULD HAVE BECOME A MAN, LIKE BIGBY DID. AND I WOULD'VE HAD MORE THAN ENOUGH TIME TO WIN SNOW WHILE HE WAS AWAY.
WHO ARE YOU AGAIN? DO WE EVEN KNOW EACH OTHER?
AM I DOING THE RIGHT THING?
AM I ABOUT TO MAKE A BIG MISTAKE?

YOU MAY *KISS* THE BRIDE.

*S*O THEY FEASTED.

*A*ND TOASTED EACH OTHER.

TO THE FINEST MAN AND THE FINEST WOMAN IT HAS BEEN MY *GOOD* FORTUNE TO KNOW.

*A*ND CELEBRATED THE JOYOUS DAY.

WHERE ARE MOMMY AND DADDY GOING NOW?

SOME-WHERE YOU'RE NOT INVITED, WOLFLING.

THAT'S ODD. HE DOES SEEM FAMILIAR--AS IF WE'D MET BEFORE.

EPILOGUE: MR. AND MRS. WOLF

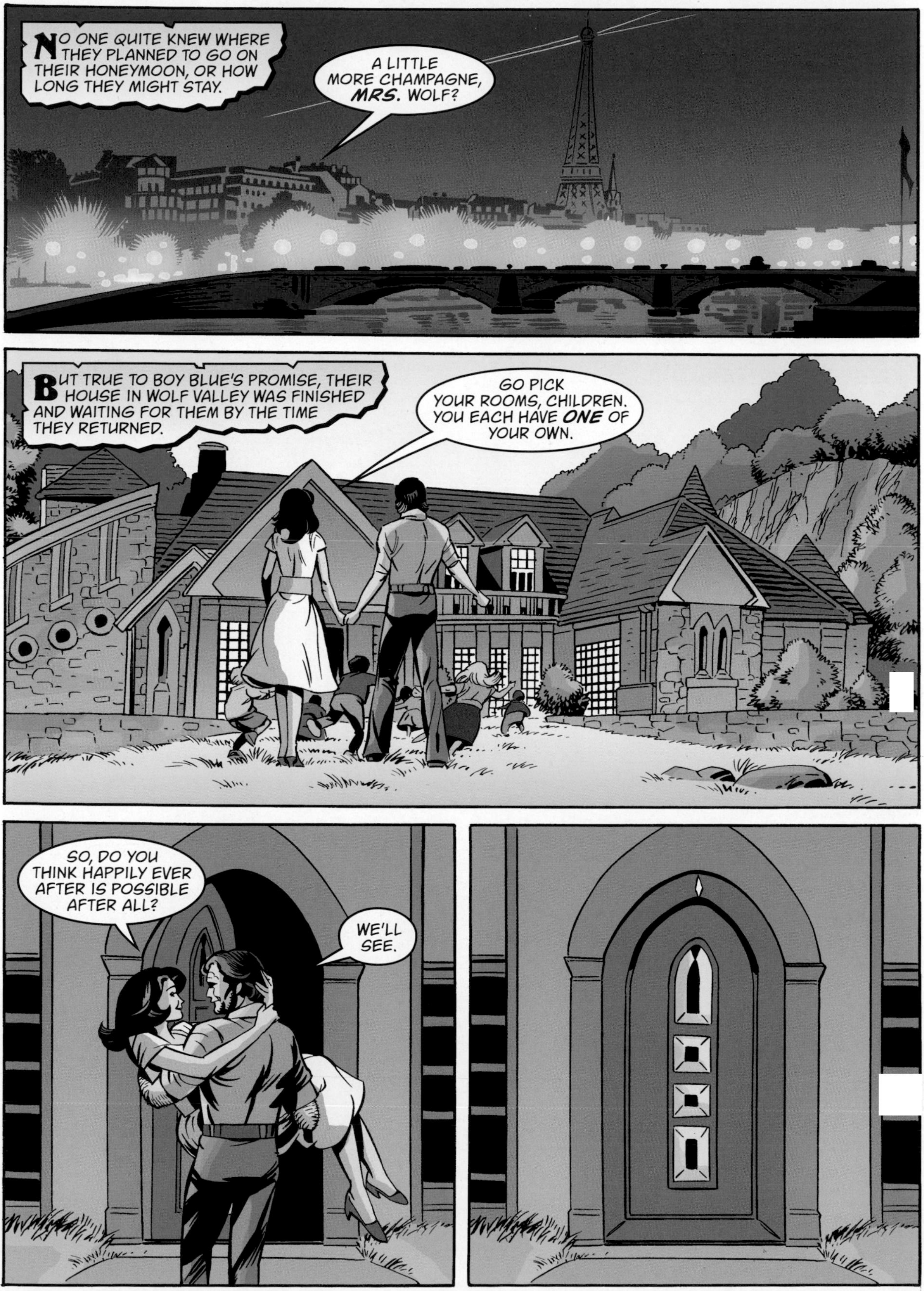
NO ONE QUITE KNEW WHERE THEY PLANNED TO GO ON THEIR HONEYMOON, OR HOW LONG THEY MIGHT STAY.
A LITTLE MORE CHAMPAGNE, *MRS.* WOLF?
BUT TRUE TO BOY BLUE'S PROMISE, THEIR HOUSE IN WOLF VALLEY WAS FINISHED AND WAITING FOR THEM BY THE TIME THEY RETURNED.
GO PICK YOUR ROOMS, CHILDREN. YOU EACH HAVE *ONE* OF YOUR OWN.
SO, DO YOU THINK HAPPILY EVER AFTER IS POSSIBLE AFTER ALL?
WE'LL SEE.

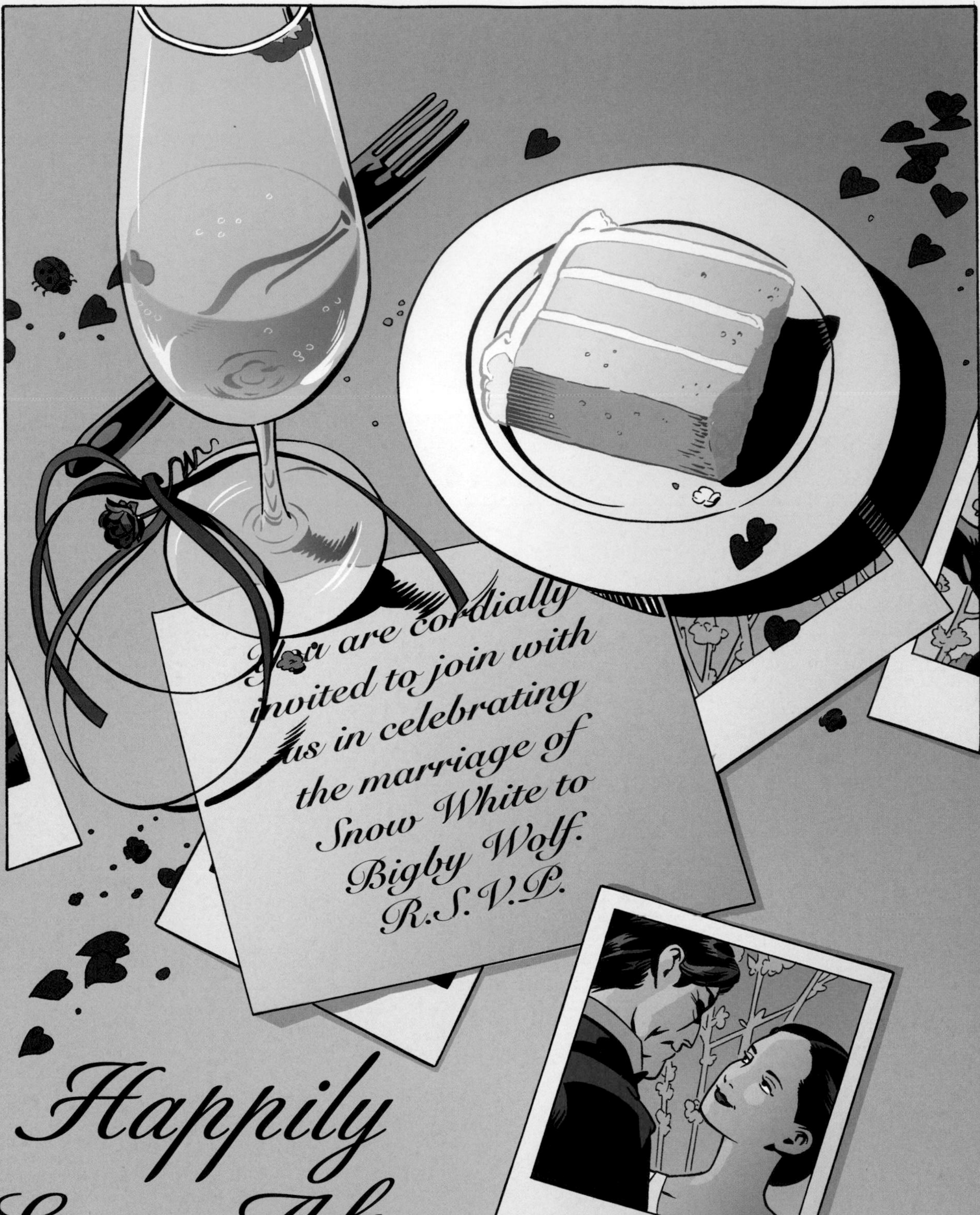
You are cordially invited to join with us in celebrating the marriage of Snow White to Bigby Wolf. R.S.V.P.

Happily Ever After

Bill Willingham: writer/creator
Mark Buckingham: penciller
Steve Leialoha & Andrew Pepoy: inkers
Lee Loughridge: colors
Todd Klein: letters
James Jean: cover
Angela Rufino: assistant editor
Shelly Bond: editor

The creators and publishers of Fables would like to thank you, our readers, for your loyalty, encouragement and reliable "what happens next" interest in these first fifty issues. We'll see you next month when the next fifty begin.

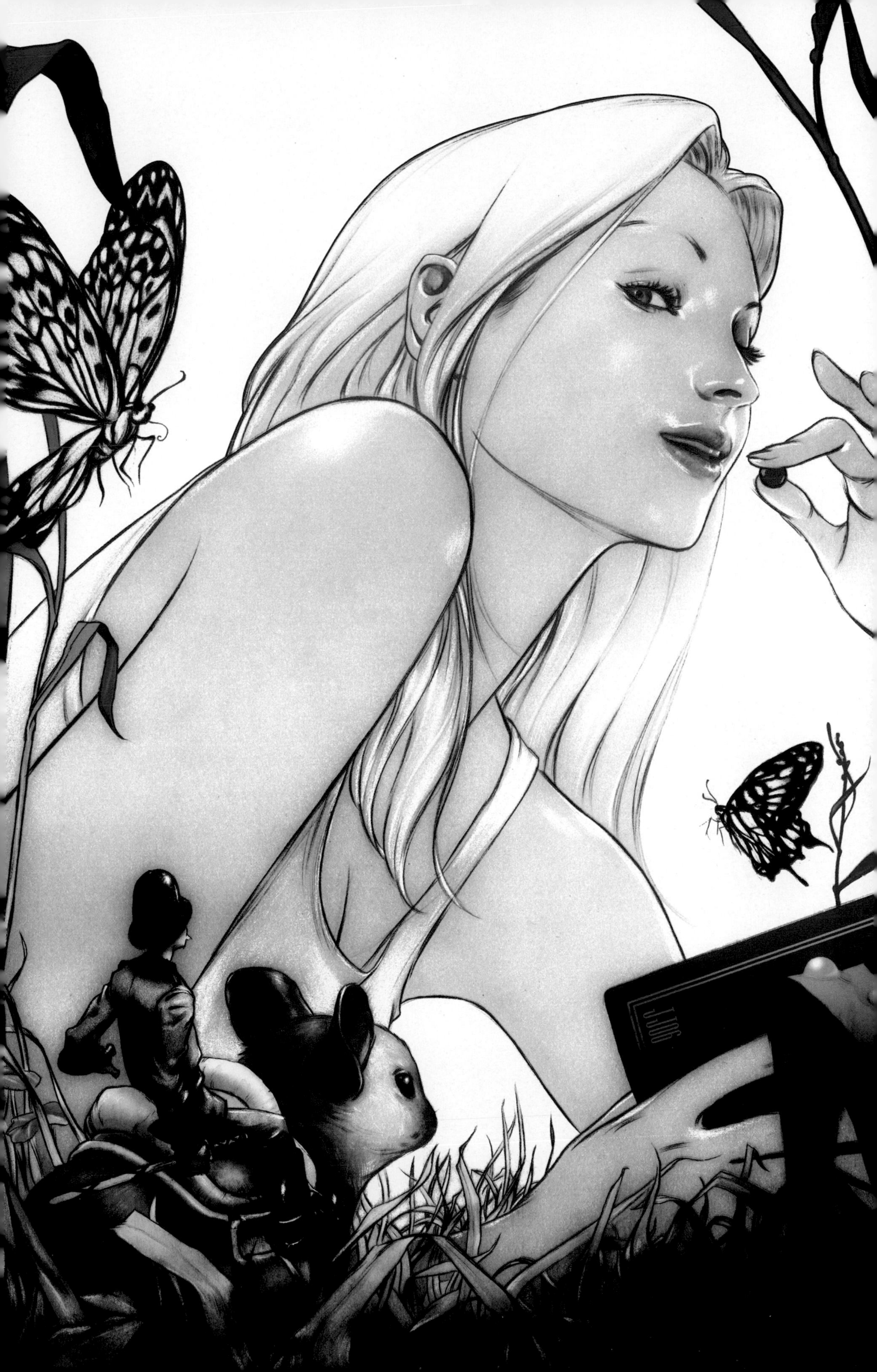

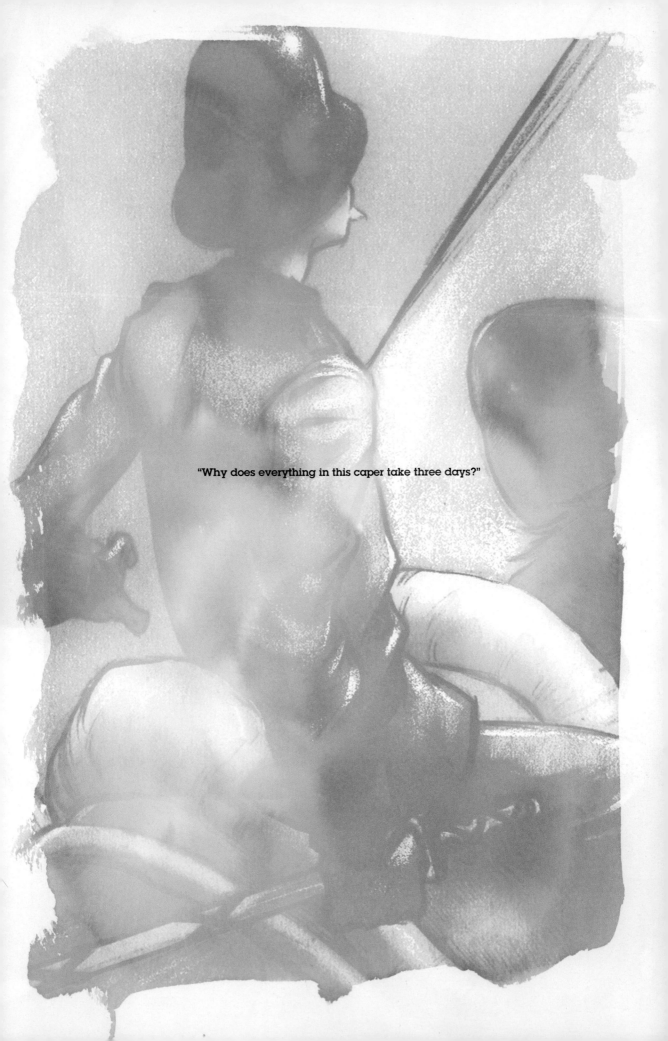

"Why does everything in this caper take three days?"

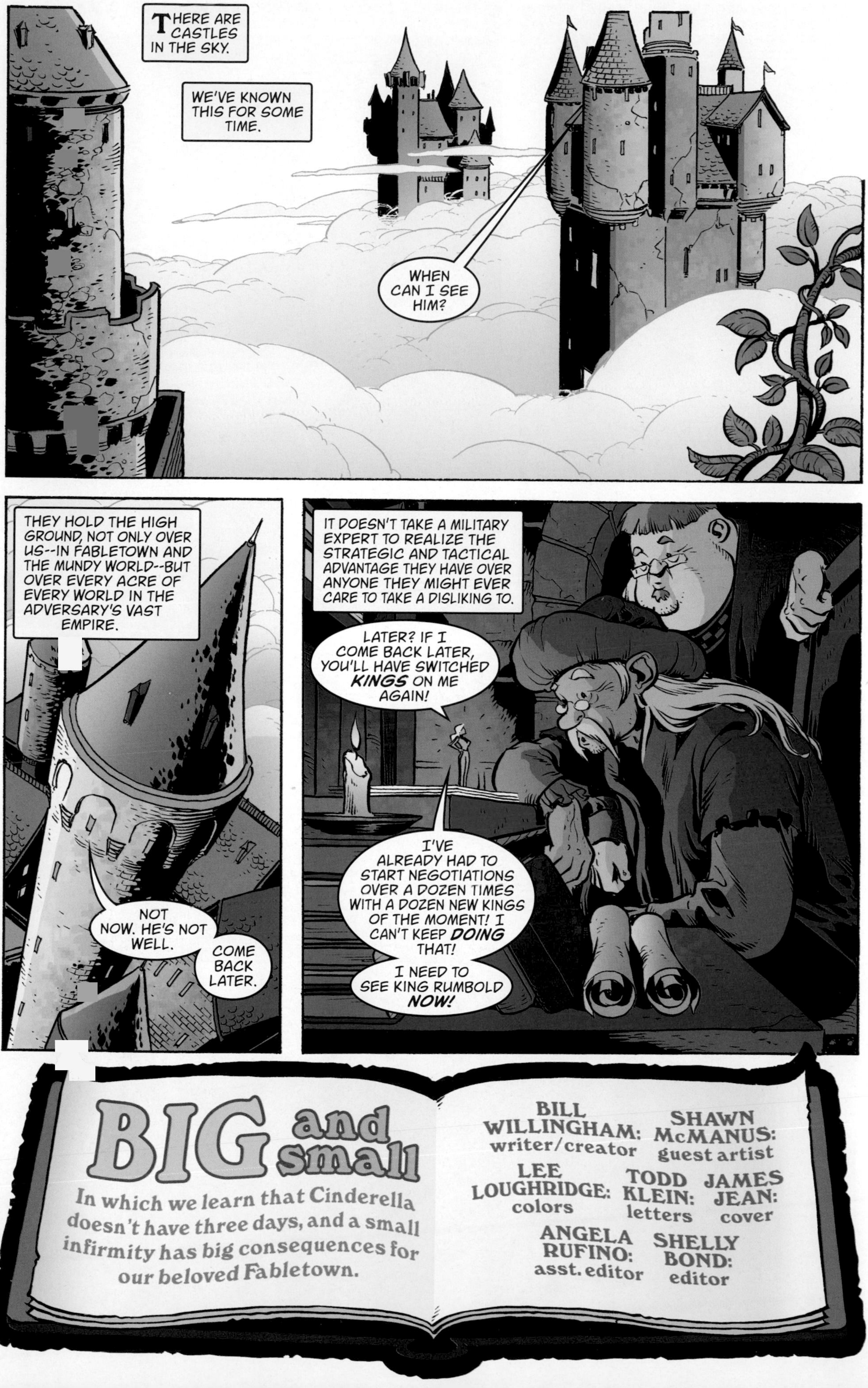
THERE ARE CASTLES IN THE SKY.
WE'VE KNOWN THIS FOR SOME TIME.
WHEN CAN I SEE HIM?
THEY HOLD THE HIGH GROUND, NOT ONLY OVER US--IN FABLETOWN AND THE MUNDY WORLD--BUT OVER EVERY ACRE OF EVERY WORLD IN THE ADVERSARY'S VAST EMPIRE.
NOT NOW. HE'S NOT WELL.
COME BACK LATER.
IT DOESN'T TAKE A MILITARY EXPERT TO REALIZE THE STRATEGIC AND TACTICAL ADVANTAGE THEY HAVE OVER ANYONE THEY MIGHT EVER CARE TO TAKE A DISLIKING TO.
LATER? IF I COME BACK LATER, YOU'LL HAVE SWITCHED KINGS ON ME AGAIN!
I'VE ALREADY HAD TO START NEGOTIATIONS OVER A DOZEN TIMES WITH A DOZEN NEW KINGS OF THE MOMENT! I CAN'T KEEP DOING THAT!
I NEED TO SEE KING RUMBOLD NOW!
BIG and small
In which we learn that Cinderella doesn't have three days, and a small infirmity has big consequences for our beloved Fabletown.
BILL WILLINGHAM: writer/creator
SHAWN McMANUS: guest artist
LEE LOUGHRIDGE: colors
TODD KLEIN: letters
JAMES JEAN: cover
ANGELA RUFINO: asst. editor
SHELLY BOND: editor

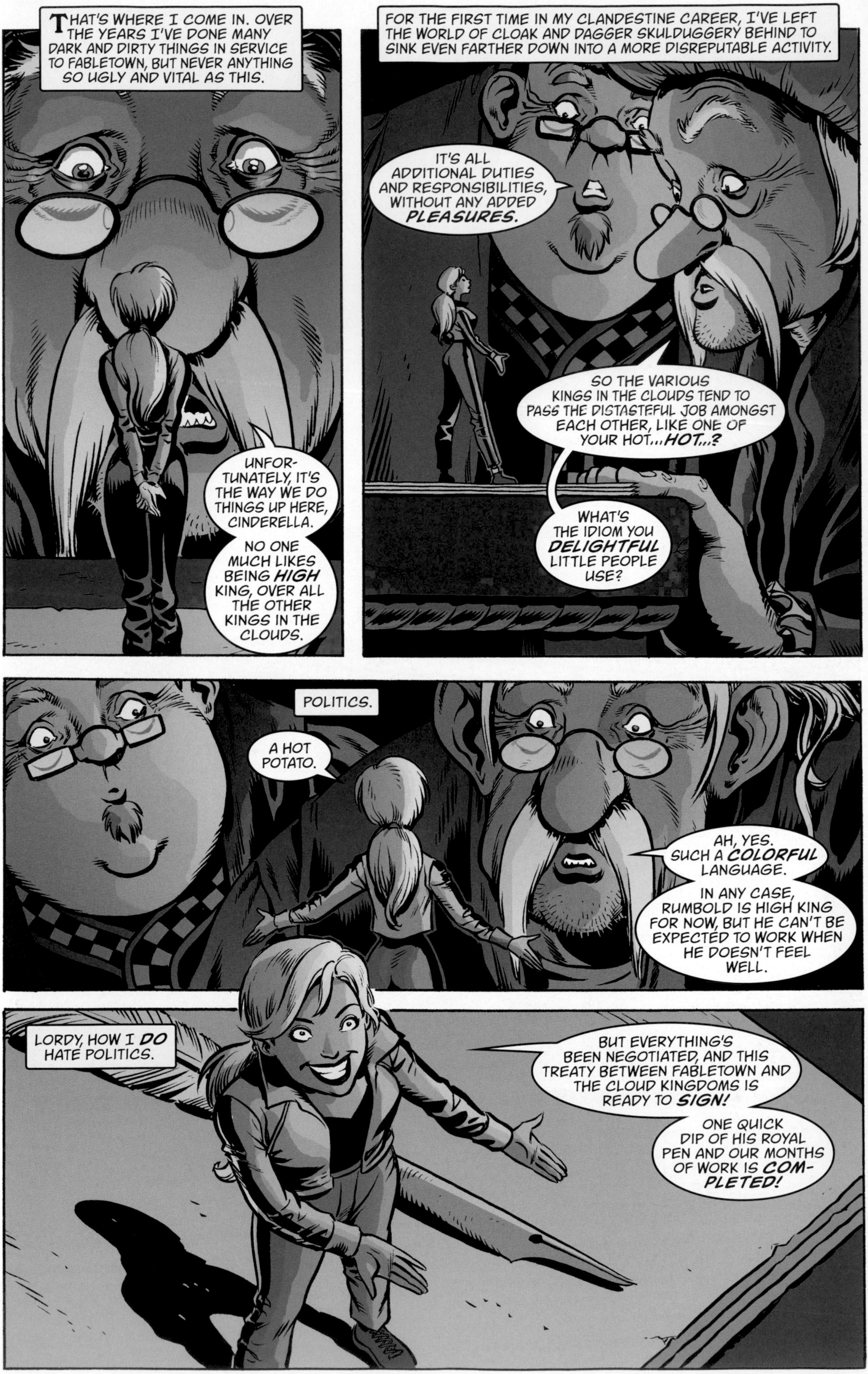
THAT'S WHERE I COME IN. OVER THE YEARS I'VE DONE MANY DARK AND DIRTY THINGS IN SERVICE TO FABLETOWN, BUT NEVER ANYTHING SO UGLY AND VITAL AS THIS.
UNFORTUNATELY, IT'S THE WAY WE DO THINGS UP HERE, CINDERELLA.
NO ONE MUCH LIKES BEING HIGH KING, OVER ALL THE OTHER KINGS IN THE CLOUDS.
FOR THE FIRST TIME IN MY CLANDESTINE CAREER, I'VE LEFT THE WORLD OF CLOAK AND DAGGER SKULDUGGERY BEHIND TO SINK EVEN FARTHER DOWN INTO A MORE DISREPUTABLE ACTIVITY.
IT'S ALL ADDITIONAL DUTIES AND RESPONSIBILITIES, WITHOUT ANY ADDED PLEASURES.
SO THE VARIOUS KINGS IN THE CLOUDS TEND TO PASS THE DISTASTEFUL JOB AMONGST EACH OTHER, LIKE ONE OF YOUR HOT... HOT...?
WHAT'S THE IDIOM YOU DELIGHTFUL LITTLE PEOPLE USE?
POLITICS.
A HOT POTATO.
AH, YES. SUCH A COLORFUL LANGUAGE.
IN ANY CASE, RUMBOLD IS HIGH KING FOR NOW, BUT HE CAN'T BE EXPECTED TO WORK WHEN HE DOESN'T FEEL WELL.
LORDY, HOW I DO HATE POLITICS.
BUT EVERYTHING'S BEEN NEGOTIATED, AND THIS TREATY BETWEEN FABLETOWN AND THE CLOUD KINGDOMS IS READY TO SIGN!
ONE QUICK DIP OF HIS ROYAL PEN AND OUR MONTHS OF WORK IS COMPLETED!

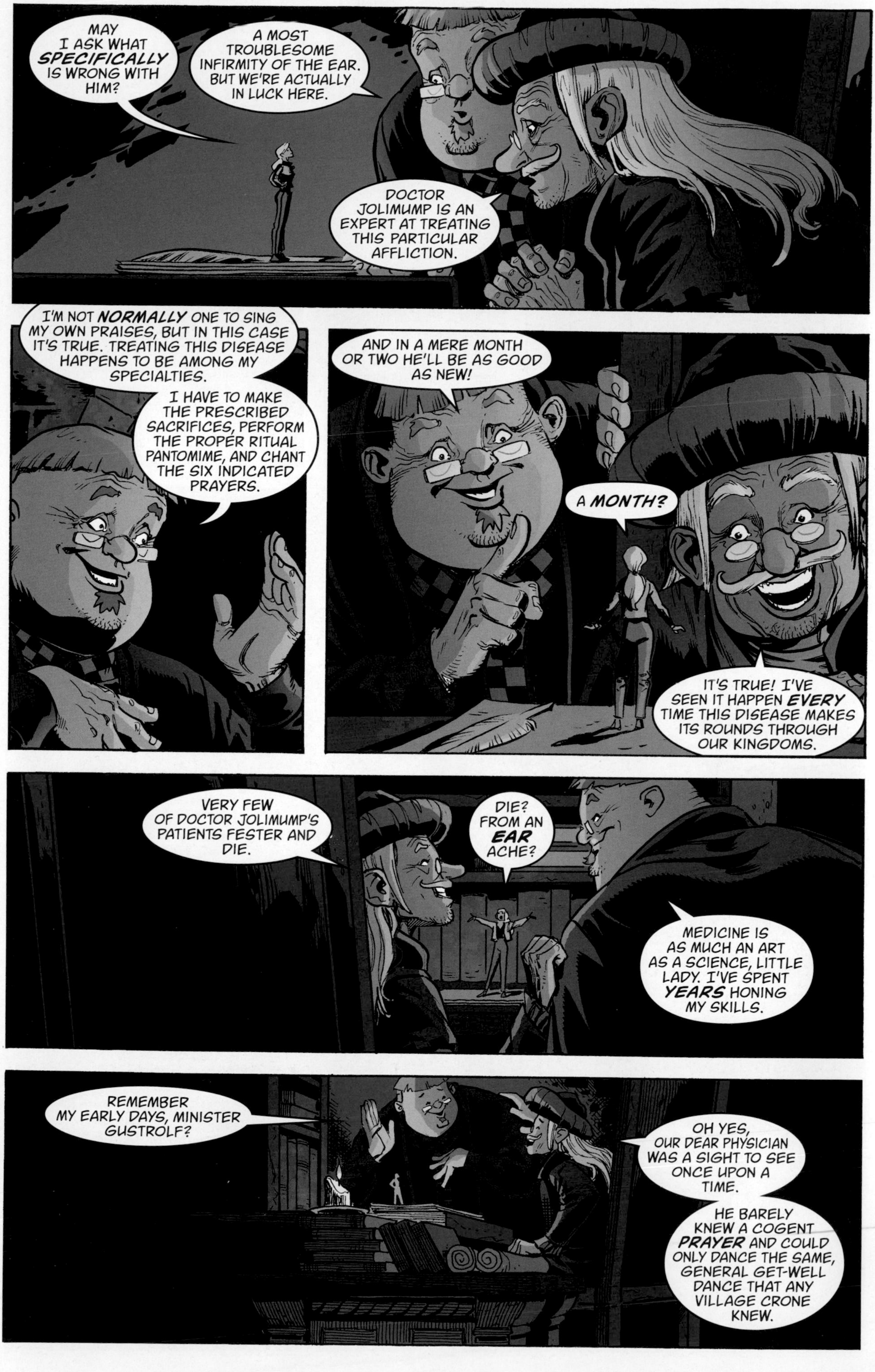
MAY I ASK WHAT SPECIFICALLY IS WRONG WITH HIM?
A MOST TROUBLESOME INFIRMITY OF THE EAR. BUT WE'RE ACTUALLY IN LUCK HERE.
DOCTOR JOLIMUMP IS AN EXPERT AT TREATING THIS PARTICULAR AFFLICTION.
I'M NOT NORMALLY ONE TO SING MY OWN PRAISES, BUT IN THIS CASE IT'S TRUE. TREATING THIS DISEASE HAPPENS TO BE AMONG MY SPECIALTIES.
I HAVE TO MAKE THE PRESCRIBED SACRIFICES, PERFORM THE PROPER RITUAL PANTOMIME, AND CHANT THE SIX INDICATED PRAYERS.
AND IN A MERE MONTH OR TWO HE'LL BE AS GOOD AS NEW!
A MONTH?
IT'S TRUE! I'VE SEEN IT HAPPEN EVERY TIME THIS DISEASE MAKES ITS ROUNDS THROUGH OUR KINGDOMS.
VERY FEW OF DOCTOR JOLIMUMP'S PATIENTS FESTER AND DIE.
DIE? FROM AN EAR ACHE?
MEDICINE IS AS MUCH AN ART AS A SCIENCE, LITTLE LADY. I'VE SPENT YEARS HONING MY SKILLS.
REMEMBER MY EARLY DAYS, MINISTER GUSTROLF?
OH YES, OUR DEAR PHYSICIAN WAS A SIGHT TO SEE ONCE UPON A TIME.
HE BARELY KNEW A COGENT PRAYER AND COULD ONLY DANCE THE SAME, GENERAL GET-WELL DANCE THAT ANY VILLAGE CRONE KNEW.

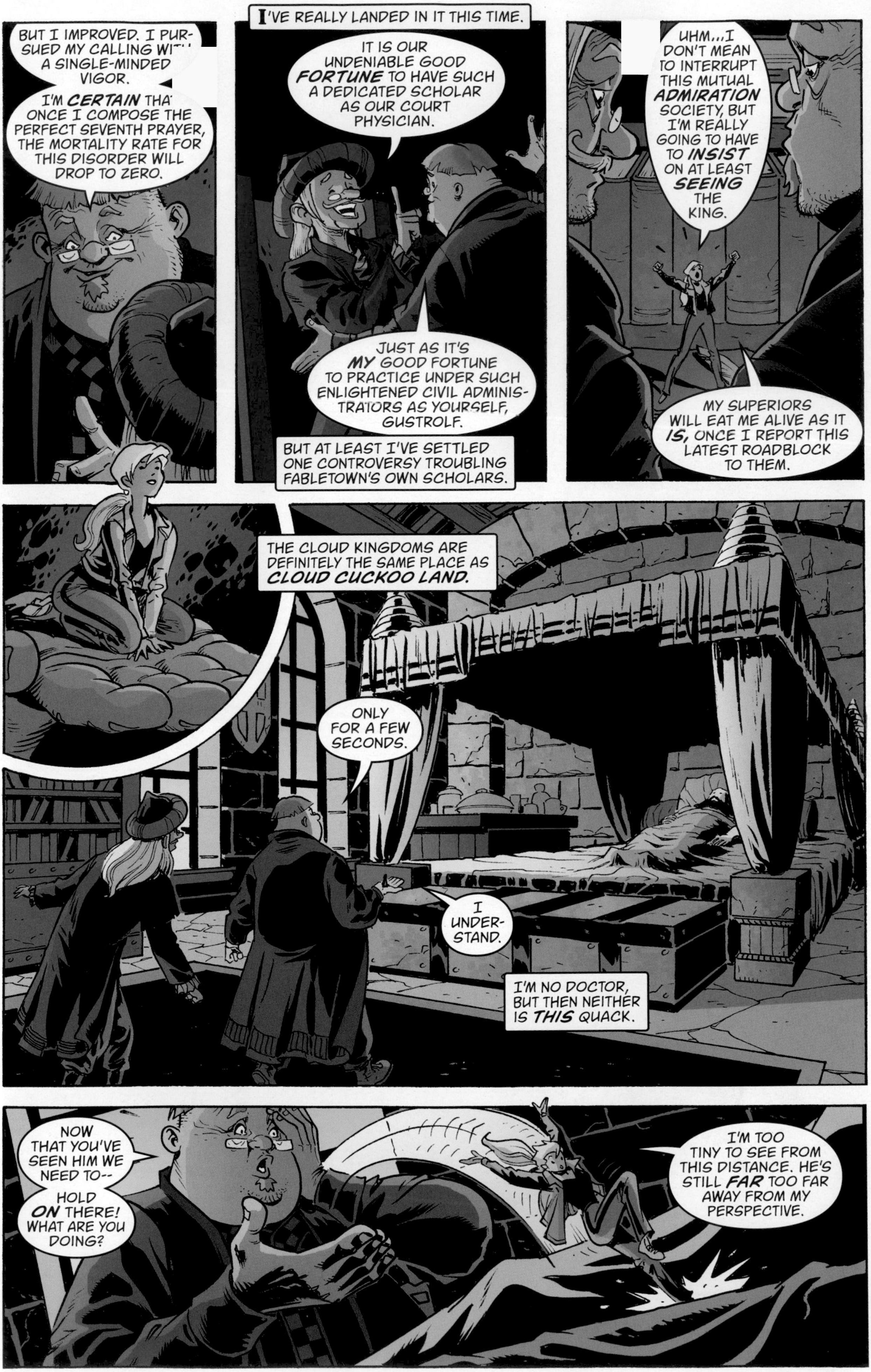

BUT I IMPROVED. I PURSUED MY CALLING WITH A SINGLE-MINDED VIGOR.
I'M CERTAIN THAT ONCE I COMPOSE THE PERFECT SEVENTH PRAYER, THE MORTALITY RATE FOR THIS DISORDER WILL DROP TO ZERO.
I'VE REALLY LANDED IN IT THIS TIME.
IT IS OUR UNDENIABLE GOOD FORTUNE TO HAVE SUCH A DEDICATED SCHOLAR AS OUR COURT PHYSICIAN.
JUST AS IT'S MY GOOD FORTUNE TO PRACTICE UNDER SUCH ENLIGHTENED CIVIL ADMINISTRATORS AS YOURSELF, GUSTROLF.
BUT AT LEAST I'VE SETTLED ONE CONTROVERSY TROUBLING FABLETOWN'S OWN SCHOLARS.
UHM...I DON'T MEAN TO INTERRUPT THIS MUTUAL ADMIRATION SOCIETY, BUT I'M REALLY GOING TO HAVE TO INSIST ON AT LEAST SEEING THE KING.
MY SUPERIORS WILL EAT ME ALIVE AS IT IS, ONCE I REPORT THIS LATEST ROADBLOCK TO THEM.
THE CLOUD KINGDOMS ARE DEFINITELY THE SAME PLACE AS CLOUD CUCKOO LAND.
ONLY FOR A FEW SECONDS.
I UNDERSTAND.
I'M NO DOCTOR, BUT THEN NEITHER IS THIS QUACK.
NOW THAT YOU'VE SEEN HIM WE NEED TO--
HOLD ON THERE! WHAT ARE YOU DOING?
I'M TOO TINY TO SEE FROM THIS DISTANCE. HE'S STILL FAR TOO FAR AWAY FROM MY PERSPECTIVE.

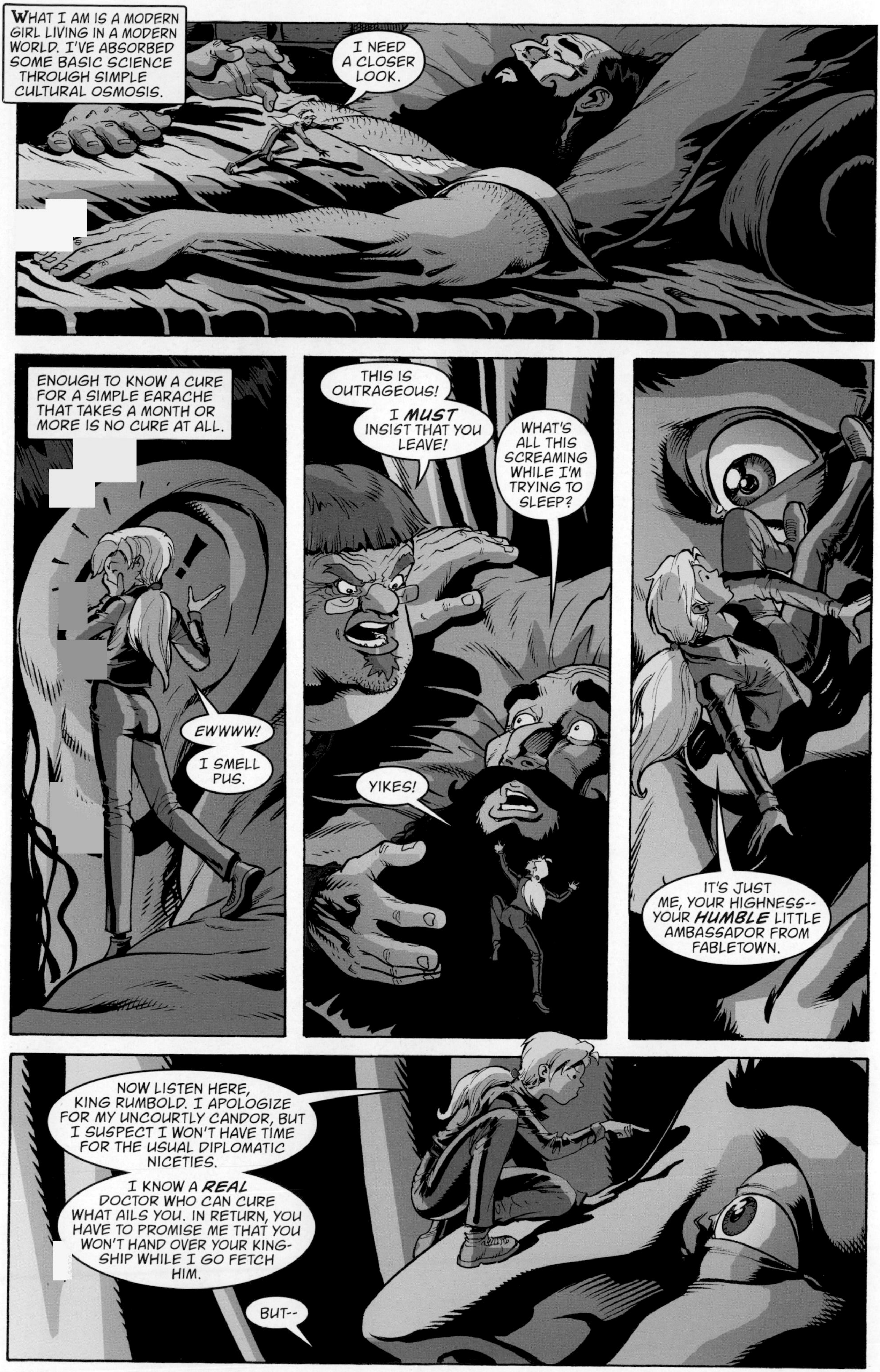
WHAT I AM IS A MODERN GIRL LIVING IN A MODERN WORLD. I'VE ABSORBED SOME BASIC SCIENCE THROUGH SIMPLE CULTURAL OSMOSIS.
I NEED A CLOSER LOOK.
ENOUGH TO KNOW A CURE FOR A SIMPLE EARACHE THAT TAKES A MONTH OR MORE IS NO CURE AT ALL.
!
EWWWW!
I SMELL PUS.
THIS IS OUTRAGEOUS!
I MUST INSIST THAT YOU LEAVE!
WHAT'S ALL THIS SCREAMING WHILE I'M TRYING TO SLEEP?
YIKES!
IT'S JUST ME, YOUR HIGHNESS-- YOUR HUMBLE LITTLE AMBASSADOR FROM FABLETOWN.
NOW LISTEN HERE, KING RUMBOLD. I APOLOGIZE FOR MY UNCOURTLY CANDOR, BUT I SUSPECT I WON'T HAVE TIME FOR THE USUAL DIPLOMATIC NICETIES.
I KNOW A REAL DOCTOR WHO CAN CURE WHAT AILS YOU. IN RETURN, YOU HAVE TO PROMISE ME THAT YOU WON'T HAND OVER YOUR KING-SHIP WHILE I GO FETCH HIM.
BUT--

I'VE NEVER SEEN DOCTOR JOLIMUMP SO ANGRY.

I HAVE THAT EFFECT ON **MOST** MEN. HE'LL GET OVER IT.

ARE YOU SURE YOU CAN MAKE IT BACK BEFORE KING RUMBOLD TRANSFERS HIS POWER? THE NEXT ONE IN LINE IS KING PINEHEART WHO'S **PROUDLY** ILLITERATE.

YOU'D HAVE TO WAIT FOR AN ENTIRE NEW KING AGAIN FOR ANY CHANCE TO GET YOUR TREATY SIGNED.

OH *JOY.*

MY LIFE GETS BETTER ALL THE TIME.

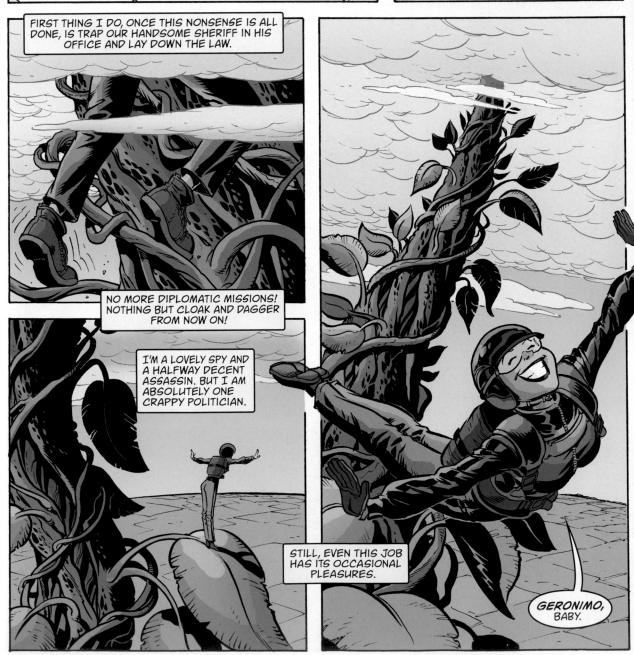

FIRST THING I DO, ONCE THIS NONSENSE IS ALL DONE, IS TRAP OUR HANDSOME SHERIFF IN HIS OFFICE AND LAY DOWN THE LAW.

NO MORE DIPLOMATIC MISSIONS! NOTHING BUT CLOAK AND DAGGER FROM NOW ON!

I'M A LOVELY SPY AND A HALFWAY DECENT ASSASSIN. BUT I AM ABSOLUTELY ONE CRAPPY POLITICIAN.

STILL, EVEN THIS JOB HAS ITS OCCASIONAL PLEASURES.

GERONIMO, BABY.

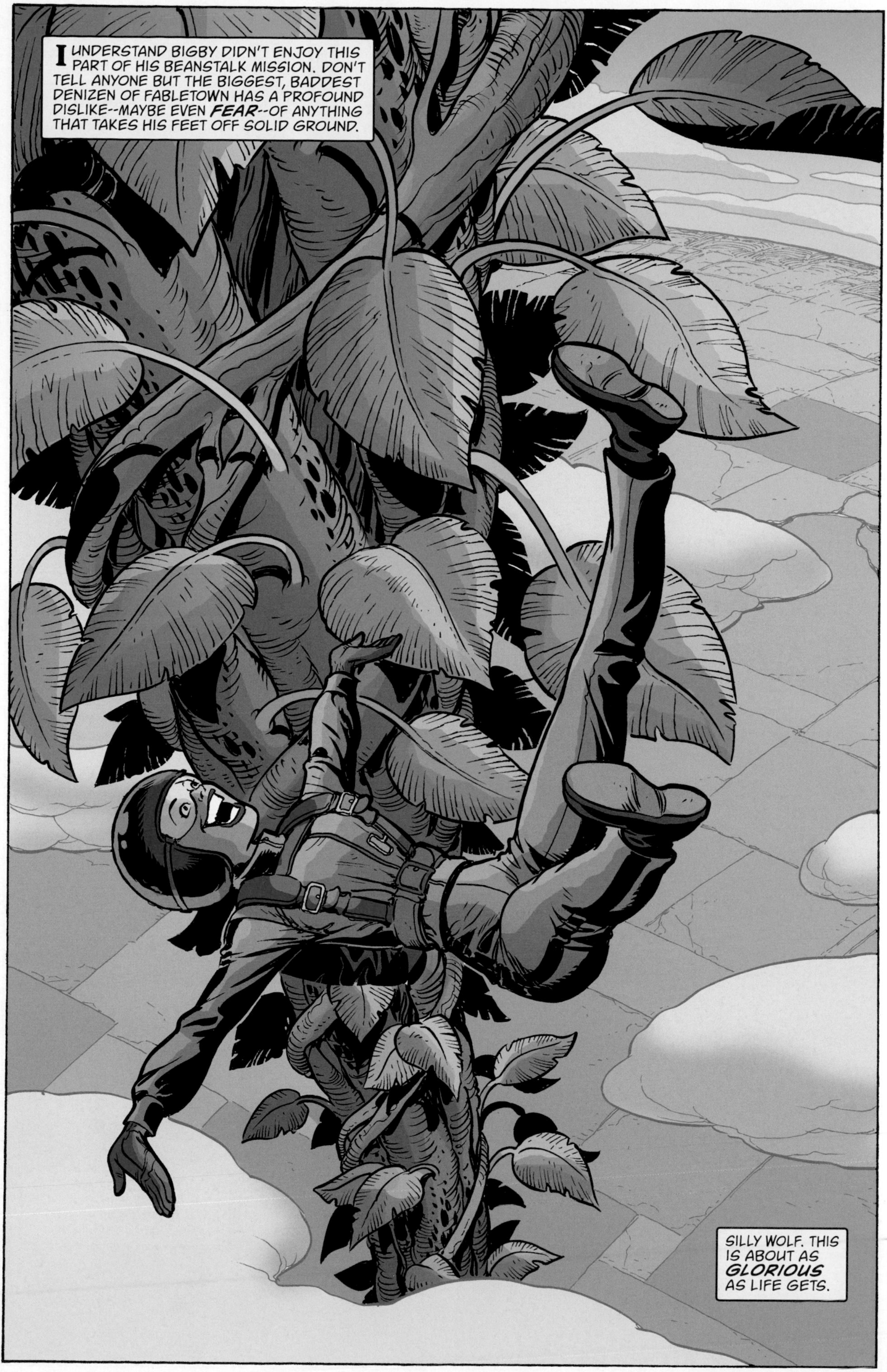
I UNDERSTAND BIGBY DIDN'T ENJOY THIS PART OF HIS BEANSTALK MISSION. DON'T TELL ANYONE BUT THE BIGGEST, BADDEST DENIZEN OF FABLETOWN HAS A PROFOUND DISLIKE--MAYBE EVEN FEAR--OF ANYTHING THAT TAKES HIS FEET OFF SOLID GROUND.
SILLY WOLF. THIS IS ABOUT AS GLORIOUS AS LIFE GETS.

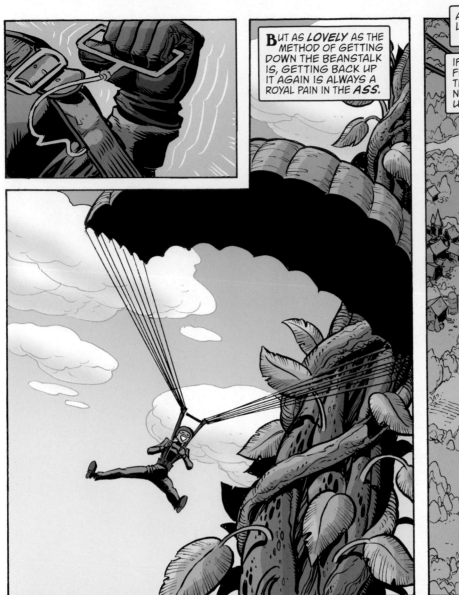

BUT AS *LOVELY* AS THE METHOD OF GETTING DOWN THE BEANSTALK IS, GETTING BACK UP IT AGAIN IS ALWAYS A ROYAL PAIN IN THE *ASS.*

AND ARMS AND LEGS AND LOWER BACK AND...WELL, YOU GET THE PICTURE.

IF WE'RE GOING TO MAINTAIN FREQUENT RELATIONS WITH THE BOYS UPSTAIRS, WE NEED A BETTER WAY TO GET UP THERE THAN CLIMBING.

I MEAN, COME *ON!* IT MAY *STILL* BE THE DARK AGES UP THERE, BUT DOWN HERE WE'VE GOT ADVANCED TECHNOLOGY OUT THE WING-WANG.

WOULD IT REALLY *KILL* US TO RIG UP SOME SORT OF ELEVATOR ATTACHED TO THE BEANSTALK?

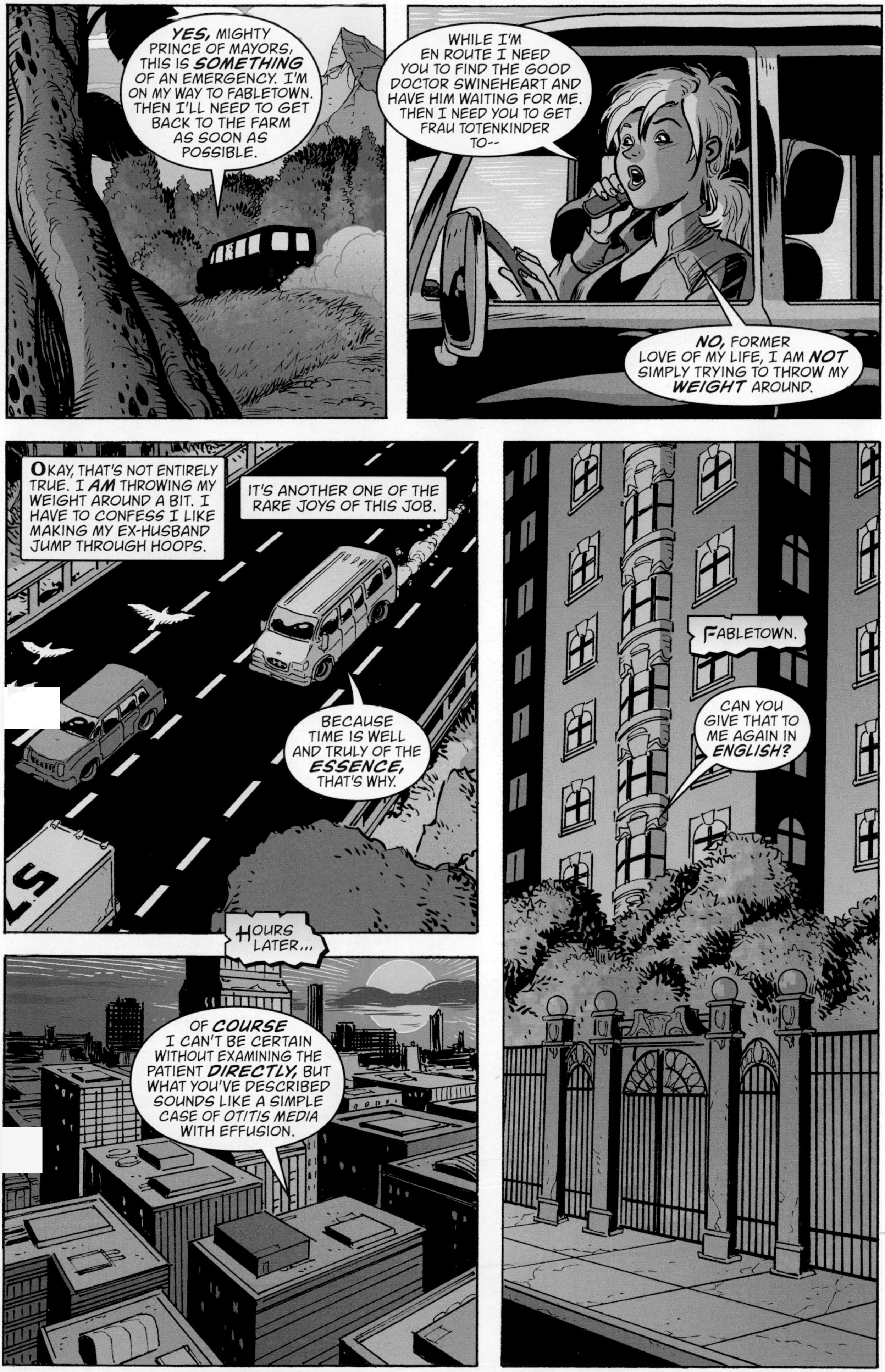
YES, MIGHTY PRINCE OF MAYORS, THIS IS SOMETHING OF AN EMERGENCY. I'M ON MY WAY TO FABLETOWN. THEN I'LL NEED TO GET BACK TO THE FARM AS SOON AS POSSIBLE.
WHILE I'M EN ROUTE I NEED YOU TO FIND THE GOOD DOCTOR SWINEHEART AND HAVE HIM WAITING FOR ME. THEN I NEED YOU TO GET FRAU TOTENKINDER TO--
NO, FORMER LOVE OF MY LIFE, I AM NOT SIMPLY TRYING TO THROW MY WEIGHT AROUND.
OKAY, THAT'S NOT ENTIRELY TRUE. I AM THROWING MY WEIGHT AROUND A BIT. I HAVE TO CONFESS I LIKE MAKING MY EX-HUSBAND JUMP THROUGH HOOPS.
IT'S ANOTHER ONE OF THE RARE JOYS OF THIS JOB.
BECAUSE TIME IS WELL AND TRULY OF THE ESSENCE, THAT'S WHY.
HOURS LATER...
OF COURSE I CAN'T BE CERTAIN WITHOUT EXAMINING THE PATIENT DIRECTLY, BUT WHAT YOU'VE DESCRIBED SOUNDS LIKE A SIMPLE CASE OF OTITIS MEDIA WITH EFFUSION.
FABLETOWN.
CAN YOU GIVE THAT TO ME AGAIN IN ENGLISH?

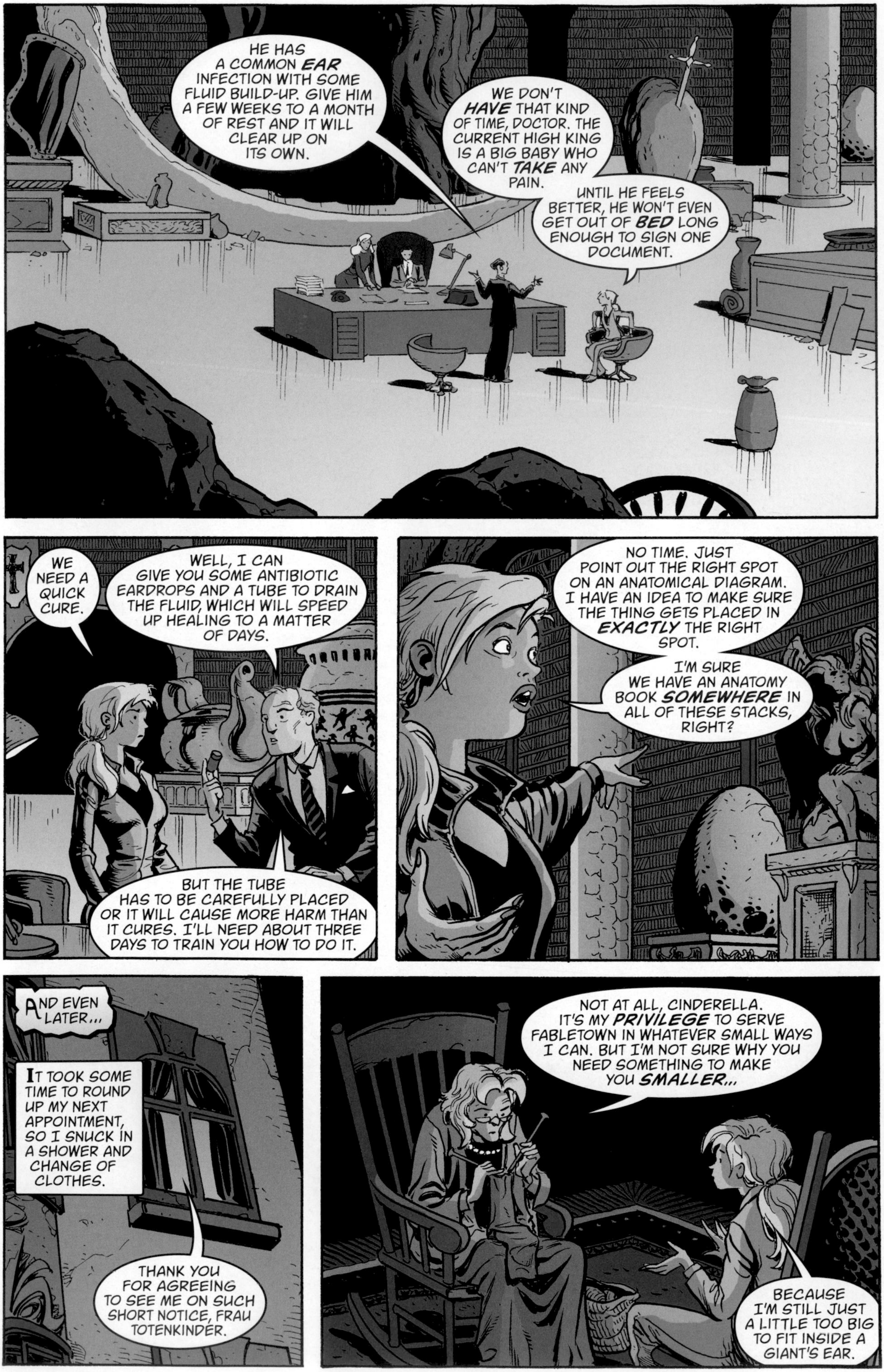
HE HAS A COMMON EAR INFECTION WITH SOME FLUID BUILD-UP. GIVE HIM A FEW WEEKS TO A MONTH OF REST AND IT WILL CLEAR UP ON ITS OWN.
WE DON'T HAVE THAT KIND OF TIME, DOCTOR. THE CURRENT HIGH KING IS A BIG BABY WHO CAN'T TAKE ANY PAIN.
UNTIL HE FEELS BETTER, HE WON'T EVEN GET OUT OF BED LONG ENOUGH TO SIGN ONE DOCUMENT.
WE NEED A QUICK CURE.
WELL, I CAN GIVE YOU SOME ANTIBIOTIC EARDROPS AND A TUBE TO DRAIN THE FLUID, WHICH WILL SPEED UP HEALING TO A MATTER OF DAYS.
BUT THE TUBE HAS TO BE CAREFULLY PLACED OR IT WILL CAUSE MORE HARM THAN IT CURES. I'LL NEED ABOUT THREE DAYS TO TRAIN YOU HOW TO DO IT.
NO TIME. JUST POINT OUT THE RIGHT SPOT ON AN ANATOMICAL DIAGRAM. I HAVE AN IDEA TO MAKE SURE THE THING GETS PLACED IN EXACTLY THE RIGHT SPOT.
I'M SURE WE HAVE AN ANATOMY BOOK SOMEWHERE IN ALL OF THESE STACKS, RIGHT?
AND EVEN LATER...
IT TOOK SOME TIME TO ROUND UP MY NEXT APPOINTMENT, SO I SNUCK IN A SHOWER AND CHANGE OF CLOTHES.
THANK YOU FOR AGREEING TO SEE ME ON SUCH SHORT NOTICE, FRAU TOTENKINDER.
NOT AT ALL, CINDERELLA. IT'S MY PRIVILEGE TO SERVE FABLETOWN IN WHATEVER SMALL WAYS I CAN. BUT I'M NOT SURE WHY YOU NEED SOMETHING TO MAKE YOU SMALLER...
BECAUSE I'M STILL JUST A LITTLE TOO BIG TO FIT INSIDE A GIANT'S EAR.

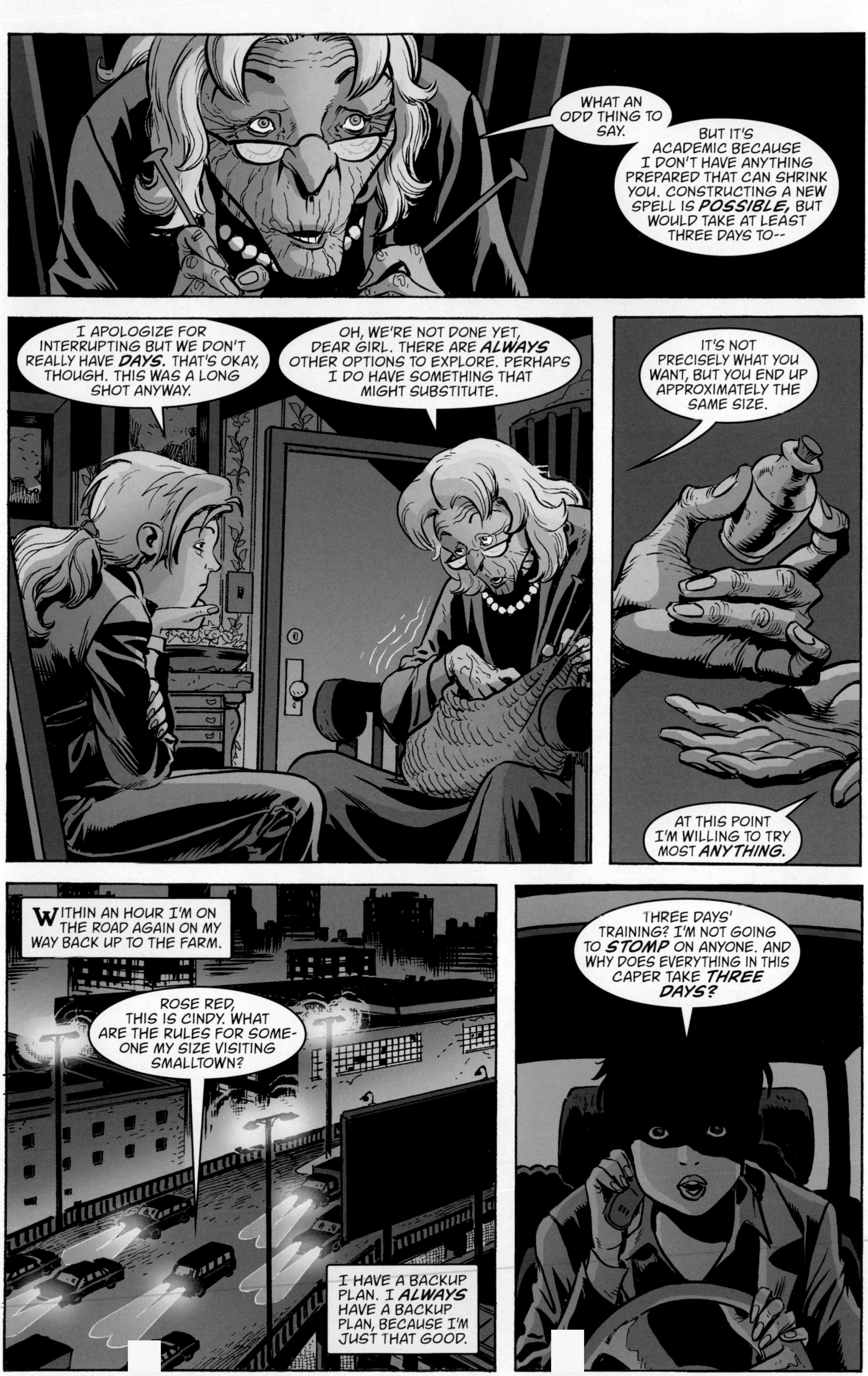
WHAT AN ODD THING TO SAY.
BUT IT'S ACADEMIC BECAUSE I DON'T HAVE ANYTHING PREPARED THAT CAN SHRINK YOU. CONSTRUCTING A NEW SPELL IS POSSIBLE, BUT WOULD TAKE AT LEAST THREE DAYS TO--
I APOLOGIZE FOR INTERRUPTING BUT WE DON'T REALLY HAVE DAYS. THAT'S OKAY, THOUGH. THIS WAS A LONG SHOT ANYWAY.
OH, WE'RE NOT DONE YET, DEAR GIRL. THERE ARE ALWAYS OTHER OPTIONS TO EXPLORE. PERHAPS I DO HAVE SOMETHING THAT MIGHT SUBSTITUTE.
IT'S NOT PRECISELY WHAT YOU WANT, BUT YOU END UP APPROXIMATELY THE SAME SIZE.
AT THIS POINT I'M WILLING TO TRY MOST ANYTHING.
WITHIN AN HOUR I'M ON THE ROAD AGAIN ON MY WAY BACK UP TO THE FARM.
ROSE RED, THIS IS CINDY. WHAT ARE THE RULES FOR SOME-ONE MY SIZE VISITING SMALLTOWN?
I HAVE A BACKUP PLAN. I ALWAYS HAVE A BACKUP PLAN, BECAUSE I'M JUST THAT GOOD.
THREE DAYS' TRAINING? I'M NOT GOING TO STOMP ON ANYONE. AND WHY DOES EVERYTHING IN THIS CAPER TAKE THREE DAYS?

THREE DAYS TO LEARN HOW TO PLACE A DRAINAGE TUBE! THREE DAYS TO BUILD A SHRINKING SPELL! THREE DAYS TO LEARN HOW *NOT* TO STEP ON TINY PEOPLE!

GODS ABOVE, WILL EVERYONE *PLEASE* GET IT THROUGH YOUR COLLECTIVE SKULL THAT *I...* *DON'T...HAVE...* *THREE...* *DAYS!*

NO, ROSE, I'M SORRY. I WASN'T SPECIFICALLY YELLING AT *YOU.* IT'S THE ENTIRE *UNIVERSE* THAT'S PISSING ME OFF RIGHT NOW.

A FEW HOURS LATER...

TRUST ME. I WON'T BE *BIG* ENOUGH TO STOMP ON ANYONE.

JUST GUIDE ME TO THE EDGE OF THEIR TERRITORY AND I'LL TAKE IT FROM THERE, ROSE.

AND I'M WILLING TO TAKE YOUR WORD ON THIS *WHY* EXACTLY?

BECAUSE I'M SMART AND LOVELY AND CLEARLY THE LEADING LADY OF THIS PARTICULAR TALE. AND MY HEART, AS ALWAYS, IS *PURE.*

AND BECAUSE OUR SECRET TREATY WITH THE CLOUD KINGDOMS IS ON THE LINE.

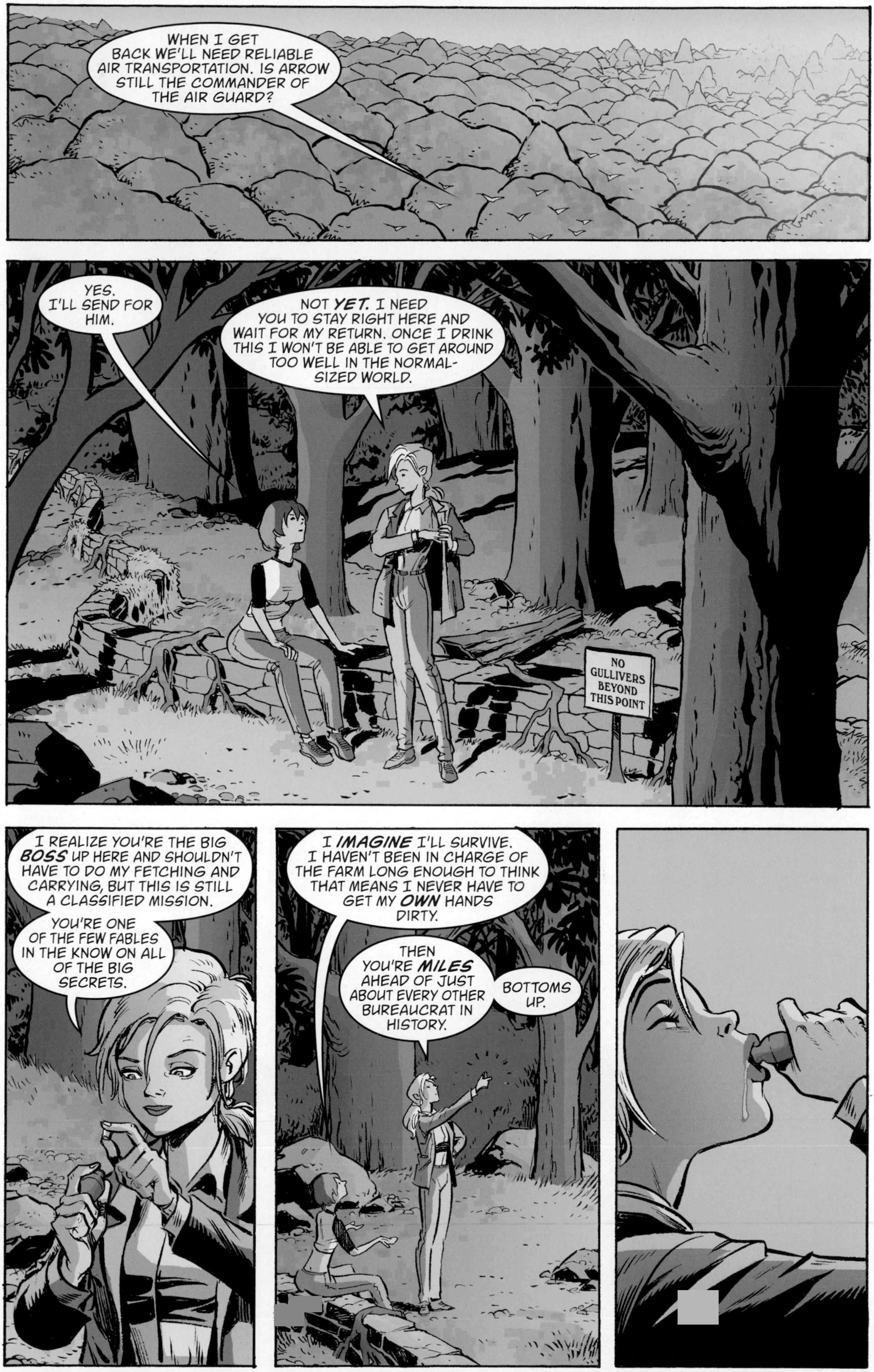
WHEN I GET BACK WE'LL NEED RELIABLE AIR TRANSPORTATION. IS ARROW STILL THE COMMANDER OF THE AIR GUARD?
YES. I'LL SEND FOR HIM.
NOT YET. I NEED YOU TO STAY RIGHT HERE AND WAIT FOR MY RETURN. ONCE I DRINK THIS I WON'T BE ABLE TO GET AROUND TOO WELL IN THE NORMAL-SIZED WORLD.
NO GULLIVERS BEYOND THIS POINT
I REALIZE YOU'RE THE BIG BOSS UP HERE AND SHOULDN'T HAVE TO DO MY FETCHING AND CARRYING, BUT THIS IS STILL A CLASSIFIED MISSION.
YOU'RE ONE OF THE FEW FABLES IN THE KNOW ON ALL OF THE BIG SECRETS.
I IMAGINE I'LL SURVIVE. I HAVEN'T BEEN IN CHARGE OF THE FARM LONG ENOUGH TO THINK THAT MEANS I NEVER HAVE TO GET MY OWN HANDS DIRTY.
THEN YOU'RE MILES AHEAD OF JUST ABOUT EVERY OTHER BUREAUCRAT IN HISTORY.
BOTTOMS UP.

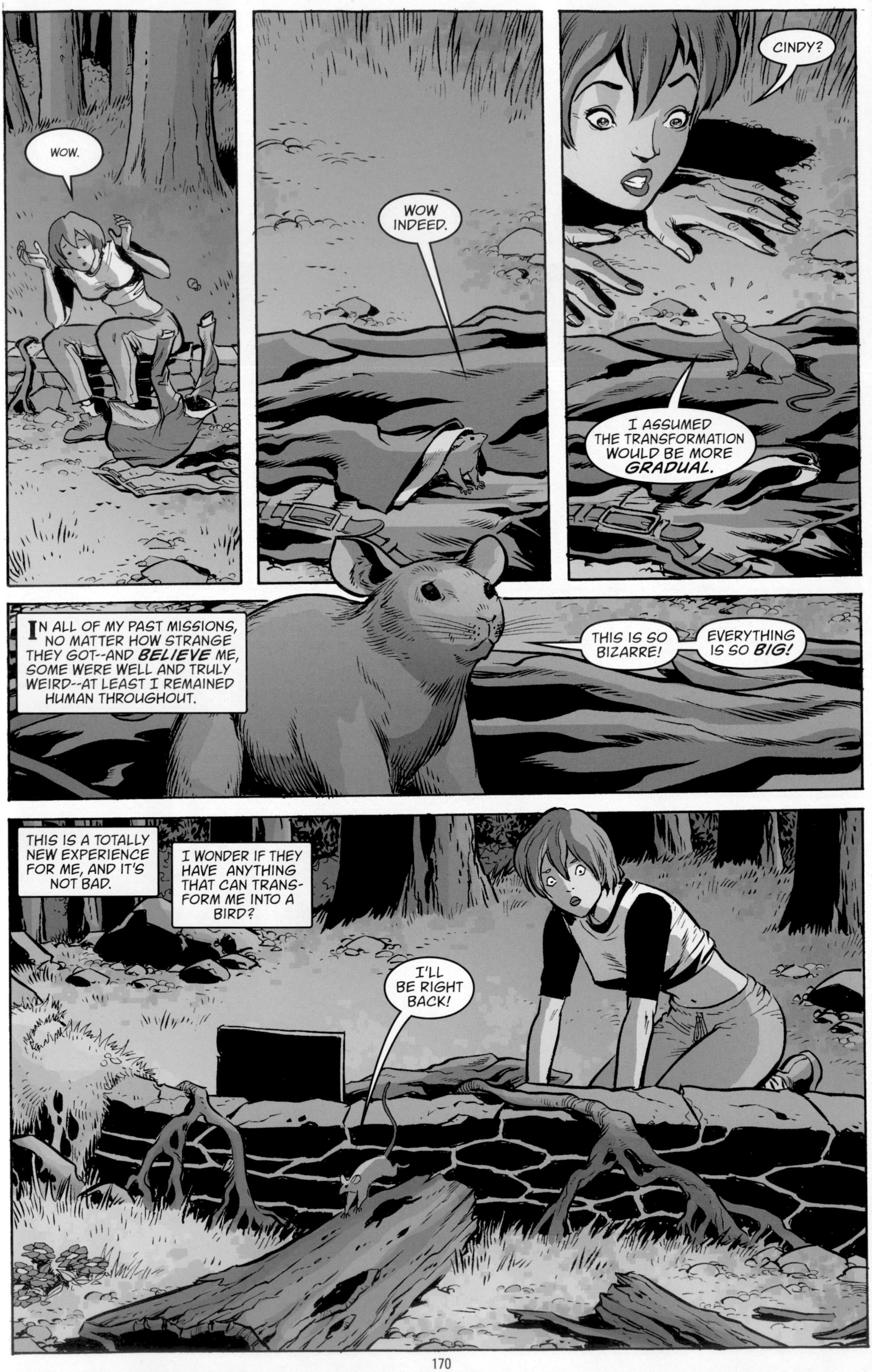
WOW.
WOW INDEED.
CINDY?
I ASSUMED THE TRANSFORMATION WOULD BE MORE GRADUAL.
IN ALL OF MY PAST MISSIONS, NO MATTER HOW STRANGE THEY GOT--AND BELIEVE ME, SOME WERE WELL AND TRULY WEIRD--AT LEAST I REMAINED HUMAN THROUGHOUT.
THIS IS SO BIZARRE!
EVERYTHING IS SO BIG!
THIS IS A TOTALLY NEW EXPERIENCE FOR ME, AND IT'S NOT BAD.
I WONDER IF THEY HAVE ANYTHING THAT CAN TRANS-FORM ME INTO A BIRD?
I'LL BE RIGHT BACK!

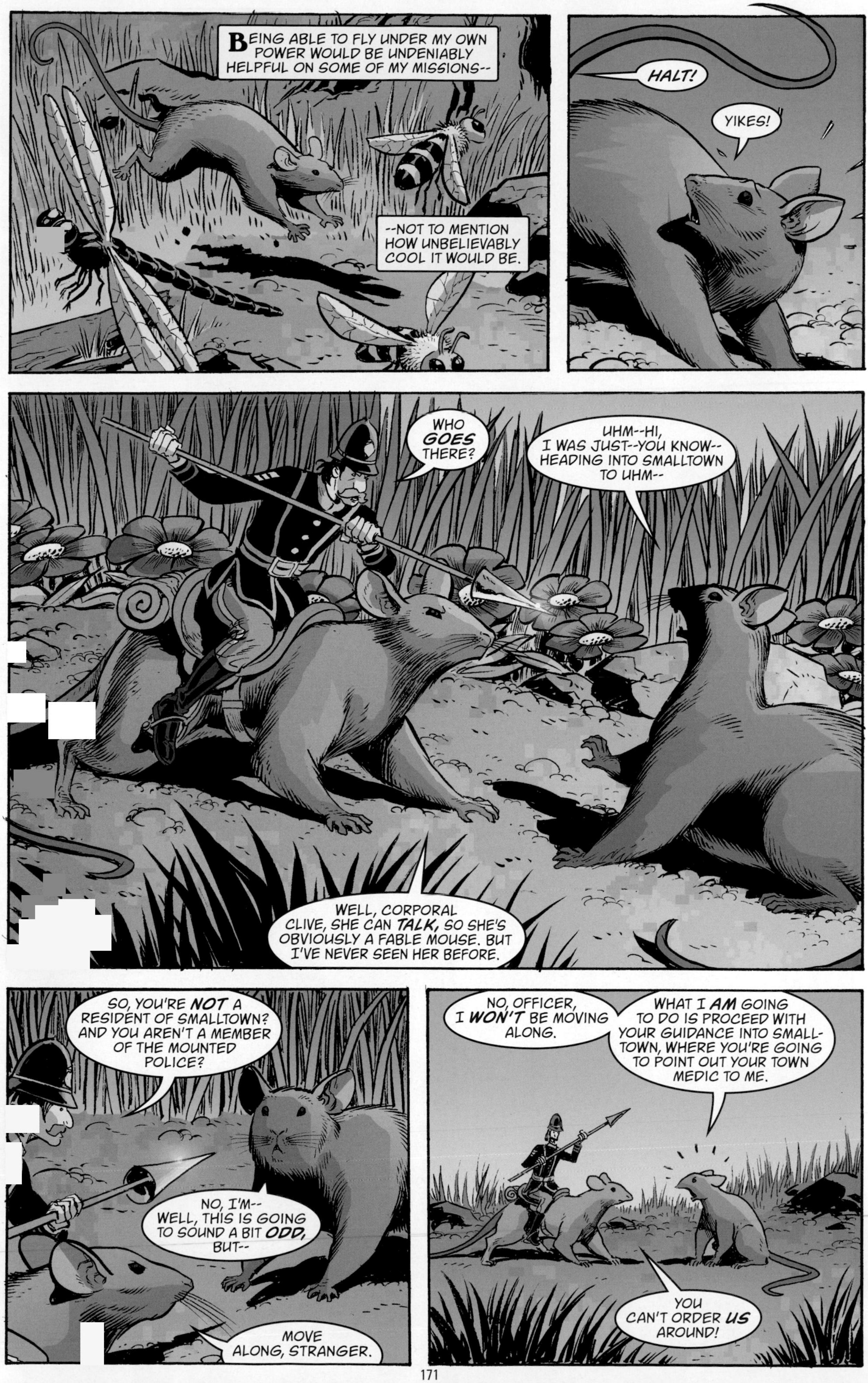
BEING ABLE TO FLY UNDER MY OWN POWER WOULD BE UNDENIABLY HELPFUL ON SOME OF MY MISSIONS--
--NOT TO MENTION HOW UNBELIEVABLY COOL IT WOULD BE.
HALT!
YIKES!
WHO GOES THERE?
UHM--HI, I WAS JUST--YOU KNOW--HEADING INTO SMALLTOWN TO UHM--
WELL, CORPORAL CLIVE, SHE CAN TALK, SO SHE'S OBVIOUSLY A FABLE MOUSE. BUT I'VE NEVER SEEN HER BEFORE.
SO, YOU'RE NOT A RESIDENT OF SMALLTOWN? AND YOU AREN'T A MEMBER OF THE MOUNTED POLICE?
NO, I'M-- WELL, THIS IS GOING TO SOUND A BIT ODD, BUT--
MOVE ALONG, STRANGER.
NO, OFFICER, I WON'T BE MOVING ALONG.
WHAT I AM GOING TO DO IS PROCEED WITH YOUR GUIDANCE INTO SMALL-TOWN, WHERE YOU'RE GOING TO POINT OUT YOUR TOWN MEDIC TO ME.
YOU CAN'T ORDER US AROUND!

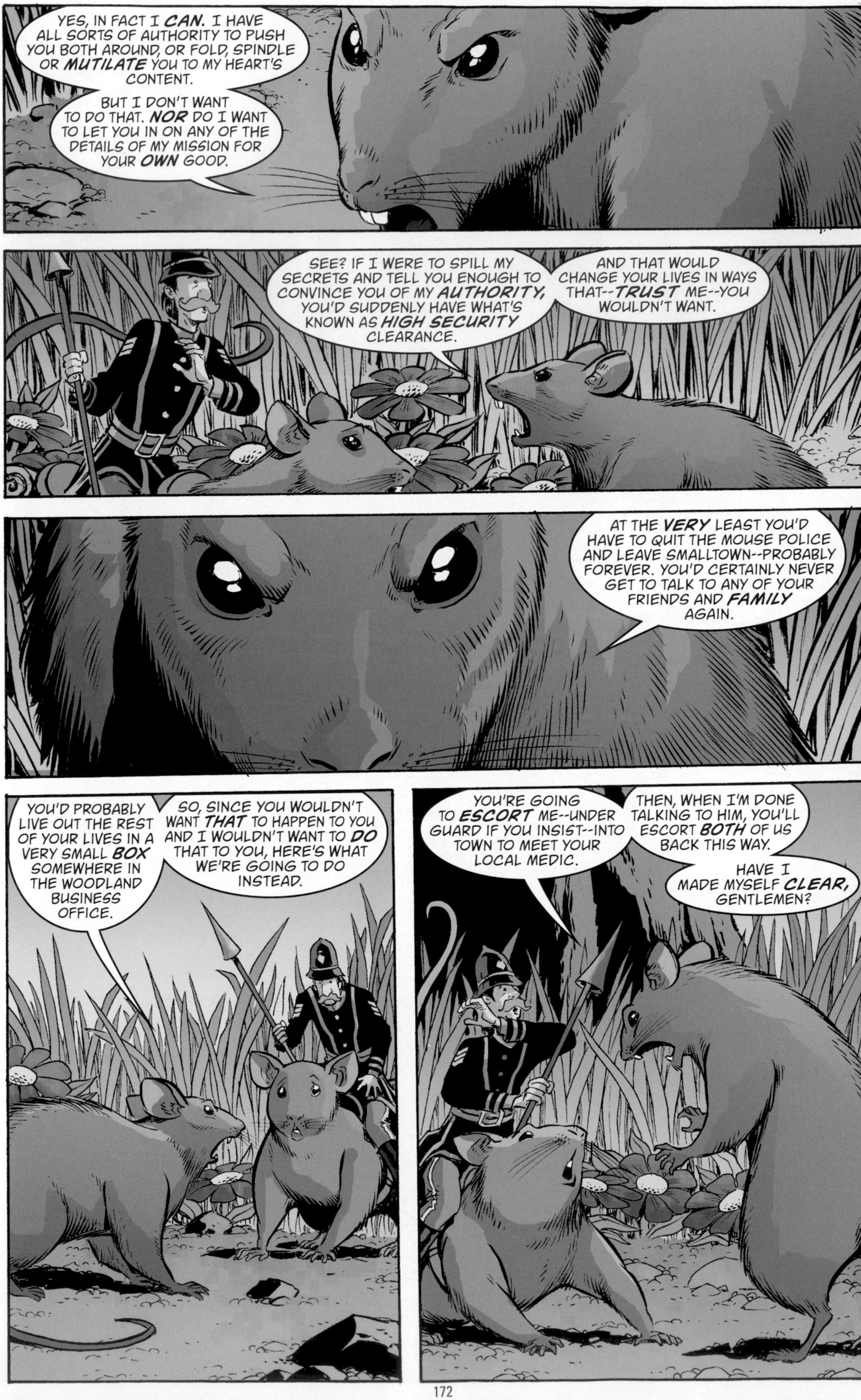
YES, IN FACT I CAN. I HAVE ALL SORTS OF AUTHORITY TO PUSH YOU BOTH AROUND, OR FOLD, SPINDLE OR MUTILATE YOU TO MY HEART'S CONTENT.
BUT I DON'T WANT TO DO THAT. NOR DO I WANT TO LET YOU IN ON ANY OF THE DETAILS OF MY MISSION FOR YOUR OWN GOOD.
SEE? IF I WERE TO SPILL MY SECRETS AND TELL YOU ENOUGH TO CONVINCE YOU OF MY AUTHORITY, YOU'D SUDDENLY HAVE WHAT'S KNOWN AS HIGH SECURITY CLEARANCE.
AND THAT WOULD CHANGE YOUR LIVES IN WAYS THAT--TRUST ME--YOU WOULDN'T WANT.
AT THE VERY LEAST YOU'D HAVE TO QUIT THE MOUSE POLICE AND LEAVE SMALLTOWN--PROBABLY FOREVER. YOU'D CERTAINLY NEVER GET TO TALK TO ANY OF YOUR FRIENDS AND FAMILY AGAIN.
YOU'D PROBABLY LIVE OUT THE REST OF YOUR LIVES IN A VERY SMALL BOX SOMEWHERE IN THE WOODLAND BUSINESS OFFICE.
SO, SINCE YOU WOULDN'T WANT THAT TO HAPPEN TO YOU AND I WOULDN'T WANT TO DO THAT TO YOU, HERE'S WHAT WE'RE GOING TO DO INSTEAD.
YOU'RE GOING TO ESCORT ME--UNDER GUARD IF YOU INSIST--INTO TOWN TO MEET YOUR LOCAL MEDIC.
THEN, WHEN I'M DONE TALKING TO HIM, YOU'LL ESCORT BOTH OF US BACK THIS WAY.
HAVE I MADE MYSELF CLEAR, GENTLEMEN?

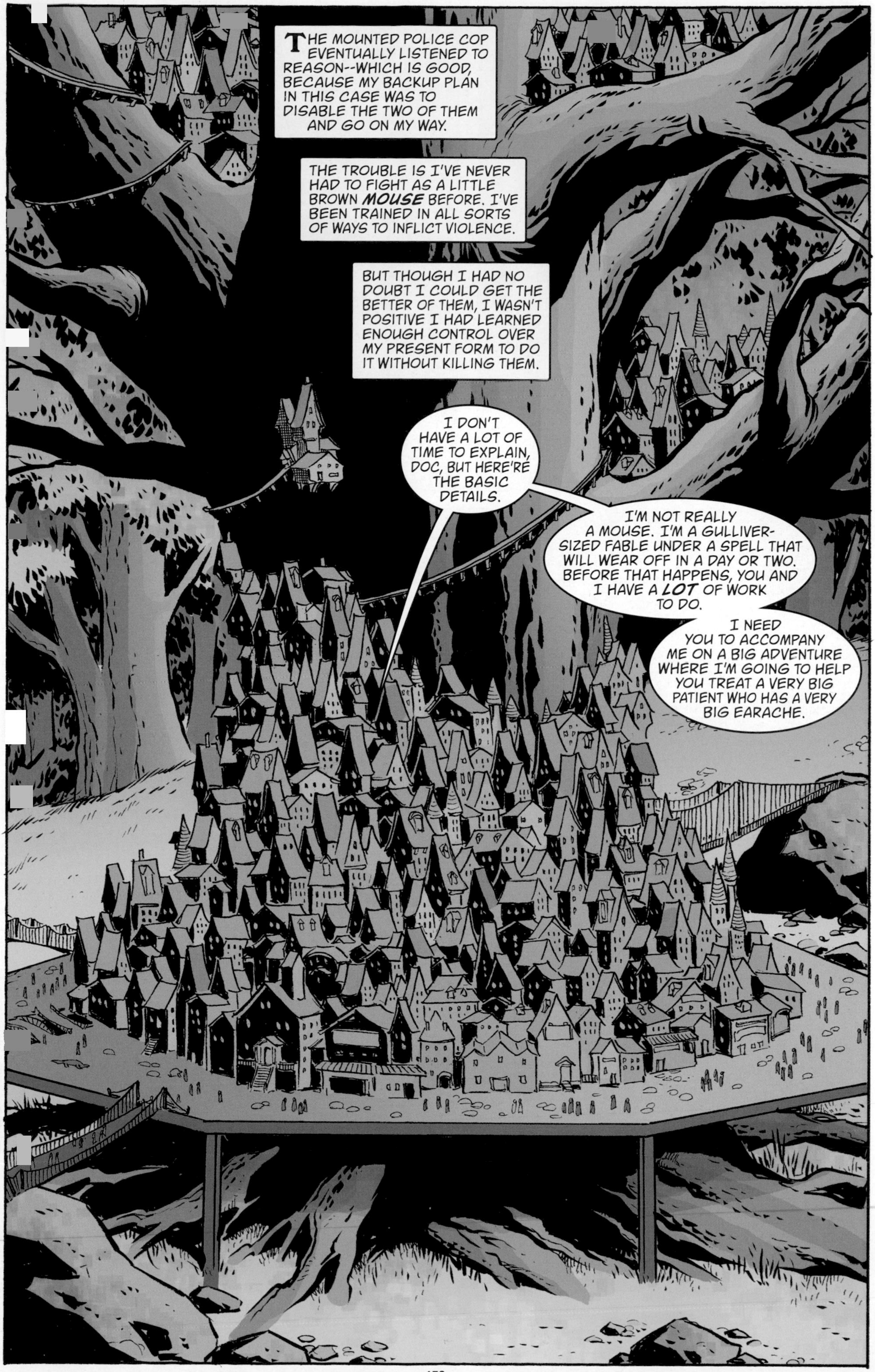
THE MOUNTED POLICE COP EVENTUALLY LISTENED TO REASON--WHICH IS GOOD, BECAUSE MY BACKUP PLAN IN THIS CASE WAS TO DISABLE THE TWO OF THEM AND GO ON MY WAY.
THE TROUBLE IS I'VE NEVER HAD TO FIGHT AS A LITTLE BROWN MOUSE BEFORE. I'VE BEEN TRAINED IN ALL SORTS OF WAYS TO INFLICT VIOLENCE.
BUT THOUGH I HAD NO DOUBT I COULD GET THE BETTER OF THEM, I WASN'T POSITIVE I HAD LEARNED ENOUGH CONTROL OVER MY PRESENT FORM TO DO IT WITHOUT KILLING THEM.
I DON'T HAVE A LOT OF TIME TO EXPLAIN, DOC, BUT HERE'RE THE BASIC DETAILS.
I'M NOT REALLY A MOUSE. I'M A GULLIVER-SIZED FABLE UNDER A SPELL THAT WILL WEAR OFF IN A DAY OR TWO. BEFORE THAT HAPPENS, YOU AND I HAVE A LOT OF WORK TO DO.
I NEED YOU TO ACCOMPANY ME ON A BIG ADVENTURE WHERE I'M GOING TO HELP YOU TREAT A VERY BIG PATIENT WHO HAS A VERY BIG EARACHE.

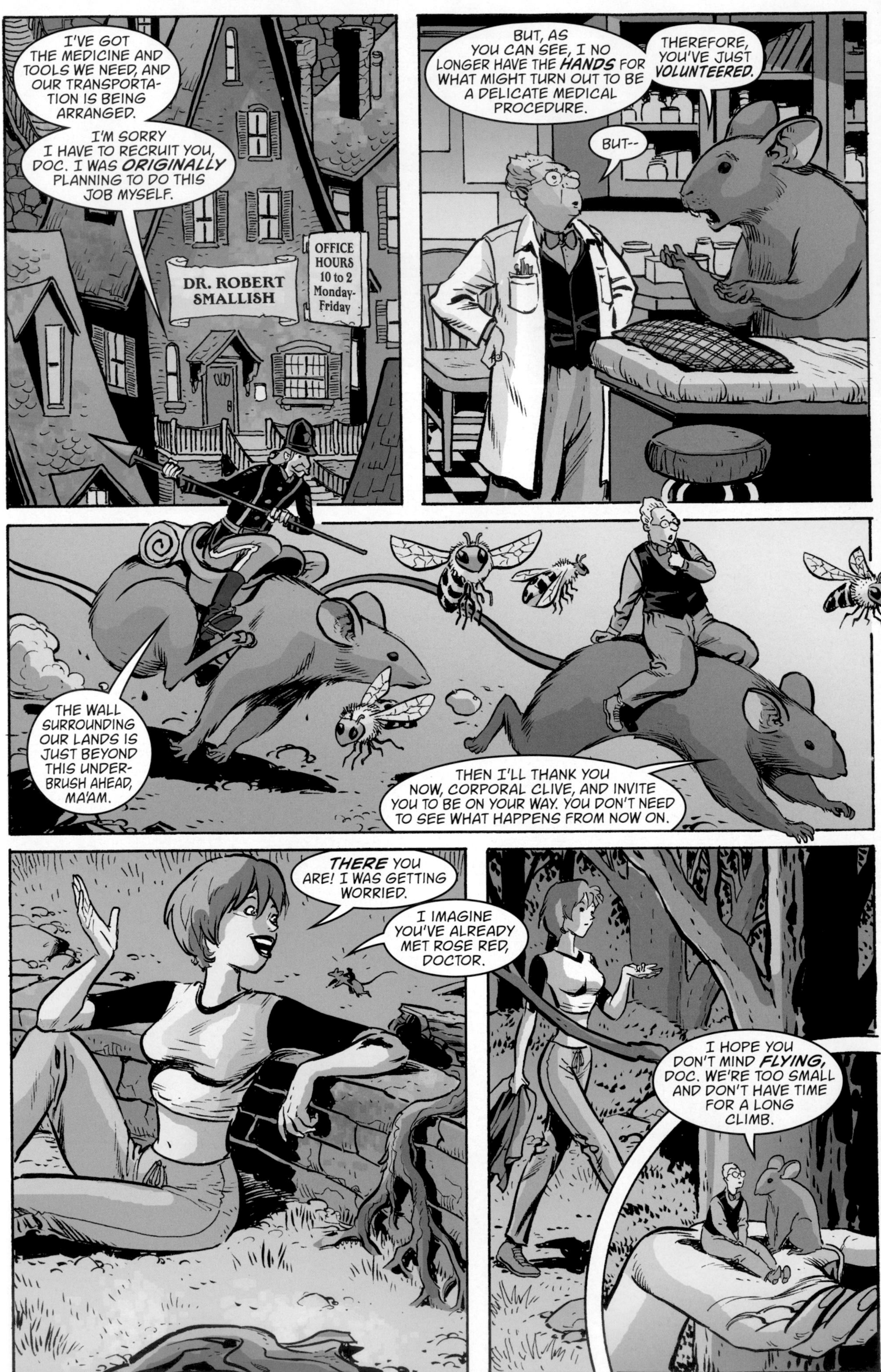

I'VE GOT THE MEDICINE AND TOOLS WE NEED, AND OUR TRANSPORTATION IS BEING ARRANGED.
I'M SORRY I HAVE TO RECRUIT YOU, DOC. I WAS ORIGINALLY PLANNING TO DO THIS JOB MYSELF.
DR. ROBERT SMALLISH
OFFICE HOURS 10 to 2 Monday-Friday
BUT, AS YOU CAN SEE, I NO LONGER HAVE THE HANDS FOR WHAT MIGHT TURN OUT TO BE A DELICATE MEDICAL PROCEDURE.
THEREFORE, YOU'VE JUST VOLUNTEERED.
BUT--
THE WALL SURROUNDING OUR LANDS IS JUST BEYOND THIS UNDERBRUSH AHEAD, MA'AM.
THEN I'LL THANK YOU NOW, CORPORAL CLIVE, AND INVITE YOU TO BE ON YOUR WAY. YOU DON'T NEED TO SEE WHAT HAPPENS FROM NOW ON.
THERE YOU ARE! I WAS GETTING WORRIED.
I IMAGINE YOU'VE ALREADY MET ROSE RED, DOCTOR.
I HOPE YOU DON'T MIND FLYING, DOC. WE'RE TOO SMALL AND DON'T HAVE TIME FOR A LONG CLIMB.

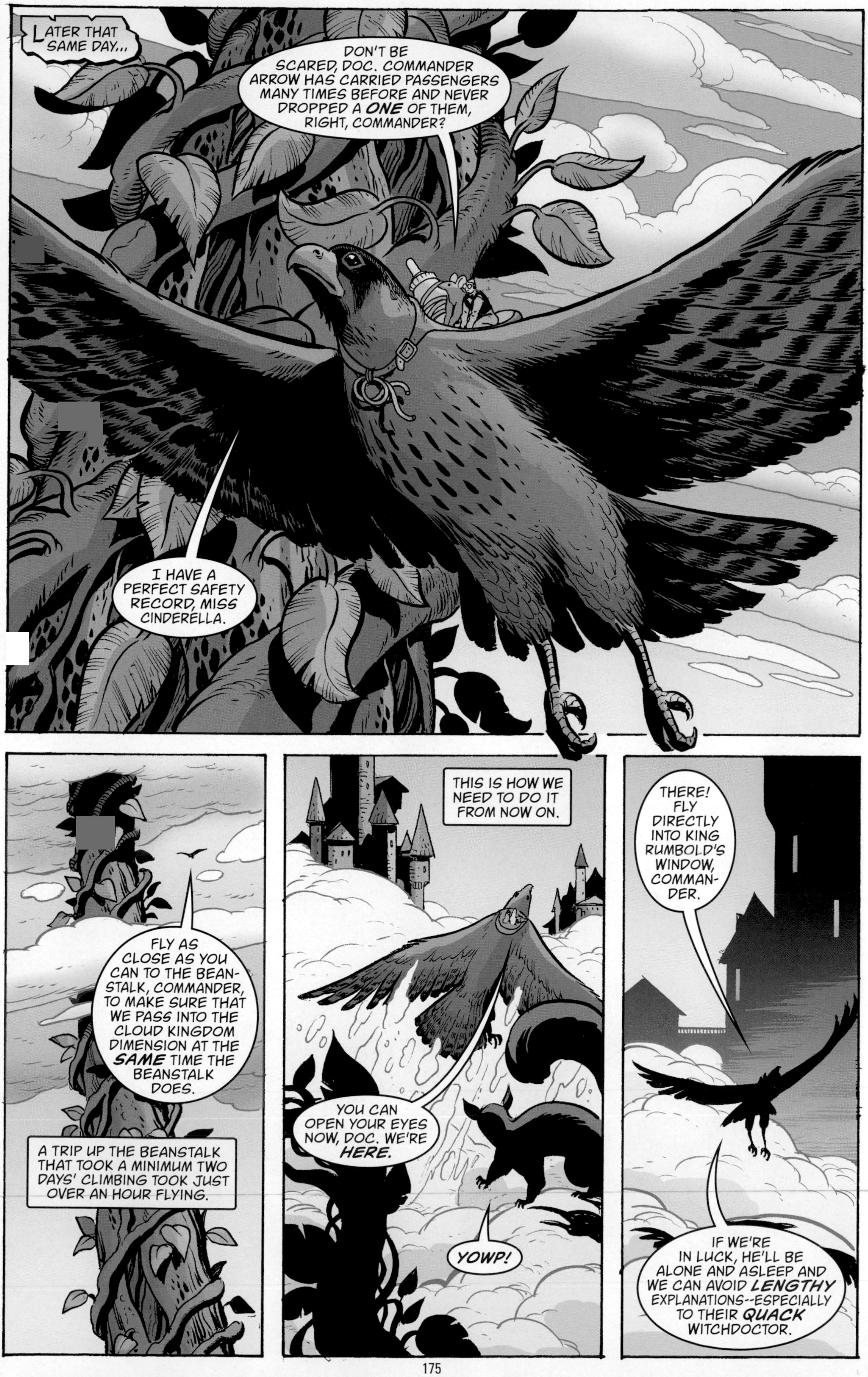
LATER THAT SAME DAY...
DON'T BE SCARED, DOC. COMMANDER ARROW HAS CARRIED PASSENGERS MANY TIMES BEFORE AND NEVER DROPPED A ONE OF THEM, RIGHT, COMMANDER?
I HAVE A PERFECT SAFETY RECORD, MISS CINDERELLA.
FLY AS CLOSE AS YOU CAN TO THE BEAN-STALK, COMMANDER, TO MAKE SURE THAT WE PASS INTO THE CLOUD KINGDOM DIMENSION AT THE SAME TIME THE BEANSTALK DOES.
A TRIP UP THE BEANSTALK THAT TOOK A MINIMUM TWO DAYS' CLIMBING TOOK JUST OVER AN HOUR FLYING.
THIS IS HOW WE NEED TO DO IT FROM NOW ON.
YOU CAN OPEN YOUR EYES NOW, DOC. WE'RE HERE.
YOWP!
THERE! FLY DIRECTLY INTO KING RUMBOLD'S WINDOW, COMMAN-DER.
IF WE'RE IN LUCK, HE'LL BE ALONE AND ASLEEP AND WE CAN AVOID LENGTHY EXPLANATIONS--ESPECIALLY TO THEIR QUACK WITCHDOCTOR.

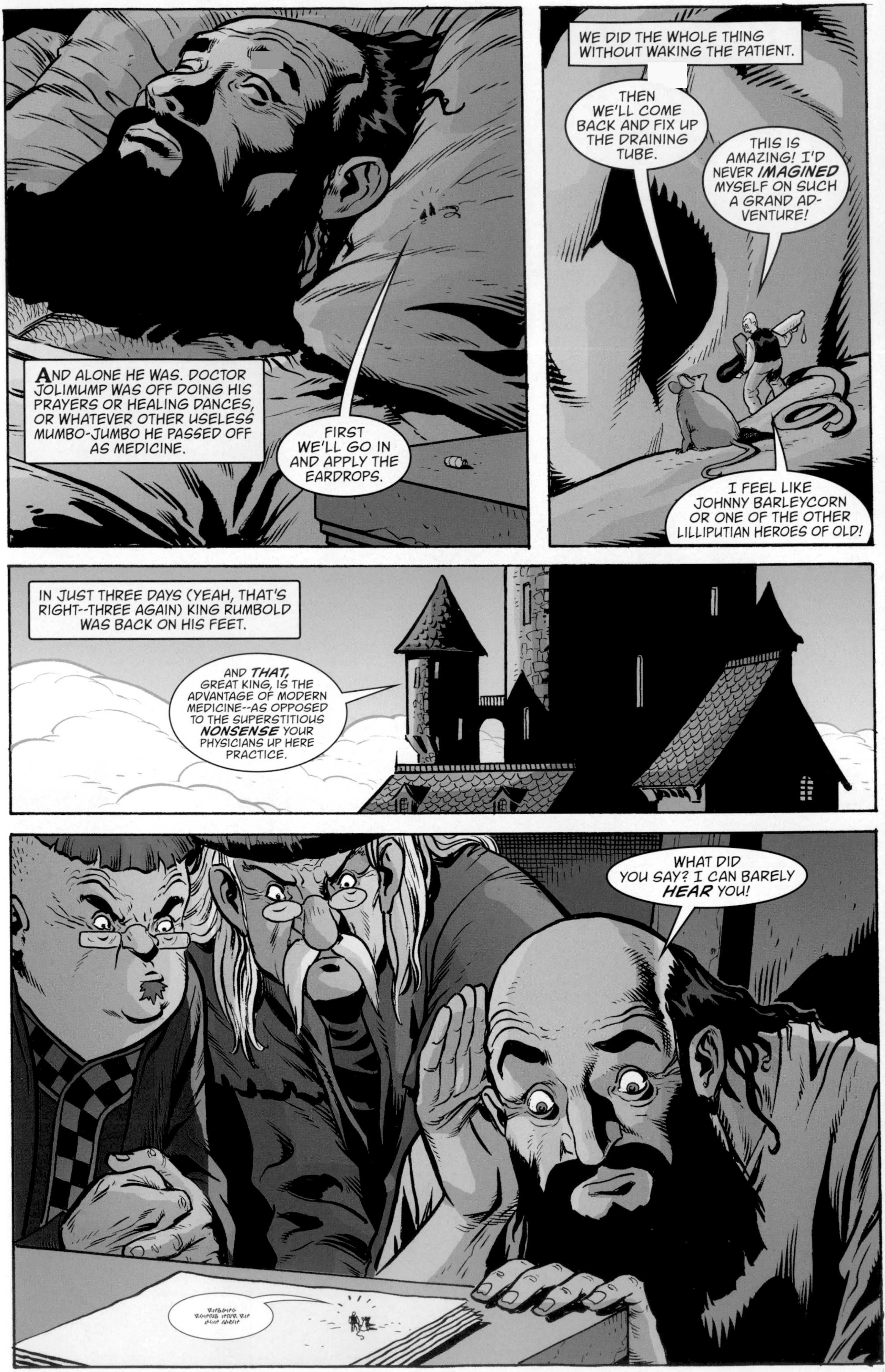
AND ALONE HE WAS. DOCTOR JOLIMUMP WAS OFF DOING HIS PRAYERS OR HEALING DANCES, OR WHATEVER OTHER USELESS MUMBO-JUMBO HE PASSED OFF AS MEDICINE.
FIRST WE'LL GO IN AND APPLY THE EARDROPS.
WE DID THE WHOLE THING WITHOUT WAKING THE PATIENT.
THEN WE'LL COME BACK AND FIX UP THE DRAINING TUBE.
THIS IS AMAZING! I'D NEVER *IMAGINED* MYSELF ON SUCH A GRAND AD-VENTURE!
I FEEL LIKE JOHNNY BARLEYCORN OR ONE OF THE OTHER LILLIPUTIAN HEROES OF OLD!
IN JUST THREE DAYS (YEAH, THAT'S RIGHT--THREE AGAIN) KING RUMBOLD WAS BACK ON HIS FEET.
AND *THAT,* GREAT KING, IS THE ADVANTAGE OF MODERN MEDICINE--AS OPPOSED TO THE SUPERSTITIOUS *NONSENSE* YOUR PHYSICIANS UP HERE PRACTICE.
WHAT DID YOU SAY? I CAN BARELY *HEAR* YOU!

WHAT I *SAID* WAS, MODERN MEDICINE IS ONLY *ONE* OF THE ADVANTAGES WE WILL BE BRINGING TO OUR NEW ALLIANCE--ONCE YOU *SIGN* THE *TREATY!*

I DON'T THINK HE'S GOING TO BE ABLE TO *HEAR* US, MISS.

GUESS NOT-- AT LEAST NOT UNTIL I GROW BACK INTO MY--

¡URP!¿

I THINK I MAY BE ABOUT TO--

YOW!

OH MY GOODNESS! YOU'RE A *GIANT!*

ZOUNDS!

A TINY NAKED *MIRACLE* APPEARS BEFORE US!

UHM-- DO ANY OF YOU GENTLEMEN HAVE A *HANKY* I COULD BORROW?

OF COURSE I MADE TWO ENEMIES THAT DAY. GUSTROLF DIDN'T LIKE ME GOING BEHIND HIS BACK, AND DOCTOR JOLIMUMP DIDN'T LIKE BEING EXPOSED AS A FRAUD.

WE NEED TO KEEP AN EYE ON THEM IN THE FUTURE.

YOU CAN *BET* THEY'LL TRY TO CAUSE US GRIEF SOONER OR LATER.

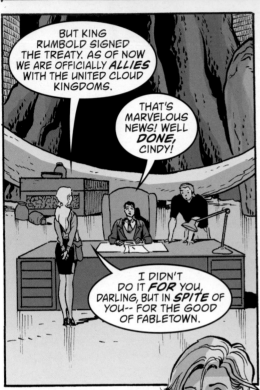

BUT KING RUMBOLD SIGNED THE TREATY. AS OF NOW WE ARE OFFICIALLY *ALLIES* WITH THE UNITED CLOUD KINGDOMS.

THAT'S *MARVELOUS* NEWS! WELL *DONE*, CINDY!

I DIDN'T DO IT *FOR* YOU, DARLING, BUT IN *SPITE* OF YOU-- FOR THE GOOD OF FABLETOWN.

ALL THE SAME, WE'RE INDEBTED TO YOU, CINDERELLA.

THEN KINDLY REWARD ME, SHERIFF, BY *NEVER* GIVING ME ANOTHER DIPLOMATIC MISSION.

WHAT I DIDN'T TELL THEM (AND WON'T INCLUDE IN MY OFFICIAL REPORT) IS THE PRICE FRAU TOTENKINDER CHARGED ME FOR HER MAGIC POTION, WHEN SHE KNEW SHE HAD ME OVER A BARREL.

THAT'S CERTAINLY GOING TO COME BACK TO HAUNT ME.

THE END

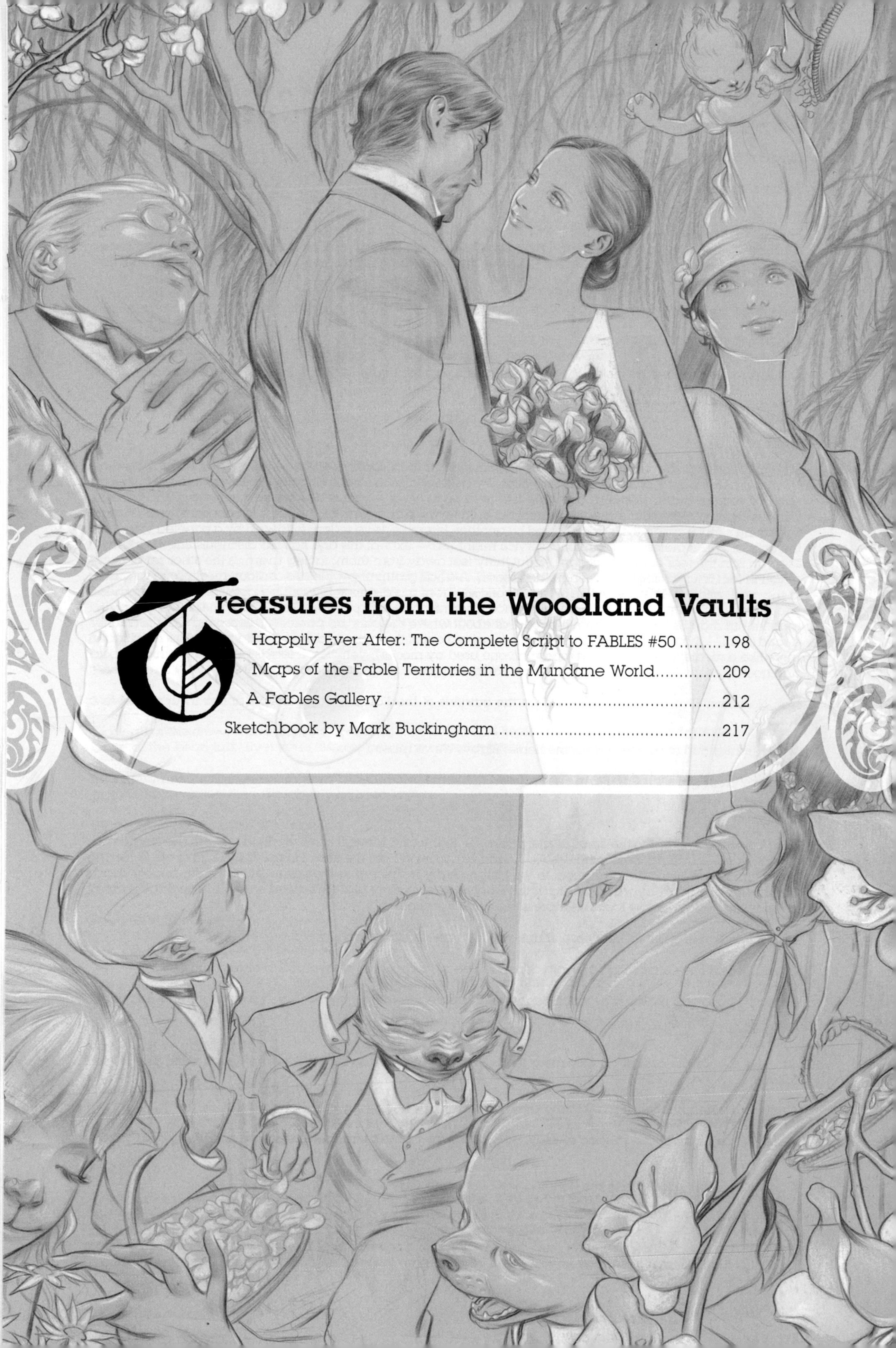

Treasures from the Woodland Vaults

Cap: And celebrated the joyous day.

One of the Kids: Where are Mommy and Daddy going now?

Rose Red: Somewhere you're not invited, wolfling.

Riding Hood (to Fly): That's odd. He does seem familiar — as if we'd met before.

Page Forty Seven (four panels)

Panel One

This isn't really a panel. It's the space you need to leave at the top of the page for the final chapter title.

Title (display lettering): Epilogue: Mr. and Mrs. Wolf

Panel Two

We see Paris at night, all lit up.

Cap: No one quite knew where they planned to go on their honeymoon, or how long they might stay away.

Voice (from city): A little more champagne, Mrs. Wolf?

Panel Three

Now we return to daytime and Wolf Valley. In the background we see their new home. It's a wonderful and sprawling one-story thing: part cabin and partly made of dressed stone and lots of real glass windows and stone chimneys and enough rooms so that each kid gets his own room. Mark: keep in mind that however you design this, you're likely to be drawing it every once in a while, until the end of time. Here and there, away from the house, there are odds and ends of the construction materials still on site, as if it were just finished minutes before the new family arrived. In the foreground we see Bigby and Snow, hand in hand, walking away from us, walking towards the house. Ahead of them the six kids race like hellions towards the house, so that they can be the first to pick their rooms. This is long after the wedding, so Snow and Bigby and all the kids will be dressed differently than when we last saw them.

Cap: But true to Boy Blue's promise, their house in Wolf Valley was finished and waiting for them by the time they returned.

Snow: Go pick your rooms, children. You each have one of your own.

Panel Four

Now the kids have long disappeared into the house's open front door. Bigby has lifted Snow up into his arms to carry her over the threshold.

Snow: So, do you think happily ever after is possible after all?

Bigby: We'll see.

Panel Five

Same exact scene, but now everyone has entered the house and we see the door close behind them, signaling that they have left the series — for now.

No captions or dialogue in this panel.

Page Forty Eight (one panel)

This is a full-page splash, leaving only enough room at the bottom of the page, as the final thing on this page, for this issue's title and credits. We are looking down on the surface of one of the feasting tables at Snow and Bigby's wedding. We see a fine plate with some partially-eaten wedding cake on it. We see a crystal champagne flute with some champagne still in it and a lipstick stain on the rim of the glass. We see a little bit of this and that — like a used fork and maybe a few Polaroid snapshots of the wedding and feast that followed. In the center of this untidy scene we see one of the wedding invitations, which reads as follows (in a fine script, please): You are cordially invited to join with us in celebrating the marriage of Snow White to Bigby Wolf. And under that: R.S.V.P.

Title (display lettering in fine script): Happily Ever After

Credits (in the same script)

Cap (not to be repeated in the collected version): The creators and publishers of Fables would like to thank you our readers for your loyalty, encouragement and reliable "what happens next" interest in these first fifty issues. We'll see you next month when the next fifty begins.

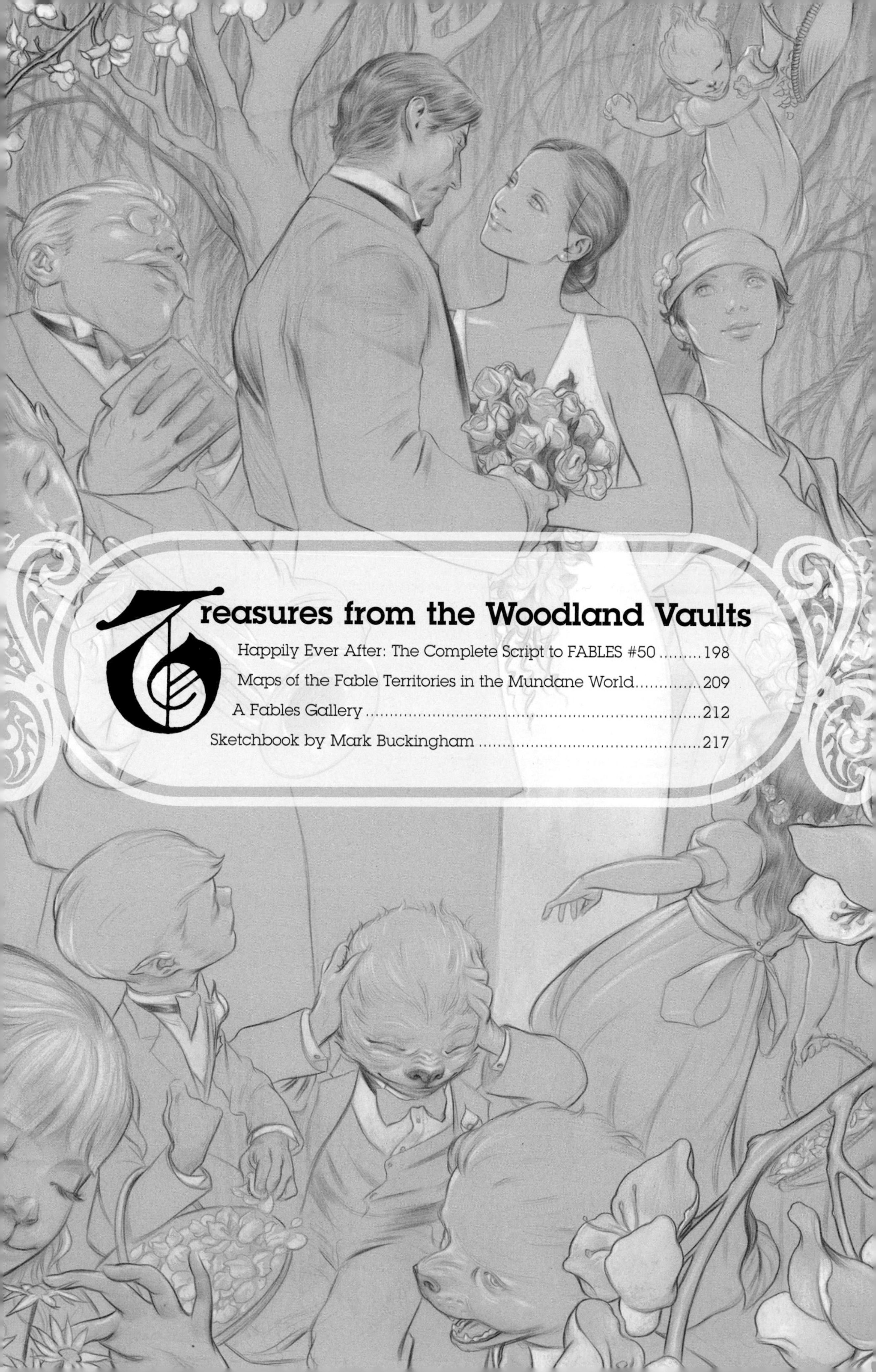

Treasures from the Woodland Vaults

Fables

Issue Fifty

Title: Happily Ever After

By Bill Willingham

48 Pages

Artist and Lettering Note: In a break from tradition, the main titles and credits for this issue will appear in the back of the book, rather than the front. However, there will be chapter titles and we'd like them all in the same general font as the main title.

Page One (five panels)

Panel One

This isn't really a panel. It's the space you need to leave at the top of the page for this section's chapter title.

Display Lettering: Chapter One: Secret Agent Man

Panel Two

It's early morning. We see a lonely two-lane (at most) dirt road somewhere in upstate New York. This is far away from any sign of civilization or habitation. Two sets of cars are parked in the middle of this road, facing each other from a distance of about thirty feet from each other — sort of like when competing underworld families have a clandestine meeting in an out-of-the-way place. One of the sets of cars consists of Prince Charming's sports car, in the lead, followed by another, less expensive sedan, followed by a paneled van, like the type of van a professional janitorial service might use — except this one has no distinguishing markings. The van is in the rear of this set of cars. About thirty feet away from them, facing them, is the other set of cars, which in fact is just a single undistinguished sedan. A small group of people are on foot, meeting each other, in the road, midway between each of the sets of cars. From this distance it won't be possible to tell who these people are, but they are: Bigby; Mowgli; Prince Charming; Beast; and Rose Red. One other note: An even rougher dirt road branches off from this road, at about where the cars are parked. This second road is hardly a road at all — more like two parallel wheel ruts carved out of the grass and weeds and brush. This road looks more like a medieval wooded cart road than one used by modern vehicles. It leads off of the main dirt road and goes towards the deep forest area of the Farm. It's a cool, late summer morning.

Non Narration Cap: A lonely side road on the outskirts of the Farm — Fabletown's annex in upstate New York.

Voice (from group of people): Welcome home, Bigby. We've missed you.

2nd Voice (from same group): Farm's never been my home, Mr. Mayor. This is as close as I've been to it.

Panel Three

Now we move in closer to the small cluster of people. Bigby and Mowgli have walked up from the single car, to join Prince Charming, Beast and Rose Red, who've come up from the line of cars. They're all dressed for the cool morning and for tramping about in the rough. Bigby is dressed in the same black T-shirt, hiking shorts and hiking boots that he was wearing in the Storybook Love story arc. He's close enough to civilization that he's smoking again. Bigby looks unimpressed with this gathering.

Charming: Fair enough. In any case, thank you for agreeing to return.

Bigby: Considering Bagheera's freedom depended on it, I didn't really have much choice, did I?

Mowgli: I hope you realize how much Baggy and I appreciate it.

Panel Four

Another shot of the group, as Charming leads Bigby to the van at the end of the line of cars. The others follow.

Charming: I imagine you'll want to see Snow and your kids before —

Bigby: Nope. If this secret mission of yours goes bad, why cause them the extra grief and worry? Let's get it done first.

Charming: Then follow me to the van and we'll be on our way.

Panel Five

We return to a wide shot, overhead view, looking down at the parked cars, as the van pulls around the car in front of it and bumps its way over the edge of the road onto the rougher (wooden cart track) road, headed towards the woods. Basically everyone is in the one van now, leaving the other cars where they're parked.

Voice (from van): Pardon the bad road, but we're headed to the most remote and restricted section of the Farm.

Page Two (one panel)

Panel One

This is a full-page splash. In the foreground we see the tiny van heading along the bumpy, twisty forest road, towards something huge in the background. In the background we see a giant magic beanstalk rising from the forest and reaching clear off the top of the page, going all the way up into the sky. The base of the beanstalk is huge — as big around as the base of giant redwood trees. But unlike such trees, the beanstalk is a twisted rope of several impossibly-thick strands imperfectly twined together. All kinds of thick stems reach out from the main stalk, some just ending in a curl of stem and some ending in huge leaves — big enough that a grown human can bunk in one like it was a hammock (which is important in a few pages). This beanstalk is in a very remote area of the Farm. No part of the civilized part of the Farm can be seen from here. In fact, no sign of civilization (except the van and the bad road) can be seen at all.

Voice (from van): Wow! That's a —

2nd Voice (from van): That's right, Rose Red, it's a beanstalk — one of the magic ones from Jack's original magic bean stash.

Same 2nd Voice (connected balloon): Which is why we never paid much attention to Jack when he claimed to still have some of the beans. He didn't know we had them all along.

Page Three (five panels)

Panel One

The van pulls up near the base of the beanstalk. The side door opens and we see Rose Red getting out, followed by Beast. Rose Red keeps looking up at the giant stalk, amazement and disbelief in her eyes.

Rose Red: So this is what you've been up to out here for the past two years? All the secret comings and goings? Why didn't you tell me?

Beast: Until now, you didn't need to know.

Panel Two

Now all of the crew: Charming, Bigby, Mowgli, Rose Red and Beast, are out of the van and standing near the base of the beanstalk. Everyone else seems unimpressed, except Rose Red who can't stop looking up at it.

Beast: Bigby taught me that much. Compartmentalization is the be all and end all of the spook game. No one gets to know unless they absolutely need to know.

Bigby: Basic operational doctrine, kid.

Panel Three

Closer on Rose Red. She's starting to freak out.

Rose Red: But this — !

Rose Red: You can't — !

Rose Red: It sticks out like a sore thumb! A giant sore thumb! This is going to attract all kinds of mundy attention to the Farm!

Panel Four

Beast lays some calming (not intimate) hands on Rose Red.

Beast: Not at all. It's completely imaginary until you get close enough.

Beast: No one can see it from a distance. A mundy pilot can fly within 300 feet of it and never know it's there.

Panel Five

Wider shot. Rose is calmer now, but still impressed by the sight of the beanstalk. Bigby looks up at it too, but for a different reason. He's judging the spaces between leaf stems (which are as thick as a normal tree's branches), to see if he can climb it without ropes and climbing gear. They are indeed close enough to free climb, by the way.

Charming: And since no flight paths pass within twenty miles of this place, we're fine.

Beast: The beanstalk's basic structure is transdimensional.

Page Four (five panels)

Panel One

Another group shot, concentrating on Charming, who's still teaching Rose Red about beanstalk lore, and Bigby, who looks at Charming.

Charming: Though the roots are firmly in our world, somewhere along the way it ends up poking its way into the Cloud Kingdoms.

Bigby: This is all very informative, but can we get to the practical business?

Panel Two

Bigby looks back up at the beanstalk, flicking his cigarette away as he does so. The closest leaf stems (branches) are well over his head. Beast at least is in this shot as well.

Bigby: I assume I'm going to climb this thing?

Beast: Exactly.

Bigby: Where's my gear?

Panel Three

Same basic shot, but including Charming now as well.

Charming: It's waiting for you upstairs, along with your specific instructions. We thought it better that way, to further guard against anything leaking out.

Beast: Your contact will meet you at the top.

Panel Four

Bigby leaps up and grabs the lowest leaf stem, hanging from it. Rose Red can be seen in the group below him.

Bigby: Then I might as well get started.

Rose Red: Are you sure there isn't anything you want me to tell Snow?

Bigby: I'm sure, Rose.

Panel Five

Now Bigby easily pulls himself up on the leaf stem he was hanging from. He's begun his climb. It's still pretty early in the morning.

Bigby: If I don't return, I was never here in the first place.

Bigby: If I do, I can tell her myself.

Page Five (four panels)

Panel One

We switch scenes slightly to follow Bigby on his climb up into the sky. In this panel he's pretty damned high, but we can still see the forested land far below him. Maybe now we can see some of the familiar details of the Farm off in the distance. Bigby is climbing pretty steadily, keeping a good pace, without getting tired. It's still daytime.

No captions or dialogue in this panel.

Panel Two

Same scene, but hours later. Now there is nothing but cloud below Bigby. He's passed through at least one cloud layer and is still going strong. The beanstalk is still as big around as a giant redwood tree trunk.

No captions or dialogue in this panel.

Panel Three

It's nighttime and Bigby is sleeping comfortably in one of the giant beanstalk leaves (see, I told you it would be important), which easily holds his weight. It's big enough that he could roll over a couple of times and still have no worry about falling.

No captions or dialogue in this panel.

Panel Four

It's another day and Bigby is climbing again. It's so high up now that snow is falling. Since Bigby doesn't feel the cold, he just keeps climbing away.

No captions or dialogue in this panel.

Page Six (five panels)

Panel One

We switch scene to another daytime establishing shot of the Farm — this time we see that part of the Farm we normally see, with the central village area. It's daytime.

Voice (from town square): Wake up, Bagheera, it's emancipation day for all imprisoned Fables of the black pantheresque persuasion.

Panel Two

We move down into the Farm's town square, and the big tiger cage that's been the centerpiece of the town for far too many issues. Prince Charming, Mowgli, Rose Red and Boy Blue are all there, as Rose has just unlocked the cage and is swinging the cage door wide open. Charming is holding up some sort of official-looking document in his hands. Mowgli and Boy Blue simply look happy. Charming, Mowgli and Rose Red are dressed differently than they were at the beginning of this issue, to show that this is not the same day. Bagheera is in his cage, yawning with sleep and only tentatively moving towards the open doorway, as if he doesn't quite believe he's free.

Bagheera: Really? I'm free to go?

Mowgli: You're officially sprung, buddy.

Charming: Here's your pardon — signed and sealed.

Panel Three

Bagheera springs out of the cage right onto Mowgli's chest, flattening him onto his back, onto the ground. Even though the wind's knocked out of him, Mowgli is still grinning like a fool. Bagheera is obviously quite happy and this is no attack — it's roughhousing with a good friend.

Bagheera: I can go anywhere I want?

Charming: Anywhere on the Farm, at least.

Mowgli: Get off of me, you giant rat!

Panel Four

Now, like a bullet, Bagheera springs into action, running for the edge of town, heading full speed towards the nearest forest areas. The others watch him as he goes. Blue is helping Mowgli get up off of the ground. Charming is shouting at Bagheera's retreating back.

Charming: Anywhere not restricted, that is!

Blue: Where's he off to like a rocket?

Rose Red: Someplace that doesn't resemble a cage, I imagine.

Panel Five

Bagheera is long gone, leaving only a cloud of dust in his wake. Rose Red looks at the cage, while Blue talks to Mowgli as he dusts himself off.

Rose Red: Speaking of which, let's get this thing dismantled today. It's been a blight on our town square for entirely too long.

Blue: He'll probably remember to thank you, once he's settled down a bit.

Mowgli: I expect.

Page Seven (four panels)

Panel One

This isn't really a panel. It's the space you need to leave at the top of the page for this section's chapter title.

Display Lettering: <u>Chapter Two: Castles in the Sky</u>

Panel Two

We switch scenes back to Bigby, who's just reached the top of his climb. This is from the point of view of the Cloud Kingdoms, which is basically a land in the sky whose land is all the top side of fluffy white clouds. In this panel we see a fairly close shot of the very top strands of the beanstalk — which have gotten pretty small in diameter by now — twining and twisting, poking through the top of the billowing clouds, ending just about twelve feet above the clouds. We can just see one of Bigby's arms reaching out of the clouds for his next handhold of beanstalk. It is daytime but we can't see too many details of the land yet.

Non Narration Cap: Three days later…

Bigby (from cloud): I better be near the top. I'm running out of beanstalk.

Panel Three

We pull back just a bit farther to see that Bigby has now climbed to the very top of the beanstalk, which is thin enough that it can barely hold his weight now. Bigby is about four or five feet off of the "ground" of the billowing cloudscape around him. He's clutching the beanstalk pretty tight, not willing to jump down and test his weight on the cloud tops. A voice talks from behind Bigby (off panel), but Bigby can't turn to see who it is without shifting his weight on his precarious perch. For the first time ever we might even see a small bit of fright on Bigby's face (not too much fright — more like just some advanced nervousness).

Voice (from off-panel behind Bigby): Yes, you're at the top, Bigby.

Bigby: Who's that? I don't think I can turn around without shifting too much weight. This thing's ready to snap off under me as it is.

Panel Four

This is the big panel of the page. We now pull out to see a wide shot of Bigby and the surrounding area. Cinderella (Cindy) is standing on the rolling cloud tops, right behind Bigby. She's dressed for outdoor living — perhaps in some variation of the track-suit thingie she was wearing when we last saw her (in the Mean Seasons story arc, when she was helping Bigby and Beast interrogate the wooden heads). Behind Cindy we can see that she has a small tent and semi-permanent campsite set up, all pitched on one of the hills of the rolling cloudscape. She's clearly been camping out here for awhile, near the top of the beanstalk, waiting for someone to arrive from below. In the background all we can see so far is a rolling landscape of cloud tops, with a clear blue sky above it. Cindy looks a bit amused to see Bigby looking so nervous.

Cindy: You can step down now, Bigby. The cloudscape is solid beneath you.

Bigby: It wasn't when I was climbing up through it.

Bigby: Is that you, Cindy?

Page Eight (five panels)

Panel One

Closer on Cindy, as she smiles up at Bigby, still clinging to the beanstalk. She's having fun teasing him. Maybe we can also see Bigby's feet in this panel — at about head height to Cindy — wrapped securely around the stalk.

Cindy: Yes, it's me, and you really can get down. It's solid from the top, even though you could pass through from below. That's the way the enchantment works.

Cindy: Honestly, I don't think I've ever seen you afraid of anything before, Bigby.

Panel Two

Closer on Bigby, still clinging to his perch. He looks a bit cranky now at what Cindy said in teasing him.

Bigby: And you still haven't. Nervous isn't the same as scared.

Bigby: Remember, me and mine didn't evolve from monkeys like you and yours. I don't have climbing hardwired into me from a million generations past.

Panel Three

Wider shot as Cindy bounces up and down on the bit of cloud nearest to where the beanstalk has thrust through — to show Bigby it's safe and he won't fall through. She's still smiling, enjoying this moment.

Cindy: Point taken, but you really can get down. See? I'm jumping up and down right next to you without falling through.

Cindy: Trust me. I've been living up here for months, preparing the way for you with the locals.

Panel Four

Bigby is finally risking a look down to the cloud tops just below him. He's screwing his courage up to jump down from the beanstalk.

Cindy: There's really no need to be scared.

Bigby: Nervous.

Cindy: Right. Nervous. That's what I said.

Panel Five

Bigby finally lets go and falls the few short feet to the cloud top landscape below him. Cindy deftly steps out of the way. She's still smiling and still teasing him.

Bigby: Okay, here goes nothing.

Cindy: If you do fall through, you'll have a long time to regret listening to me on the way down.

Page Nine (five panels)

Panel One

Now Bigby stands up on wobbly feet. He looks like he's trying to stand on a very soft, constantly-shifting, surface. Cindy, having gotten used to the footing long ago, stands just fine.

Bigby: Very funny. You've got quite the cruel streak in you, Cindy.

Cindy: Which is why we always got along so well. How does it feel?

Bigby: Shifty. Like trying to stand on a ground made of damp sponge.

Panel Two

Cindy watches as Bigby tries to stand, like a drunk man, nearly falling over with every minor shift of his weight.

Cindy: Yeah, it's odd, but you'll get used to it. It didn't take me much more than a day up here to get my sea legs — or cloud legs actually.

Cindy: Truth is, since this is a giant land with giant distances, you won't be doing much walking up here anyway.

Panel Three

Cindy turns and calls out, and a giant squirrel's head suddenly appears, popping up from behind the next hump of cloud. This squirrel is big enough for both Bigby and Cindy to ride if they needed to (but they won't). This is a land of the giants and this squirrel, named Radiskop, is to scale with everything and everyone they are about to encounter. Bigby is a little taken aback by the sudden appearance of the huge beast.

Cindy: Radiskop!

Radiskop: Yes, Cinderella?

Cindy: Can you go inform our host the guest of honor has arrived?

Panel Four

Radiskop the giant squirrel goes bounding away from (us) Cindy and Bigby, enthusiastically leaping and bouncing off of the sponge-like cloud as if it were a series of puffy trampolines.

Bigby: He seems enthusiastic.

Cindy: Rady's a big sweetheart.

Bigby: Big is right — big enough to swallow us both in two or three bites.

Panel Five

Wider shot. Radiskop is gone. Cindy turns back towards her campsite. Bigby follows behind her on very shaky legs.

Cindy: Help me break camp, while we wait for our transport to arrive.

Cindy: We won't be coming back this way.

Page Ten (four panels)

Panel One

This is the big panel of the page, taking up at least half of the page. We switch scenes to a shot of a giant named Humberjon striding across this vast cloudy land. Humberjon is a young giant — basically a teenage boy. He's only going to be seen on this page, and one other panel later, so you can design him pretty much any way you like. As he walks, Humberjon is holding one arm out, with his palm up. Cinderella and Bigby are riding in that open palm, high above the cloudy ground below. All of Cindy's camping gear is packed up, rolled up and riding in the giant's open palm along with them. Note that there needs to be lots of gear shown — because it includes all of Cindy's camping gear plus all of the gear Bigby will be taking with him into the Homelands on his mission (the specifics of which are described in a few pages). Basically we need to see lots of stuff here. Humberjon is walking towards a big, dark wizard's castle (a giant wizard's castle) in the background. Also, now that we have a high vantage point, we can see other castles and towns scattered in the distance. It's still daytime.

Non Narration Cap: Less than an hour later...

Cindy (from giant's hand): Young Humberjon is taking us to the wizard Ulmore's castle. That's our staging area for the mission.

Bigby (from giant's hand): Nice view.

Panel Two

Closer on Cindy and Bigby riding in the giant's open palm. Cindy hands Bigby a multi-page document bound together with little brass fasteners (which we call brads over here on our side of the pond) — bound like movie screenplays are bound. This is the written mission plan that Bigby has to read and memorize. It's at least twenty pages thick.

Cindy: Here. We'll be awhile getting there, so you can start reading. These are your mission orders.

Panel Three

Same scene. Bigby starts reading.

Cindy: You'll have to memorize all of your instructions before you go. We can't let you take the physical documents with you.

Bigby: Standard procedure.

Panel Four

Closer on Bigby who is deep into reading the document now.

Lettering Note: Todd: From now on (until about halfway through this issue) all captions, unless otherwise noted, are the written instructions that Bigby is reading, or has memorized for his mission. Can we have a serif font for these captions, please? Not a fake typewriter font though, since Fabletown is modern enough not to use old-fashioned typewriters anymore. Thanks

Cap (mission text): Operation: Israel. Stage One: Preparation.

Cap (mission text): You will make contact with your Mission Operator at the summit, who will direct you to friendly elements in the Cloud Kingdoms.

Page Eleven (four panels)

Panel One

We switch scenes to an exterior shot of the wizard's giant castle. Some time has passed and so it's nighttime now. We can see a light showing from one of the higher tower windows.

Cap (mission text): Your primary contact among the giants will be the wizard Ulmore, who will prepare you for insertion.

Voice (from lighted tower window): Since you're not a magician, I'll have to try to explain things to you in layman's terms.

Panel Two

Big panel. Now we switch scenes inside the giant tower room to see the wizard Ulmore seated at a wooden table with a candlestick set on it, with a lit candle burning in it. The tiny forms of Cinderella and Bigby are seated on the table, looking up at Ulmore's giant face. Ulmore has to lean down to hear them, just the way Prince Charming had to lean close to hear his Mouse Police spies in the Storybook Love arc. Basically the giants are on the same scale to Bigby and Cindy as normal-sized Fables are to Lilliputian-sized Fables.

Cap (mission text): Extreme care should be taken not to do or say anything that might jeopardize the new and fragile diplomatic relations between Fabletown and the Cloud Kingdoms.

Ulmore: Even though the Cloud Kingdoms exist in their own dimension, in a seemingly paradoxical way they also exist in the sky over every known world.

Panel Three

Closer on Ulmore and the two Fables on the table.

Cap (mission text): Securing them as allies is vastly more important than the needs of this particular mission.

Ulmore: There's a corresponding location up here for any location down below, whether in your Mundy world or any world of the Empire.

Ulmore: Our task then is to find the location that looks down on their imperial capital.

Panel Four

Same scene.

Bigby: And just drop down on them from above?

Ulmore: Precisely. So far, the only way to bridge dimensions from below, coming upwards, is to travel via one of the magic beanstalks.

Page Twelve (four panels)

Panel One

Same scene. The candlelight conversation between Ulmore, Bigby and Cinderella continues.

Ulmore: That's kept us safe so far from the Adversary's armies.

Ulmore: But the dimensional doorways are always open going in the other direction.

Panel Two

We switch scenes to another part of the cloud kingdom. The giant wizard Ulmore is kneeling next to a large hole in the cloud floor being dug by the giant boy Humberjon, wielding a giant spade. Bigby and Cinderella are standing in one of Ulmore's open palms. Bigby is now laden down with all sorts of equipment. He is wearing a huge backpack of gear high on his back. Just below that (at about small-of-the-back or butt height) is strapped the first of two parachute packs. This is his main chute pack. On his belly is strapped his reserve parachute pack. Held in his arms is a fourth big bag of gear, called a musette bag. Once he makes his parachute jump, Bigby will release the musette bag, which will drop below him to be suspended about ten feet below him by two long straps, so that this bag will hit the ground before Bigby does and that loss of weight will allow Bigby's chute to slow down a tad bit more in the important few feet before landfall.

Here's some photo reference for a modern musette bag, but this is a small one. The one Bigby is carrying needs to be about twice as big and with longer straps: http://www.gr8gear.com/index.asp?PageAction=V IEWPROD&ProdID=3469

Here's a shot from the TV series Band of Brothers that shows some of the parachute troops beginning to strap on all of the gear they'll be taking with them for their D-Day jump. Note the very large musette bag on the ground in front of one of the troops: http://www.wingsamerica.com/webart/products/small/579.jpg

Here's a close-up shot of one of the troops getting onto the plane. You can just get a hint of how much gear is strapped to them. They have so much stuff on that they can barely walk on their own and what you can't see is the two troops below him that have to push on his butt to hoist him up into the doorway: hltp://www. dday-overlord.com/img/bob/film/imgfilm/band_of_brothers_c47_parachutistes_americain.jpg

Note that Bigby won't need the helmet and guns. But he's wearing as much equipment (all inside of packs) as you can physically draw on him.

Non Narration Cap: Three days later...

Ulmore: We shouldn't need anything but gravity to do the trick.

Cinderella: Are you ready to go, Bigby? Got all your equipment?

Humberjon: The hole's dug, sir.

Panel Three

Closer on Bigby and Cindy in Ulmore's palm. But in the background we can also see Humberjon using both hands to lift himself out of the hole he's dug. Now we can really see the immensity of the amount of gear strapped to poor Bigby.

Humberjon: I almost slipped through myself.

Bigby: I hope so. There's no room for anything else.

Panel Four

Ulmore holds his palm over the hole in the clouds and Bigby hops off of it and immediately starts falling towards the open hole. With all that gear, Bigby can barely give a small hop off of Ulmore's palm. He's still holding the musette bag in his arms.

Bigby: Better hold your hand directly over the hole, Ulmore. I can't jump far under all this weight.

Cindy: Be careless down there!

Page Thirteen (five panels)

Panel One

Now we switch scenes to the underside of the cloud layer. Dropping like a stone, Bigby comes hurtling out of the clouds into the open sky below, almost puncturing a hole in the clouds, trailing cloud vapor in his wake. He's still holding the musette bag in his arms. Oddly enough, though it was daytime up in the Cloud Kingdom, it's nighttime under the clouds in this new sky.

Cap (mission text): Stage Two: Insertion.

Cap (mission text): You will parachute into the Empire district of Calabri Anagni.

Panel Three

Still dropping towards the land far, far below, Bigby releases his musette bag which drops below him, the long straps (connecting the bag to his gear) trailing between them.

Cap (mission text): Be sure to pick a wilderness location for your drop zone.

Panel Four

The musette bag reaches the end of its two straps and snaps taught between the bag and Bigby above it.

Cap (mission text): And drop at night to avoid detection.

Panel Five

Closer on the still-plummeting Bigby, as he reaches for the rip-cord handle strapped to his chest and pulls it hard.

No captions or dialogue in this panel.

Page Fourteen (six panels)

Panel One

This isn't really a panel. It's the space you need to leave at the top of this page for the chapter title

Title (display lettering): Chapter Three: Behind Enemy Lines

Panel Two

Now Bigby's chute has deployed and Bigby drifts down to the land below, the musette bag hanging about ten to twelve feet below him.

No captions or dialogue in this panel.

Panel Three

We switch our angle of view so that we can look down to see the land far below Bigby. Directly below him we can see Bigby headed for a hilly, forested area. Off in the not too far distance we can see the Imperial City.

Bigby will be coming down a few miles from Geppetto's hut and the magic grove of trees.

Cap (mission text): Pick a landing site close enough to your target area to be within a day's travel, making sure that you stay far away from the Imperial City.

Panel Four

Down in a very remote area of forest at night, the musette bag hits the forest floor hard, as Bigby drifts down nearly on top of it.

No caption or dialogue in this panel.

Panel Five

Now Bigby hits the earth (and rolls), narrowly avoiding the musette bag.

No caption or dialogue in this panel.

Panel Six

Just a few minutes later Bigby has un-strapped from all of his gear and is gathering up the limp parachute by rolling it up in his arms. His copious gear lies near him.

Cap (mission text): Immediately bury your expended chute and reserve chute pack. You won't be needed them any longer.

Cap (mission text): Inspect all remaining gear.

Page Fifteen (five panels)

Panel One

Now a bit later, still devoid of his gear, Bigby is kneeling over a small hole in the dirt he has dug with his hands, in order to plant a single magic bean in the hole. This is still in some remote part of the nighttime forest.

Cap (mission text): Plant your extraction bean in some remote location. Take note that it will take approximately twelve hours to fully deploy.

Panel Two

Now, about an hour later, Bigby, still in human form, is running lithely through the nighttime forest. He's wearing one backpack on his back and holding the big musette bag in his arms again.

Cap (mission text): Travel only at night.

Panel Three

Now in another part of the forest, we see Bigby hiding behind some rocks or trees as a trio of armored goblin soldiers pass by on a forest path. They are very close to Bigby, but have no idea he's there. It's still nighttime.

Cap (mission text): Avoid all enemy contact.

Panel Four

Now it's daytime. We see Bigby lurking in the trees, looking down out of the forest towards Geppetto's hut and the grove of trees surrounding it. Maybe we can see Geppetto puttering around in his front yard, but this isn't vital.

Cap (mission text): If you arrive at the target site during daylight hours, wait until late the next night to begin operations.

Panel Five

It's nighttime again. Now we switch scenes to a shot of Bigby coming silent out of the woods, approaching a guard who is on foot, patrolling the area of Geppetto's hut and the magic grove of trees. Bigby is still in human form but has no packs on now. The guard isn't a goblin, but is a human guard. Remember that Geppetto doesn't like the so-called lower races around his home? The guard has no idea Bigby's coming up behind him.

Cap (mission text): Stage Three: Preliminary Objectives.

Cap (mission text): First remove all guards from the area.

Page Sixteen (four panels)

Panel One

With a single deadly move, using only his bare hands, Bigby twists the guard's neck, breaking it instantly. In fact he nearly rips the guard's head entirely off of his body. Make this scene as graphic as we can. I want to stress the animal brutality of Bigby, when he's doing dirty deeds.

Sfx (guard's neck breaking — not too loud please): — *ckricck* —

Panel Two

In another spot we see a naked Bigby in mid-transformation to his wolf form. His clothes and gear are around his feet.

No captions or dialogue in this panel.

Panel Three

A bit later, in another part of the nighttime grove of magic trees, Bigby, in giant wolf form now, leaps out at a trio of guards, who are just turning to notice the danger they are in.

Cap (mission text): It's vital that you kill swiftly and silently...

Panel Four

This is the same scene just a few seconds later. All three guards are under Bigby being ripped to shreds. Bigby, still in wolf form, stands over his kills with a blood-painted muzzle. His attention is on his kills below him. Note that there will be some overhang of the forest in this panel so that two more guards (about to be seen in the following panel) can leap down on Bigby, who is too distracted by the ones he is dealing with now.

Cap (mission text): ...so that no alarm can be raised in the woodcarver's cabin.

Page Seventeen (three panels)

Panel One

Same scene but now two more guards leap down towards Bigby's unprotected back, with swords or long knives brandished to plunge right into his back by the weight of their fall. Bigby just has time to look up at them, but there seems no way for Bigby to avoid their attack.

Guard #1: Devil spawn!

Panel Two

The guards don't fall. Suddenly they're both suspended in midair halfway between the ledge they leapt off of and Bigby's back. The panic in their faces shows that they hadn't planned this. Bigby is still looking up at them, unconcerned about their predicament.

Guard # 1: What's this?

Guard # 2: Dire sorcery!

Bigby: Not at all, gentlemen.

Panel Three

Same scene from another angle. Bigby is done with the other three kills and now watches as the two invisibly-suspended guards now fall (mostly on their heads) down at Bigby's feet.

Bigby: It's just my son, guarding my back.

Bigby: You can drop them now, boy. I'm ready for them.

Page Eighteen (five panels)

Panel One

Now we see Bigby, dressed again and in human form again. He has picked up the larger musette bag from his pile of gear and is walking away from us, into the depths of the grove itself.

Cap (mission text): Next enter the grove of magic trees and prepare them with the Special Packages — spaced for maximum effect.

Panel Two

It's still the same nighttime. We switch scenes a bit to see a wide shot, establishing shot of the forest trail leading up towards Geppetto's hut, from the Imperial City in the valley below. Basically this is the same view as in the Homelands collection, page 177, except that now there's no wagon or gob lizard riders on the trail. Instead we see one very drunk Pinocchio staggering up the trail, coming home alone from a late night spent in the town below. He's so drunk he can barely walk upright and is holding a bottle of some liquor in one hand.

Cap (mission text): Stage Four: Primary Objectives.

Cap (mission text): When the grove is prepared you can enter the woodcarver's hut.

Pinocchio (singing drunkenly): If the ocean were whiskey and I was a duck...

Panel Three

Closer on the drunken Pinocchio staggering up the night trail from the city below. Not that it's important, but this is the same drinking song Jack was singing when he came out of the Branstock Tavern in the March of the Wooden Soldiers story arc. I wonder if anyone will notice?

Pinocchio (singing drunkenly): I'd dive to the bottom and drink it all up.

Panel Four

From another angle we now see Pinocchio staggering up to the front door of Geppetto's cabin.

Pinocchio (drunkenly and quietly to himself): b — be very quiet now, Pin — Pinocchio.

Panel Five

Now we switch scenes to the inside of Geppetto's hut, specifically the workroom we saw so much of in the Homelands arc. There's no big cage in the center of the workroom now, but otherwise it looks much the same. It's very dark in here and we can't see Bigby at all. In the small light coming from the open doorway we can barely see Pinocchio. He is turning and making the shushing gesture with one finger to the wooden owl perched just inside the door.

Pinocchio (drunkenly and quietly): *Shhhhhhhh*, Mr. Woody Owl. It's very important we don't wake my da — my da — don't wake the evil, bloody-handed Adversary.

Page Nineteen (three panels)

Panel One

Close on Pinocchio in the very dark room, striking a match with one hand and holding up a candle with the other.

Pinocchio (drunkenly and quietly): Kindly old conquerors need their sleep.

Panel Two

This is the big panel of the page. Except for the small panel above and the small panel below it is nearly a splash page. In the foreground, facing away from us, Pinocchio has lit the candle. In the background we can see what Pinocchio sees: The work room is illuminated now and we see Bigby, in human form. standing semi-crouched at the open closet door that contains the imprisoned Blue Fairy. He has turned away from the Blue Fairy and is making the same shushing gesture towards Pinocchio that he made towards the wooden owl. Pinocchio's body language shows us that he is quite surprised to see Bigby here.

Cap (mission text): If possible, try to free the Blue Fairy from her imprisonment. If that fails, try to destroy her.

Pinocchio (normal volume now): Bigby?

Bigby (quietly): *Shhhhhhh*, Pinocchio. Geppetto's sleeping only two rooms away and we don't want to wake him.

Panel Three

Closer on Pinocchio and Bigby at the open closet door showing the withered Blue Fairy in the closet. The surprise of discovering Bigby here seems to have sobered Pinocchio up some.

Pinocchio (quietly): What are you doing here, Bigby?

Bigby (quietly): Trying to murder your dad's power source. Didn't work though.

Page Twenty (four panels)

Panel One

Another shot of Bigby and Pinocchio as Bigby quietly closes the door with the Blue Fairy inside it, a look of resignation on Bigby's face.

Pinocchio (quietly): The spells protecting her are nearly as complex as those protecting my dad.

Bigby (quietly): The very same conclusion I came to about twenty seconds ago.

Panel Two

Bigby turns to talk to Pinocchio, who looks deeply conflicted by what Bigby tells him.

Cap (mission text): Only if an opportunity presents itself, without jeopardizing the main mission, attempt to recruit Pinocchio into returning with you to Fabletown.

Bigby (quietly): I also came to get you, if you're ready to come home now.

Panel Three

Another shot of Bigby whispering to Pinocchio who looks like what he's saying is killing him to admit.

Cap (mission text): Our sorcerers' best theory is that his second transformation to flesh probably included the same loyalty bonds that infect all new puppet creations.

Pinocchio (quietly): How can I do that, Bigby?

Panel Four

Big panel. Wide shot. Suddenly the room gets brighter, as Geppetto appears in the other doorway — the one connecting this room to the rest of the cabin — holding a lantern up. Geppetto looks sleepy and is wearing his nightgown and slippers and nightcap.

Geppetto: My goodness.

Geppetto: What's going on in here?

Bigby: Geppetto!

Pinocchio: Oh no!

Page Twenty One (five panels)

Panel One

This isn't really a panel. It's the space you need to leave at the top of this page for the next chapter title.

Title (display lettering): <u>Chapter Four: The Israel Analogy</u>.

Panel Two

With a sour and accusing look on his face, Geppetto steps further into the room with Bigby and Pinocchio.

Bigby: You might as well come on in, Geppetto. I'm ready for you now.

Geppetto: You're the Fabletown werewolf, aren't you?

Pinocchio: His name is Bigby, dad.

Panel Three

With the hand not holding the lantern, Geppetto points commandingly to the front door. Bigby looks relaxed and content to wait.

Geppetto: Pinocchio, son, go outside and summon the guards.

Bigby: Good luck with that. They're all dead.

Pinocchio: Be real careful, dad. Bigby's a stone cold killer.

Panel Four

Geppetto still looks pissed as he turns to accuse Bigby, who sits on the edge of one of the work tables, like an old friend who just popped in for a visit.

Geppetto: You won't be able to kill me. And my son is nearly as protected.

Pinocchio: I've still got years of spell treatments to catch up, but —

Bigby: Relax. You're both safe from me.

Panel Five

Closer on Bigby and Geppetto.

Bigby: I'm here to deliver a message from Fabletown.

Geppetto: Then say what you came to say and get out.

Bigby: Sure. How familiar are you with the Mundy world?

Page Twenty Two (five panels)

Panel One

Another shot of Bigby and Geppetto, who still looks cranky but also now looks a little confused as to what Bigby might be trying to get at.

Bigby: Ever hear of a country called Israel?

Geppetto: Who knows? Maybe. Why's that important?

Bigby: Here's what you need to know about it.

Panel Two

Bigby and Geppetto continue their adversarial conversation.

Bigby: Israel is a tiny country, surrounded by much larger countries dedicated to its eventual total destruction.

Geppetto: And why should that concern me?

Panel Three

Closer on Bigby. His expression shows that he admires the country he's talking about.

Bigby: Because they stay alive by being a bunch of tough little bastards who make the other guys pay dearly, every time they do anything against Israel.

Bigby: Some in the wider world constantly wail and moan about the endless cycle of violence and reprisal.

Panel Four

Another shot of Bigby telling his tale.

Bigby: But, since the alternative is non-existence, the Israelis seem determined to keep at it.

Bigby: They have a lot of grit and iron. I'm a big fan of them.

Panel Five

We pull back for another two-shot of Bigby and Geppetto, who is getting tired of the speech. Geppetto shows no fear in Bigby's presence. He entirely trusts the spells protecting him.

Geppetto: Are you near to being done? I'd like to go back to sleep.

Bigby: Here's the part that concerns you. Fabletown has decided to adopt the Israel template in whole.

Bigby: You've no doubt guessed that you guys play the part of the vast powers arrayed against us.

Page Twenty Three (five panels)

Panel One

Now we close in on Bigby and his look is deadly serious.

Bigby: Every time you hurt us we're going to damage you much worse in return.

Bigby: It will always happen. Always. You're the only one who can end the cycle.

Panel Two

Now Bigby smiles a small, sly, predator's smile.

Bigby: And keep this in mind. You have a huge empire to protect.

Bigby: Guard the ten million most likely targets and there will still be a hundred million ripe, unprotected targets we can hit.

Panel Three

We widen out to another group shot. Since it's been awhile since we've seen Pinocchio, let's include him in this shot too. Bigby is reaching into one of the oversized pockets in his shorts.

Geppetto: Okay, I understand now. I'll ponder your threat.

Bigby: Not so fast, old gaffer. Accounts aren't balanced yet. You still have the wooden soldier raid against Fabletown to pay for.

Panel Four

Closer on Bigby and Geppetto. Bigby has pulled a small radio transmitter (the kind used to set off bombs) out of his pocket and holds it up for Geppetto to see.

Geppetto: But you already know you can't hurt us.

Bigby: Think so? I'm about to stick it to you where it hurts most. See this? It's Mundy magic, which they call high-tech. It's a radio transmitter.

Panel Five

With a smile, Bigby pushes the red button on the face of the small transmitter.

Bigby: It's about to talk to another bunch of Mundy magic called plastic explosive, formed into about three dozen bombs strapped to tree trunks.

Bigby: This would be a good time to duck, because when I push this little red button —

Page Twenty Four (one panel)

Panel One

This is a full-page splash. We move our view to the exterior of the woodcarver's hut, with a wide enough shot to take in as much of the magic grove as you can show us. All at once the entire grove goes up in a series of explosions. The blasts aren't directed at the cabin, but the cabin is too close to escape all damage. The entire grove goes up in massive blasts that already show the fires to come.

No captions or dialogue in this panel. No sound-effects either. We can have the art tell the entire story on this page.

Page Twenty Five (five panels)

Panel One

It's about an hour later. Morning has just begun. This is another exterior shot of the same area shown in the previous panel. What little remains of the magic grove is still on fire. The cabin has suffered considerable damage and is also starting to burn.

Non Narration Cap: Sometime later…

Voice (from cabin): Come on, old man. Your cabin's started to burn.

Panel Two

Closer on the sagging front door of the cabin, Bigby comes out, literally carrying Geppetto under one arm and Pinocchio under the other.

Bigby: And even if those spells protect you from burning up with it, I doubt you'll want to wait for them to find you two under the scorched remains.

Geppetto: *cough — cough!*

Panel Three

Bigby unceremoniously dumps the two on the ground, a safe ways away from the fire. All characters are covered with dust and ash from the explosions.

Bigby: I've just taken your magic grove away from you.

Bigby: Yeah, I know it'll grow back — eventually — but I suspect it'll be at least a generation before you can produce new wooden children from it.

Panel Four

As Pinocchio and Geppetto begin to sit up, Bigby bends down to speak his final words to them.

Bigby: That's your punishment for invading Fabletown. See how we did much worse to you than what you did to us?

Bigby: Do yourself a big favor and learn the lesson here.

Panel Five

In our final panel of this scene, Pinocchio and Geppetto, still a bit dazed from their ordeal, are in the foreground, beginning to pick themselves up off the rough ground. In the background Bigby is walking away from them, towards the nearest unburned woods.

Bigby: That was the stick, now here's the carrot. Most of the heads from your invasion force are still alive.

Bigby: We might be willing to exchange them for things we want — if you can convince us you're inclined to be nice from now on.

Page Twenty Six (five panels)

Panel One

It's later in that same day. Bigby is in wolf form, running through the deep woods as fast as he can. Make sure we can see he's carrying his shorts in his mouth.

Cap (mission text): Stage Five: Extraction.

Cap (mission text): After completion of all objectives, return to the extraction point as quickly as possible, no matter the time of day.

Panel Two

Bigby is at his extraction point — the spot where he planted the magic bean several pages ago. He's back in human form and wearing the pair of shorts he brought back with him. Now a huge beanstalk has grown in the same spot. It's as big as the one growing up from the Farm at the beginning of the issue. Bigby is crouching at the base of the beanstalk, attaching another set of plastic explosive bombs to the base of the stalk. He's placing them so that the leaves or something will conceal them, when he's done placing them. Make sure we can see the remaining backpack here where the remaining bombs were stashed.

Cap (mission text): The beanstalk should have fully deployed by the time you reach it. Plant the remaining bombs at its base in places of concealment...

Panel Three

Naked except for his shorts, Bigby is now high above the forest, climbing up the beanstalk towards the sky. Down below him we can see goblin troops climbing after him.

Cap (mission text): ...to avoid detection from any forces that might give chase.

Panel Four

Now we see a closer look at all of the goblin and other Empire forces climbing up after Bigby. At least one of the enemy troops needs to be a human-looking captain.

Guard Captain: Climb faster, you filthy gobs, or the Emperor will kill every bloody one of you!

Panel Five

Bigby is near the top, climbing up to just below cloud level. With one hand he's holding out the radio transmitter. With the other hand he's reaching for the end of a rope that's dropping down from the clouds above, paralleling the beanstalk.

Cap (mission text): Be sure to activate the radio detonator while still in the Empire dimension, to ensure a good signal.

Page Twenty Seven (five panels)

Panel One

Down at the base of the beanstalk, we see more explosions go off, blasting the base of the beanstalk to smithereens.

Cap: And celebrated the joyous day.

One of the Kids: Where are Mommy and Daddy going now?

Rose Red: Somewhere you're not invited, wolfling.

Riding Hood (to Fly): That's odd. He does seem familiar — as if we'd met before.

Page Forty Seven (four panels)

Panel One

This isn't really a panel. It's the space you need to leave at the top of the page for the final chapter title.

Title (display lettering): Epilogue: Mr. and Mrs. Wolf

Panel Two

We see Paris at night, all lit up.

Cap: No one quite knew where they planned to go on their honeymoon, or how long they might stay away.

Voice (from city): A little more champagne, Mrs. Wolf?

Panel Three

Now we return to daytime and Wolf Valley. In the background we see their new home. It's a wonderful and sprawling one-story thing: part cabin and partly made of dressed stone and lots of real glass windows and stone chimneys and enough rooms so that each kid gets his own room. Mark: keep in mind that however you design this, you're likely to be drawing it every once in a while, until the end of time. Here and there, away from the house, there are odds and ends of the construction materials still on site, as if it were just finished minutes before the new family arrived. In the foreground we see Bigby and Snow, hand in hand, walking away from us, walking towards the house. Ahead of them the six kids race like hellions towards the house, so that they can be the first to pick their rooms. This is long after the wedding, so Snow and Bigby and all the kids will be dressed differently than when we last saw them.

Cap: But true to Boy Blue's promise, their house in Wolf Valley was finished and waiting for them by the time they returned.

Snow: Go pick your rooms, children. You each have one of your own.

Panel Four

Now the kids have long disappeared into the house's open front door. Bigby has lifted Snow up into his arms to carry her over the threshold.

Snow: So, do you think happily ever after is possible after all?

Bigby: We'll see.

Panel Five

Same exact scene, but now everyone has entered the house and we see the door close behind them, signaling that they have left the series — for now.

No captions or dialogue in this panel.

Page Forty Eight (one panel)

This is a full-page splash, leaving only enough room at the bottom of the page, as the final thing on this page, for this issue's title and credits. We are looking down on the surface of one of the feasting tables at Snow and Bigby's wedding. We see a fine plate with some partially-eaten wedding cake on it. We see a crystal champagne flute with some champagne still in it and a lipstick stain on the rim of the glass. We see a little bit of this and that — like a used fork and maybe a few Polaroid snapshots of the wedding and feast that followed. In the center of this untidy scene we see one of the wedding invitations, which reads as follows (in a fine script, please): You are cordially invited to join with us in celebrating the marriage of Snow White to Bigby Wolf. And under that: R.S.V.P.

Title (display lettering in fine script): Happily Ever After

Credits (in the same script)

Cap (not to be repeated in the collected version): The creators and publishers of Fables would like to thank you our readers for your loyalty, encouragement and reliable "what happens next" interest in these first fifty issues. We'll see you next month when the next fifty begins.

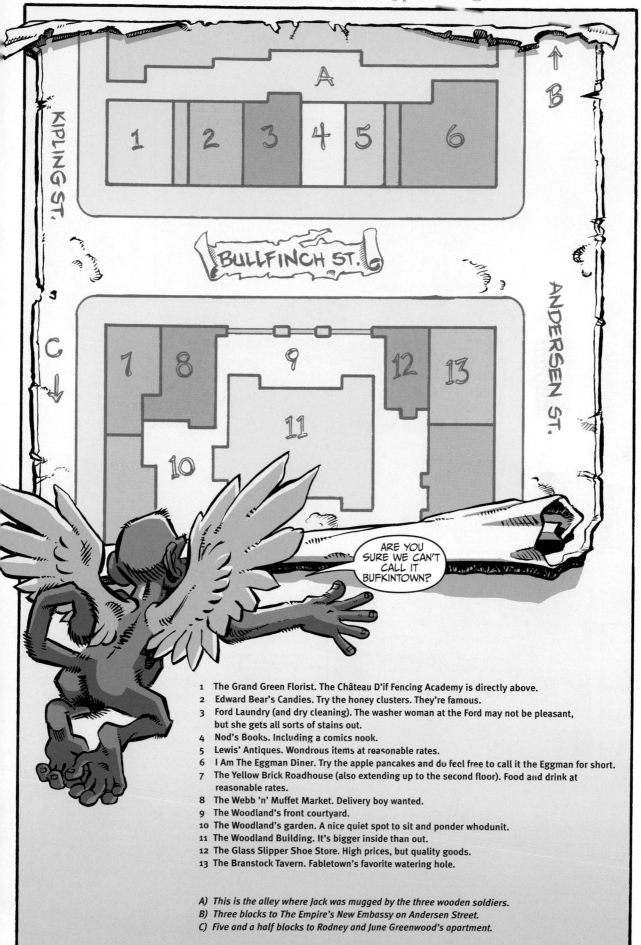

FABLETOWN

KIPLING ST.

ANDERSEN ST.

A

1 2 3 4 5 6

BULLFINCH ST.

7 8 9 12 13

10 11

ARE YOU SURE WE CAN'T CALL IT BUFKINTOWN?

B

C

1   The Grand Green Florist. The Château D'if Fencing Academy is directly above.
2   Edward Bear's Candies. Try the honey clusters. They're famous.
3   Ford Laundry (and dry cleaning). The washer woman at the Ford may not be pleasant, but she gets all sorts of stains out.
4   Nod's Books. Including a comics nook.
5   Lewis' Antiques. Wondrous items at reasonable rates.
6   I Am The Eggman Diner. Try the apple pancakes and do feel free to call it the Eggman for short.
7   The Yellow Brick Roadhouse (also extending up to the second floor). Food and drink at reasonable rates.
8   The Webb 'n' Muffet Market. Delivery boy wanted.
9   The Woodland's front courtyard.
10 The Woodland's garden. A nice quiet spot to sit and ponder whodunit.
11 The Woodland Building. It's bigger inside than out.
12 The Glass Slipper Shoe Store. High prices, but quality goods.
13 The Branstock Tavern. Fabletown's favorite watering hole.

A) This is the alley where Jack was mugged by the three wooden soldiers.
B) Three blocks to The Empire's New Embassy on Andersen Street.
C) Five and a half blocks to Rodney and June Greenwood's apartment.

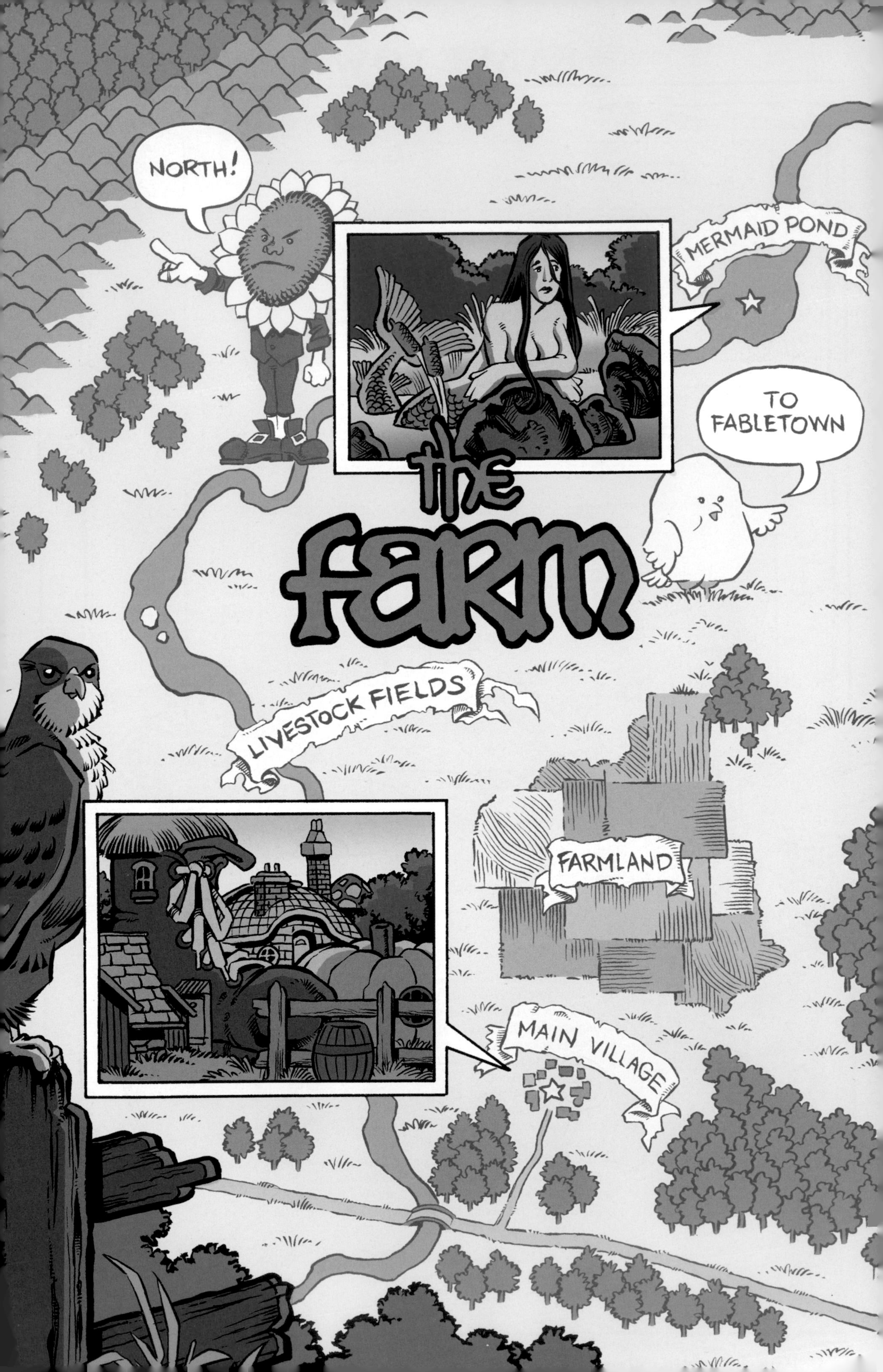
NORTH!
MERMAID POND
TO FABLETOWN
the farm
LIVESTOCK FIELDS
FARMLAND
MAIN VILLAGE

- A FABLES GALLERY -

ADVERSARY
WARRIORS
BY
ERIC POWELL

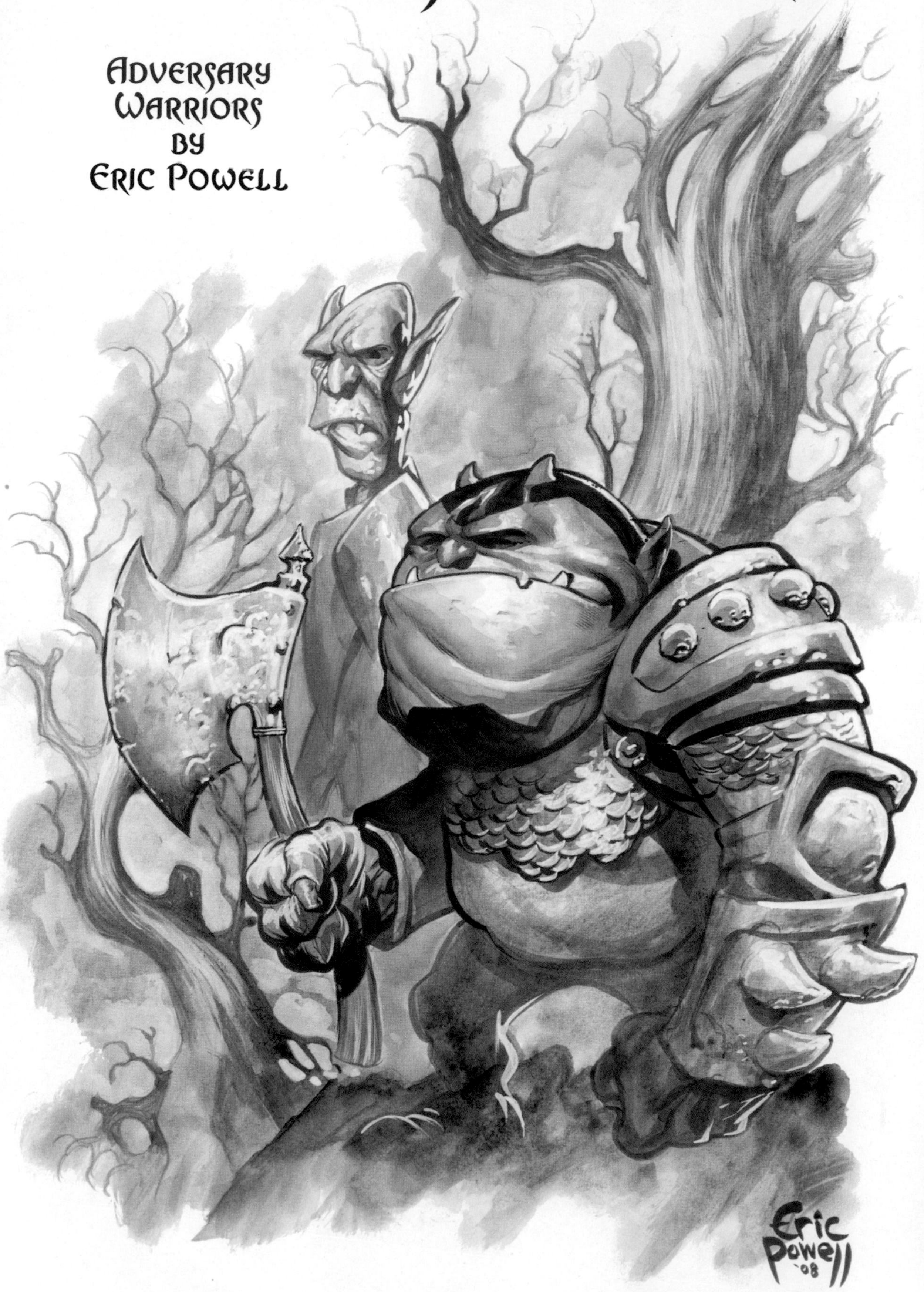
Eric
Powell
'08

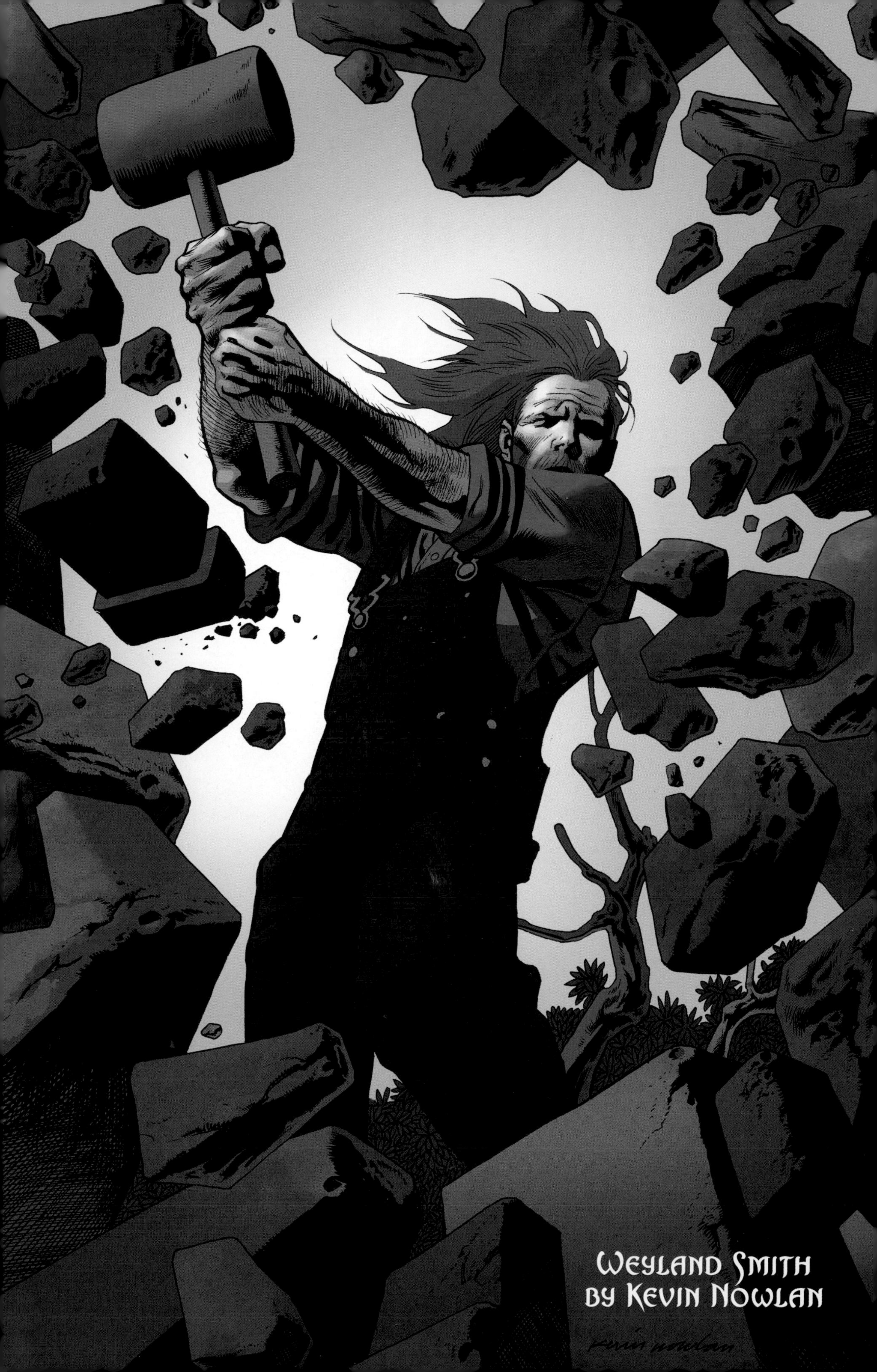

Weyland Smith
by Kevin Nowlan

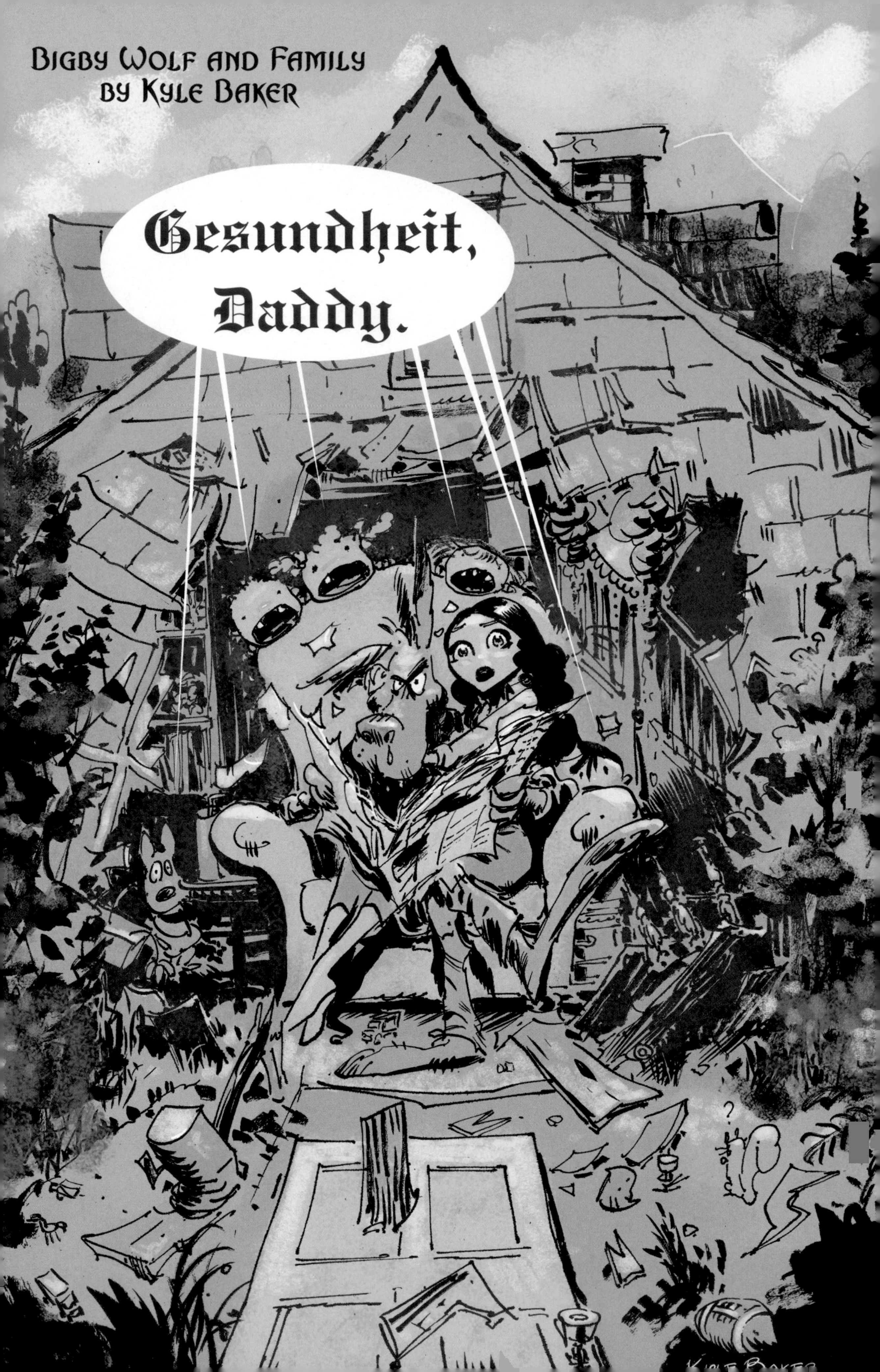
BIGBY WOLF AND FAMILY
BY KYLE BAKER
Gesundheit, Daddy.